S0-BNT-594

Liquid Relations

Liquid Relations

Contested Water Rights and Legal Complexity

EDITED BY

DIK ROTH

RUTGERD BOELENS

MARGREET ZWARTEVEEN

RUTGERS UNIVERSITY PRESS

NEW BRUNSWICK, NEW JERSEY, AND LONDON

Library of Congress Cataloging-in-Publication Data

Liquid relations : contested water rights and legal complexity / edited by Dik Roth, Rutgerd Boelens, and
Margreet Zwarteveen.
    p. cm.
    Includes bibliographical references and index.
    ISBN-13: 978-0-8135-3674-3 (hardcover : alk. paper) – ISBN-13: 978-0-8135-3675-0 (pbk. : alk.
paper)
    1. Water rights. I. Roth, Dik, 1954- II. Boelens, Rutgerd. III. Zwarteveen, Margreet.
    K3496.L57 2005
    346.04'32–dc22

2005004405

A British Cataloging-in-Publication record for this book is available from the British Library

This collection copyright © 2005 by Rutgers, The State University

Individual chapters copyright © 2005 in the names of their authors

All rights reserved

No part of this book may be reproduced or utilized in any form or by any means,
electronic or mechanical, or by any information storage and retrieval system, without
written permission from the publisher. Please contact Rutgers University Press, 100
Joyce Kilmer Avenue, Piscataway, NJ 08854-8099. The only exception to this
prohibition is "fair use" as defined by U.S. copyright law.

Printed with the Support of the Ford Foundation New Delhi Office and WALIR
Manufactured in the United States of America

CONTENTS

ACKNOWLEDGMENTS

Liquid Relations is the fruit of solid relations of fellowship, research collaboration, and friendship. It is the result of efforts of individual researchers and professionals engaged in this collective endeavor, who have joined their visions, ideas, and concepts as well as points of debate, consensus, and contradiction. Our common purpose was to shed light on a largely unexplored domain that now receives growing attention: the field of research and action concerning the role of legal pluralism in water control.

Since we organized a panel on water rights and legal pluralism at the XIIIth International Congress on Folk Law and Legal Pluralism in Chang Mai, Thailand in 2002, many persons have supported and encouraged us to continue working on this issue and deepen the understanding of the dynamic relationships among water rights, power, and legal complexity. Therefore, we are most grateful to the organizers of the congress, Franz von Benda-Beckmann, Keebet von Benda-Beckmann, Melanie Wiber, Sunita Thapa, and particularly to Rajendra Pradhan, who also compiled three impressive volumes containing the overall congress results.

A number of other friends and colleagues have also greatly contributed to this book. We gratefully acknowledge Paul Gelles, WALIR/University of California at Riverside, and Gilbert Levine, Mario Einaudi Center for International Studies/Cornell University, for reading the chapters and giving very insightful, constructive comments to an earlier version of the book. Next, we very much appreciated the thought-provoking, stimulating debates with our colleagues at the departments of Irrigation and Water Engineering, and of Law and Governance, both at Wageningen University. Both departments and their staff take interdisciplinary work seriously and give it their full support. This book continues a longer history of cooperation between the two departments on issues such as water rights and legal pluralism. We hope that more will follow. Special thanks are due to Maria Pierce and Gerda de Fauw for their support to this book.

We also would like to express our gratitude to the academic and action-research networks and institutions that have supported research and publication. This book was published with the support of the New Delhi office of the Ford Foundation, for which we would like to express our gratitude. Further, this book could not have been realized without the research support and facilitation provided by the Commission on Folk Law and Legal Pluralism, the Water Law and Indigenous Rights program (WALIR), and the Water Unit of the Netherlands Ministry of Foreign Affairs. We kindly acknowledge the supportive role of the Max Planck Institute for Social Anthropology in Halle, Germany. Last but not least, we are grateful to both departments of Wageningen University for financially supporting our participation in the Chiang Mai conference and for granting us time to work on the conference and the book.

Most of all, we thank our coauthors Vishwa Ballabh, Pranita Bhushan Udas, Bryan Bruns, Ingo Gentes, David Getches, Armando Guevara, Nitish Jha, Barbara van Koppen, Ruth Meinzen-Dick, Rajendra Pradhan, Anjal Prakash, Amreeta Regmi, and Patricia Urteaga. Our effort to bring together crucial theoretical concepts and analytical frameworks could never have materialized without their contributions. Their rich experiences with water issues all around the world have provided us with several important lessons, not just from the books but most of all from the field.

And it is through our fellow authors that we also want to thank the water users and communities they have worked with. The sharing of their experiences and insights has provided the basic inputs and fundaments for this book. We hope that, indirectly, and in a spirit of solidarity, the results of this book may somehow contribute to changing the unequal power relations, discrimination, and oppression that too often characterize current water control, water policies, and water legislation.

ABBREVIATIONS

ADB	Asian Development Bank
CBO	community-based organizer
CEDLA	Centre for Latin American Research and Documentation
CEJIS	Centro de Estudios Jurídicas e Investigación Social
CEPAL	Economic Commission for Latin America (United Nations)
CGWB	Central Ground Water Board (India)
CMAs	catchment management agencies
DG	director general
DHM	Department of Hydrology and Meteorology (Nepal)
DIO	District Irrigation Office (Nepal)
DOI	Department of Irrigation (Nepal)
DWAF	Department of Water Affairs and Forestry (South Africa)
GWRDB	Groundwater Resources Development Board (Nepal)
GWRDC	Gujarat Water Resources Development Corporation (India)
HYVs	high-yielding variety seeds
IIMI	International Irrigation Management Institute (Colombo)
ILRI	International Institute for Land Reclamation and Improvement (The Netherlands)
IMTA	Instituto Mexicano de Technologia del Agua
ITDG	Intermediate Technology Development Group
IWMI	International Water Management Institute (Colombo)
MHPP	Ministry of Housing and Physical Planning (Nepal)
MLD	million liters per day
MOWR	Ministry of Water Resources (Nepal)
NGO	nongovernmental organization
NR	Nepalese rupee
NWSC	Nepal Water Supply Corporation
ODI	Overseas Development Institute (London)
PUCP	Pontificia Universidad Católica del Perú
RD	regional director
SISP	Second Irrigation Sector Project (Nepal)
TU	tertiary unit

VDC	village development committee
VIKSAT	Vikram Sarabhai Centre for Development Interaction
WALIR	Water Law and Indigenous Rights
WED	water extracting device
WUA	water users' association

Liquid Relations

1

Legal Complexity in the Analysis of Water Rights and Water Resources Management

RUTGERD BOELENS
MARGREET ZWARTEVEEN
DIK ROTH

Since the 1990s, water problems have been high on national and international policy agendas. Climate change, population growth, urbanization, industrialization, and intensification of agriculture are putting increasing pressures on the resource (see Gleick et al. 2002; Gupta 2004; Petrella 1999). Growing scarcity, overexploitation, and pollution coincide with an ever-increasing demand, leading to competition for resource control between people, sectors, and countries. Unavoidably, these trends have generated sociopolitical tensions and conflicts between users at various levels. They also prompt the call for new approaches to water governance and management that are adapted to the changing use conditions of the resource in a rapidly changing world.

Especially during the last decade, water policy discourse has become truly global (see Brans et al. 1997; Cosgrove and Rijsberman 2000). Problems increasingly tend to be framed and phrased in global terms, and standardized solutions are promoted that are assumed to have general and global applicability. In the field of irrigation, for instance, a global discourse of irrigation sector reforms characterized by "model" and "tool-box" approaches has become hegemonic.[1] In water management in a more general sense, characterized by competition between multiple uses and users, the common wisdom treats as givens the river basin as a "natural" management unit and the treatment of water as an economic good. It is assumed that the formulation and enforcement of national legal frameworks will facilitate a uniform implementation of such policy principles, and thus provide backing to the water reform process. Yet these standardized approaches face a fundamental criticism: complex problems require a more contextualized understanding (Donahue and Johnston 1998; Wester and Warner 2002). Rights-based approaches to problems of water scarcity attempt to construct water rights as a (globally defined) human right, but fail to provide an answer to more context-specific questions: what are the contents and meaning of a water right? For which uses and users, and under which circumstances, should such a right be defined? How can such rights be exerted and operationalized in specific societal contexts in which other, local definitions of water rights exist? (see F. and K. von Benda-Beckmann 2003).

An important starting point of this book is that issues such as water scarcity and competition are not standard problems for which universally valid solutions can be formulated. Although partly attributable to the same causes, and although increasingly urgent in many places of the world, water problems are inherently local and context-specific in their manifestations. They are not simply reducible to natural and physical processes of water extraction and storage and do not follow universal economics or natural laws. Water control problems are both physical-ecological and human-made, the locally specific outcome of social and political histories and processes.

In order to be effective at all, solutions to water-related problems framed in an increasingly global water policy discourse will have to be accepted and adopted in local settings of water use and water rights definitions. It is precisely in this field of tension between various levels of governance and management that water-related policy measures and interventions are contested, reinterpreted, and transformed under the influence of locally specific sociocultural normative systems and relations of power and control. This highlights the need for the contextualized study and analysis of water problems and for the formulation of context-specific solutions. These should pay attention to power relations, culturally defined meanings and patterns of resource use, and definitions of water rights (see Donahue and Johnston 1998).

Law is one potentially important tool in regulating water allocation. The role of law in processes of water resources regulation has remained underexposed. In the fields of development studies and natural resource management, law tends to be treated rather one-dimensionally as an instrument of regulation that belongs exclusively to the state. In such views, state-made legal and institutional arrangements simply do their job: they generate the kind of societal changes they were designed for. More often than not, the crucial role of law and normative points of departure of policy making and water regulation remain hidden behind apparently neutral terms like "appropriate practices" or "efficient use." Water rights and the legal dimensions of water use have long been treated either within the paradigm of state-defined and centralized water control, or within a market-focused neoliberal paradigm. A third, nowadays popular, current emphasizes the need for decentralized platform structures for negotiating local water rights and mediating conflicts among multiple users and uses, but often fails to address fundamental power differentials. Even where local rights to water are recognized by state law, such recognition tends to be

Janus-faced. The flip side of recognition tends to be incorporation, control, oppression, or downright eradication.

In this book we actively engage with such contemporary issues of water use, management, and governance. We take as our point of departure the fact that we are dealing with complex interventions in resource tenure with an equally complex legal dimension. In the field of water resources, for instance, finding a solution to the problems of growing water demand and scarcity will inevitably entail the redistribution of established water rights and definition of new rights to this resource. In mainstream approaches that treat water as a tradable commodity, market efficiency has become the panacea. But because water use for irrigation is the least beneficial in market terms, such market-focused policies often entail water transfers from rural agricultural use toward urban and industrial uses. The transfer of water between sectors, users, and uses is not, however, simply a process mediated by market forces. Market-focused approaches tend to overlook the fact that water is not only a commodity to be redistributed and allocated in accordance with market principles but also a crucial resource in rural livelihoods, and that security of (land and water) tenure forms the backbone of these livelihoods. In addition, water is a fundamental source of cultural meaning, identity, and social identification.

Thus, we believe that there is a great need for more critical appreciation of the complexities involved in water resources regulation and processes of development. Interventions in water resources such as irrigation reforms or intersectoral transfers of water are based not only on legal regulations and a variety of forms of sociolegal engineering (F. von Benda-Beckmann 1993; Crook 2001) but also on normative conceptions of the ideal ordering of resource tenure and management. Various social groups in society may hold differing conceptions of legitimate rights and forms of regulation. There is a growing awareness of the multilevel character of water governance, the tensions between various levels and sources of regulation, and the consequences of this multiple character of legal ordering for intervention, control, and planned change in the water sector.

In this introductory chapter, we explore the general field of legal pluralism and water resources management. Although other water uses receive attention in some chapters, we will be mainly concerned with water use for irrigation in this introduction as well as in the book. In the second section of this chapter, we discuss the gradual emergence of legal pluralism as a field of study and policy attention. We also critically review some of the contributions that insights about law and legal pluralism can make to understanding and improving complex water use and management realities. In our view, attention to law and legal complexity increases analytical understanding of natural resource use. Insights derived from conceptualizations of law that take into account the existence of

legally plural conditions also provide a refreshing and necessary counterbal-
ance to the general tendency in the world of policy making to be prescriptive
and normative rather than descriptive and analytical, to state what should be
done rather than to understand what is at stake first.

In the third section, we review main(stream) approaches to the analysis of
water management. As we will show, irrigation and water management professionals and policy makers have been slow to adopt insights from studies of legal
pluralism. Most scholars and practitioners in the field do not acknowledge the
various and complex normative and legal dimensions of water control. We focus
our discussion on four main bodies of thought that prevail in water resources
and irrigation studies: traditional engineering approaches, new institutionalism, common property resources management, and empowerment.

This overview raises the question of how insights on plural legal conditions
in society can contribute to the understanding of complex water use and management realities. We conclude the third section of this chapter with a short
discussion of more recent trends in the irrigation and water management literature in which a genuine interest in the analytical value of the concept of legal
pluralism has become visible, and which guides attempts to bring the social,
legal, and policy worlds closer together.

In the fourth, final section of this chapter we provide an introduction to the
book itself. A short overview of all the chapters is preceded by more general
introductory remarks on the case-study focus, as well as on the common themes
and interests shared by the contributing authors.

Law, Legal Pluralism and Natural Resources Management

As is the case with the social sciences in general, social scientific approaches to
law have undergone radical changes in the last decades. Central to these
changes is a shift of focus away from exclusive attention to formal structures,
regulations, and routines of implementation toward an interest in how and by
whom they are produced, reproduced and transformed. This has generated an
interest in how people experience law in the context of their own local society
and use it as a crucial resource in their day-to-day aspirations and struggles, and
in the relationship between law and human behavior, in the real-life manifestations of law in specific interaction settings (see Cotterrell 1992; Crook 2001;
Spiertz 2000).

Legal Pluralism and Approaches to Natural Resource Management

Acceptance of a broad conceptualization of law and of the existence of legally
plural conditions in society are part of these changes. "Legal pluralism" or "legal
complexity" refers to the existence and interaction of different (usually state

and nonstate) normative orders in the same sociopolitical space.[2] Before the 1980s, in a period in which "the dominant theories about law . . . were antagonistic to all notions of legal pluralism" (Woodman 1998: 22), the concept was still in a state of "combative infancy" (Griffiths 1986: 1). Its spread during this period is closely associated with what Griffiths calls the objective "to combat the ideology of legal centralism and its denial of the character of law to normative orders other than that of the state" (Woodman 1998: 33).[3]

It is not surprising that attention to legal pluralism has advanced so rapidly in the fields of development and natural resource management studies. The complex relationships between planned change and legal regulation, on the one hand, and actual human behavior and practices, on the other, are a major problem in efforts to engineer human behavior. Intellectual efforts at understanding these complex relationships have paved the way for the concept of legal pluralism to emerge and expand so that its relevance for development policy and natural resource management is now broadly recognized (see Boelens and Dávila 1998; Bruns and Meinzen-Dick 2000; Crook and Houtzager 2001; Pradhan et al. 1997, 2000; Pradhan and Meinzen-Dick 2003; Roth 2003).

A major topic of discussion within the field is the relative performance of various property regimes in terms of developmental norms and values such as productivity, efficiency in management, sustainability, and equity (see F. von Benda-Beckmann 2001). After a long period in which development strategies were exclusively biased toward either state or private property regimes and against common property (cf. Hardin 1968), the emergence of common property resources theory was an important step forward. However, such approaches and their more or less explicit neoinstitutionalist flavor (see below) have been rightly criticized for being economistic, one-dimensional, and instrumentalist, and for not being able to cope with the historicity, the sociopolitical and sociocultural embeddedness of resource use and management practices (see Cleaver 2000; McCay and Jentoft 1998; Mehta et al. 1999). Too often, analysis and understanding are sacrificed for the sake of policy-driven searches for new forms of social engineering.

The increasing recognition of the relevance of legal complexity is related to a more general trend toward allowing for complexity, contingency, ambivalence, and conflict in the analyses of resource exploitation and management settings. Such analyses focus, for instance, on rethinking the concepts of community (Agrawal and Gibson 1999; McCay and Jentoft 1998; Mosse 1997), on local knowledge (Agrawal 1995), and on the existence of multiple legal and institutional frameworks (Mehta et al. 1999; Spiertz and Wiber 1996). How can approaches and analyses in terms of legal complexity contribute to the study and analysis of natural resource management realities? What are its strengths and weaknesses? Some major contributions as well as points of criticism are summarized below.

MORE THAN ONE LEGAL ORDER IN SOCIETY. The concept of legal pluralism allows for the possibility of the existence of more than one legal order in society and often unpredictable forms of interaction between such orders. It implies a broad conceptualization of law and legal phenomena. Further, a focus on function rather than on form and typology makes the a priori distinction between state and nonstate forms of normative ordering rather pointless. Thus, the concept of law is no longer exclusively reserved for state law, but expands to a variety of more or less formalized and institutionalized forms of normative ordering in society. Examples of nonstate normative orders are, for instance, customary law, religious law, "project law," and forms of self-regulation. Not all these normative frameworks have the same coercive means and power of enforcement with respect to the rules and regulations they produce and represent, nor do all enjoy the same degree of legitimacy and respect for their rules, rights, and authority. Therefore, analysis of the relationship between law and power, as well as of perceptions and relations of legitimacy in legally plural situations is crucial (see F. von Benda-Beckmann 1997, 2002; Merry 1992; Spiertz 2000).

LAW, SOCIAL PROCESS, AND HUMAN AGENCY. A second contribution of legal pluralism studies is their attention to the relationship between law and behavior as well as to issues related to social process. Rather than merely assuming a direct relationship between legal rules and behavior—an assumption often implicitly or explicitly present in development policies and interventions—sociological and legal anthropological analyses tend to address this relationship through empirical research. Interest in the social significance of law for (groups of) people in specific social arenas has replaced rule-centred approaches to law (Houtzager 2001; Moore 1978, 2001).

Approaches to law as a social resource require a human-agency focus on social actors and their interests, options, constraints, dilemmas, and choices. In strategizing to reach their goals, people have multiple legal options at their disposal, deriving from a variety of state and nonstate sources. Though differences in power, capacity, and knowledgeability play a role, in principle all actors in society are in a position to weigh various legal options in view of their enabling and constraining characteristics. Thus, they can make selective, context-bound, and strategic use of these options, a phenomenon known as legal shopping or forum shopping (K. von Benda-Beckmann 1981). In such specific contexts, law ceases to be a mere abstraction and assumes its actual social meaning and significance. Therefore, the understanding of the social significance of law should start from human experience and behavior (see Spiertz 2000).[4] For resource management studies, the important point is that people are constrained by law, but that they can also use it as a resource, interpret it, and change it.

THE DYNAMIC AND HYBRID CHARACTER OF LAW. The gradual shift away from structure-centered, systemic conceptualizations of law toward more dynamic, interactive, and ambivalent ones has made the law's hybrid character clearly visible. "Legal systems" in legally plural conditions not only coexist, they also interact and are permeable to the extent that this interaction changes them. Interactions may even produce new, hybrid, forms of law that have incorporated elements of two or more legal systems into a totally new form of "local law." In such hybrid forms it is almost impossible to distinguish separate constitutive elements, such as state law and customary law. This attention to hybridity as a new dimension of legal pluralism is a relevant contribution to the analysis of property rights and provides a necessary warning against simplistic conceptualizations of law and against the uncritical use of oppositions such as state versus customary and traditional versus modern.

THE VARIOUS LEVELS AT WHICH THE SOCIAL MEANING OF LAW SHOULD BE STUDIED. Attention to legal pluralism and the social meaning of law in general can help to increase awareness of legally complex conditions in an analytically more sophisticated way than by using distinctions such as formal and informal rights, or de facto and de jure rights (Schlager and Ostrom 1992). More refined distinctions are needed for a greater understanding of the actual social meaning of rights in specific social contexts. F. and K. von Benda-Beckmann propose to distinguish between categorical and concretized rights. Categorical rights define in general terms "the legal status of categories of persons and property objects as well as the type of rights and obligations among persons with respect to property objects." These are distinguished from concretized rights, rights that are "inscribed and become embodied in a social relationship among actual persons with respect to actual property objects" (F. and K. von Benda-Beckmann 2000: 18–19). In a legally plural setting, where such rights may also be multiply defined, it is important to pay attention to the various levels at which such rights are given meaning for all legal systems.[5]

Law and Irrigation Studies

People experience law in daily life not primarily in its abstract, decontextualized, and delocalized form but rather in setting-specific rules and norms. More often than not, a wide gap exists between intended outcomes, on the one hand, and actual practice, on the other. For irrigation and water management policies, this insight suggests that we need to question an assumed congruence between technical and managerial designs and models, on the one hand, and users' interpretations and perceptions, on the other. Moreover, written laws regulating irrigation are frequently—and quite wrongly—seen as the main or only manifestation of law and the legal order in any society.

The Engineering Roots of Irrigation Studies

Until twenty years ago, engineers dominated thinking about irrigation development.[6] Irrigation development was conceived and discussed primarily in engineering, agronomic, and economic terms. Problems of low performance were consequently diagnosed as technical problems, which could and should be solved through "modern" and supposedly better designs, just as optimal performance levels were derived from what could hypothetically be realized if an irrigation design would function as originally planned. In this technocratic period the maintenance and rehabilitation of colonial irrigation systems as well as new designs for large-scale systems were to be based on the latest hydraulic insights. Water management was seen as the operation and maintenance of technical infrastructure, a task that necessarily had to be performed by highly skilled technical engineers or automated infrastructure (Plusquellec et al. 1994). The role of the users was to adapt their practices to the technology and to follow the rules decreed from above (cf. Nobe and Sampath 1986; Scheer 1996; Uphoff 1986).

The gradual emergence of an international irrigation management debate in the 1970s was partially responsible for the demise of the technocratic approach. This debate emerged from an increasing awareness of the many nontechnical causes of the poor performance of (large) irrigation systems. Existing irrigation approaches were also criticized because of the negative socioeconomic effects of the Green Revolution, of which irrigation was a pillar. Studies revealed that irrigation development was often accompanied by processes of social differentiation (Chambers 1988, 1994; Esman and Uphoff 1984; Uphoff 1986), especially around the axis of gender (K. von Benda-Beckmann et al. 1997; Jackson 1998; Koppen 1998; Lynch 1993; Meinzen-Dick and Zwarteveen 1998; Zwarteveen 1994a, 1994b, 1997). This critique translated into concerns about the role of irrigation in rural transformation, phrased differently in different periods: basic needs, small farmer approaches, poverty alleviation, equity, livelihood security, and most recently sustainable development.

In the 1970s and 1980s the irrigation management literature mainly focused on the organization of water distribution and maintenance and the organization of users in water users' associations (WUAs) at the local, tertiary unit or outlet command area level. Most of these efforts continued to disregard the existing institutional environment. Instead, they derived recipes for efficient management from general management theories combined with engineering ideas about the optimal performance of irrigation systems. At about the same time, development NGOs began to emphasize the development of small-scale irrigation systems with "appropriate technology," paying explicit attention to existing "indigenous" irrigation systems (Coward 1986; Hunt and Hunt 1976; Maass and Anderson 1978). Participatory irrigation design and development approaches emerged but often turned out to be incompatible with the prevailing technocratic approaches to design (cf. Diemer and Huibers 1996; Scheer 1996; Ubels and Horst 1993).

Although the two last decades clearly show a gradual shift from technocratic to more people-centered approaches to irrigation and water management, the technocentric roots and biases of irrigation thinking have remained clearly visible in the instrumental manner in which laws and rules are conceptualized. For irrigation systems to become functioning wholes, laws, rules, and institutions have had to be engineered by knowledgeable specialists—social engineers—in the same way that hydraulic infrastructure has had to be designed by civil engineers. If only institutional design principles were added to the technical design principles, so the logic went, these together would guarantee efficient use. Approaches mainly developed by economists, such as rent-seeking analysis and game theory, were often used for understanding institutional processes (Repetto 1986; Ostrom 1992).

Law and Legal Pluralism in Contemporary Irrigation Thinking

The Changing Water Management Panorama

To understand how the law is treated in irrigation, it is helpful to trace the roots of contemporary bodies of irrigation thought. Here, we identify four such bodies of thought that have had and continue to have a visible influence on thinking about water and rights in professional irrigation circles. In addition to the classic—and still very powerful—technocratic engineering approach outlined above, contemporary models draw on the new institutionalism,[7] common property resources theory, and empowerment approaches. In actual policies and most writing on irrigation, arguments from all four bodies of thought are used eclectically, interchangeably, and in a complementary fashion. All have influenced and continue to influence irrigation policies, discourses, and intervention practices.

NEW INSTITUTIONALISM. New institutionalism derives theoretical insights from neoliberal economics and political theory. In the context of natural resources management policies, it primarily focuses on the creation of financial and other incentives by markets and institutions to improve the economic efficiency of resource use (cf. Ostrom 1992, 1997; Saleth 1994b). Poor performance of irrigation systems is diagnosed as the result of perverse incentives. A major source of perversity lies in the way irrigation systems are (or have been) funded. Many irrigation agencies in the world are (or used to be) dependent upon external donors to finance new construction and recurrent costs of irrigation. This leads to a disregard of local farmers and users' needs and interests, a preference for capital-intensive investment in construction and rehabilitation (rather than in water management and conservation), and the absence of agreed performance levels (Nijman 1993). The fact that irrigation agencies are normally dependent for their budgets on a central treasury rather than on user fees creates additional management anomalies. Since there is no direct link between the quality of the services provided by irrigation agency staff and the amount they earn, they have no performance incentive. Instead, the professional rewards of irrigation managers in centrally financed, hierarchical agencies are best secured through conformity to higher authorities (Vermillion 1991).

Cost recovery, accountability, and financial autonomy are the central concepts in the neoinstitutionalist solution to these perverse incentive structures. Irrigation agencies should, as it were, sell their services to those clients who are willing and able to pay for them and thereby recover management and part of the investment costs from the users. The principle of cost recovery questions the public nature of irrigation, which was earlier taken for granted and justified heavy subsidies. Some neoinstitutionalists advocate further measures, such as treatment of water as an economic good, tradability of water rights, and water pricing as means to save water and use it more efficiently (Briscoe 1996; Rosegrant and Binswanger 1994. See also Moore 1989, 1991; Perry et al. 1997). Accountability refers to the extent to which the performance of all irrigation managers and staff at all levels is subject to monitoring and control by water users (Uphoff et al. 1991). A lack of accountability is often identified as one of the key causes of low performance in irrigation systems (Merrey 1996). Financial autonomy is, together with cost recovery, the most important mechanism (as identified by neoinstitutionalists) to bring about accountability.[8]

Neoinstitutionalist irrigation thinking stresses the importance of well-defined and enforceable water rights. The existence of clear water rights is identified as a necessary condition for the emergence of water markets (Perry et al. 1997; Rosegrant and Binswanger 1994; Meinzen-Dick and Bruns 2000), following the widely accepted contention of liberal economists that "market allocation will be efficient, given well-defined and non-attenuated initial property rights and zero transaction costs" (Coase 1960, cited in Rosegrant and Binswanger 1994: 1,616). Water rights are seen as the legal complement to technical infrastructure and institutions, the three of which are necessary for an effective allocation and distribution of water. Thus, the conceptualization of water rights in the neoinstitutionalist school is primarily prescriptive. It focuses on what a water rights system should look like if water management is to improve (in terms of water use, allocation, efficiency, investment, security, and so on). Existing water rights systems are seen and analyzed against this model, and generally judged not to fulfill the necessary conditions for well-defined property rights to water. These models rarely recognize or discuss the existence of legally plural conditions; if they do, they typically identify its fuzziness and seemingly chaotic character as major obstacles to the desired conditions of transparency deemed necessary to achieve well-performing systems.

COMMON PROPERTY RESOURCE MANAGEMENT. Common property resources thinking is rooted in the continuing debate about the "tragedy of the commons" (Hardin 1968), revived by growing concerns about the environment. Past concerns about the tragedy of the commons, following Hardin's analysis, led to recommendations favoring the abolition of common property. More recent empirically grounded analyses, associated with the common property resources school, increasingly recognized the existence and importance of forms of regulation, cooperative behavior, and collective action associated with local management of natural resources.

A key concept in these approaches is, of course, property, "a claim to a benefit (or income) stream. . . . Property is *not* an object but is rather a social relation that defines the property holder with respect to something of value (the benefit stream) against all others" (Bromley 1992: 4). Common property regimes are characterized by the fact that specific resources are owned collectively, where the collective has relative autonomy and authority to establish the rules, rights, obligations, and procedures regarding resource management and distribution. Individual members' rights and obligations are derived from this collective right to use and regulate the common resource. In common property regimes it is often difficult to exclude outside users, even though each person's resource use reduces its availability for others (Lam et al. 1993). Most irrigation systems display essential characteristics of a common property regime.

In these common property systems, maintaining an appropriate balance between the rights and responsibilities associated with irrigation is a key principle of sound and successful management. Responsibilities include mobilization of labor, materials, and funds required for operation and maintenance, while rights mainly refer to a timely and adequate supply of irrigation water (cf. Gerbrandy and Hoogendam 1998; Hoogendam 1995; Ostrom 1992; Yoder 1994). Rights thus play a central role in the analysis: it is argued that those who most need access to a resource should also be granted the rights of access and control of its management (Cleaver 2000; Guillet 1992; Hendriks 1998; Pradhan et al. 2000; Schlager and Ostrom 1992; Zwarteveen and Meinzen-Dick 2001). Without secure rights to the resource, users will be less motivated to act collectively and make the long-term investments that are a precondition for higher productivity and efficiency.[9]

Common property resources scholars place excessive faith in the effectiveness of local and traditional rights systems. Their proposals for improving water management often include pleas for recognition of existing regulatory frameworks. Discussions about the potential of common property regimes sometimes tend toward ideologically inspired romanticism (a simplistic "return to the commons") as the way to achieve both environmental and social sustainability. Such approaches often see common property regimes as inherently more equitable than private property regimes. For analytical and practical purposes such analyses have many shortcomings. A case in point is their conceptualization of community, characterized by an a priori assumption of unity, homogeneity, and solidarity, at the cost of a more realistic appreciation of internal diversity and conflict, as well as the dynamics, fluidity, and complexity of legally plural forms of regulation.[10]

EMPOWERMENT. This body of thought is concerned with fostering more participatory ways of development from a perspective that questions unequal power relationships, often out of a concern with equity, democracy, and social justice (cf. Friedmann 1992; Hoebink et al. 1999; Nelson and Wright 1995; Scott 1985; Slocum et al. 1995). It is argued that if people (rather than states or development agencies) have the power to decide for themselves what is best for them, chances for equitable development are higher. In this line of thinking, a main cause of poor irrigation management performance lies in the fact that users— and especially the least powerful groups such as peasants, indigenous water users, and women—have too little control over water and related resources (Boelens and Hoogendam 2002; Bolin 1990; Gelles 1994, 1998; Mollinga 2003; Zwarteveen and Meinzen-Dick 2000). Control and power are central concepts in the empowerment line of thinking. As in new institutionalist analysis, the fact that agencies are not accountable to farmers also figures prominently in the analysis. However, these theories focus on political rather than financial mechanisms as the main cause of poor accountability. Political or organizational control of water and infrastructure are identified as the key determinants of successful WUAs. The empowerment orientation conceptualizes irrigation management in a broader rural development perspective, explicitly connecting water distribution to other dimensions of development (Ferguson 1990; Guillet 1992; Meinzen-Dick et al. 1997; Scott 1985; Wood 1985; Zwarteveen and Endeveld 1995). Consequently, the success of WUAs is not judged only on the basis of irrigation management performance criteria but also on whether and how these organizations can increase the influence and power of farmers' groups and their ability to deal with issues among themselves as well as with agencies and other external groups.

In this approach to irrigation, property rights are seen as an important reflection of prevailing social relations of power. Property rights are conceptualized as social relations between people, whereby power structures influence both the contents and the distribution of water rights, as well as the ways in which they are contested. Differences in access to and control of resources are recognized as a main determinant of wider social inequities and injustices. Although this approach recognizes the importance of law as a manifestation of social relations of power, it tends to undervalue the importance of existing normative frameworks in codetermining and shaping the social organization of irrigation. Moreover, it pays little attention to how norms and laws structure the ways in which needs and interests are articulated and negotiated. The existence of a plurality of norms and laws that may both enable and constrain people has only recently received more attention in analysis (F. von Benda-Beckmann et al. 1998; Boelens and Doornbos 2001; Bruns and Meinzen-Dick 2000; Hendriks 2002; Mosse 1997; Pradhan et al. 1997, 2000; Roth 1998, 1999; Spiertz and Wiber 1996).

Legal Pluralism between Scientific Analysis and Policy-making

From the short overview presented above, it should be clear that current approaches to irrigation and water management, with the possible exception of the more sophisticated versions of empowerment thinking, share a rather instrumentalist and functionalist approach to law. In technocratic or neoinstitutionalist approaches, the existence of complex sociolegal conditions is either completely disregarded or merely treated as an obstacle to a desired efficient future condition. Even in common property resource theory, in which property rights are recognized as a central element in determining the use and management of natural resources, plural legal conditions tend to be reduced to dichotomies such as formal versus informal and de jure versus de facto (cf. Schlager and Ostrom 1992). Empowerment scholars—while recognizing the importance of law and rights in social behavior and relations of power—often leave the fluidity and dynamics of plural legal conditions unexplored.

This general lack of attention to legal pluralism in mainstream natural resources management approaches is regrettable, since attention to legal pluralism provides important insights for the understanding of water rights. Water resources and irrigation systems are often used and managed under legally plural conditions, in which rules and principles of different origins, legitimated by different legal and normative frameworks, coexist and interact. Water policies and intervention strategies often create additional layers of rules and additional sources of legitimation. The interactions between various existing norms, rules, and rights, and forms of regulation, exploitation, and management form an intrinsic part of water management realities, and thus require study. Indeed, understanding legally plural conditions may be the first step toward finding location-specific solutions to existing problems of scarcity, overexploitation, and redistribution. If the aim is to contribute to progressive social change in water rights and control, it can only be accomplished if the complexity of norms and rights is well understood and taken as a point of departure. In any case, it has become clear that intervening in water resources use, management, or governance without understanding such conditions is a recipe for failure.

Whereas water management professionals have been slow in adopting insights about legal pluralism, legal anthropologists, mainly concerned with scientific analysis and averse to policy involvement, have made little effort to make their insights useful to water management. Is it possible for legal anthropologists and water professionals to meet and interact in more productive ways? And, taking a step further, how can a better understanding of the complexities of water use and management realities improve policy making and practices of intervention in water control?

Recent developments in the debates on water rights suggest that there is at least some common ground between anthropologists and water professionals. We are therefore hopeful about the chances of productive meetings between the two. A growing body of literature, exploring the boundary area between academic and policy-related professional work, and among irrigation studies, sociolegal studies, anthropology, economics, and political sciences, actively engages with the sociolegal aspects of water issues. This body of research and literature gives such a prominent place to analysis of the role of legal pluralism in water use, management, and governance that a sound basis for policy making seems to be in the making.

Such recent work recognizes the existence and strategic use of multiple definitions of water rights originating from various normative frameworks to support conflicting resource claims, and stresses the importance of negotiated approaches in processes of water allocation and legislation under conditions of growing demand. Analyses that incorporate the existence of a multiplicity of rights not only better reflect daily reality as experienced by resource users but also give a better insight in the ways in which resource users adapt to changes in their resource environments. The existence of legally plural conditions is not exclusively a recipe for chaos, as many neoinstitutionalists would have it. Plurality may also increase the capacity of resource users to adapt flexibly to changes and various forms of uncertainty (see Bruns and Meinzen-Dick 2000; Meinzen-Dick and Pradhan 2001a; Pradhan and Meinzen-Dick 2003).

This kind of approach and analysis moves away from the narrow prescriptive perspective of state legislation and grants agency to other water actors. It also links the rights discussion in a useful way to debates on institutionalized behavior and the role of institutions in resource management. However, the almost exclusive focus on the agency and the capacity of water users to use law as a resource in strategic action may overlook the role of power. Where the relationships between various legal orders are characterized by power differences that are a serious constraint to human agency, resource users are confronted with legal uncertainties about their rights to a resource. Situations of water scarcity and water reforms almost always entail redistribution of water, and when some get a larger share it unavoidably means that others get less. This is why water rights and regulations are always contested and the object of more or less open struggles. The policy-induced focus on strategic actions, the search for negotiated outcomes, and the promotion of problem solutions through stakeholder platforms still tend to neglect or ignore these conflicts and struggles.

Indeed, what these debates and approaches show is how turning legal pluralism from an analytical concept into a policy-relevant one creates the danger of diluting the concept to turn it into yet another buzzword of the development policy world. We will return to this issue in the concluding chapter.

The Chapters in This Book

Common Themes and Case Study Focus

In this book we present a collection of in-depth case studies about the role of law and legal pluralism in water resources management from Africa, Asia, Latin America, and the United States. Some contributions are based on experiences with practical development-related work, others on academic research yielding rich and detailed ethnographic case material. There is a strong focus on water for agricultural use, that is, for irrigation. This is mainly for the following reasons: First, irrigation is among the historically oldest and, in terms of rights, most established and socially embedded forms of water use. Second, far more water is used for irrigation than for anything else. Irrigated agriculture is responsible for between 70 and 80 percent of fresh water consumption. Third, and related to the first point, the redefinition of water rights and the resulting transfer of water from agriculture to other uses tends to generate conflicts about water rights, usually fought in terms of conflicting legal definitions of such rights. Indeed, global proposals often suggest that water be transferred from agriculture to "more productive uses." Irrigation is also perceived to be the largest waster of water. Although it does not attempt to refute such statements, this book is premised on the belief that the real value of much water used in agriculture is ill captured by such recipes. This belief stems from our common interest in, and in-depth knowledge of, the ways that rural livelihoods are transformed by irrigated agriculture.

Most of the contributors to this volume participated in a panel on water rights and legal pluralism at the thirteenth international congress on folk law and legal pluralism, held in Chiang Mai, Thailand, in April 2002. The constructive discussions during the panel sessions made us decide to engage in this collaborative effort, and to ask other authors who did not participate in the panel but have widely published on the theme to contribute chapters to this volume. The primary focus of all authors contributing to this book is a socio-legal one. That is, all authors deal with the sometimes explicit, sometimes more implicit role of law in issues of water rights and water resources management.

The authors of all chapters in this book, whether more engaged in academic work or deeply involved in development and policy-related activities, take as their point of departure the possibility of existence of legal pluralism, multiple definitions, and interpretations of legitimate rights in various social fields or levels of governance. All authors share a fundamental interest in the working of law in real life, in law in society or law in practice. Therefore, all chapters cover in some way the issue of the relationship between legal regulation originating from a diversity of sources of authority, on the one hand, and actual human behavior in the field of water resources use and management, on the other.

The authors engage with the topic of legal pluralism and water rights in a variety of ways. They offer different perspectives on analytical approaches, on the debate about recognition, on ways to operationalize the concept in policy worlds, and on combinations of these. Together, they help to create a broader awareness of the role of law in resource use and management, and contribute to a wider acceptance of the plural character of regulation of water resources. The case studies illustrate the analytical value of the concept. Second, the focus on recognition shows that the sheer acceptance of legal pluralism as a social fact does not automatically or straightforwardly solve problems of water governance. On the contrary, coping with plural rights in practice raises fundamental questions about the scope of recognition, about power relations, about identities, and about norms and values. They plunge the researcher back into the real and messy world of politics and of difficult distributional questions for which there are no easy and clean academic answers.

Short Overview of the Chapters

Chapters 2 to 5 illustrate the contradictions, limitations, and dangers inherent in state recognition or construction of local rights. In chapter 2, using case material from Nepal, Bhushan Udas and Zwarteveen discuss the tensions between national policies and legal regulations aimed at redressing gender disparities in WUAs for irrigation management, on the one hand, and local realities in which such higher-level regulation is given meaning and transformed, on the other. To what extent can national regulations redress gender imbalances in irrigation management that reflect wider power imbalances between men and women? Investigating the influence of national quota rules for women's representation and participation on local management realities, the authors critically question the degree to which paper rights or categorical rights are turned into concretized rights actually exerted by women.

In chapter 3, Getches deals with the legal recognition and protection of native Indian water rights in the United States. Legal complexity is manifested in contradictory intrasystemic legal pluralism, where federal and state law confront each other in the establishment of regulations concerning the limitations and faculties of indigenous rights systems. Tenure security of the latter is largely dependent of the nonindigenous settlers' interest in clearly defining their encroachment opportunities and investment security. By showing that recognized indigenous rights largely lead a paper life, this case study again underlines the importance of making a distinction between categorical and actualized rights.

In chapter 4, Roth analyzes irrigation management among migrant Balinese farmers in a state-built irrigation system in Indonesia. These practices have developed in the tension between state-defined norms, organizational and technical blueprints, and Balinese conceptions of irrigation management. This case study shows the limits of social engineering approaches to local irrigation management. Within the void created by a highly abstract and generalized legal definition of rights and responsibilities, specifically Balinese perceptions and practices continue to play a crucial role even in this "modern" system.

In chapter 5, Boelens and Zwarteveen critically discuss neoliberal theories and models that inform water reform in the Andes. Water reform in Andean countries tends to follow the neoliberal privatization recipe. The authors argue that such reforms and the language used to justify them closely resemble those of colonial and postcolonial "civilizing" efforts. Today's thinking about water is strongly rooted in an Enlightenment tradition, based on a strongly normative assumption of rational individuals, on the decoupling of power from knowledge, and on an association of private property rights with civilization and progress. The chapter shows that neoliberal terminology is ill-suited for understanding water realities, for visualizing the effects of reforms on local water rights, and for informing water legislation and management. An analysis that pays due attention to legal pluralism provides many useful ingredients for an alternative approach to water reforms.

The case studies in chapters 6 to 9 illustrate the fact that local struggles over water are also struggles over definitions of rights. Thus, these chapters highlight the relevance of the concept of legal pluralism by analyzing the tensions between various definitions of water rights that originate from multiple sources. The case studies show how different actors strategically use and manipulate different regulatory and legal frameworks to claim and secure water. Chapter 6 somewhat deviates from the other chapters in dealing with urban groundwater use in Kathmandu, Nepal, rather than with agricultural water use. Regmi analyzes how modern extraction technology affects the existing rules and rights regimes to water, and shapes peoples' perceptions of rights. Since groundwater is primarily seen as private property, the right to use it is restricted (or individualized). Once again, we find a wide gap between formal regulation and actual water use practices. The author proposes an allocational framework for water that could help to address this gap by recognizing the diverse and interlinked forms of access and technologies.

In chapter 7, Boelens, Gentes, Guevara Gil, and Urteaga deal with the complex issue of recognition and negation of local and indigenous rights in the

Andean sociocultural and political context. For the last decade, peasant and indigenous rights frameworks have received constitutional backing in most Andean countries. Yet, after centuries of discrimination and destruction of local water management rules, the tension between official and nonofficial water rights repertoires lingers on. The authors argue that special legislation to solve the contradiction tends to foster subordination of marginalized sections of society and to essentialize invented concepts of ethnicity and community.

Chapter 8 deals with groundwater in an agricultural context. Prakash and Ballabh present an analysis of groundwater extraction for irrigation in Gujarat, India. Groundwater tables are rapidly declining due to increasing use. The case study shows that this water scarcity has put many at a disadvantage, while giving others an opportunity: rich farmers who have invested in deep tube wells. Mediated by access to increasingly expensive pumping devices, access to groundwater is ultimately determined by the hierarchic social and economic relationships associated with caste rather than by effective legal regulation of the resource on the basis of social or environmental goals.

After this set of case studies, the book proceeds with a set of chapters (9, 10, and 11) that were written by authors actively engaged in the world of water policy making and consultancy, and attempting to match their professional activities with the analytical concerns of legal pluralism. In chapter 9, van Koppen and Jha take up another regionally specific dimension, the national politics of water reforms in South Africa. Since the demise of the apartheid regime, South Africa has embarked on a road of impressive legal and policy reforms that should help to redress the color-biased injustices of resource allocation during the apartheid regime and contribute to poverty eradication. Can these policy reforms in the framework of the new National Water Act contribute in a meaningful way to the creation of a more equitable and just society? As this case study on the formation of catchment management agencies shows, this remains an open question.

In chapter 10, Bruns asks how rights-based approaches that start from a neoinstitutionalist perspective can be combined with an approach that pays attention to legal complexity. Using examples from Southeast Asia, the author shows that development of water rights could rely on demand-driven processes that emphasize voluntary initiative, local knowledge, self-governance, and negotiation among stakeholders. According to the author, adaptive strategies for water reform based on the existence of multiple definitions of water rights can form a viable alternative to the usual focus on water pricing, water markets, and the establishment of uniformly formalized forms of water tenure.

In chapter 11, Meinzen-Dick and Pradhan broaden the discussion by tackling the issue of intersectoral water transfers, usually away from agricultural use toward nonagricultural uses. Exclusive attention to rights based on state law in such water transfer processes tends to favor the politically and economically most powerful groups in society. Taking examples from various sources and uses of water under a diversity of legal regimes in several countries, the authors argue in favor of greater attention to legal pluralism in water policy, especially in the context of water transfers. Recognition of local water rights, according to the authors, favors access to water, livelihood, and the bargaining position of the poor.

In the concluding chapter to this book, Zwarteveen, Roth, and Boelens highlight a number of important issues that emerge from the case studies in the earlier chapters. With a general focus on issues of analysis of legally complex settings, on debates about the pros and cons of recognition of local water rights, and on the consequences for water resource governance and management practices, the authors present a number of key reflections, conclusions, and recommendations pertaining to law and legal complexity, water rights, and water policies based on the case study chapters.

NOTES

1. For examples, see www.gwpforum.org and www.worldbank.org/wbi/pimelg/. For a critical approach to water reforms in irrigation, see Mollinga and Bolding 2004.
2. Though other uses of the concept are possible, we will refer here to its use for analytical purposes, that is: accepting the theoretical possibility of the existence of such a multiplicity of legal orders (see F. von Benda-Beckmann 1997, 2001; Merry 1988, 1992). Important recent discussions of the history and the concept of legal pluralism are Roberts 1998 and Woodman 1998. See also Hooker 1975; Griffiths 1986; Merry 1988. For an important conceptual precursor of legal pluralism, see S. F. Moore 1973, 1978. A distinction can be made between those who have elaborated and discussed the concept (mainly legal scholars), and those who are interested in its empirical and analytical qualities (largely sociologists and anthropologists) (see Woodman 1998; Merry 1992).
3. Even today, many legal theorists reject the concept of legal pluralism. It has remained the subject of fierce and often rather unproductive academic debates among legal anthropologists and legal scientists (see F. von Benda-Beckmann 2002; Tamanaha 1993).
4. It has proved impossible to capture these more messy properties of law in neatly systemic terms. Attempts at localizing law in terms of systems related to a distinct geographical or other space have, not surprisingly, remained problematic (Woodman 1998). This is reflected in a hodgepodge of terms such as "legal systems," "orders," "mechanisms," "phenomena," "frameworks," "domains," "discourses," and "repertoires" to convey the basic idea of the approach. However, a term such as "repertoire" is an apt expression of the fact that actors have a variety of legal options on the shelf, to be activated in specific contexts and interaction settings.
5. In the case of water rights, this subdivision can be further refined by distinguishing between reference rights, activated rights, and materialized rights, a distinction that matches the one between water allocation, water scheduling, and actual water distribution (see Boelens and Zwarteveen 2002).
6. We focus here on the professional irrigation and irrigation management literature. In addition to this literature, there is also what could be called a more academic

literature, which is much less linked to irrigation intervention practices. It consists of historical, geographical, socioanthropological, political-economic, and other studies on irrigation, which aim at understanding ongoing processes rather than desiring to intervene directly in these processes (e.g., Barnett 1981; Geertz 1972; Gelles 1998, 2000; Guillet 1992; Lansing 1991; Maass and Anderson 1978; Mitchell and Guillet 1994; Mosse 1997). In these studies there is more attention to water laws as well as to the normative and legal dimensions of irrigation development. However, their influence on irrigation professionalism has remained limited at best.

7. New institutionalism and rational choice theory refer to a family of approaches also referred to as "rational choice paradigm," "new political economy," "public choice theory," and "economics of politics." Game theory is an important tool in these approaches.

8. Financial autonomy is defined as a condition such that the irrigation agency must rely on user fees for a significant portion of the resources used for operation and maintenance, and has expenditure control over the use of funds generated from these charges (Small and Carruthers 1991).

9. Under conditions of insecurity, the ability to invest in the resource may also be less, due to a lack of control and poor access to support services such as information and credit, which are often linked to ownership.

10. See also Leach, Mearns, and Scoones (1997), Agrawal and Gibson (2001), Goldman (1998), and Boelens and Zwarteveen (2002) for elaboration of this point. Mosse (1997) provides an interesting historical analysis of community management of tank irrigation systems in south India, which demythologizes some persistent beliefs about the greater equality of traditional common property institutions in irrigation.

2

Prescribing Gender Equity? The Case of the Tukucha Nala Irrigation System, Central Nepal

PRANITA BHUSHAN UDAS

MARGREET ZWARTEVEEN

This chapter discusses the potential of law to contribute to progressive social change in water management by looking at legal attempts to improve the gender balance in water users' associations (WUAs) in Nepal. The gap between women's responsibilities in irrigation and their voice in local irrigation management organizations is well documented, in Nepal as well as elsewhere. Existence of this gap is often seen as an indicator of gender inequity, reflecting wider power imbalances between men and women. In Nepal, the need for bridging this gap has been realized in the last decades on grounds of efficiency, equity, and sustainability. More recently, participation of women in resource management organizations is also linked to concerns of democracy and justice. In recognition of these concerns, the government of Nepal has incorporated in its policies and laws explicit rules and measures aimed at improving the gender balance in WUAs. Nepal's eighth five-years plan first mentioned the need to promote women's participation in agricultural and forest cooperatives. Partly reflecting the intentions of the five-years plan, the irrigation policy of 1992 included a provision to the effect that executive committees of WUAs should have at least 20 percent female members (HMG/MWR 1992). The Irrigation Regulation of 2000 finally made women's representation in executive committees of WUAs mandatory by statutory law. It stipulates the compulsory presence of at least two women members in executive committees of at most nine members.

Through the example of a WUA in the Tukucha Nala irrigation system, this chapter explores the effects of these quota rules on actual participation of women in decision making. It looks at how national policies are used and how they receive meaning in the actual practices and negotiations of engineers, project staff, and water users at different levels of bureaucratic planning and project implementation. How are rights on paper or categorical rights turned

21

into actual, concretized rights? This chapter adopts a broad conceptualization of law, not exclusively reserving this term for state law but expanding it to include other more or less formalized and institutionalized forms of normative ordering in society. The study has made the relationship between legal rules and policies, on the one hand, and human behavior and outcomes, on the other, the object of investigation, rather than assuming them (see Long and van der Ploeg 1989). It is through actual practices and in actual negotiations that rules and laws assume their social meaning and significance. The chapter thus uses a definition of policy as process, treating policy formulation and implementation as political processes in which many interests are at stake and many actors are involved. Implicit in this approach is the treatment of all people (and not just experts) as knowledgeable and capable actors, thus allowing for a serious consideration of their actions, skills, concerns, and perspectives (Bourdieu 1977; Giddens 1984; Long and van der Ploeg 1989).

The final objective of this chapter is to reflect on wider questions of gender equity and water management. Water management regulation and irrigation development processes are essentially about generating or redefining control over water and (re-)structuring power relations (cf. Boelens and Hoogendam 2002; Mollinga 2003; Roth 1999; Zwarteveen 1997). Water is power, and "changing water" is changing power. As regards gender relations in Nepal, the question that poses itself is whether and how progressive laws and regulations, that is, the quota system in the Irrigation Regulation, can lend support to local political action for water control by women. How and by whom are irrigation authorities held accountable to the rules and guidelines regarding women's participation?

The next section of the chapter describes the implementation process, from the drafting of the memorandum of understanding between the Asian Development Bank (ADB) and the Department of Irrigation (DOI) to the actual registration of the Tukucha Nala WUA. The third section discusses WUA activities, with a focus on participation of women. The fourth section looks at the WUA from the perspective of female water users, and shows why they are (or are not) interested in participating. In the concluding section, the question of the title is further reflected upon.

From Paper and Policies to People and Practices

Donor agencies have had considerable influence in raising the issue of women's political representation in offices and public decision making.[1] Donor organizations have also been instrumental in influencing formulation and implementation of development policies.[2] This starts with negotiations in the Foreign Aid Co-ordination Committee at the Ministry of Finance, in which donors and the government discuss future and current irrigation projects. Other participants in these discussions are the Ministry of Water Resources, the DOI, and the National Planning Commission. One such project was the Second Irrigation Sector Project (SISP), financed by the ADB, part of which called for rehabilitating the Tukucha Nala irrigation system.

The Second Irrigation Sector Project

The Second Irrigation Sector Project was one of the thirty programs of DOI in 2001. SISP was the largest irrigation project in Nepal, targeting an area of 41,000 hectares.[3] It aimed at the provision of irrigation services to the Eastern and Central Development Region in Nepal, primarily through the rehabilitation of existing farmer-managed irrigation systems, and was a continuation of the First Irrigation Sector Project launched in 1989. A recognized weakness of the first project was institutional development and one of the reasons for embarking on SISP was to redress this mistake. Thus, institutional strengthening through support of WUAs in 180 irrigation systems was a major focus (CRID 2001). Active participation of irrigators in planning, design and construction, and operation and maintenance of the rehabilitated systems was an important objective.

SISP was executed from 1996 to 2002. A group of consultants named SILT was hired by the Asian Development Bank to assist DOI in implementing the project. SILT prepared regular progress reports for ADB and DOI, and was involved in preparing the operational procedural manual.[4] This manual provides details for project implementation, and serves to smooth out and avoid contradictions between national irrigation policies and donor objectives.

According to a project review mission in 1998 (after two years), progress made with the establishment of WUAs was disappointing, and funding was temporarily stopped. Two studies were commissioned to identify how to best strengthen WUAs. The studies concluded that the appointment of a local person as community-based organizer was an effective strategy to consolidate and strengthen WUAs, more effective than involving NGOs. Another proposed change was the creation of an institutional development team, consisting of an agronomist and a social scientist, at the Regional Irrigation Directorate. The institutional development team was to give special support to WUAs.

The memorandum of understanding of the SISP project contains the following section on gender:[5]

> Although women are widely involved in farming activities, particularly in the Hills, they have traditionally had little involvement in irrigation system operations. In many cases, irrigation management is thought to be a task for men, and women would prefer not to be involved. However, they do have needs for water, particularly for washing and bathing, and would like to have these needs recognized. The project approach therefore

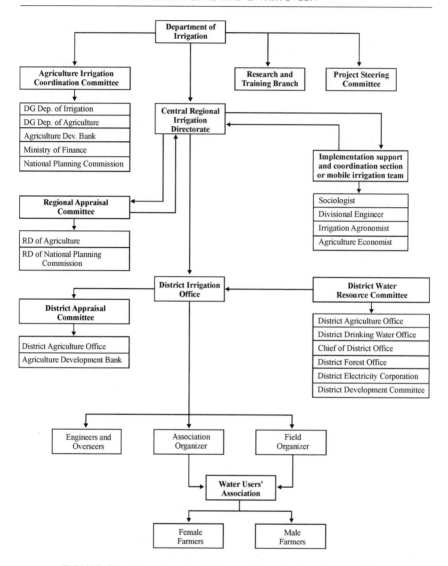

FIGURE 2.1. Actors involved in irrigation project implementation.

needs to be flexible. Encouragement will be given to the involvement of women in the design and implementation of the project. To achieve this objective:

- Female sociologists, association organizers (AOs), field organizers (FOs) and consultants will be hired by DOI to assist in the formation and strengthening of WUAs in each subproject;[6]
- DOI, DOA and WUA officials will be trained in gender awareness and in recognizing the needs and role of the women in the community;
- Training packages for women will be prepared by DOI;

- An appropriate provision concerning women's participation in project implementation will be included in the memorandum of agreement between DOI and each WUA;
- Linkages between the project and ongoing Women in Development projects will be strengthened.

In contrast to this explicit attention to gender in the memorandum of understanding, the project operational procedural manual, the main reference for project staff in their day-to-day work, does not provide any details on how to address gender concerns. The manual does provide detailed and step-by-step instructions on many other matters such as the mobilization of labor for system construction and maintenance.

The Tukucha Nala Irrigation System

The Tukucha Nala irrigation system is located in the Tukucha Nala Village Development Committee, in the northwest of the Kavre District of the Bagamati Zone in the Central Development Region. It lies at a distance of approximately thirty-four kilometers east of Kathmandu and ten kilometers west of Dhulikhel, the district headquarters. The Punyamata River, which feeds the system, is a perennial nonsnow-fed river with a catchment area of 6.5 square kilometers, which meets the Rosi River at Panauti and is part of the Sunkoshi River basin in the south. In 1982, a small group of farmers started irrigating from the Punyamata River on their own initiative. After a violent flood in 1992, which washed away most of the fertile land, the District Irrigation Office first intervened in the area through the provision of financial support for emergency relief and rehabilitation. Through collective voluntary labor efforts of both female and male irrigators, the farmers managed to save 10,000 rupees of the allocated office's budget for wage labor.[7] In the next year, the river was extremely dry and, because of the drought, the harvests very poor. The president of ward three, together with other local leaders from the same ward (all men), came together and took the lead in diverting water from the river for what is the head end section of the current irrigation system. Women farmers actively participated in the digging of the canal. Using the saved money, cemented casting pipes were bought to divert water from the canals to the fields. The pipes were not very effective, as they often got clogged, while cleaning proved quite cumbersome. This prompted the local farmer leaders to request support for rehabilitation to the District Irrigation Office in 1996. This rehabilitation was undertaken in 1997 and 1998 as part of the SISP project. From 2001 onward, a community-based organizer from the village was appointed by the District Irrigation Office as part of the institutional strengthening component of this same project.

At present, Tukucha Nala irrigation system has a command area of thirty-four hectares. The main canal is designed to carry a discharge of eighty-five liters per second. It has no fixed diversion structure, except for the side intake situated at the left bank of the river (DIO 1997). The length of the main canal is a little over two kilometers. At the time of construction, sixty-seven households used the canal to irrigate their lands. This has now increased as a consequence of splitting up of households and formation of new ones. The system irrigates three wards out of a total of nine in the village: the whole of ward three and parts of wards two and four. The head works are situated in ward four, which lies at the highest altitude. Ward three lies a bit lower, and ward two lies almost at the foothills. Thus, ward four users are the head enders, whereas ward two users are the tail enders. The majority (forty-five) of the households belong to the dominant Newar caste, living in wards three and four. Thirteen of the remaining households are Mijar, Magarati, Sarki, and Tamang, all castes that are considered as lower in social status. All of them live in ward number two, in the tail end. The remaining nine households are Chettris of higher social status, who live in ward four.[8]

The introduction of irrigation in Tukucha Nala made an increase in cropping intensity possible. Farmers grow paddy now from April to September. After harvesting paddy, two crops of potatoes are planted, the first from October to December and the second from January to March. Potatoes are grown as a cash crop; it has considerably increased the incomes of irrigating households.

The Water Users' Association

As mentioned above, the Tukucha Nala WUA came into formal and registered existence as a result of a request from the villagers for rehabilitation support. Obtaining this support was not just a matter of complying with formal requirements, but was very much the result of skillful political networking.[9] The first president of the WUA was also the president of ward three (and was later elected as the area representative in the district development committee). At the time of application for rehabilitation support, he was an active local leader with important political connections. In order to increase the chances of obtaining the requested support, he approached a parliament member who belonged to his political party. This member of parliament successfully lobbied with DOI for approval of the project. At the time the request was made to the District Irrigation Office, some other village groups from irrigation systems in the same village development committee had also applied for District Irrigation Office support. One of those requests, pertaining to an irrigation system upstream of Tukucha Nala, was already selected by the district irrigation office for a prefeasibility study. Yet, because of the pressure of the political leader, DOI decided to approve the Tukucha Nala system, in the process changing its name from Phanalpat to Tukucha Nala, instead of basing its choice on the original names of the systems under consideration. Tukucha Nala thus got the support

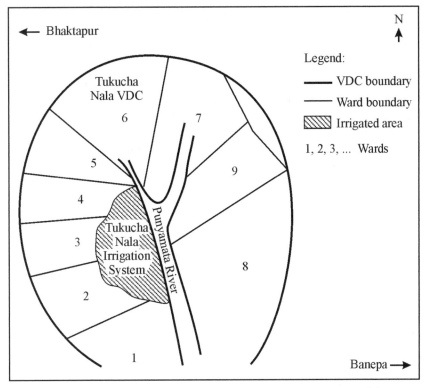

FIGURE 2.2. Tukucha Nala irrigation system (not according to scale).

originally intended for the upstream system where the prefeasibility study had already started.

Formal Registration and Establishment of the Water Users' Association

Thus, the WUA came into existence because of the villagers' request for funds for rehabilitation, an initiative of the ward three president and two other local leaders, all of whom were male. An association organizer from the District Irrigation Office informed the local leaders of the approval of their request, and started the process of formal registration. The first meeting to establish the Tukucha Nala WUA was called by the same association organizer from the District Irrigation Office, on April 22, 1996. Almost naturally, it was decided that the president of ward three would become the president of the new WUA, while the two other local leaders who had been involved in submitting the request to DOI were to become the secretary and vice secretary. Among the three of them, and with the help of the association organizer, they nominated the other committee members among those present at this first meeting. No women were present.

However, thanks to the organizer's suggestion that some women were needed in the committee, one woman was nominated by the president. Two days later, on April 24, the proposed executive committee (of eleven members) was approved in a meeting in which fifty-eight people were gathered, eleven of whom were women. According to the association organizer, it was not easy to interest women in coming to the meeting; the villagers understood the business of attending meetings as a responsibility of men and household heads. It was all right for women to actively participate in canal cleaning and construction, but discussing matters in public meetings was seen as something to be done by educated male leaders.

Drafting the WUA constitution was an all-male affair, involving two local leaders (the president and the secretary of the WUA) together with the chief district engineer and district engineers at the District Irrigation Office.[10] The constitution was based on the format provided by the office. According to the adopted format, a WUA member is "a farmer who is more than eighteen years old and who holds land under cultivation, tenancy or any other landholder without tenancy relation or any farmer who has obtained the right from the landholder to farm within the irrigated area." WUA membership is thus based on land utilization rather than ownership. Formal titles to land are not necessary for membership, removing one of the often-mentioned barriers to female participation in users' organizations. The constitutional rule for membership could even be interpreted to mean that membership applies to households or families rather than to individuals. In the case of Tukucha Nala, the rule is interpreted to apply to heads of households, in most cases men. Evidence so far also shows that there is no problem when formal members are replaced by either male or female close relatives. Yet the adopted WUA constitution is silent about female representation in the committee.

Hardly anyone involved in the process of organizing and registering the WUA was aware of the contents of the constitution. Its drafting as well as its ratification by WUA members in September had the character of a ritual that needed to be performed in order to become eligible for financial support rather than a decision-making process where the rules and internal functioning of the WUA are negotiated and agreed upon. The staff from the District Irrigation Office supposed to guide this ritual was primarily guided by the operational procedural manual that had been made especially for SISP. Although most staff members were quite familiar with the national policies, in their day-to-day actions they followed the project manual. It is illustrative in this regard that the head of the District Irrigation Office, when asked, did not have printed copies of national policy documents. The project operational procedural manual, in contrast, was carefully kept in a locked cupboard. This was the document the district irrigation officer referred to when explaining his actions and decisions. The manual is important when the project evaluation team of the donor and the DOI visit the field. As noted above, the manual did not reflect national policies in that it was silent on gender issues.[11] In addition, project officials justified their lack of efforts to achieve more female participation in meetings by referring to the Water Resources Act of 1992 and the Water Regulation of 1993, in which gender issues are not mentioned. Although they were aware of the stipulation in the 1992 Irrigation Policy that 20 percent of the seats in executive committees need to be reserved for women, they did not consider this as mandatory. Selective and strategic use of regulations ("shopping") is thus not restricted to resource users but is also a practice of officials.

It is interesting that the quota system for women was the only guideline of the Irrigation Policy that was thus questioned; all the other guidelines were accepted. This can be partly explained by the fact that many of the other guidelines more directly reflected concerns expressed by those water users who were involved in negotiations. They are, for instance, keen on having fixed and clear rules on how much labor they are expected to provide, since they want to be sure that they do not pay more than other WUAs. Whether or not women participate in the stipulated way did not provoke the same level of concern. Therefore, WUAs do not tend to demand strict enforcement of that rule.

Members of the project team were not against inclusion of women in WUAs, nor did they dispute the importance of women in irrigated agriculture. Yet many of them perceived women to be in need of special male protection, rather than seeing the need for gender equity-enhancing measures. This perception is illustrated by the example of a woman who had come to the District Irrigation Office. She had traveled for two hours by bus, and walked for five hours to get there. She wanted to request an iron mesh that was made available through the river control program. In an honest attempt to be nice and polite, the irrigation engineer dealing with the request asked the woman: "Oh, you took so much trouble coming here. Do you not have any male in your village to come and make this request?" He did not intend to discourage the woman, but the subtext of his remark was that the woman herself was not as well suited for doing this job as her male counterparts.

In actual practice, the responsibility for actively promoting female participation seems to have primarily been with the association organizer. This is an unregistered officer at District Irrigation Office. At the time of conducting this study, the association organizer for Kavre District was on unpaid leave, and the post was thus vacant. In an interview, this organizer explained that he had felt rather isolated among the other irrigation staff. He complained about his high workload: he was responsible for all irrigation projects in the district. He felt that he had been posted to Kavre because the person who replaced him in the office in Kathmandu (a better-liked working station) had good political connections. He went on unpaid leave to start work somewhere else for a higher wage, closer to his family. About the participation of women in WUAs, he felt he had made some real efforts to encourage women to come to the meetings. "Women will not come by themselves, they need to be forced to become members of the committee," he commented. In addition to referring to prevailing beliefs that allocate the tasks of public decision making to men, he also doubted the importance of the WUA for irrigators: "what people want is funds for rehabilitating their irrigation system. They are not interested in the WUA."

Possibilities for networking with government and nongovernment agencies outside the village may have been another important reason for wanting to join the WUA. In most cases, after rehabilitation the WUAs continue working in informal ways irrespective of the WUA constitution. How WUA meetings are held and how irrigation-related decisions are made seems to be less a function of formal rules and regulations than of existing customs and practices that are tightly interwoven with local hierarchies of power and existing networks and alliances (on this same trend in Bali, see chapter 4). The overall low literacy rate is obviously also a factor in explaining why the constitution hardly matters.

In official project implementation plans, achievements and results of efforts to involve women in WUAs were to be monitored through field observations. A special benefit monitoring evaluation format was developed in which these observations could be reported in a systematic fashion. The agronomist of the institutional development team at the Regional Directorate was to keep these forms and analyze them. However, as he was absent for months, this never happened. In the absence of such information, it became impossible for DOI or ADB to hold project officers accountable for the achieved results.

Toward the end of 1996, the Tukucha Nala WUA was formally registered at the District Water Resource Committee. After two years of SISP, a monitoring team declared that the implemented project was not achieving acceptable irrigation efficiencies because of poor WUA performance. In response to this evaluation, in 2001 a community-based organizer (CBO) was hired locally. The man, who had until then been the secretary of the WUA, was appointed on a one-year basis and with a remuneration of NRs 2,400 per month plus NRs 300 stationary allowance. His main task was to strengthen the WUA at the local level. He was also to provide the main link between the village level and the District Irrigation Office. He had to resign from his post as WUA secretary to become CBO, as demanded by the official rules of the District Irrigation Office. The WUA committee accepted his resignation with the understanding that he would again serve as WUA secretary after completion of his role as CBO.

WUA Activities

According to the official organizational structure of the WUA, the General Assembly meeting of the WUA should be held twice a year, once before the rainy season and a second time before the winter season. Meetings of the WUA committee are to be held at least four times a year. The WUA is expected to appoint five teams, headed by committee members. These teams are formed to guide the execution of specific tasks such as system maintenance and operation, provision of agricultural inputs, institutional development, training, and networking with line agencies such as the District Agricultural Office, district cooperatives, and district women's organizations. In the general assembly meetings, the users are to select these teams, which are to operate for two years.

In Tukucha Nala, from the time of registration in 1996 until 2001, only three general assembly meetings of the WUA were held. The first was held in 1996, the second in 2000, and the third in 2001. The WUA committee formed in 1996 was only changed in 2000, even though the constitution mentions a working period of two years.

The actual functioning of the WUA responded more to the needs of the irrigators than to constitutional requirements; the WUA committee met when it was time for canal cleaning, just before the start of the season when canal sedimentation due to the rains of June and July was high. Since all irrigators wanted to grow potatoes in October, there was a clearly felt need for the canals to be cleaned before that time. Organizing canal cleaning activities was, in fact, the main activity of the Tukucha Nala WUA. The stipulated teams existed on paper, but none of the committee members remembered to which of the teams they belonged. In 1997, when the WUA had just come into being, it was also involved in system construction activities, which were organized with help from the District Irrigation Office. Some committee members attended training about system operation and maintenance, and networking. None of the other activities mentioned in the WUA constitution were carried out by the WUA. An initial attempt to distribute seeds through the WUA ended when SISP support to the District Agriculture Office was stopped. Even the canal cleaning activities had a rather ad hoc character. During the field research it was observed that there was an upstream drain that ran directly into the main canal, depositing sediments in it and thus increasing the amount of labor required for cleaning. Diverting the upstream drain would have been a time-saving and more structural solution to problems of canal sedimentation, but the WUA was not involved in regular monitoring and did not have a more structural maintenance plan. Collection of water fees and distribution of membership cards started with the appointment of the former secretary as the community-based organizer, in 2000. In 2001, sixty households had received membership cards, leaving eleven still without. Fees had been collected from only twenty-eight members. The plan was to collect in 2002 the rest of the fees for 2001 and those for 2002.

Both men and women participated in canal-cleaning activities. In the cleaning activities that took place in September 2001, on the first day representatives of forty-five households participated, fifteen of whom were women. On the second day, only eleven people showed up, two of whom were women. In this cleaning campaign, fifty-six of the seventy-one member households contributed labor. On the face of it, men's and women's labor inputs were considered of equal value. On closer inspection, it turned out that some cleaning activities were gendered. For instance, cleaning of human feces was indirectly left to the women. Women accepted this without any complaint.

As has been said, the physical involvement of women in construction and canal-cleaning activities was much more normal than their involvement and participation in public decision making. Very few women, if any, participated in the early informal get-togethers and more formal meetings that led to the creation of the WUA. Over the years, however, the number of women present at meetings gradually increased. At the first formal meeting, held in 1996 in the presence of the association organizer, only men were present. Female participation at the first, second, and third general assembly meetings was 9, 13, and 17 percent, respectively. In 2001, at the time of the field research, the letter that was distributed by the community-based organizer to call the third general assembly meeting explicitly mentioned that either men or women of a household could attend. Earlier letters had just invited household heads.[12] The first WUA committee only counted one woman among eleven members (9 percent), whereas the second committee counted three women (27 percent). It was the fierce insistence of the first president of the WUA that led to the appointment of three women in the second committee. His insistence stemmed from his awareness of the stipulation in the Local Governance Act that all development organizations need to have at least 30 percent female participation if they are to receive support from government and nongovernmental sources. During the assembly meeting, he announced the need for female participation and started nominating three women.

The first female committee member was appointed at the suggestion of the association organizer, who was present at the first meetings. The president of that time nominated her, a Chhettri woman of about forty years old whose husband worked in Kathmandu in the police force. In the absence of her husband, she was the household head and also in charge of farming. In 2001, her husband retired from his job and returned to the village. From that time onward, he took her place in the WUA committee, a decision that had her full support as well as that of the other committee members. She explained that the position in the committee had never been her own choice anyway, since she had been nominated by the president of that time. Also, she felt it was logical and appropriate that her husband, now that he was around, represent the household. She was happy that he was back and could resume his roles for the household, but also regretted that she would no longer be getting information on what was happening in meetings.

The process of appointing women for the second committee at the third general assembly meetings went as follows: the CBO first explained the need to reappoint a committee, as the first committee had already served for four years whereas the constitution stipulates a period of two years. In response to the CBO, the president explained that he wanted to step down as president, because his activities as area representative for the district development committee already took too much of his time. He nevertheless mentioned his willingness to represent Tukucha Nala at the national federation of WUAs, if Tukucha Nala decided to become a member of the federation. The vice secretary then proposed himself as the new secretary, a post he had already effectively assumed after the previous secretary had become the CBO. The president and the CBO then proceeded with the nomination of other committee members, and all present agreed to these nominations. Male representatives from the head, middle, and tail end section were thus selected. After this, the president announced the need to have women members in the committee. He said that this was needed in order to get support and approval from governmental and non-governmental organizations. The president nominated three women, all of the Newari caste, but all three refused. The first said she might not be able to attend meetings if her husband were at home. The other two refused because they felt diffident about participating: they referred to their lack of education and their inability to read and write. They were reluctant to assume the responsibility. When they had thus refused, and no other women were nominated, a middle-aged woman from the Sarki caste (a lower caste) quickly nominated her daughter-in-law as committee member. All agreed to this nomination. This woman is a widow of forty-six years old, who lives with her son and his wife. She was eager to have her daughter-in-law as a representative in the committee, because she thought that this would help them receive relevant information from outside the village. In the recent past, she had experienced tremendous difficulties in transferring her husband's land to her name after his death. She attributed these problems, at least partly, to her illiteracy and lack of access to information and connections. Because her daughter-in-law went to school until grade six, she believed she would be better able to assume a position in the committee than she would herself. After the appointment of her daughter-in-law, the president appointed two other women present at the meeting (both Newari women), who agreed by remaining silent. Their nomination was accepted by the others present.

Observations during the third general assembly meeting shed some further light on women's participation. The meeting was held outside at the Ganesh temple ground, a usual place for village meetings. The meeting started two hours late, at twelve o'clock noon instead of ten o'clock. Thirty-seven men and eight women were finally gathered. Since the grass at the back of the temple, in the shade, was not suitable to sit on, two women went to get floor mats. They gave floor mats to the community-based organizer, the president, and some other important men. One remaining mat was used by the eight women, who all sat together behind the local leaders. An important discussion during the meeting concerned the rules for labor contributions to canal cleaning. The absence of fines for not contributing labor was questioned. Some of those present (those with smaller landholdings) also felt that contributions should be proportional to the size of irrigated landholdings rather than being the same for all. A large landholder loudly protested against this proposal, and argued that contributions should be proportional to family size and thus to the availability of labor. Since all have about the same family size, he argued, the existing rule is good enough. The discussion about this topic was lively, and many of the men present participated. The women just whispered among themselves, and refrained from publicly articulating their opinions. Some of the poorer men also kept quiet. When the meeting was in full swing, a potato buyer from outside the village passed by and interrupted the meeting to find out whether farmers still had potatoes for sale. Most farmers had already sold all of their harvest, except for the large landholder, who had stored part of his harvest to wait for prices to rise. He eagerly embarked on a discussion with the potato buyer, thus interrupting the meeting for fifteen minutes. None of the participants had the presence of mind or courage to ask him to conduct his negotiations somewhere else, outside the meeting. It was the president who finally stopped him.

These observations illustrate that physical presence at meetings by itself is not enough to guarantee equal participation. Existing social relations of power and social divisions based on caste, gender, or size of landholding govern modes of conduct inside as well as outside meetings. Articulating opinions in public is not just difficult and considered inappropriate for women, it often is also unwise for poor men and women to openly disagree with (or question) those on whose favors they depend.

WUA Participation: For Whom?

How do men and women themselves understand their (non-)involvement in irrigation decision making? When discussing their low levels of participation in group discussions, many village women agreed that they did not see the use of participating in meetings. In their opinion, the only decision of importance made at the meetings relates to the dates for canal cleaning. Many women said that it would be a waste of time for them to spend hours at a meeting just to find out about this decision, which they can also come to know through the CBO. On the basis of the date, they can decide among the family members who will participate in canal-cleaning activities.

Prevailing notions about how men and women can and should behave do influence how people interpret and value participation in the WUA. A much-heard understanding about women in the village is that "women are uneducated, do not know official matters, and are poor in accounting." The strength of this belief can be illustrated by an observation made in a women's group (of sixteen members) of the participatory district development program. The district provided the group with a loan through the rural credit program. The female manager of the group left, as she felt unable to solve the quarrels that emerged among the women after having received this loan. The other women then decided to request male assistance to keep their accounts. They felt unable to do this themselves, even though two women of the group had five and six years of formal education. The vice secretary of the WUA agreed to take on this role. When he talked about his role in the women's group, he said he had to help the women, as they were unable to help themselves. In practice, the two women who were educated did the writing part of the bookkeeping. The vice secretary of WUA just guided and facilitated the meeting.

Another influential perception in Tukucha Nala is that women are physically weak and sexually vulnerable. Daughters usually are not allowed to go far from home after puberty, whereas sons of the same age are expected to explore the outside world. A village girl, for instance, wanted to go to Banepa, the nearest market, to collect sheep wool for spinning. Her mother only allowed her to go if some female friends would accompany her. Finally she suggested sending her brother to collect the wool. The idea that women are physically weak is also reflected in lower wages for women: for similar work, wages for women in the community are half those of men. In wards two and four the daily wage for labor is NRs 120 for men and NRs 60 for women, whereas that in ward three is NRs 100 and NRs 50, respectively. Gender ideologies further have it that women are particularly good in cooking and other kitchen-related work. People claim that, in the past, the roles and activities of women were restricted to indoor household activities. How accurate these memories are is hard to tell. In any case, today's women are prominently involved in all kinds of outdoor agricultural activities.

Gender norms and values vary with caste. The first people involved in water diversion from the Punyamata River were mainly Brahmin men. Brahmin (high-caste) women were hardly involved in the construction of the first diversion, since their tasks were confined to indoor activities, seed sowing, weeding, and harvesting. Carrying stones and digging canals was considered typically male work. Whereas many other families in the village, for lack of labor and money, could seldom afford to stick to this gender division of labor, the Brahmin families involved in constructing the first diversion were wealthy enough to be able to do without the labor of wives and daughters. Women did participate in the rehabilitation works that were organized after the 1992 floods. Those that worked alongside men to reconstruct the canals and diversion were mostly from the Newar, Mijar, and Sarki castes, all castes that have much less stringent gender divisions of tasks. Women from Brahmin castes were also less likely to participate in canal-cleaning activities.

Being a Household Head

The large majority of women who attended WUA meetings were heads of households. In discussing the issue of participation, woman members of male-headed households expressed a clear preference for being represented by their male partners in WUA meetings, whereas women of female-headed households stressed the importance of having women participants. Women from female-headed households emphasized that, without male partners, they lacked access to knowledge on official matters and also lacked access to decision makers. At the time of the study, out of the seventy-one irrigator households, fourteen (20 percent) were effectively headed by women (this is more than the national average of 10 percent).[13] In these households, women managed the farms. They were also the ones to take most of the day-to-day agricultural and irrigation decisions. Normally, activities such as spraying pesticide, cleaning canals, going to meetings, and managing outdoor official activities are done by men, but in their absence women also do them. Plowing is the only work women do not do. Three of the female heads of households were widows (de jure female heads of households) who cultivated part of their land and leased out the remainder to tenants. These three women usually did attend WUA meetings, and were more or less aware of what happened inside the WUA. None of them, however, participated in the executive committee, although two of the three women who were selected in the last general assembly meeting did come from female-headed households. They were from the eleven de facto female-headed households. The senior men from these households either worked as government staff or as a police officer, were in the army, or carried out business away from home.

As already mentioned, men are seen as the ones to represent the household in public meetings, including those of the WUA. Indeed, of the twenty-two households interviewed, in sixteen households only men had attended the WUA meetings, in three households only woman had attended, and in another three both men and women had attended. As to cleaning canals, from nine households only men participated, from four households only women, and from another nine households both men and women participated at different times. Attending WUA meetings is thus much more associated with masculinity than cleaning of canals and construction work.

Mothers, Daughters, and Daughters-in-Law

In addition to the distinction between women whose husbands are present and those whose husbands have migrated or died, women's interests and perceptions about participating in WUAs varied depending upon their position within households. Women could be broadly categorized into three groups: mothers, daughters, and daughters-in-law. Their respective influence in intrahousehold decision making, management, and control over household resources and incomes varied greatly among the three groups. The distinction helps explain how different women looked at their involvement in WUAs.

Mothers include most women between the ages of forty and sixty. In the village, all women in this group were illiterate and never went to a formal school. They spent most of their working lives as family farm laborers on household farms, cultivating food crops. Nowadays many of them work in potato fields, and thus help to earn cash income. In addition, many of them work as wage laborers in the village. They use the money earned through wage labor to increase the family income. Unlike the income derived from the family farms, they themselves control the money they earn as laborers and usually spend it on the children. Although the possibility of engaging in farm labor and earning an individually controlled income suggests some degree of autonomy from husbands, women themselves sketch the intrahousehold situation as one in which their husbands (if they are still alive and around) are the undisputed bosses. Women, for instance, say that they hardly discuss incomes and farm activities with their husbands. Instead "we wait for our husbands to make suggestions. Unless our husbands ask us to do things, we do not engage in new activities." Mothers are obviously important in conveying behavioral norms to their children. For instance, they teach their daughters never to allow their husbands or brothers to work in the kitchen. As referred to earlier, in the absence of husbands, mothers take on their roles and responsibilities.

Daughters are mostly women in the age group of eighteen to twenty years, many of whom have had at least some years of formal schooling before marriage. Dropout from school was higher for girls than for boys, because when farm labor was scarce most people would ask their daughters rather than sons to help them in the fields. Frequently missing classes, many girls got poor results on their exams. The embarrassment and shame this provoked was for many a reason to leave school altogether, once they reached grade five or six. After having dropped out of school, girls focused on learning skills such as knitting, sewing, weaving, and spinning from their neighbors and sisters-in-law. They hoped to earn money by knitting sweaters or spinning wool fibers for traders in nearby villages. Unlike their mothers, daughters hoped to keep this income for themselves, and use it to join in training activities, for instance. It is the rule that a good daughter obeys her mother and gives her due respect by giving over her earnings. Some daughters felt that, if they did not do this, their mothers might not allow them to engage in wage-labor activities in the future. Mothers were seen to be anxious about the whereabouts of their daughters, and tended to be rather controlling, imposing restrictions as to when and where they wandered. For many young women, engaging in wage-labor activities was as much a way to temporarily escape from this control as it was a way to earn money. Many daughters felt isolated within their houses, and some of them looked forward to getting married, seeing marriage as a road to freedom.

Daughters-in-law came into the family through either a formal or an informal marriage (marriage without permission of the parents and without a social marriage ceremony). How well they were treated and respected by other household members appeared to be related to how much they contributed to the household. There seemed to be a clear preference for daughters-in-law who come into the family through a formal marriage, as they then bring Daijo property (gifts from their maternal home), adding to the social prestige of the family of the bridegroom. Compared to mothers and even daughters, daughters-in-law had the least control over farm income. To access their incomes, they were dependent on their mothers-in-law, who in turn depended on their husbands. The communication between husbands and wives in younger couples was often better than that between their mothers and fathers. In some cases, literate daughters-in-law openly admitted interfering with their husbands' farm activities—something their mothers-in-law would never do.

Who Wants to Participate in WUAs?

When asked in individual interviews and group discussions, most women in the study area did not really consider their involvement in the WUA as important. Mothers were the least interested of all three categories of women, with the notable exception of the widows among them. They strongly felt that it was not their role to attend meetings and discuss irrigation matters, but that of their husbands. Yet at the same time, mothers were very concerned about the well-being of their families, which is why some of them indicated that they would certainly attend the meeting if it would benefit them. Daughters and daughters-in-law felt themselves not to be in a position to represent their households in meetings, since the elders in their homes were the ones to make most important decisions. Yet many daughters-in-law did say that they would like to have the opportunity to attend meetings as a way of getting to know more about what happens in the village. They were interested in receiving information about possible programs and projects that might benefit them, and saw WUA meetings as one possible avenue for obtaining this information. Some younger women (daughters as well as daughters-in-law) remarked that there was little chance of obtaining such information, or any other benefits, from the WUA meeting since these meetings were only held to decide upon the date for canal cleaning.

Prescribing Gender Equity?

To what extent has the stipulation in Nepal's Irrigation Regulation 2000, stating that at least two members of the executive committee of WUAs should be women, been successful in increasing women's voice and visibility in water management? The data at the regional level show that there is some participation of women in WUAs: the policy objective of having at least 20 percent female members has been achieved in 27 out of 108 WUAs. This means that, when expressed in numbers, the rate of success of the policy was 25 percent (SILT 2001). The Tukucha Nala case also shows how the policy has helped create space for at least some women to step forward and occupy a seat in the water users' committee. It also provided legitimate possibilities for some implementers to raise the issue of gender balance and promote women's participation. Yet we argue here that the degree of success might have been more impressive if the need for more female participants in WUA committees was felt and demanded not only by donor organizations and high-level government bureaucrats but also by implementers and, even more important, by water users. Although the Irrigation Regulation provides the justification for demanding attention to gender concerns, its active implementation and enforcement crucially requires willingness as well as gender awareness of implementers. Further, for female participation in meetings to become more than a numerical policy concern, the WUAs need to be organized in such a way that they meet demands and needs of women. The proportion of women in WUAs maybe an easy-to-use indicator and policy objective for gender equity from the point of view of policymakers and donors, but in itself says little about what participation means (or could potentially mean) to female irrigators. Trying to find out and address what women themselves want and need in terms of irrigation and water rights is a crucial missing element in the current policy. Such a query, of course, touches on larger questions about what gender equity is, and according to whom, and about the linkages between what Moser (1989) has called practical and strategic needs. It requires, in short, an analysis of the social relations of power in and through which WUAs function and operate.

In the process of implementing the regulation, its contents were reinterpreted and negotiated on the basis of the views of those involved. For instance, during the formulation of the memorandum of understanding between ADB and DOI, the section about gender stressed women's participation in the design and implementation of the project, but included little specification about women's inclusion in water-related decision making. The Tukucha Nala agreement between WUA and the District Irrigation Office was silent on gender issues, as was the WUA constitution. In fact, the overall influence of the written agreements between ADB and DOI (the memorandum of understanding) on actual project implementation was negligible. In day-to-day practice, project implementation was guided more by the project operational procedural manual, which did not contain any instructions about gender issues.

At the time the Tukucha Nala WUA came into being, promotion of women's involvement happened because of the enthusiasm of the association organizer.

The rest of the staff involved in the project did little or nothing to comply with the rule of 20 percent female participation. This was not because of malevolence or ignorance, but largely because water users of the different communities did not push project staff for compliance, in itself a sign that among water users the question of female involvement was not considered of high importance. Further, project staff was not held accountable to the female participation objective by DOI or ADB: the formal benefit evaluation format that was designed for the purpose was never used in practice. Project staff was aware of the Irrigation Regulation, and modestly positive about supporting gender objectives. Yet their actual behavior often did not reflect such support. The fact that all members of the implementation team except the association organizer and the project sociologist were engineers may have made a difference here. Irrigation engineers are educated in a professional culture that is technically oriented and strongly associates professionalism with masculinity.[14] For engineers to promote gender objectives and female participation more actively would have involved questioning their own gendered assumptions, norms, and practices, and thus their own expertise and professional identity. Unless explicitly encouraged and rewarded institutionally to do so, this is unlikely to happen.

Although the rule for female participation was not included in the WUA constitution, there were three women appointed as members of the second committee. This was not the result of the Irrigation Regulation, but stemmed from the fact that the WUA president, an active and ambitious local leader with political connections, was aware of the Local Governance Act. The main reason for wanting female participation was to provide the WUA with legitimacy and credibility in the eyes of outsiders, and there appeared to be no awareness of its underlying motives of gender equity, representation, and transparency. Female participation was considered a separate issue, something to be dealt with only after the male representatives of the different sections of the irrigation system were nominated. In spite of this, the local leader's insistence on having women did provide an opportunity for a lower-caste woman to step forward and nominate her daughter-in-law as a member.

With the exception of this woman, no other women present at the committee election said anything or indicated any interest in participation. Most of the women felt that there was little to be gained from participating in WUA meetings or from becoming active as a member of its committee. Lack of education and literacy were clearly identified by all women as a handicap that prevented them from participation. They felt that if they were more educated and literate, they would feel more confident to play an active role in the WUA. Yet, their lack of enthusiasm not only stemmed from various gendered constraints but was also the result of the overall functioning of the WUA. In fact, after rehabilitation the only matter that seemed to require agreement between water users, and that thus justified holding a meeting, was the issue of canal cleaning. It can be safely assumed that many of the important decisions were not taken at the meetings of the WUA but continued to be taken at more or less formal gatherings of male village leaders. Many women, and also many men, did not perceive the meeting as a place where they could voice their concerns and opinions. Because of their lower social status and dependency on the bigger and more vocal men, most people remained silent at meetings and just listened to what the more literate and articulate people had to say. Many water users continued to perceive public decision making as an affair of "important men." The idea of a democratic meeting where people can deliberate as if they were equals was rather alien to both the practice and the ideas of water users, whether male or female.

The women most interested in WUA affairs were those who headed farms and households, about 20 percent of all households in Tukucha Nala. Although these women also doubted the relevance of the actual WUA, and although many of them were also rather shy and diffident about their participation, they also realized the potential benefits of a well-functioning WUA, and were interested in contributing to as well as benefiting from it. Women from male-headed households felt less sure about the usefulness of their involvement. Most felt that having one household member participate in WUA meetings would be enough, and almost all agreed that it was more appropriate for men than for women to go. Yet, women's level and degree of interest also depended on their position within the household. The older category of mothers was less enthusiastic and felt most strongly that public decision making was men's business. Daughters and daughters-in-law were slightly more positive, and identified the WUA as one possible avenue for channeling their concerns to NGOs and government agencies outside the village. Some younger women and especially daughters-in-law, most of whom had not grown up in the village, also saw the WUA as a means to get acquainted with other villagers and thus to feel less isolated. Overall, the activities of political networking and public decision making are very much seen as typically male activities. Leadership attributes are also associated more with men than with women. Women's current lack of participation in decision-making bodies is rooted in and reflects wider gender inequities and divisions.

The quota rule for women's participation in WUA committees in the Irrigation Regulation came about as a result of donor pressures and in response to more general political demands from several Kathmandu-based women's organizations. Although its existence provided support to those implementers interested in changing male dominance of water-related decision making, the norms of gender justice and equity that it reflects and to which it hopes to contribute are not well institutionalized and internalized among implementing agency personnel. The existence of the regulation will, by itself, not do much in creating such gender awareness. The fact that some women are now committee members and the discussions this generated at village level can be seen as first steps in a much longer process of raising awareness among male and female irrigators. Achieving real and more lasting changes in unequal gender relations, and fostering changes so that women themselves actively demand for rights and voice in water decision making, cannot be expected to just happen as a mere effect of increasing the number of women in WUA committees. These structural changes require more general development efforts aimed at the empowerment of women, most of which would require broadening the scope of what is normally considered to belong to the professional domain of irrigation. Literacy and education for women, and prevention of school dropout of young girls, are possible entry points for such efforts. Further strengthening WUAs, and possibly expanding their range of activities to make them more attractive for dealing with women's needs is another.

NOTES

This chapter is based on field research carried out by Pranita Bhushan Udas, in institutional collaboration with the Irrigation and Water Engineering Group of Wageningen University.

1. National NGOs and women's organizations based in the capital Kathmandu have also played an important role. See, for instance, Karki Singh 2000; Bhattachan 2001.

2. To illustrate the importance of donor agencies: ten donor agencies were supporting DOI in 2001–2002, and donor-funded projects accounted for 74 percent of the total area targeted for improvements by DOI (excluding feasibility studies). Until the ninth plan period, 59 percent of irrigation development investment loans came from various donor agencies (Shah and Singh 2001).

3. SISP is not necessarily a typical program, nor is Tukucha Nala necessarily a typical project. SISP was chosen for this study because of its importance; among all surface irrigation programs in Nepal, this is the largest in terms of area covered. An additional reason to choose SISP was that because it is a continuation of the first Irrigation Sector Project (1989–1994) it allowed a longer retrospective. Tukucha Nala was selected because of the relatively long history of registered women members in its committee (DOI 2001).

    The total budget of the SISP project is US$33.3 million, of which the contribution of the government of Nepal is US$4.2 million and farmers' contributions are US$4.1 million. The rest (US$25 million or 75 percent of the total budget) is covered by the ADB (CRID 2001)

4. Each project under DOI has a slightly different operational procedural manual depending, for instance, on the type of technology, the location of the project, and on the specific demands of the funding agency. The manual guides the implementation procedure. DOI and consultants from donor agencies design the operational procedural manual.

5. Memorandum of Understanding, Second Sector Irrigation Project (1996–2002). Loan No. 1437 NEP (SF), His Majesty's Government, Nepal and Asian Development Bank, Manila, Philippines.

6. Community-based organizers (CBOs), village-level facilitators whose task it is to

strengthen WUA activities, were recruited in 2000. Out of sixty-eight CBOs appointed, only five were women; source: SISP, Tenth Progress Report (SILT 2001).

7. In 1992, 1 US dollar was equivalent to 40 Nepalese rupees (NRs). During the research period, the exchange rate increased to 74 NRs to the dollar.

8. Prior to the Indo-Aryan influence in Nepal, the caste system did not exist. The system divided Nepal into four groups: Brahmin, Chettris, Baisya, and Sudra, based mainly on occupation. The Indo-Aryan migrants imposed this stratification upon other, mostly non-Aryan, ethnic groups as well. Though the caste system is not strictly upheld by these groups, it does influence social positioning. Despite the antidiscrimination provisions in the 1990 constitution, caste discrimination is still felt in Nepalese society.

9. The official procedure is that the district irrigation office, together with the district agriculture office, identifies irrigation systems eligible for assistance and carries out prefeasibility studies. The district irrigation office then forwards the prefeasibility report to the district appraisal committee, which after appraisal forwards it to the regional approval committee. The latter then decides whether or not to recommend the project to the Project Steering Committee of the Department of Irrigation (DOI). After approval, the WUA is officially registered at the District Water Resource Committee under the 1992 Water Resource Act and the 1993 Water Resource Regulation 1993. At present, after the formulation of the Irrigation Regulation 2000, WUAs are registered at the district irrigation offices.

10. In the context of Tukucha Nala, the local leaders were not from the local elites. They came forward during the political movement to change a thirty-years-old single panchayat party system to a multiparty democracy. These leaders, either from the United Marxist Lenist Party or from the Nepali Congress, replaced the elite panchayat leaders, and distinguished themselves basically because of their relatively higher education. They are very much aware of the need to satisfy their constituency, and of their dependency on public support.

11. Ironically, the benefit monitoring evaluation format at the end of the manual requests information about the number of female participants in WUA meetings. This format is to be used after project completion and thus does not guide project implementation.

12. The presence of a researcher constantly asking questions about women's participation in the WUA activities has undoubtedly influenced both the phrasing of the CBO's invitation letter and the awareness of villagers about female involvement in decision making.

13. CBS 1999.

14. See also Khanal 2003, 233. Reflecting on his own working experience as an implementation engineer working in the Terai in Nepal, he states: "I was hardly aware of the issue at first because of my technocratic background and bureaucratic orientation."

3

Defending Indigenous Water Rights with the Laws of a Dominant Culture

The Case of the United States

DAVID H. GETCHES

The United States is one of the few nations of the world to provide distinctive and apparently robust legal recognition to the water rights of its indigenous peoples. On rivers in the arid, western United States where most ethnic groups reside, indigenous peoples have rights to water that are superior to those of their nonindigenous neighbors. If dominant societies do not extend legal dignity to the water rights of indigenous peoples, this can impede or doom their struggle to hold and use their territories. The integrity of these territories is essential to indigenous cultures and livelihood strategies. Yet the protection of the so-called Indian water rights in the United States remains an imperfect model.

The apparently generous recognition of significant legal rights for indigenous peoples to water for their lands and families has produced more paper documenting legal rights than usable water for indigenous peoples and lands. A fundamental problem is that legal rights were announced a century ago, but after that the national government and the states, whose laws dominate water allocation, promoted non-Indian use of water. Nowadays, if local Indian kinship groups attempt to use the large quantities of water to which the law entitles them, they face formidable economic and political barriers because non-Indians are already using most of the water.

The principles of Indian water rights—as developed in the legal system of the Unites States—were created to advance national policies, not simply to achieve justice for indigenous peoples or ensure the survival of their cultures. As is often the case, the realization of the law's beneficence in the future will depend on the dominant culture's willingness to make readjustments that affect negatively the nonindigenous majority of water users. To many, Indian water rights seem anomalous (see chapter 5 for a parallel situation in the Andes).

Whether courts and politicians will honor those rights is a test of their commitment to the rule of law and willingness to comprehend justice in the light of cultural values alien to the dominant culture. So far, the results are mixed. The courts have modified Indian water rights in some cases rather than enforce them fully. The federal and state governments, however, have shown some willingness to invest money in protecting and developing Indian water uses—so long as non-Indian uses are preserved in the process.

Those seeking to learn from the United States experience with indigenous water rights, like those attempting to improve the application of the system in the United States, confront the classic moral struggle between realpolitik and theoretical concepts of justice and morality. The advantage of paper rights to water, even if they promise more than they deliver, is that they provide an open door to the legal system, allowing the intercultural dialogue to begin there and not outside the system. The struggle to apply them in a way that ensures cultural and socioeconomic survival continues, nonetheless.

In this chapter I will first discuss United States Indian law and policy. Second, I will look at Indian legal rights against the background of changing and conflicting policies. I will focus here on the theory and practice of Indian rights, conflicts with non-Indian users, and the role of the state courts in deciding on the scope of Indian rights. In the following section I will discuss the role of negotiation as a recent alternative to litigation. Next, I will focus on a number of important current water rights issues: finality of determination of rights, water marketing, tribal water codes and administration, the use of rights for new purposes, and the mismatch between law and Indian culture. In the final section I present a short conclusion.

United States Indian Law and Policy

The foundational principles of Indian law in the United States were announced by the Supreme Court in the early days of the nation.[1] They have roots in the international law created among European colonizing nations. As such, there is a mix of pragmatism allowing orderly conquest of the New World and equitability concerns for the people found there. The latter concerns were partly motivated by the morality of the people and religious leaders involved in the colonial effort, and partly by the reality that a harsh policy would meet with Indian resistance, which would frustrate colonization (see similar considerations in the Andes, chapters 5 and 7).

The United States Supreme Court's decisions clearly recognized rights of Indian communities to occupy and govern their own territories. It also defined a fiduciary relationship in which the national government was charged with protecting indigenous collective rights. The same Supreme Court decisions gave the Congress broad powers to implement this obligation but also to extinguish

Indian rights when lawmakers determined that it was in the interest of the country to do so. This great federal power in the area of Indian affairs has been frequently invoked to limit private or state efforts to encroach on the property rights and self-governing authority of ethnic groups within their territory. But it was also invoked by Congress to extinguish land titles and limit the self-governing powers of local indigenous societies. The latter typically gave up lands in treaties with the United States. When they resisted, the United States had the power to take their lands anyway. As indigenous populations were confined to smaller and smaller reservations of land in successive transactions and legislation, their rights to retained lands were to be respected, at least until more land was needed by the nation. Thus, the nation was settled.

As it divested the indigenous first nations of most of their historic lands, the United States adopted a series of conflicting policies, ranging in their purposes from isolation to integration of Indian peoples. Neither type of program worked well. For cultural separation to work, indigenous territories would have to retain enough land and resources to be self-sufficient and have adequate protection from avaricious settlers to exist with reasonable security. For much of the nineteenth century, most of the continent was underpopulated and barely governable. This made protection of Indians and their land, to keep settlers away from Indian lands, politically and practically impossible. The government was, after all, pursuing a national policy of expansion. The intensity of the settlers' hunger for land was supported by official policies designed to settle the entire continent.

Policy was adapted in light of this reality and to open up the reservation enclaves of the indigenous peoples. It was thought that they should be assimilated into the larger society. However, policies of integration were frustrated by the racial biases of whites and the inexorable desire of indigenous people to adhere to cultural and religious traditions that link them to specific lands and to one another (see also issues of cultural traditions and racial bias in the Andes and South Africa, chapters 7 and 9).

In the nineteenth century, national policy sought first to confine Indians to reservations so that settlers could move into the lands ceded by the diverse indigenous kinship groups, collectivities, and nations, or "tribes" as they are commonly referred to in the United States. Tribes of the Great Plains were placed on reservations and told to give up the vast territory where they conducted their far-ranging hunts, to open up those lands for white settlement. Later, when settlers also coveted reservation lands, Congress adopted a new program to break up tribal land holdings and promote individual farm cultivation. It was designed to assimilate Indians into the mainstream of society by ending their communal landownership and activities. Within the reservations, each Indian family would be allotted a parcel of the tribe's land. Lands not "needed" by the Indians would be made available to non-Indian homesteaders.

The architects of this allotment policy envisioned integrated communities of Indian and non-Indian farmers, each holding land in individual ownership within reservations. They assumed that tribes and their cultures would then wither away. This did not happen, even in the reservations where farms failed because farming was appropriate neither to the land nor to the culture of the people. The reservations were (and still are) refuges for the tribes where people can live together and attempt to eke out an existence (on the mismatch between planners' visions and on-the-ground practice in Indonesia and South Africa, see also chapters 4 and 9).

Elsewhere, government officials understood that it would not be feasible to promote agriculture. Some tribes were culturally and economically so dependent on hunting and fishing that the reservation policy of the time took account of the tribes' preferences. In the Northwest and Great Lakes regions, treaties created reservations that limited the extent of territories but allowed the historic fishing pursuits of indigenous peoples to continue. The tribes retained reservations on waterways or kept only small reservations but retained rights to fish in lands that they ceded to the government.

It should be evident that the government's reservation policy could not succeed without water for Indian use. Adequate amounts of water were needed for irrigation on reservations that were created to promote Indian (and non-Indian) agriculture. For fishing tribes, flowing water in streams was essential to maintain the habitat needed to sustain fish life. Tribes with agricultural reservations as well as those with on- or off-reservation fishing rights that required water encountered encroaching populations of non-Indians. The resulting competition for water and water-dependent resources threatened the Indians' ability to survive on their reservations. But the non-Indians who came with the support of national policies intended to establish new communities, and they were given property rights to the land. These non-Indian settlers worked hard, developed farms, and obtained water rights under state law, as the government had encouraged them to do. Their established water uses now compete with the capacity of Indians to use water and natural resources that depend on water. Consequently, the nation's Indian policy, which was and is one of promoting self-sufficiency, is threatened, while the policy encouraging non-Indian homesteading and settlement has been fulfilled. What does the legal system do in the face of such conflicting policies?

Indian Legal Rights in the Face of Conflicting Policy

In 1908 the United States Supreme Court announced a remarkable doctrine of water rights that favored Indian tribes in their attempts to secure sufficient water to make their reservations useful. The "reserved rights doctrine," announced in the case of *Winters v. United States*, guaranteed tribes the right to use all the water they needed to fulfill the purposes for which their reservations were established. The right could be exercised any time in the future, even if non-Indians had used the water first and had been granted rights under state law. This was shocking to some because the prevailing law in the western United States was that the first person to use water had the strongest right to use it in the future, a right better than that of everyone who started using water later.

The history of the tribes' exercise of their ostensibly bold and potent reserved water rights for Indian reservations has been problematic. In practice, non-Indians were able to develop water first on the streams shared with Indians because they had access to capital. The tribes, however, lacked capital to put their water rights to use and were left to compete with non-Indians who built their economies using the water to which the Indians were rightfully entitled under the Winters decision. Tribes on most reservations have remained in a state of poverty, and their lands are largely undeveloped. Theoretically, they have "better" rights than their non-Indian neighbors. Although they have not actually used the water—a key issue in the law and culture of the West—the teaching of Winters is that they have rights superior to the non-Indians and can use the water whenever they need to in the future (see Shurts 2000).

Modern national policy favors use of water by these tribes, too. For the last fifty years federal policy toward Indian tribes has favored self-determination and economic self-sufficiency. Increasingly, tribes have pressed for a vindication of their theoretically strong but actually underutilized water rights. The non-Indians know that the inchoate rights of the tribes pose a threat to their economic security. Because investments and property values are undermined by uncertainty, non-Indians and the western states that tend to support non-Indian interests have also urged that Indian water rights should be legally determined.

Judicial processes are now under way in most states. These proceedings are lengthy and expensive. In recent years, water rights of several tribes have been resolved in negotiated settlements and implemented through federal legislation. This remains the preferred method of quantifying tribal water rights, primarily because it infuses federal funding into solutions that enable tribes to use their water rights, and it protects established non-Indian uses.[2]

Indian Reserved Water Rights in Theory and Practice

The Winters case arose on the Fort Belknap Indian Reservation in Montana, where the Indians had been placed after a series of treaties that had limited them to a small fraction of their former territory. The Court recognized the government's intention of "civilizing" the Indians by turning them into individual farmers and breaking up communally held tribal lands (chapter 5 considers similar intentions in the Andes). The government plan involved dividing up the reservation lands into individual land holdings, allotting the land to heads of Indian families to be cultivated, and then opening the rest of the land on and off the reservation for non-Indian homesteaders. Without sufficient irrigation water for the reservation, this civilizing scheme would fail. If the individual allotment policy fell, lands desired by settlers—the so-called surplus lands on reservations and former reservations—would not be available for white settlement.

The fundamental legal principle giving rise to Indian water rights is stated simply: the establishment of a reservation results in an implied reserved right to take water sufficient to fulfill the purpose of reserving the land for the Indians. The United States Supreme Court articulated the rationale as follows:

> The reservation was a part of a very much larger tract which the Indians had the right to occupy and use and which was adequate for the habits and wants of a nomadic and uncivilized people. It was the policy of the Government, it was the desire of the Indians to change those habits and to become pastoral and civilized people. If they should become such the original tract was too extensive, but a smaller tract would be inadequate without a change of conditions. The lands were arid and, without irrigation, were practically valueless. . . . The Indians had command of the lands and the waters—command of all their beneficial use, whether kept for hunting, "and grazing roving herds of stock" or turned to agriculture and the arts of civilization. Did they give up all this? Did they reduce the area of their occupation and give up the waters which make it valuable or adequate?[3]

It would have been grossly unfair to the Indians to confine them to reservations without the means to pursue a livelihood. The decision was surely a courageous one for the local court to make and for the Supreme Court to uphold. But the bold decision ostensibly favoring Indians at a time when they lacked political power or popular sympathy can be explained as promoting a broader purpose. The plan for obtaining and distributing former Indian land to non-Indians would have failed if the tribes could not survive on their reservations. Indeed, on the Fort Belknap Reservation non-Indians held a considerable area of land and were already doing much of the farming. Denying the reservation sufficient water would have limited their uses. The conflict between reservation use of water and off-reservation use can be seen as a conflict between non-Indians off the reservation and non-Indian farmers on the reservation.

The reserved rights doctrine of Winters became the cardinal rule of Indian water rights. It was later applied to protect the federal government's own rights to water on federal lands reserved for parks, forests, military bases, and other public uses.[4] As with Indian lands, the quantity of water reserved depended on the purposes for which the reservation was established.

Over the years, the reserved rights doctrine has promised more than it has delivered. The government has rarely applied it in litigation to assert rights against non-Indian water users. The Indians themselves, until about thirty years ago, often lacked their own attorneys to represent them in protecting their water rights. Government attorneys sometimes represented them in water litigation although the government often had a conflict of interest because it had sponsored water projects for non-Indians on the same waterways where tribes claimed rights.

Meanwhile, non-Indians built dams and diverted water from streams and initiated uses that depended on that water. Non-Indian water development was often planned and paid for by the federal government, which is ironic considering the well-established legal principle in American Indian law that the government is charged with the responsibility of a trustee to act for the benefit of Indian tribes. The National Water Commission found in its 1973 report that:

> Following Winters . . . the United States was pursuing a policy of encouraging the settlement of the West and the creation of family-sized farms on its arid lands. In retrospect, it can be seen that this policy was pursued with little or no regard for Indian water rights and the Winters doctrine. With the encouragement, or at least the cooperation, of the Secretary of the Interior—the very office entrusted with the protection of all Indian rights—many large irrigation projects were constructed on streams that flowed through or bordered on Indian Reservations, sometimes above and more often below the Reservations. With few exceptions the projects were planned and built by the Federal Government without any attempt to define, let alone protect, prior rights that Indian tribes might have had in the waters used for the projects. . . . In the history of the United States Government's treatment of Indian tribes, its failure to protect Indian water rights for use on the Reservations it set aside for them is one of the sorrier chapters. (National Water Commission 1973, 474–475)

Conflict with Non-Indian Users

Many decades after the Supreme Court first articulated the reserved water rights doctrine, Indian water rights finally gained considerable attention when the Court issued its opinion.[5] The case involved an allocation of the Colorado River's flow among three of the states that touch the river. The United States, which was involved in the case because the river also crosses extensive Indian and federal lands, claimed reserved rights for five tribes along the river. The Supreme Court awarded those tribes 900,000 acre-feet of water per year—a huge quantity of water—which it determined by calculating how much water would be required to irrigate all the practicably irrigable acreage on the five reservations. This sent a strong message to water users all over the West that

Indian claims could be made to formidable amounts of water. The reserved rights doctrine had been largely idle since Winters, but it was far from dead.

The historical method for allocating water in the American West, known as prior appropriation, was enshrined in state laws. Although this doctrine has been altered in various ways and embellished with rules that satisfy important public purposes, most of the West's water was allocated under it long ago, giving the prior users—those who put it first to a beneficial use—the best rights. The most valuable rights are the oldest because in times of shortage the holders of those rights can insist on delivery of the full quantity of water to which they are entitled. Accordingly, when senior users assert their rights, the most junior users often must curtail their water uses.

The Supreme Court actually created reserved water rights to fit into the priority system. Although the requirement of use does not apply, a tribe with reserved rights does have a priority date. Instead of being the date on which water was first used, it is the date when the tribe's reservation was established. Because most reservations were established more than one hundred years ago, the accompanying water rights are usually quite senior. All users after that date must ensure that the tribe gets all the water to which it is entitled—enough to fulfill the purposes of the reservation—before those junior users can take any water.

The tribe's position in the system of priorities is easy to determine because it is determined by the date of the reservation. But the scope of the right—the amount of water the tribe is guaranteed—remains uncertain until the quantity of water to which the tribe is entitled can be determined. Quantifying non-Indians' water rights as established in the prior appropriation system is relatively simple because the quantity of their rights is determined on the basis of the amount of water actually used in the past. But for Indian reservations the task is much more difficult. Reserved rights exist without a history of actual use but must be quantified according to reservation purposes that are rooted in old government policies. The question is, then, how much water it takes to fulfill the reservation's purposes. The resulting uncertainty is disturbing to neighboring non-Indian water users because it frustrates their investments and undermines their security.

One solution to this uncertainty is to quantify Indian reserved rights. This can be done judicially by asking a court to decide how much water is necessary to fulfill the purposes of a reservation. Where the purpose of setting up the reservation was to allow the Indians to pursue agriculture, the courts follow the Supreme Court's formulation.[6] The Court said that the amount of water necessary for agricultural purposes can be calculated on the basis of the reservation's practicably irrigable acreage. In arid areas the amount of water needed to produce crops is enormous; in adopting this formula, the Supreme Court opened the way for tribes to claim huge quantities of water. The Court expressly rejected the idea that tribes should just get merely a "fair share" of the water in a river or that rights should be determined on the basis of reservation populations. The Court said that rights should not meet present needs but future needs, and therefore be set according to the reservation's full capacity to use water.

A court seeking to determine how much land is irrigable and how much water is required for irrigation must examine evidence of soil type, structure, and depth, topography, salinity content, possible crops, and climate, as well as the technology and irrigation efficiencies that are assumed to be used in the future. As this information is usually based on expert studies in hydrology, soil science, engineering, and economics, trials can be long and expensive. Given the importance of scarce water, the process of establishing the quantity of water to which a tribe is entitled can also be contentious, and hence expensive.

State courts decide the scope of Indian rights. The United States has two separate court systems, state and federal. The individual court systems of the fifty states have local courts with general jurisdiction and appellate court systems to review local decisions. These state courts usually handle water rights matters arising within a particular state. The United States generally is not subject to the jurisdiction of state courts, and the principle of sovereign immunity provides that the United States cannot be sued without its consent. Thus, ordinarily state courts would not be able to adjudicate federal water rights. Similarly, Indian tribes are also considered sovereign governments with sovereign immunity from suit without their consent or the consent of the United States Congress.

Federal district courts sitting in every state, and with a separate system of appeals, have more limited jurisdiction than state courts. The primary task of federal courts is to adjudicate "federal questions" including interpretation and application of federal laws. This can include determining how much water a tribe would be entitled to use for a reservation established under a treaty or agreement with the United States. The United States Congress passed a law in the 1950s, however, saying that when a state court takes jurisdiction over the adjudication of all water rights in a river, the United States will waive its sovereign immunity to suit and the state court can determine all federal water rights. The law authorizing state courts to adjudicate Indian reserved rights is called the McCarran Amendment.[7]

Congress recognized in the McCarran Amendment the importance to non-Indians of clearly knowing the extent of water rights of others with whom they compete for water in times of shortage under the prior appropriation doctrine. The law applies to all water rights of which the United States is the "owner." Although the United States technically only holds title to Indian water rights in trust for the tribes, the Supreme Court held that Congress intended to extend state jurisdiction over those rights whenever the rights to an entire river were being adjudicated.[8]

Being subjected to state court jurisdiction to adjudicate their water rights caused great concern for tribes. They understandably feared that state courts were likely to be less equitable to them than federal courts. Indeed, there is a history of tension between tribes and states. The Supreme Court long ago described the situation of Indians relative to states: "They owe no allegiance to the states, and receive from them no protection. Because of local ill feeling, the people of the states where they are found are often their deadliest enemies."[9]

After the Supreme Court made it clear that Indian water rights were subject to determination in state courts, many states initiated "general stream adjudications," legal proceedings that sometimes involved tens of thousands of water rights claimants in an entire river basin. The cost and complexity of these proceedings have proven burdensome to everyone. Some adjudications have continued for over twenty years and are still not near completion. Today, there are over sixty Indian water rights cases pending in state courts.

Although Indians believed that state courts would not provide fair trials for their water rights claims, the results have varied. In most cases the tribes have been able to prevail on the United States as their trustee to furnish lawyers and expert witnesses. Alliances of government and tribal lawyers have presented cases competently to the courts. In some cases, the state courts have awarded tribes impressively high quantities of water. Yet the overall record is not reassuring to critics who say that relegating tribal rights to the mercy of state courts is bound to be unfair to Indians.

In the adjudication of the Big Horn River, for example, the Wyoming Supreme Court affirmed the right of the tribes of the Wind River Reservation to some 400,000 acre-feet of water, most of the water in the river.[10] Undeniably, the amount of water, based on a lower court determination of the irrigable acreage on the reservation, is enormous. Yet the state supreme court rejected the tribes' claims for water to be used for mineral development, fisheries, wildlife, and aesthetics. It also rejected the tribes' attempt to extend their reserved water rights to groundwater. Many scholars and at least some other courts differ with each of these holdings. Whether or not the state court erred in defining the scope of the tribes' reserved water rights, it nevertheless awarded them enough water to overshadow the impacts of those parts of the decision. The state challenged the decision in the United States Supreme Court but the state court decision was upheld, although barely; the justices on the Supreme Court were divided by a vote of four to four.

The Big Horn case is the only state court adjudication of Indian water rights that has proceeded through final judgment and appeal to the Supreme Court. Other state courts have handed down rulings in general stream adjudications, some favorable and some unfavorable to Indian tribes. In Arizona, the state supreme court has held that the treatment of groundwater under state law as a resource that is allocated and managed under a regime entirely separate from surface water could not affect any rights the tribes had to groundwater under the reserved rights doctrine because those rights were a matter of federal law.[11] In Idaho, however, the state courts have rejected tribal claims to exemption from the state adjudication process under the McCarran Amendment.[12]

Negotiated Settlement of Indian Water Rights Claims: An Alternative to Litigation

The results of state court adjudications for Indian water rights vary, but all are terribly costly and take years to conclude. The combination of unpredictability and the burdens of litigation have induced all parties to seriously consider negotiation as an alternative to litigation. Since the 1980s there have been about eighteen negotiated settlements of Indian water rights. Settlement negotiations usually are commenced after a tribe or the United States becomes involved in litigation with a state and non-Indian water users. Sometimes this is part of a general stream adjudication started by a state under the McCarran Amendment. It can also follow litigation in federal courts brought by the tribe or the United States. In a few cases, settlement negotiations have begun without litigation.

Negotiations typically allow for all interested parties to participate. Sometimes they require court decisions to decide basic legal questions like the tribe's priority date. Negotiations are most useful when there are factual disagreements based on technical data. Rather than dwell on these contests, the parties seek to craft a solution that will generally satisfy their respective needs. Instead of an all-or-nothing court decision with a clear-cut victory for one side, they seek ways to provide recognition for tribal water rights without jeopardizing existing water uses. Although the tribes may not receive the full quantities of water originally or potentially claimed, they often get money—mostly from the federal government—to enable them to build facilities to put their quantified water rights to use.

The lubrication of federal funding has been a key element in most Indian water rights settlements. It has allowed for tribes to secure not only paper water rights but also "wet water" delivered through irrigation systems and pipelines for domestic supplies. At the same time, non-Indians have gained assurance that they can continue using water under water rights that are junior to tribal water rights. Sometimes federal or state funding is also assured for projects that benefit non-Indian water users. Because funding is usually part of a settlement package, an agreement reached by the various parties in negotiation usually must be approved and monies appropriated by Congress. Thus, settlements are almost always accompanied by federal legislation, and sometimes accompanying state legislation. Although each Indian water rights settlement is unique, some examples will illustrate how they work.

Congress has approved two water settlements in Arizona. In the first case, in 1978, the Ak-Chin Indian Community agreed with the secretary of the interior to forgo a substantial amount of water claims against non-Indian users in exchange for 85,000 acre-feet of irrigation water provided by a federal well-field water project.[13] Using the well water on the Ak-Chin reservation, however, would deplete the groundwater under another reservation. In order to avoid this problem, the Department of Interior renegotiated a water contract with an irrigation district that received its water from the Colorado River, to deliver its surplus water to the tribe. In the second case, in 1982, the San Xavier Band of the Tohono O'Odham Nation first settled its groundwater claims without involving the federal government in the settlement process. However, the tribe could only proceed after securing federal government participation and financial support in the final water settlement. The bill was ultimately approved.[14] These water settlements exemplify successful water negotiations, which provide tribes with promises for delivered water and a consideration of their reserved water rights.

Each settlement is different because the legal, geographic, and economic situations of tribes vary; and so do the political factors. The ability of a tribe and its neighbors to achieve a settlement will differ with the relative power of the members of Congress that represent that state. The receptiveness of Congress to settlements and the need to appropriate federal funds will also vary, depending on the economic health of the federal government at the time a settlement package is presented. Notwithstanding the inevitable differences among them, a review of the Indian water rights settlements to date shows characteristics that are common to many of them:

- Federal investment in water or water facilities: by providing funds to build dams and delivery works, the settlement can ensure delivery of water to both Indians and non-Indians.
- Nonfederal cost-sharing: a typical condition for the provision of federal funds is that state or local governments bear a portion of the cost of the settlement.
- Creation of tribal trust fund: cash funds are usually appropriated for the use of the tribes. Sometimes the money is to be used for water development, sometimes it is available for general economic development.
- Limited off-reservation water marketing: for various reasons, tribes that are entitled to water rights cannot or do not want to use all water on their reservations. Allowing them to lease water for use by non-Indians off the reservation can provide cash income that can help build the tribe's economy while allowing non-Indians to use water they need. Under the legal systems governing water in the West, water-rights can be transferred with few restrictions beyond protection of

other water-rights holders. Some argue that denying tribes the same right would be inequitable. Most settlement packages allow the tribes to market their water, but nearly all impose stronger restrictions than those applying when non-Indians transfer water rights.

- Deference to state law: often settlements concerning Indian water rights make use of state water law, at least when the water is used off the reservation. Where two or more states enter into a compact allocating the use of a river that also satisfies tribal water claims, the Indian water rights settlement agreement and accompanying legislation usually provide that the compact will govern water use.
- Concern for efficiency, conservation, and the environment: less pervasive among the settlements but included in many of them is a provision for improving the efficiency of water use and advancing environmental values.
- Benefits for non-Indians: the viability of Indian water settlements depends on producing benefits for non-Indians. At a minimum, non-Indians should receive certainty that their established water uses can continue. If the United States agrees to build water facilities, non-Indians also get access to water that will allow new uses. In some cases, non-Indians have been able to obtain federal funding for a project that otherwise would have been politically impossible. By "wrapping it in an Indian blanket" they can make a project politically viable.

Current Indian Water Rights Issues

Finality of Determinations

One of the goals of non-Indians in seeking quantification of Indian rights is to provide the certainty they themselves need in order to make investments and to borrow money to build water projects. This was surely a motive for enactment of the McCarran Amendment. Tribes can also benefit from knowing the extent of their rights as they try to attract investments in water facilities and otherwise to realize value from their water rights. The tribes whose water rights have been adjudicated learned that they must suffer the consequences if they have inadequate legal representation in the litigation of their claims. Even if mistakes are made they cannot later return to have their water rights adjusted, because that would disrupt non-Indian expectations. The likelihood that the outcome of an adjudication will be permanent raises a serious concern for any tribe embarking on a quantification of its water rights.

In two cases where tribes had their rights fixed in the past and wanted to reopen cases to expand their rights, the Supreme Court refused to allow any change in tribal rights. In *Arizona v. California,* five tribes along the Colorado

River had been represented against the states by the United States Department of Justice.[15] The federal attorneys failed to claim all of the tribes' practicably irrigable acreage. Thus, the tribes' water rights were limited to the quantity needed for the irrigable lands that had been claimed by the government. The tribes later hired their own lawyers and experts and reopened the case. They claimed that additional lands were irrigable and asked the Supreme Court to award a greater quantity of water. But in 1983, twenty years after the original decision, the Supreme Court held that the quantification could not be changed except where there was actually a judicially recognized error in boundaries.[16] The Supreme Court said there is a "strong interest in finality" in western water law, and therefore it would be unfair to the non-Indians who had relied on the earlier decision if the tribes were allowed to increase their claims.

In another case, the Pyramid Lake Paiute Tribe also had depended on the United States for the protection of its interests in court. The tribe historically depended on fishing, and its reservation consisted almost entirely of a large lake. Early in the twentieth century, the United States Bureau of Reclamation built a federal irrigation project to benefit nearby non-Indian farmers. The federal water project diverted nearly all of the water from the single stream that supplied water to the lake. The United States went to state court to secure the necessary water before building the project. Purporting to represent both the tribe and the irrigation project, the federal government claimed only an amount of water sufficient to irrigate the Indian lands in the narrow ring of land around the lake, and claimed no water to maintain the Indian fishery. Without water to sustain the fishery and the lake level, the lake shrunk and the fish started to die.

Years later the tribe, through its own attorneys, proved that the United States had failed to claim sufficient water rights due to its conflict of interest, and got a lower court to order the government to take action consistent with its trust responsibility and stop diverting all water to the reclamation project. The United States also was forced to reopen the old case that had given the tribe inadequate water rights. But, on appeal, the United States Supreme Court refused to let the case be reopened, citing the interest of the non-Indians in having certainty in their water rights.[17]

The outcomes in these two cases make it imperative for tribes whose reserved water rights are being determined in an adjudication to participate fully and aggressively in asserting their rights. This is difficult for tribes with limited financial resources. However, in recent times the United States has provided funding for some tribes to hire lawyers and experts, even when it has also represented the tribes as a trustee.

The daunting specter of a final and unalterable judgment may provide an argument against seeking an adjudication of reserved water rights. In most cases, however, tribes have no choice whether to adjudicate their rights, because under the McCarran Amendment the United States can be sued any time a state initiates a general stream adjudication and must claim all federal and Indian water rights. Although a tribe, as a sovereign government, remains immune from being sued, the rulings of the Supreme Court teach that if the tribe abstains from litigation it does so at its peril.

Water Marketing

One of the most controversial questions concerning Indian water rights is whether tribes can sell or lease their water to non-Indians outside their reservations. In many cases, the government decided that Indians should become farmers, and moved them to reservations for that purpose. Some of these tribes do not have a cultural tradition that is based on agriculture, however, or are unable to produce a livelihood because they were put on reservations that were too small or had poor lands for farming. This has led some tribes to consider allowing others to use their water off the reservation. As explained earlier, most of the negotiated settlements of Indian water rights provide for some off-reservation use of tribal water rights, although the marketing of water is typically restricted in location and scope.

Non-Indians control the best agricultural lands on many reservations. The allotment policy opened up the reservations to non-Indian settlement; today, non-Indians cultivate 69 percent of all farmland and have 78 percent of the irrigated acreage on reservation lands throughout the nation. Moreover, in the last one hundred years, the allotments issued to individual Indians have descended through inheritance to an unwieldy number of heirs. The only way to put these lands to use is to lease them, usually to non-Indian farmers. A share of the tribe's reserved water rights often attaches to allotted land, and the right to use this water accompanies the lease to non-Indians.[18]

There is considerable debate about whether tribes should have the legal right to allow their water rights to be used outside their reservations. Opponents of Indian water marketing argue that the nature of the reserved right is to make reservation lands useful and this purpose is not fulfilled when water is used elsewhere. Proponents say that the ultimate purpose of all reservations was to provide a territory where Indians could be self-sufficient. This goal may be best achieved if tribes can enter the marketplace and realize the economic value of tribal resources. Off-reservation Indian water marketing could provide a way to continue and expand non-Indian uses. Simply by paying Indians for the right to use their water, non-Indian users could buy the certainty they now lack. Nevertheless, non-Indians who have depended on using undeveloped Indian water without charge do not want to be forced to start paying for it. This is why some of them have tried to raise policy and legal arguments against marketability.

The most substantial legal question about Indian water marketing is whether a tribe has the legal right to convey what is essentially a tribal property right. One of the oldest rules of Indian law is that tribes cannot transfer land or rights in land to non-Indians without the participation or approval of the United States government.[19] Any legal doubts on this point can be resolved by obtaining congressional consent. Such consent was granted in several negotiated Indian water settlements that allowed water marketing. Action by Congress also moots the issue of whether there is a fundamental conflict between the Supreme Court's original rationale for reserved water rights and a tribe's use of them outside the reservation. In any event, the basis of the legal restraint on alienation of Indian property is to ensure protection of Indian rights from encroachment by non-Indians or the states. Therefore, the primary concern in whether Indian water is marketable should be whether the tribes have been dealt with fairly. Presumably, congressional approval should depend on a finding that the transaction is in the best interests of the tribe.

Some observers have proposed that Congress authorizes tribes to lease their water rights subject to the approval of the secretary of the interior, just as tribes can now lease tribal lands with secretarial approval. One of the arguments offered in favor of Indian water leasing is that non-Indians may freely transfer their water and water rights so long as the rights of others are not harmed. It is argued that it is inequitable to deny tribes the same attributes for its water rights. As yet, Congress has not seriously considered legislation allowing Indian water leasing.

Tribal Water Codes and Administration

As sovereigns with jurisdiction over their members and territory, Indian tribes can promulgate and enforce legislation and regulations concerning water rights. Their ability to do so has been frustrated, however, by political impediments to the federal government's approval of tribal water codes and by recent decisions of the Supreme Court that limit the reach of tribal regulatory authority over non-Indians on reservations.

It is clear that a state has no jurisdiction to regulate Indian use of Indian water rights. This is part of a 150-year legal tradition of maintaining tribal jurisdiction over Indians and their property on reservations, free from state control. The harder question is under what circumstances non-Indians on an Indian reservation can be controlled by tribes and when they are subject to state jurisdiction. Generally, if non-Indians are on Indian land they, like Indians, can be subjected to tribal jurisdiction.

Recent Supreme Court decisions, however, have created doubts about whether tribes can regulate non-Indians, especially if they are on non-Indian owned land. One case says that a tribe may have jurisdiction over a non-Indian on its reservation, even on the non-Indian's fee land, if the non-Indian's conduct would threaten or have a "direct effect on the political integrity, the

economic security, or the health and welfare of the tribe."[20] The use of waterways on a reservation presumably would affect some or all of these interests. But
in a case dealing specifically with the applicability of a tribal water code, the
court held that the tribe lacked the requisite interest in the subject matter and
could not regulate non-Indian water use.[21] This was because the stream in question originated outside the reservation, ran only a short way along the reservation boundary, then turned away and joined the Spokane River outside the
reservation.

In *Holly v. Confederated Tribes and Bands of the Yakima Indian Nation*, the
same court upheld the application of a tribal water code to non-Indians using
water on their land within the reservation where the stream was entirely on the
reservation.[22] The court added, however, that the tribe could not control "excess" water used by non-Indians—presumably water not subject to reserved water rights.

It would appear that tribes with comprehensive, well-developed codes and
regulations governing waters on their reservation would be better able to demonstrate the need to regulate non-Indian water to further tribal interests. The
United States Supreme Court upheld, for instance, the exclusive authority of the
Mescalero Apache Tribe to regulate game and fish on its reservation, including
hunting and fishing by non-Indians, where the tribe had a comprehensive fish
and game conservation and regulatory program.[23] This case did not deal with
regulation on non-Indian land, but the court did emphasize the importance to
the tribe of having unified regulation of a resource such as wildlife.

Tribes attempting to enact legislation to regulate water resources on their
reservations do not have support from the United States Department of the Interior. Perhaps half of the tribal constitutions have provisions that require certain tribal legislation to be approved by the secretary of the interior before it
will be effective. For twenty-seven years the department has maintained a
moratorium on approval of any tribal water codes that would extend to non-
Indian water use. On two occasions the department circulated draft regulations
governing the approval of such codes, but they were met with a firestorm of
opposition from western senators and congressmen. The federal government
has departed from the moratorium in only a few cases to approve tribal codes as
part of negotiated water settlements approved by Congress.

President Clinton's administration voiced sympathy for the tribal effort to
regulate water resources, but did not change the policy. Secretary Bruce Babbitt
said that if a tribe wanted to enact a water code and confronted a requirement
for secretarial approval, as is included in many tribal constitutions, all the tribe
needed to do was to amend its constitution to remove the requirement for secretarial approval of ordinances, and the secretary would approve the amendment removing the approval requirement so that the tribe could adopt a code
without the need for federal approval. Although not all tribes have a secretarial

approval requirement for tribal codes, and those that do may have a means to remove the impediment, the apparent policy of the Department of the Interior disfavoring tribal codes could portend difficulties if code enforcement is challenged by a non-Indian and a court is called upon to examine the tribe's authority to enact the provision.

Notwithstanding the uncertain area of tribal water code enforcement over non-Indians within a reservation, many tribes have sophisticated codes. Some have well-trained professionals on the staffs of water resources departments that do water resources planning and enforce water rights among those who share in the use of water on the reservation.

Use of Rights for New Purposes

Reserved water rights are quantified according to the purposes for which the federal government established an Indian reservation. As described earlier, the most commonly expressed purpose for creating reservations was to enable the Indians to pursue agriculture. However, reserved rights can arise from other purposes. For example, in historically important fishing and hunting regions reservations were located to provide access to rivers and lakes to enable the continuation of these traditional lifestyles. In *United States v. Adair*, the court found that a treaty provision guaranteeing the Klamath Tribe the exclusive right to hunt, fish, and gather on its reservation showed the primary purpose for creating the reservation.[24] Other parts of the treaty mentioned agriculture; the court found that encouraging the Indians to take up farming was a second essential purpose of the reservation. Although state law did not allow water rights for fishing and hunting, the court held that the Indians had such rights and they could be enforced to prevent non-Indians from depleting streams below levels needed to maintain stream flows for fish and game.

A more difficult question arises when a tribe wants to use water for purposes other than those for which its reserved water rights were quantified. For instance, if rights were quantified for agricultural uses, can a tribe use the water for industrial purposes, for a fishery, or to water a golf course? In *Arizona v. California*, the Supreme Court appointed a Special Master to determine the tribes' claims that they were entitled to enlarge the quantity of their reserved water rights on the Colorado River, on the basis of increased acreage on their reservations.[25] The Court rejected most of the Master's recommendations regarding quantification, refusing to reopen the issue of the extent of practicably irrigable acreage. It did not disapprove the Master's finding, however, that the tribes' future uses of water were not limited to the agricultural purpose that had been the basis for quantifying tribal rights in the first place.

Not all courts have followed this approach. In the *Big Horn* adjudication, the court quantified the tribes' reserved rights on the basis of irrigable acreage.[26] The Wind River Tribes decided to use a portion of these rights to restore stream flows within the reservation and build up the fishery. They recognized an opportunity to recover the natural ecosystem and to reap economic benefits from tourism and recreational uses by attracting anglers. Non-Indian water users on the reservation who would have had to leave water in the stream instead of diverting it for irrigation objected and took the matter before the court. The state supreme court rejected the tribes' attempt to use water for instream flows, saying that any change in use would have to be in accordance with Wyoming state law, which does not recognize such instream uses as "beneficial."[27] The United States Supreme Court did not review the decision.

If a tribe changes its water rights to uses that were not the basis for a quantification of reserved rights and this must be approved under state law, the state court can review the decision under the so-called "no injury" rule. This rule applies to all changes in use under the prior appropriation system. Limiting tribes to a single type of use and prohibiting all changes would be inconsistent with that system of water rights. But when prior appropriators change their use they must show that no other water users are hurt by the change. If the no injury rule were applied to Indian reserved water rights, it could render them useless. Recall that tribes generally have not been able to raise the capital needed to put water rights to use. On the Wind River Reservation, for instance, the federal government financed an irrigation system that served mostly non-Indian farmers on the reservation. Commencing Indian uses on Wind River and in other river basins where the investments of hundreds of non-Indian water users depend on using water that the tribe, as the senior water rights holder, could have claimed, is bound to cause injury to the non-Indians.

There is no doubt that the equities of established non-Indian water users deserve consideration. The non-Indian irrigators are neighbors and generally not responsible for the way the system from which they benefit was developed, nor for the fact that it has operated to the detriment of the Indians. The government created the system, and the non-Indians inherited the situation. They reasonably expected that the present conditions would continue. On the other hand, they have been using Indian water to build their wealth. In these circumstances, it seems inappropriate either to ignore the no injury rule or to apply it mechanically.

Walker and Williams propose that tribes like those on the Wind River Reservation exercise their authority to administer and regulate water rights on their reservations, and in doing so take control over the "change of use" question. They can adopt criteria for "sensible water use policies for all reservation citizens," non-Indian as well as Indian (Walker and Williams 1991, 5: 10). Some non-Indians have relied on state permits to use water diverted on the reservation that are over eighty years old. Walker and Williams urge that tribes "balance the complex interests of these non-Indians against . . . the unique historical circumstances of water development on Indian reservations [that] may well compel compromise" (Walker and Williams 1991, 5: 9). They say that one such compromise would be for tribes to adopt a public interest standard for tribal reservation water administration and apply it in a way that considers and weighs, along with other equities, the injury to juniors of changing the use of reserved water rights.

A Mismatch of Law and Culture?

The entire reserved water rights doctrine is not based on Indian values but on federal legislative purposes (see the similar situation in the Andes, described in chapter 7). The very existence of any water rights as well as the quantity of those rights depends on federal purposes derived from treaties, agreements, statutes, and executive orders. Typically, if not always, the terms were dictated by federal negotiators and federal policy in situations where the Indians had little bargaining power (see the comparable situation in South Africa, chapter 9). The integrity of land, water, and the natural world is at the heart of nearly all tribal cultural and spiritual life. Traditional Indian cultures surely needed water; yet *legal* rights to water are tied to fulfillment of national policy goals and not to cultural protection.

Although reserved water rights are not intended to protect tribal cultural values, uses of water that are secured by reserved rights can nevertheless further cultural values. Indian value systems sometimes create demands for water that can be satisfied by rights to water recognized by the law. In the desert Southwest, some tribes had established irrigation cultures using the sparse and seasonal streams. Like the tribes that were forced into agriculture by government policy, they needed irrigation water. In other situations, water reserved for agriculture according to national policy can be switched to other uses that satisfy Indian cultural demands, such as subsistence fisheries or spiritual purposes. The struggle of the Wind River Tribes described in the preceding section demonstrates that this is not always possible.

Conclusion

The Indian reserved water rights doctrine is certainly a potent force for tribes. Yet its application has not justified worries that assertion of Indian water rights will displace non-Indian established uses. This is partly because only a handful of tribes—fewer than thirty—have finally determined the extent of their rights through litigation or negotiation. Of those, only a few have actually put a significant portion of their water rights to use. Consequently, non-Indians have not been affected adversely by Indian water use. As Richard Collins wrote, "this situation has generated powerful political and financial forces that oppose Indian development, of which there has been very little. There have been extravagant claims of the threat posed by Indian water claims, but actual conflict has been almost entirely a war of words, paper, and lawyers. Indian calls are not shutting anyone's head gates" (Collins 1985, 56: 482).

The doctrine is strong in theory and the challenge to lawyers and tribal leaders is to give it potency in practice. A tribe is more likely to get attention if it brings a lawsuit. Litigation by tribes creates a credible threat because of the reserved rights doctrine. Yet proceeding in court to a conclusion can be prohibitively expensive for many tribes. There are other forums for asserting Indian reserved water rights, but all are expensive and arduous, including adjudication and negotiation. They also produce uneven results. Success can depend on the quality and impartiality of the court. If negotiation and legislation are needed it will depend on the political power and skill of the state's congressional delegation and the timing relative to the nation's economic health.

Even after tribal water rights are quantified, they will often remain unused because of a shortage of capital to finance water development, restrictions on marketing, and limits on changes of use. Sometimes the only uses available under applicable law are not those that the tribe would pursue to further its cultural values. The tribes may need to exercise comprehensive control over the water, against non-Indian users within the reservation, in order to protect tribal resources and values. Jurisdictional barriers in United States Indian law can impede attainment of this goal.

The United States reserved water rights system appears to provide substantial legal rights, yet it is fraught with complications. It is the product of policies that were not aimed at support for the creation of indigenous peoples' territories and livelihoods but that have actually been inimical to their culture. These problems challenge local ethnic groups and their lawyers. Nevertheless, achieving justice and equity for indigenous peoples and furthering cultural integrity depends primarily on having an ample legal foundation for asserting legal rights. The reserved rights doctrine is an invaluable asset for indigenous populations in the United States. It provides a mechanism within the dominant culture's legal system for territorial groups and communities to claim rights to large quantities of water. By contrast, indigenous peoples in many other countries lack any effective legal recognition for their water rights.

NOTES

Research for this chapter has been carried out in the framework of the international WALIR (Water Law and Indigenous Rights) program that contributes to counteracting the discrimination and undermining of local and indigenous water access and control rights by national laws and policies. The program is coordinated by the Irrigation and Water Engineering Group of Wageningen University and the United Nations Economic Commission for Latin America and the Caribbean. In this action-research alliance the United States of America is studied as a comparative to Mexico, Ecuador, Peru, Bolivia, and Chile.

1. Indian law and indigenous or Indian water rights in the United States legal tradition fundamentally refer to the principles by which indigenous rights have been codified in the positive legal system—not to the multiple, diverse, and dynamic sociolegal repertoires, rules, and rights that are applied and developed for locally regulating water control by indigenous communities or ethnic groups themselves.

2. For Indian water rights issues, see also Burton 1991; Getches et al. 1998; McCool 1987.

3. *Winters v. United States*, 207 U.S. 564, 576 (1908).

4. *Arizona v. California,* 373 U.S. 546 (1963).

5. Ibid.

6. Ibid.

7. McCarran Amendment of 1952, 43 U.S.C.A. sec. 666.

8. *Colorado River Water Conservation District v. United States*, 424 U.S. 800, 810 (1976).

9. *United States v. Kagama*, 118 U.S. 375, 384 (1886).

10. *In re General Adjudication of All Rights to Use Water in the Big Horn River System*, 753 P.2d 76, affirmed, *Wyoming v. United States,* 492 U.S. 406 (1989).

11. *San Carlos Apache Tribe v. County of Maricopa*, 972 P.2d 179 (Ariz. 1999).

12. *In re Snake River Basin Water System*, 764 P.2d 78 (Idaho 1988).

13. Public Law No. 95–328, 42 Stat. 409 (1978); Public Law No. 98–530, 98 Stat. 2698 (1984); Public Law No. 102–497, 106 Stat. 3528 (1992).

14. Public Law No. 97–293, 96 Stat. 1274 (1982).

15. *Arizona v. California,* 373 U.S. 546 (1963).

16. *Arizona v. California,* 460 U.S. 605 (1983).

17. *Nevada v. United States,* 463 U.S. 110 (1983).

18. *Skeem v. United States,* 273 Fed. 93, 9th Cir. (1921); 25 U.S.C. sec. 415.

19. *Johnson v. McIntosh,* 21 U.S., 543 (1823); Non-Intercourse Act, 25 U.S.C.A. sec. 177.

20. *Montana v. United States,* 450 U.S. 544, 566 (1981).

21. *United States v. Anderson,* 736 F.2d 1358, 9th Cir. (1984).

22. *Holly v. Confederated Tribes and Bands of the Yakima Indian Nation,* 655 F. Supp. 557, E.D. Wash. (1985); affirmed subnom, *Holly v. Totus,* 812 F.2d 714, 9th Cir. (1987), certiorari denied, 484 U.S. 823 (1987).

23. *New Mexico v. Mescalero Apache Tribe,* 462 U.S. 324 (1983).

24. *United States v. Adair,* 753 D.2d 1394, 9th Cir. (1983), certiorari denied, *Oregon v. United States,* 467 U.S. 1252 (1984).

25. *Arizona v. California,* 439 U.S. 419 (1979).

26. 753 P.2d 76, 98,Wyo. (1988); affirmed, *Wyoming v. United States,* 492 U.S. 406 (1989).

27. *In re General Adjudication of All Rights to Use Water in the Big Horn River System,* 835 P.2d 273, Wyo. (1992).

4

In the Shadow of Uniformity

Balinese Irrigation Management in a Public Works Irrigation System in Luwu, South Sulawesi, Indonesia

DIK ROTH

Technocratic approaches to irrigation development and management have gradually given way to participatory but still largely instrumental approaches, with a focus on how water users should perform local irrigation management tasks and functions. Thus, joint management is often characterized by devolution of day-to-day managerial tasks and responsibilities to local water users' associations (WUAs) of the tertiary units (TUs) in irrigation systems. In the same way, water rights are often paid attention to in an instrumental manner on the basis of preconceived assumptions about the efficiency of exploitation and management under specific property regimes (F. von Benda-Beckmann et al. 1996; Spiertz 2000). The ultimate objective of such approaches is to create supposedly ideal conditions of governance, management, and exploitation through combinations of physical and sociolegal engineering. From the 1980s on, these issues were increasingly approached from an economic point of view: deregulation and cost reduction have put management turnover, cost recovery, and the introduction of market principles high on the irrigation management agenda.

Fortunately, there is also a growing attention to the sociolegal aspects of irrigation (see also chapter 1).[1] Many studies on irrigation and water rights are now openly posing the question of how to cope with legally complex water use and management situations and the new forms of interaction and problems of governance and management emerging from them.[2] Such studies often focus on farmer-managed irrigation systems and problems of rehabilitation, incorporation, and redefinition of water rights against a background of increasing pressure on water resources and competition between multiple uses and user groups. In these settings, the existence of multiple sources and definitions of rights—for instance between state law and customary law—is the rule rather than an exception.

Less attention has generally been paid to the sociolegal aspects of irrigation systems designed, built, and operated by state agencies (see Meinzen-Dick and Bruns 2000). However, the seeming uniformity of such systems based on modern engineering technology, in which rights to land and water are allocated, and material infrastructure and users' organizations designed and built by state agencies, should not blind us to the fact that these systems may hide a considerable diversity of norms and rules, forms of knowledge, organizational arrangements, and practices that do not by definition neatly and harmoniously fit in with "the system." Engineering norms, rules, and definitions of rights emerging in such systems may differ considerably from those of the users. The existence of an ethnically heterogeneous farmer population within one command area as a consequence of migration, for instance, may add to these complexities.

This chapter explores the sociolegal landscape of irrigation management in such a setting. I describe and analyze the role of the traditional Balinese irrigators' institution of the subak in irrigation management among Balinese settlers in the command area of the Kalaena irrigation system, a public works system in Luwu, South Sulawesi, Indonesia (see figure 4.1). I transcend (sub-)disciplinary boundaries that select either "the legal," "the technical," or "the organizational" as an exclusive focus of analysis. Approaches that stress the socially constructed or heterogeneous character of technology are one way out of such disciplinary approaches. Any human use of technology entails processes of sociotechnical stabilization. Bijker and Law (1992: 293) remark that "the concern with sociotechnical stabilization . . . is close to . . . the problem of securing the social order." Irrigation systems can also be analyzed as sociotechnical systems, intricate complexes of physical-technical, organizational, and normative-legal dimensions of water control in a wider agroecological, economic, sociopolitical, and cultural context.[3] There is a strong interdependence among social norms, technology, and the organization of irrigation management. A functioning irrigation system requires a sufficient degree of stability among these dimensions of norms and rights, infrastructure, and organization (see Boelens 1998). The normative and legal dimensions of irrigation, then, are important in processes of stabilization at work in irrigation systems, but should not be analyzed in isolation.[4]

In Indonesia, so-called technical irrigation systems based on civil engineering technology were built on a large scale from the 1960s.[5] This type of irrigation development is characterized by a top-down modernization approach with a focus on standardized physical construction. Contrary to "traditional" irrigation systems, the normative-legal, technical, and organizational properties of these systems are basically a product of blueprinted approaches to design, construction, and management, and therefore largely external to the life-worlds of the users. What does this mean for the processes of sociotechnical stabilization? How do Balinese farmers cope with legal, technical, and organizational

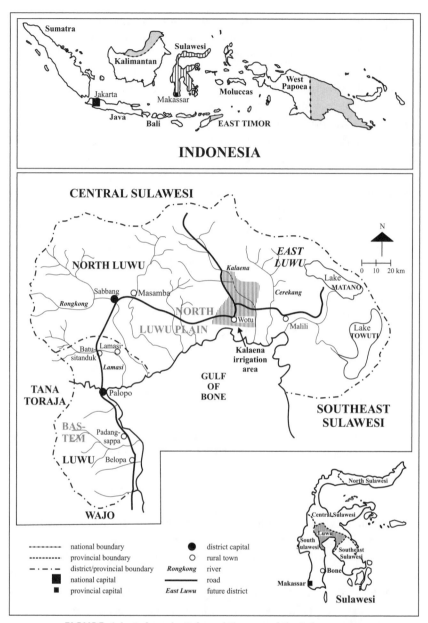

FIGURE 4.1. Indonesia, Sulawesi, Luwu, and the Lalaena area

complexity? What role do civil engineering and specifically Balinese conceptualizations of water control and irrigation management play? What are the consequences of legal and other complexities for irrigation management practices?
These are the main questions that guide this exploration.

  This chapter consists of the following sections: in the next section I describe the regional and local context, the character of the rights to land and water resources and infrastructure, and the forms of regulation in this irrigation setting. In the third section I provide more detailed information about the TU/WUA complex and the subak, both of which play an important role in this case study. In the fourth section I describe and analyze the specific ways in which Balinese irrigation management has developed. I discuss the establishment of the subak and its development in relation to the complex of TU/WUA. Further, I pay attention to the influence of the subak on the technical, organizational, and legal arrangements of the TU/WUA complex. In the fifth section I present a short conclusion.

The Regional and Local Setting

Luwu and the Kalaena Area

Luwu District (Kabupaten Luwu) is situated in the northeastern part of the province of South Sulawesi (Sulawesi Selatan; see figure 4.1).[6] Luwu is a mountainous area, except for a narrow coastal plain in southern Luwu and the more expansive North Luwu plain, a 2,500 square kilometer alluvial coastal plain bordering on the northwestern part of the Gulf of Bone. This plain, the floodplain of a large number of rivers that discharge into the Gulf of Bone, used to be covered with tropical forests, sago, and mangrove forests. In the course of the twentieth century it became a major center of exploitation of land and water resources.[7]

In the early twentieth century, the establishment of a more direct form of rule by the Dutch colonial government set in motion radical sociopolitical and economic changes, including those in the field of irrigation development. The island of Java, the center of colonial power, had long usurped most funds for agricultural and irrigation development. In the framework of Dutch "ethical policy," however, a more welfare-oriented colonial policy prioritizing education, emigration, and irrigation, islands such as Sulawesi (Celebes) attracted greater attention (Booth 1977a, 1977b; Ravesteijn 1997). In the 1930s, this colonial development agenda reached Luwu. Prospects for irrigation development were bright there. From the late 1930s on irrigation development in Luwu was introduced in combination with a "colonization" program (Ind. *kolonisasi*) for resettlement of Javanese farmers.[8]

After the end of Dutch rule, this combined strategy of irrigation development and demographic policy in Luwu was continued by the Government of Indonesia with multilateral and foreign donor aid. Thousands of families from Java and Bali were resettled in North Luwu between the late 1960s and the mid-1990s. In addition, regional development programs for irrigation development and intensification of agriculture were implemented, fitting in with the national objective of attaining self-sufficiency in rice production through the spread of Green Revolution agricultural technology.[9] This combination of transmigration and irrigation development in Luwu shows a high degree of continuity with the earlier colonial programs.

Irrigation development in the Kalaena area is part of these efforts. The Kalaena plain stretches between the northern coast of the Gulf of Bone and the mountain range that separates South Sulawesi from Central Sulawesi. The Kalaena irrigation system consists of a right bank branch (Kalaena Kanan) and a left bank branch (Kalaena Kiri), with a total irrigable potential of about 17,000 hectares. Like most public works systems, the Kalaena system consists of a diversion weir (in River Kalaena) and a network of primary, secondary, tertiary, and quaternary canals, connected by structures for measurement and regulation in the main system part, and division boxes with flap gates for rotational water distribution inside the TUs (between tertiary and quaternary canals).[10]

The Kalaena system had also been planned in the 1930s in the framework of colonization. While it was under construction, hundreds of Javanese families were resettled here between 1938 and 1941. Then a long period of political turmoil followed, between 1941 and 1965.[11] From the 1970s on, construction of the system was resumed with foreign donor aid. Irrigation development was combined with state-sponsored transmigration. With other economic opportunities, it became a major pull factor for spontaneous migrants from various areas. The area now harbors a large number of population groups, including local Pamona, Padoë and Luwu; Bugis, Makassarese and Toraja from other parts of South Sulawesi; and transmigrants from Java and Bali.

Settlement in Kertoraharjo

Three decades ago the site of Kertoraharjo, now a relatively prosperous Balinese village, was still covered with dense forest. In 1972 and 1973 several groups of Balinese and Javanese transmigrants, totaling 500 families, settled in (then) transmigration project Kertoraharjo I. The 350 Balinese families, all Hindus, arrived in four groups of 150, 100, and two groups of 50 families each (see figure 4.2). Once the settlers had cleaned their 0.25 hectare home yards, they started developing their future agricultural land. Aside from the home yard, land allocated by the state through the transmigration program consisted of one hectare of (future) irrigated fields (*sawah*) and 0.75 hectare of rainfed land (*ladang*).[12] Whereas (planned) irrigated fields were located east of the road bisecting the settlement, (planned) rainfed fields were located west of it. In the first years, the harvests of rainfed rice, maize, and other seasonal crops fell prey to rats, wild boars, and birds. The settlers were poor and produced mainly for a meager subsistence.

In the years that followed, both government-administrative and specifically Balinese village institutions took shape in this new environment. The administrative village (*desa*) and its subdivisions into hamlets (*dusun*) became the ba-

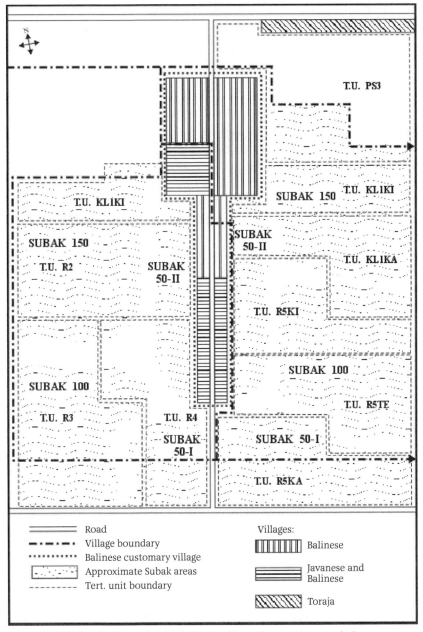

FIGURE 4.2. Kertoraharjo, tertiary units, and approximate subak areas

sic unit of government administration, and the customary village (*desa adat*) and its subdivisions (*banjar*) formed the customary administrative world. The Balinese subak was established in the initial period of land development, while the government-initiated WUAs in the TUs were only established after the irrigation system had reached Kertoraharjo in the early 1980s (see below).

State-Derived Rights and Regulation in a Newly Developed Irrigation System

The way in which property rights to water, land, and infrastructure are created, defined, and reproduced, and the balance of rights and responsibilities involved, are crucial factors in irrigation management. A relevant focus for analysis is the relationship between the normative-legal, technical-infrastructural, and organizational dimensions of water rights and water control. It will be clear that the history of water rights in the irrigation development and settlement setting analyzed here differs widely from the history of creation, development, and reproduction of rights in traditional farmer-managed systems. In such systems rights may be associated with collectivities of water users on the basis of a specific group history of land occupation and settlement expressed in customary claims, of location or prior access, or of earlier investments of time, labor, materials, or money in the establishment, operation, and maintenance of irrigation infrastructure. In the case discussed here, the state is a primary actor in land allocation, settlement, and irrigation development. Rights to land, water, and irrigation infrastructure were defined, created, and allocated by the state.

Land rights in the Kalaena transmigration settlements have developed in a specific manner under the influence of transmigration. Transmigration is based on the principle of state control over national land resources (see F. and K. von Benda-Beckmann 1999; Slaats 1999).[13] Between the late 1960s and 1990s, when transmigration was a spearhead of Suharto's New Order regime, throughout the country the state appropriated extensive areas of land previously under local customary tenure and reallocated it to transmigrants under an individual ownership title. This was also the case with transmigration in Kalaena. Thus, state interventions in land tenure are at the basis of the processes described and analyzed here. Most land of transmigrants was routinely titled after settlement.[14]

In the Kalaena system, built and—as far as the main system is concerned—managed by the state and its agencies, water rights are tied to the ownership of land in the command area of the system. Water rights are state-provided; there is hardly any contestation of this fact. Through the WUAs, the state agency has delegated to the farmers a relatively limited bundle of (mainly operational) water rights and a variety of responsibilities. Establishment of WUAs for TU management and farmer membership of these organizations is obligatory, each TU having its own WUA. The reverse side of the right of farmers to use water is their obligation to fulfill all responsibilities pertaining to WUA membership. Administrative responsibility for the WUAs lies with the village administration of the village to which the WUA belongs.

Water rights (that is, in the more restricted sense of a right to a share of the resource; see Pradhan and Meinzen-Dick 2003), defined in terms of crop water requirements per area irrigated, are allocated by the state agency responsible for main system operation. Formally, determination of water requirements takes place in a rather management-intensive process of bottom-up field data gathering involving regular contacts between representatives of the WUA and the irrigation agency. Water distribution by the agency takes place at the level of the TU (at the tertiary off-take). Inside the TU, the WUA (through its functionary, the unit water master) is responsible for rotational water distribution to the quaternary units of which the TU consists (see below). Within the quaternary units, the TU has no technology or other forms of regulation for water allocation to individual water users.

The definition of rights to infrastructure is part of the division of rights and responsibilities between the main system under agency responsibility and tertiary systems under responsibility of the WUAs. All irrigation infrastructure is owned by the state. Farmers organized in a WUA have a right to use the irrigation infrastructure of the TUs, in combination with the duty to contribute to its cleaning and maintenance. Use of the tertiary infrastructure, especially its water division structures, is narrowly circumscribed. Thus, farmers are formally not allowed to interfere with, or bring about changes to, the tertiary gate itself. The same goes for the tertiary infrastructure below the tertiary gate, which is operated and maintained by the WUAs. Farmers are formally not allowed to make any changes to the tertiary infrastructure. Their role is limited to operation, maintenance, and small repairs. Operation of the tertiary systems by changing the gate settings of the water division boxes is formally the task of the TU water master (*ulu-ulu*).

The establishment of state-defined and state-allocated rights to land, water, and infrastructure, and of regulatory arrangements for irrigation management has resulted in a *seemingly* uniform and undifferentiated landscape of government-allocated rights to resources, and related obligations and tertiary management arrangements. Before exploring the real-life sociolegal landscape as it has developed in the context of Balinese settlement and agricultural practices, in the next section I discuss the subak and WUA.

The Subak and WUA

The Balinese Subak

The subak has a long historical record but does not belong only to the past. In the 1980s, Bali counted more than 1,200 subaks encompassing over 100,000 hectares (Sutawan 1987; Sutawan et al. 1990).[15] Generalizing about subaks is difficult. Many variations in form, function, and meaning given to the subak exist in time and space. Colonial researchers stressed its combined secular and ritual functions, its relative autonomy from other institutional and political arrangements in Balinese society, and its key role as an irrigation institution (Korn 1924; Lansing 1991; Liefrinck 1969). Outside Bali, the subak served as a model for irrigation development in Java. One of the issues in colonial debates of the 1930s was whether to opt for a proportional or an absolute water division. The former originates from the Balinese subak and is based on historically established rights; the latter is characteristic of civil engineering approaches, and is based on rotational schedules in accordance with calculated crop water requirements. The proportional system has continued to draw attention as an alternative to water division based on crop water requirements and modern technology (see Booth 1977a; Horst 1996a and b; Ravesteijn 1997).

Anthropologists were also attracted to the subak. Geertz (1972, 1980) stressed the autonomy of the "village republic," of which the subak was distinguished as a "wet" variant.[16] In more recent analyses the focus has shifted from exclusive attention to the subak level to higher levels of integration of which subaks are now supposed to be part. Lansing focuses on the role of agricultural rituals as "scheduling mechanisms" and of regional networks of water temples as "managers of the terrace ecosystems" (Lansing 1987: 327; see also Lansing 1991). New functions continue to be invented for the subak. Thus, Sutawan (1998) pleads for the development of the subak into a multipurpose institution engaging in both commercial agriculture and environmental protection. Such approaches to the subak illustrate the relevance of legal-anthropological research. In legal-anthropological approaches, the subak is no longer reduced to its formal properties but analyzed in relation to the behavior of subak-related actors, government agencies and development programs in specific interactive situations. The subak, its constituent parts, or higher integrative levels can become subject to differing definitions and interpretations, and thus undergo crucial transformations (Spiertz 1992, 2000).

With all these variations in time and space in mind, and stressing diversity rather than uniformity, what are the main characteristics of the subak in Bali?[17] A subak is a complex of irrigated (sometimes also rainfed) land of between tens and hundreds of hectares. Subaks tend to crosscut village or hamlet boundaries. Physical boundaries (rivers, ravines, and so on) and hydrological factors (a shared water source), as well as sociopolitical factors play an important role in defining the subak. The head of the subak is the klian subak or pekaseh, assisted by other functionaries.[18] Important subak functions related to irrigated agriculture are: construction and repairs; operation and maintenance; water allocation and distribution; determination of cropping patterns; timing of agricultural activities; prevention and eradication of pests and diseases; temple

construction and maintenance; timing, coordination, and performance of agricultural rituals; maintenance of religious purity; collection of funds, fines, and
other contributions; conflict resolution; creation and enforcement of regulations; and application of sanctions.

Subak regulations may also include land-tenure issues. Subaks often have a
moneylending function for their members. Membership is associated with a set
of rights: to obtain water; to take part in rituals and use the services of a priest;
to elect subak leaders or be elected; and to have a say in subak affairs. Important
responsibilities and obligations are labor contributions for construction, improvement, and maintenance; to take water in accordance with allocated
shares; to follow instructions for planting and cropping schedules or rotational
arrangements; to guard against religious-ritual pollution of the fields; to attend
meetings; and to contribute to the subak funds in money or kind (Barth 1995;
Birkelbach 1973; FAO 1982; Geertz 1980; Lansing 1991; Spiertz 1991, 2000; Sutawan
1987).

A subak is characterized by specific technology such as diversion weirs,
tunnels and aqueducts, and a hierarchy of canals connected by division structures. Technology for intersubak and internal water division is mainly based on
the fixed proportional division of continuous water flows through wooden,
stone-cement, or concrete overflow weirs called temuku. An advantage of
this method is that the water flow is divided in a direction parallel to the current
and division structures are relatively transparent, the only variable being
the width of the proportional openings in the structure.[19] Water division between subaks and inside the subak is the outcome of the historical process of
the more or less proportional determination of water allocation based on area
irrigated (Horst 1996a, b; Liefrinck 1969; Spiertz 2000, Sutawan 1987; Sutawan et
al. 1990).

From the 1960s onward, the subak was discovered by development programs for the introduction of high-yielding varieties, upgrading and rehabilitation of infrastructure (dams, canals, division works), and TU development. This
often had radical consequences, deeply influencing agricultural practices
(Horst 1996a; Lansing 1987, 1991; Spiertz 1991; Sutawan 1987). Analyzing the impact of public works interventions on the subak, Horst (1996a) shows that
changes were often not accepted and led to conflicts between farmers and the
project. Relatively simple Balinese division structures were replaced by complex
ones. The proportional distribution system in combination with determination
of turns and rotations, planting dates, and cropping patterns based on local
knowledge and experience was done away with. It was replaced by a labor- and
knowledge-intensive system of data collection (for water requirements), measurement, and (too) frequent adjustment of gates, all depending on the irrigation bureaucracy. Often, the outcome was a forced retreat from engineering
technology to subak technology (Horst 1996a).

Water Users' Associations

As awareness of the bad performance of large irrigation systems all over the world grew, technocratic approaches to irrigation development gradually gave way to approaches that paid more attention to social-organizational aspects.[20] Participation of water users, organized in WUAs at the TU level, was seen as the solution. WUAs created through such policies are legal entities, usually formalized by a combination of the key elements of basic law (enabling law), bylaws, and transfer agreements (Geijer 1995; Salman 1997). The formal governance and management structure in irrigation systems with WUAs is based on this form of regulation. In Indonesia, formation of WUAs in public works irrigation systems was made compulsory by presidential decree in 1984. While the main part of the canal hierarchy (weir, primary, and secondary canals, including the tertiary gate) remained a state agency responsibility, a key role was now assigned to the WUAs. Thus, most Indonesian "technical" public works systems currently belong to the type often referred to as jointly managed or bureaucratic-communal (Chambers 1980).[21] In view of continuing problems of operation and maintenance, financing, and performance, in 1987 the Irrigation Operation and Maintenance Policy was introduced. It focused on irrigation management transfer through the turnover of irrigation systems of 500 hectares or less, the introduction of cost recovery principles through collection of irrigation service fees, and funding for operation and maintenance. The objective was a further devolution of financial and managerial responsibilities to water users. The general future trend is toward commoditification of water resources, introduction and expansion of market principles, and mixed private and public-sector investment (Bruns 2004; Geijer 1995; Oad 2001; Vermillion et al. 2000).

TUs in Indonesia cover between 50 and 150 hectares. The units are defined by design and use principles (subdivision into quaternary units, separated canal functions, rotational water distribution) and internal organization through the WUA (board with chairman, vice chairman, secretary, and treasurer; water master, quaternary unit leader; formal procedures, and so on). Turnover to the WUAs is, above all, a top-down devolution of management tasks and responsibilities to the farmers, rather than a real participatory process involving the empowerment of user groups and the establishment of strong local rights to water and infrastructure. According to the Indonesian constitution, water belongs to the state. The only right delegated is the right to use a state-owned natural resource delivered to the TUs through a public irrigation system. In many irrigation systems (including that in Kalaena), the transfer of TUs as legal entities for tertiary management has not or has only partly been realized. In practice, this means that Kalaena continued to depend on rehabilitation funds related to construction projects (Bruns 2004; Oad 2001; Vermillion 2000).

Local Development of Water Rights and
Arrangements for Irrigation Management

In this section I explore the real-life normative-legal, technical, and organizational landscape as it has developed in the context of Balinese settlement, development of irrigated agriculture, and ways of coping with a physically, normatively, and organizationally blueprinted irrigation system. First, I relate the process of interaction between WUA and subak to more general conceptualizations of management. Second, I discuss changes in water division technology under the influence of subak knowledge. Third, I give examples of the role of the subak in organizing water users at the tertiary and subtertiary levels. Thus I will show that subak plays a prominent and, for irrigation management, relevant role. Subak-derived norms and rules, technology, and forms of organization are visible behind the apparent uniformity of tertiary infrastructure, organization, and tertiary management system.

Land and Water, Subak and WUA: Different Definitions of Management

DEFINING THE SUBAK. Apart from state legal and regulatory arrangements pertaining to land, water, and infrastructure, for the Balinese settlers the institution of subak plays an important role in regulating a variety of dimensions of irrigated agriculture. Subak jurisdiction over Balinese land was established even before the first irrigation water reached the village land. When settlers were still fully engaged in land clearing, the settler groups that had arrived formed a village subak. Later, when all Balinese groups had arrived and made progress in clearing their agricultural land, the village subak was split up into four smaller ones, membership of which was defined on the basis of land allocation to the four Balinese settler groups. These subaks are generally known by reference to the settler group that initially formed their membership: 150KK, 100KK, 50KK (I), and 50KK–Tampaksiring (II) (see figure 4.2).[22] Organizationally, each subak was headed by a klian subak. Together, these four subaks formed an organization called pekaseh, headed by a functionary with the same name. Thus, the pattern of state land allocation to the four settler groups became the initial defining criterion of the subaks. Unlike the situation in Bali, the Kertoraharjo subaks bore no relation to hydrological and physical boundaries, canal structures, or branches.

The establishment of subaks before finalization of the irrigation system and the availability of irrigation water points to the central importance of their religious-ritual functions, next to their irrigation management functions in a more restricted sense (see Sutawan et al. 1990). Initially, the subaks were created mainly to arrange agricultural rituals at an early stage of land clearing and development. The forested area was still full of destructive forces and potentially dangerous spirits. These can, in the Balinese view, only be effectively combated by appropriate rituals. Subaks were also essential in controlling the planting date by determining a propitious day on the religious calendar. On a small scale, attempts were made to divert water from a natural drain by building a small weir and digging a canal. This failed under the difficult physical conditions of the early period. Weir and canal had fallen into disuse before construction activities of the irrigation system reached the area.

Thus, the subak potentially showed the same wide variety of functions known from Bali, covering ritual, agricultural practices and decision making, construction and irrigation management in the more restricted and instrumental sense understood by officials and irrigation engineers. However, there was one crucial difference from the subak in Bali. Whereas in Bali the flow of water largely determines the form and membership of subak, in Kertoraharjo it was the pattern of land allocation by the state to the various settler groups that determined subak boundaries and membership.

RESTRICTING THE SUBAK. In the late 1970s, the public works construction program reached Kertoraharjo. Construction of tertiary infrastructure was not restricted to the planned sawah area east of the road bisecting Kertoraharjo, but also covered the ladang area west of it (see figure 4.2). The transmigrants generally welcomed the irrigation system as a major contribution to their further development. Water from the new system reached Kertoraharjo land around 1983. Whatever its benefits, the introduction of the public works system had serious consequences. As explained above, the organizational arrangements for tertiary irrigation management in the new system—the WUAs—came as one package with the physical infrastructure of the TUs. TU layout, construction, and irrigation management were fully based on irrigation-technical and hydrological criteria, and did not take into account preexisting social-organizational, settlement group, or ethnic boundaries. The TU boundaries (based on design criteria) cut across the preexisting subak units which, based as they were on land allocation, had no link with irrigated agriculture and irrigation management. Under the influence of the new TUs and obligatory establishment of WUAs, the subaks gradually lost their relevance as organizations with a potential for fulfilling irrigation management functions in the new system. Nor could the often ethnically mixed new TUs fulfill that other important subak function, organizing and carrying out the rituals associated with the cycle of cultivation of irrigated rice.[23] Thus, under the influence of introduction of the TU/WUA system, the agricultural, irrigation managerial, and religious-ritual functions of the subak were torn apart. Tertiary irrigation management, narrowly conceptualized as operation and maintenance of the tertiary infrastructure, formally became the sole responsibility of the WUAs. This function was regarded as belonging to the domain of government regulation, delegated by the government agency of public works to the WUAs. Subak activities were restricted to the religious-ritual sphere; the subaks were to refrain from any interference with nonritual irrigation management functions.

The Balinese have always loyally accepted government regulations for tertiary irrigation management. The accounts of many Balinese show that they had great difficulty in making WUAs function in an acceptable way, however, without having recourse to normative-legal, technical, and organizational elements of the subak. To solve this, they attempted to copy organizational arrangements deriving from the subak to the WUA domain, and to rename them, using the idiom of the WUAs. After establishment of TUs and WUAs they created an organizational structure in which the pekaseh of the subaks also functioned as "WUA coordinator" in the village. According to stories of Balinese farmers, subak functionaries and a government functionary, subak-derived regulations pertaining to water distribution, maintenance, collective labor, and planting discipline, expressed in subak regulations (*awig-awig*) were quite successfully applied to the farmer population of the TUs and WUAs. The TUs showed rapid development, farmers invested capital and labor in their TUs, and regular contacts were maintained between the WUA coordinator (who was also pekaseh) and the Irrigation Service. However, after some years this double organizational structure generated conflicts between the pekaseh and the village administration, then under a Javanese village head.[24]

DIVORCING THE SUBAK FROM WATER CONTROL. Thus a final separation was established between irrigation management functions, formally belonging to the WUA domain, and religious-ritual functions, belonging to the subak domain. Further, the subaks in Kertoraharjo show many similarities with subaks in Bali, as described above.[25] The pekaseh has a set of regulations pertaining to ritual purity and avoidance of desecration of the irrigated areas under its control. One of the main tasks of the pekaseh is to collect funds for subak rituals. Subak members pay a seasonal subak tax per area of irrigated land (*sarin tahun*), collected in money or kind. The larger part of this tax, determined in proportion to the number of hectares of irrigated land under subak control, flows from the subak funds to the pekaseh. This is the capital used for preparing and staging of rituals related to the rice cultivation cycle. Rituals are performed by a priest specializing in rice rituals, assisted by a specialist in offerings. By providing funds, labor of the subak members and materials the pekaseh also contributes to the maintenance of the irrigation temple. Contributions to collective labor for maintenance are administered at the subak level; collective work parties are generally well attended.

Each subak has its own simple regulations, written down in a small notebook. Subak funds originate from different sources. First, there is the seasonal contribution (*sarin tahun*) of ten kilograms of unhulled rice per hectare of irrigated land (or its corresponding value in money). Second, there are fines paid by members, especially for absence from collective labor and subak meetings, or inability to participate in subak tasks due to prolonged absence from the village (*beli ayah*; "buying work"). Third, if the subak has a moneylending function, interest paid by members is an important source of income. Loans are provided for six (Balinese) months against an interest determined by the members, usually amounting to 5 percent per month. Members tend to value highly the savings and credit function of subak. These funds were often described to me as a "binding force" to make the organization function and stimulate member involvement and interest in its functioning.

Though subaks and pekaseh are not allowed to interfere with tertiary irrigation management, both play an important role in irrigated agriculture. The pekaseh determines the day on which the first irrigation water is ritually received, field preparation is allowed to start, and transplanting the rice is allowed to take place.[26] The role of pekaseh and subaks in determining the transplanting date illustrates the legal character of their regulation. As is the case with all stages of rice cultivation, the beginning of transplanting, marked by the performance of a transplanting ritual (*pengawitan*), is accompanied by regulations pertaining to transplanting and agricultural labor on the day of the ritual. Transplanting before the performance of the ritual is strictly forbidden. It is regarded as a polluting act that disturbs the harmonious relationship between nature, human beings, and the divine world. Although farmers are allowed to start transplanting directly after the ritual, any other agricultural labor in the irrigated fields is forbidden on the day of the ritual. Rules are enforced by "spies" in the irrigated fields (I met one who was the head of one of the WUAs). Transgressors are fined by their subak, and must, in addition, finance a cleansing ritual.

The rapid socioeconomic changes in recent years have also influenced the subaks. Many Balinese bought additional irrigated fields in Kertoraharjo and surrounding villages. As Balinese irrigated agriculture expanded across the initial subak and village boundaries, the subak as an organization that regulates seasonal tax collection and transplanting behavior of Balinese farmers was confronted with new tensions and threats to its authority: conflicts about subak boundaries. Some Balinese support the validity of subak regulations for all irrigated land owned by Balinese, irrespective of its location (that is, both inside and outside initial subak areas). Others do not agree with such interpretations and tend to restrict subak regulations and tax collection to irrigated land inside the initial subak areas. The economic dynamism of Kertoraharjo, in combination with its location in the midst of non-Balinese territory, make the subaks face new challenges it will have to cope with without having recourse to an important sanctioning instrument of the subak in Bali: water.

This development of subak and WUA points to the importance of the cultural dimension of water rights and irrigation management. There are marked differences between engineering and government agency approaches to irrigation management, and those associated with the subaks. The government sphere of regulation, based on civil engineering approaches, discerns a specific category of activities called "manajemen" (management). In the case of tertiary management, this includes the organization of water users in WUAs for the performance of routine operational and maintenance tasks, but excludes the religious-ritual dimension of irrigated agriculture. It classifies this as belonging to the category of religion (*agama*), as not associated with irrigation management. Balinese would never use "manajemen" to refer to the complex domain of irrigated agriculture as perceived in Balinese culture. They tend to use "persubakan" for the totality of activities pertaining to infrastructure, water control, legal regulation and organization, agriculture, and religious-ritual obligations. There are also important differences in the definition of rights pertaining to the various dimensions of irrigated agriculture. Whereas WUA rights are mainly operational rights devolved to the collectivity of the WUA, rights associated with the subak form a more comprehensive bundle of rights that does not exclude the collective choice dimensions of irrigation water rights (Ostrom and Schlager 1996). Some dimensions of these differences will be treated below: decision making about tertiary infrastructure and organization, and about WUA or tertiary boundaries; and bringing about active changes in these.

Changing the Tertiary Infrastructure

Water division technology plays a crucial role in issues of water rights and irrigation management. Ideally, water division technology reflects existing norms concerning water distribution and local notions of equity, and reproduces these norms and notions in patterns of water allocation and distribution (see Boelens 1998). Thus, general norms are turned into accepted physical patterns of allocation and distribution through technology. Whenever there is a discontinuity between normative notions and technical solutions, problems may arise in irrigation management and water control. Manipulation, destruction, or replacement of technical devices may be the outcome.[27] The use of specific forms of technology also has important consequences for how irrigation management is socially organized. Hence, it is important to pay attention to the characteristics of technology, in particular the types of rights inscribed in it, the way it is used, and the way in which people talk about technology. These may provide a clue to the relationship between technology and the normative and organizational dimensions of irrigation (see also chapter 6 for similar considerations in Nepal).

As described above, the TUs discussed here were products of the drawing table of engineers, the technical and spatial outcome of the application of standardized design criteria to a new irrigation area. Assumptions about technology, its use, and users were based in modernization thinking. Technology was regarded as a neutral instrument for development, and the relationships between technology and its users (between users or user groups through technology) as basically unproblematic. This approach does not allow for attention to different conceptualizations of water rights or norms pertaining to water distribution on which these are based. It is assumed that users will automatically accept, and adapt to, the new infrastructure provided by external intervention. Thus, from the perspective of the government, the history of irrigation development is quite simple: ready-made standard technical-infrastructural elements of the TUs are transferred to users organized in WUAs, and operated and maintained by the latter in accordance with attached recipes for use. Another basic assumption is that, upon finalization of construction, the system is "ready." In contrast, a more process-oriented approach is taken here, which defines irrigation development as an ongoing process entailing continuous transformations and adaptations. In addition, such adaptations take place in a setting in which the technology provided and the norms and principles basic to it might well be external to the life-world of the (Balinese) users of the system.

After finalization of their construction, the TUs were immediately handed over to the newly formed WUAs. According to accounts of farmers, only parts of the tertiary infrastructure were functioning. Most TUs were not ready for use but required all kinds of adaptations and changes by the farmers. Initial shortcomings involved the low quality of construction, especially the wrong position or elevation of the quaternary water division boxes. These led to rapid decay, water losses, and a seriously disturbed water distribution function of the tertiary systems. Apart from spontaneous decay of division boxes, active destruction by farmers also occurred. From the beginning, acceptance of engineering solutions such as flap-gated division boxes seems to have been low.[28] Traces of tampering with the infrastructure can be seen everywhere: locks that have been forced open; gates fixed with wire, sawn off, or completely broken out; thresholds under the gates broken away to let the water pass; gate openings filled with stones and earth or with masonry; and whole division boxes smashed to pieces. More than 80 percent of the water division boxes in the TUs with Kertoraharjo farmers can no longer perform the function for which they were designed and built: rotational tertiary water division.

Superficially, the infrastructure in all TUs makes the same degraded impression, in which it seems useless to look for any differentiation or meaning at all. However, a closer look at the (partly) Balinese TUs and discussions with Balinese farmers revealed that farmers have also actively tried to improve the infrastructure, although on a small scale.[29] Wherever Balinese farmers have created infrastructure for water division, they have used elements of subak technology. In some TUs with a Balinese farmer population, farmers have replaced the degraded division boxes with Balinese temuku structures for continuous proportional water division (see figure 4.3). These structures divide the water to an area almost similar to the quaternary units of the initial system, but with the boundaries adapted to the realities of a working irrigation system. In TU KLIki, for instance (see figure 4.2), great problems existed with technical water control as a consequence of malfunctioning boxes. One of these boxes had never functioned at all because it had been constructed at too low an elevation. Some years ago it was smashed to pieces by farmers and replaced with a stone-cement temuku upstream of the location of the old box. The temuku had been financed by the WUA, after the decision had been taken that such a construction was necessary for solving water division problems and conflicts. Many irrigated fields have better access to water after construction than before. In TU PS3, solutions to problems with the internal water division have also been sought in subak knowledge. Two temukus have been constructed to divide water in the tertiary canal among the user groups. In some of these groups, the use of the wooden temukus for water diversion from the smallest ("quaternary") canal into individual fields is also common. A wooden temuku is a piece of wood of sufficient size to be placed diagonally at the point where a water inlet or small canal leading to the individual field branches off from the canal, so as to serve as a small threshold. Using mud, farmers can close off the canal and the water inlet in proportion to the water shares involved at this level of distribution. Thus, the use of stone-cement and wooden temukus makes possible a more transparent manner of water distribution, open to public control, from the tertiary canal down to the individual fields. Like any kind of division technology, the temuku is not tamper-proof. It is easy to close off with mud one or more openings in the stone temuku, or to let water pass under the wooden one. However, what is important is the fact that, without tampering, water division takes a more transparent and controllable form than used to be the case with the division boxes of the engineering system.

Thus, farmers have sometimes actively tried to improve the infrastructure for water division. In doing so, they have made choices between engineering and subak technologies. What do Balinese farmers have to say about these choices? It becomes clear that farmers' choices are based on a complex of norms and principles pertaining to irrigation, embedded in broader Balinese social norms (see also Vermillion 1986, 2000). In the small groups of farmers who receive water from the same box or temuku canal, conformity to the norms for water distribution and appropriation is most explicitly stimulated by the group leader, and effectuated by social control. As was remarked above, water availability is not generally felt to be a major problem in Kertoraharjo. Hence, there is no felt need for very strict rules pertaining to water distribution within the small groups. However, even in the absence of such strict rules, Balinese are generally familiar with widely accepted norms and principles pertaining to water allocation and distribution. First, they should not be too greedy in appropriating water. Balinese farmers stress the importance of self-restraint and

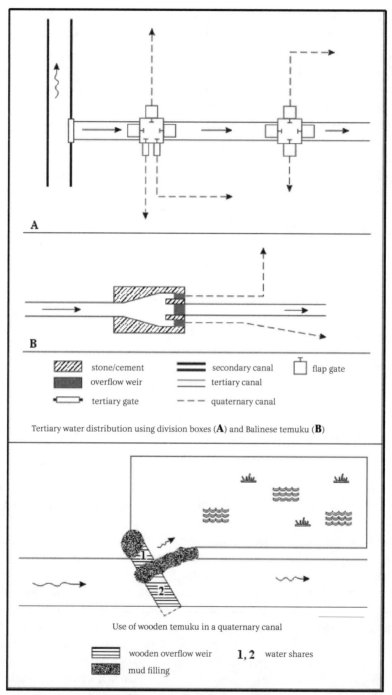

A

B

	stone/cement		secondary canal		flap gate
	overflow weir		tertiary canal		
	tertiary gate		quaternary canal		

Tertiary water distribution using division boxes (**A**) and Balinese temuku (**B**)

Use of wooden temuku in a quaternary canal

| | wooden overflow weir | **1, 2** water shares |
| | mud filling | |

FIGURE 4.3. Quaternary division box, temuki, and use of wooden temuku

moderation. Second, water appropriation should be visible. Water should not be taken by digging holes in the canal embankment. Thus, farmers are encouraged to use a wooden temuku for taking water individually. Third, under circumstances of scarcity and water shortage, farmers at the head end of a canal may be ordered to take less water, while those below are allowed to take more. Fourth, if a farmer is in acute need for water (for example, for land preparation), a larger share or even all the water may be taken for a period determined by the group leader or the other members. A farmer borrowing water must ask permission from the leader of the farmers' group or the farmer(s) affected, and is responsible for restoring the initial water distribution afterward. Some groups demand that farmers who temporarily change the water division place a stick at the point where water is taken, as a sign that no "stealing" is involved (see also Vermillion 1986).

Farmers often criticized the engineering technology represented by tertiary gates and quaternary boxes, which are most prominent in the day-to-day management experiences of farmers. Farmers tend to object to the flap-gated division boxes, in particular. Most of these had been badly constructed, were degraded, or had been destroyed. In addition, boxes are often criticized because of the rotational system and the principles of water division they represent. Closure of the box gates may cause the tertiary canal to overflow and damage the embankment. Therefore, as long as sufficient water is available, farmers have a distinct preference for a continuous flow system. Further, many farmers expressed the opinion that the division boxes are too coarse a technology of water division, especially in case of low quality of construction. If boxes do not function as they should, the water runs straight through rather than being equally divided among the box gates. Finally, farmers stressed that, with division boxes, they cannot check whether actual water division is more or less proportional to the areas irrigated. A farmer stressed that "if we use a temuku, water division is more equitable. A temuku divides the water proportionally in a just manner. If there is much water in the canal we enjoy its benefits together, if there is less, we suffer a shortage together."

One of the characteristics of TUs is that water division below the quaternary division boxes (at the level of quaternary units) is unspecified. In these areas, usually between ten and fifteen hectares, farmers have to take care of water division themselves. Though in some parts of the TUs with Balinese farmers hardly any regulation seems to take place at this lower level, in some farmers' groups the use of wooden temukus for water appropriation by individual farmers is quite common and is actively stimulated by group leaders. Thus, some degree of order is imposed upon practices of water distribution within the quaternary units, making water diversion to the individual plots more transparent and conforming to Balinese norms and principles pertaining to water distribution.

Though degradation remains a serious problem of most TUs with Balinese farmers, the conclusion seems justified that changes actively made to the water division infrastructure are based on subak water division technology and the general normative principles and cultural preferences behind it. Attempting to make water appropriation conform to the general norms about water distribution and notions of equity, Balinese farmers make use of simple but effective forms of Balinese subak technology such as the use of the temuku.

Organizing Local Management Tasks

As I have described, the broad management function of the subak, including irrigation management, agricultural decision making, and the religious-ritual dimensions of irrigated agriculture, was restricted in such a way as to separate religious-ritual functions from irrigation management and agricultural functions. However, the key issue is not this formal separation of functions at the level of organizations, but rather to what extent this separation of functions on the basis of a rather narrow officials' conceptualization of irrigation management is reflected in forms of regulation in the WUA, in social relationships between irrigators, and in irrigation practices. In the foregoing section I have shown that norms pertaining to water distribution that guide farmers' behavior in the Balinese TUs and technology based on these norms can be traced back to the subak. What about organizations for irrigation management? Even if the role of the subak as an organization is formally restricted to the religious-ritual field, how do Balinese farmers organize themselves, using which elements?

Let me take the same TUs again: PS3 and KLıki. In general, the WUAs of the TUs with Balinese farmers are not very active.[30] This is not only evidenced in the usual formal criteria such as attendance at WUA meetings (which is very low, unlike subak meetings) but also by more substantial indicators. The WUA boards have a low authority and legitimacy in the eyes of the members. Unlike the subak boards, accountability of the WUA boards toward the members tends to be low.[31] Activities for cleaning, maintenance, and repair of the tertiary infrastructure are rarely planned and implemented at WUA level. Actually, PS3 is a relatively active WUA, while KLıki conforms to the more general picture sketched above. However, in both TUs, farmers' organizations at the sub-WUA level are more active than at the WUA level. These are the small groups of farmers who receive water from the same canal emerging from a division box or temuku (in engineering terms, a quaternary unit). PS3 has four such groups, and KLıki seven. Rather than the formal organizational structure of a board, these groups have a leader (*kepala*) chosen by the members. Before the start of the season, rather informal group meetings are held, usually in a field hut and often combined with collective labor activities. Farmers tend to be willing to attend meetings only if these are combined with necessary cleaning or maintenance activities. Unlike WUA meetings, in these smaller groups time is not only spent on the formalities of a meeting but direct action is also taken. With a weak WUA lacking the means to impose sanctions, cooperative labor can be planned, organized, and controlled more effectively at this lower group level. Labor for maintenance and repairs on the small feeder canal (between box or temuku and the water diversion point to the individual sawahs), structures and farm roads are planned, organized, and implemented in these groups. Collective tasks have been decentralized as much as possible from the WUA level to these small groups. In KLIki, each group is not only responsible for its own canal from a diversion point (box or temuku), but also for a predetermined stretch of tertiary canal. Since collective labor tasks have been subdivided among the various groups into such physical shares, maintenance has improved. At this lower level, control is more effective and, if necessary, sanctions are imposed upon transgressors. Some of these groups have simple written regulations on collective labor and fines for absence or transgression of the norms for taking water.

One constraint to the efficient performance of cleaning and maintenance is the definition of responsibilities of individual farmers. As a consequence of the egalitarian initial conditions of settlement, landownership is still relatively egalitarian. However, processes of differentiation in landownership are emerging.[32] WUA regulations, based on a superficial participatory ideology in which water users figure as an undifferentiated mass, do not offer specific regulation for labor responsibilities in proportion to landownership. The Balinese tend to regard this as an inequitable system. To solve the problems of felt inequity in collective labor contributions between farmers with differential interests in land, several farmers' groups have successfully introduced a Balinese solution to this problem: "buying work" (*beli ayah* or *beli ayahan*). This term, common in the Balinese customary institution of *banjar* (customary hamlet) and in the subak as well, is used for a variety of regulations concerning financial compensation to be paid by farmers who, for one reason or another, cannot perform their fair share of labor. The arrangement is most commonly used for those who have other labor obligations in or outside the village (such as teachers) or those who temporarily live too far away from the village to perform their share but have retained all ties with the village and its institutions. In another meaning, it refers to arrangements that ensure the proportionality to area owned of labor and/or money contributions by members. Thus, in the groups in which labor on the irrigation infrastructure is organized, a standard or modal area of land (*areal patokan*) is determined for which all members are expected to perform collective labor. For land ownership exceeding that area owners have to pay a certain amount of money per 0.25 hectare. Sometimes, farmers who own less than the modal value receive compensation proportional to their deviation from standard landownership. Especially in combination with a small savings and credit function for these groups, as exists in TU KLIki, acceptance of such payments is high. The capital derived from these sources is also used for buying snacks, drinks, and cigarettes for group meetings.

Creating Law

Either implicitly or more explicitly, law plays a role in irrigation in various ways, and is closely related to technology and organization. Technical solutions, for instance, whether based on engineering or Balinese irrigation knowledge, reflect specific definitions and conceptualizations of water rights. Specific technology choices require corresponding organizational and regulatory arrangements. However, other normative and cultural dimensions play a role here, as well. What exactly is the role of law in local irrigation management? What kinds of legal rules have been created, and how do these interact in the tension field of WUA and subak? First, as discussed above, WUA formation is based on a national presidential decree. Second, even before the establishment of TUs and WUAs, the pekaseh and subaks were established. Though restricted in their functioning as a consequence of the introduction of WUAs, pekaseh and subaks continue to exert legal authority in irrigated agriculture. After introduction of the TU/WUA system, pekaseh and subaks regulate religious-ritual obligations, agricultural planning, and subak tax collection. As remarked above, the scope of their rule and authority is contested. Third, groups of Balinese farmers are also actively creating law at various levels of organization. As I have shown, small pragmatic farmers' groups exist at the sub-WUA level. These groups create their own legal rules and sanctioning systems for local management, mainly covering labor issues. Group rules may also deal with water division and religious-ritual matters. These groups are more effective than the largely inactive WUAs in organizing and performing management tasks and imposing sanctions on transgressors. Again, Balinese solutions have been introduced to solve problems that remained unsolved in the WUAs.

Sometimes, elements associated with subak rather than WUA regulations are even gradually penetrating into formal WUA regulations. One instructive case is TU PS3 (see figure 4.2), a TU with a partly Balinese and partly Toraja farmer population. The TU covers an area of some ninety hectares of irrigated land. Its boundaries cut across administrative boundaries of Kertoraharjo and a neighboring Toraja village.[33] The upstream part of the TU is located in the Toraja village and has a mainly Toraja farmer population. Balinese landownership in this part of the TU has been rapidly increasing in recent years, however. As Toraja tend to be land sellers while Balinese are active land buyers, there is a clear trend towards Balinization of landownership here. The middle and tail sections of the TU are located on Balinese village land and have a fully Balinese farmer population. The WUA falls under the formal responsibility of the Kertoraharjo village administration. In 1999, the TU counted thirty-eight Balinese and thirty-four Toraja landowners.

Though cordial relationships may exist between individual members of these neighboring groups, the mixed character of the TU can also be a source of tension and conflict. These conflicts are not so much caused by ethnic differences per se as by differing irrigation management and water use practices existing in the two groups. Three issues stand out: first, group norms about methods and transparency of water appropriation differ. Whereas Toraja often simply dig through the canal bottom or embankment to get their water— a method generally accepted within their group—Balinese tend to favor a more transparent, controlled, and equitable method. Second, conflicts about canal cleaning and maintenance recur every irrigation season. The Toraja farmers are said generally to leave the work to the Balinese (a fact recognized by Toraja community leaders). Third, in reaction to earlier tensions and conflicts the Balinese are said once to have been refused access to the tertiary weir to perform their "welcoming the water" (*mapag toya*) ritual for opening the irrigation season.

Some years ago, the Balinese decided to apply to Public Works for separation of their part of the TU from the head section with its Toraja farmer population. This was refused, of course, because the Toraja head section and the Balinese middle and tail sections share the same tertiary gate. Later, the Balinese decided at least to separate themselves off in an organizational sense. WUA leadership and membership are now wholly Balinese (with one exception, the board has always consisted only of Balinese). Members of the "new" WUA are the Balinese farmers of the middle and tail sections covering the land initially allocated to the Balinese, and those Balinese who have bought land in the (initially Toraja) head part of the TU. Just across the village boundary, on the Balinese side, the Balinese farmers owning land in the head section have constructed a temuku, from which water flows back from the tertiary canal into the head section. The water is used by the Balinese landowners who do not want to depend for their water on the field-to-field irrigation of their Toraja neighbors. Thus, even though both groups continue to be technically dependent on the same tertiary gate and canal, the WUA has become a "Balinese only" organization. Recently, the WUA has introduced new regulations that show clear traces of its Balinese character through the incorporated subak elements (see figure 4.4).

Thus, the Balinese actively create legal rules based on the subak. They do so at various levels of organization, irrespective of whether these formally belong to the field of government regulation or not. Many subak elements have thus reentered tertiary management through the back door of the WUAs. These elements seem to strengthen local management in a general setting of malfunctioning WUAs. At the same time, the case of the multiethnic TU shows the limitations of specifically Balinese solutions in a setting of crosscutting ethnic, administrative, and regulatory boundaries.

I. Collective labor (*gotong royong*)
1. those who are absent without permission will be fined Rs. 2.500
2. those who arrive too late will have to pay half of that amount
3. those who are absent on three consecutive occasions are fined twice the amount under 1

II. Absence leave
1. for ritual obligations
2. for circumstances related to death
3. those who left the village before the call for gotong royong was given
4. those who are absent for reasons unclear will have to pay up

III. Labor recompensation (*pembeli ayah*)
1. officials: Rs. 10.000 per cropping season
2. those suffering from chronic disease: Rs. 10.000
3. those who own more than one hectare have to pay labor compensation Rs. 10.000
4. those who own less than 1 hectare will receive labor compensation

IV. Cattle
1. fine for cows of members or nonmembers tended or tied up in the sawahs, causing damage to farm roads / canals: Rs. 25.000 per cow
2. cows entering the sawahs causing damage to sawah bunds: Rs. 25.000
3. cows eating the rice plants: Rs. 250 per stalk

V. Pigs, ducks, geese
1. damage to the farm roads etc.: Rs. 5.000 per animal
2. damage to the sawah: Rs. 5.000 per animal

VI. Sexual intercourse in the sawahs
1. those, either members or nonmembers, who commit sexual intercourse in the sawahs will be fined:
   a. to organize and hold a cleansing ritual (*mecaru*)
   b. payment of a Rs. 50.000 fine
2. those who are witness to people committing intercourse in the sawahs and immediately report to the head of the P3A are entitled to receive Rp. 15.000

FIGURE 4.4. Balinese subak law in a water users' association.

Source: WUA regulations

Recognizing Diversity and Legal Complexity:
The Role of the Subak in Local Irrigation Management

Irrigation systems jointly managed by a state agency and WUAs are by definition complex, as a consequence of the mix of public, common, and private property characteristics involved (F. von Benda-Beckmann et al. 1996; Meinzen-Dick 2000). I have focused here on the lower section of this complex world: TUs and WUAs with a Balinese farmer population. At first sight, all seemed clear and simple. Though tensions between head end and tail end at various levels of distribution are common, water availability is not a major problem. Though processes of differentiation are visible, this Balinese settlement is relatively egalitarian. Agrarian relations are not characterized by skewed landownership and great power differences with a determining influence on water control. Further, this is not a setting characterized by a high degree of uncertainty and insecurity pertaining to livelihoods, access, or rights to natural resources. Government-defined rights to land, water, and physical infrastructure are relatively clear, and organizations for tertiary irrigation management are in place.

The Indonesian WUA model has often been criticized for its focus on formal organizational routines and procedures rather than local decision-making and management capacities, flexibility, and effectiveness in coping with acute problems through "episodic mobilization" (Bruns 1992). Too often, form has been mistaken for content and substance (Bruns 1992, 2004; Oad 2001; Vermillion 2000). My point of departure was the wish to avoid the pitfalls of normative approaches based on a priori assumptions about the relationships between individual and collectivity, resources, and technology that also inform much policy thinking and doing (see Spiertz 2000).

Therefore, I have analyzed the relationships between regulation and farmer behavior in the technical, legal, and organizational complexes that developed in the field of tension between blueprinted approaches to irrigation management as reflected in the TU/WUA complex, and specifically Balinese cultural frameworks. This exploration of the technical-infrastructural, organizational, and legal landscape of tertiary irrigation management clearly shows the complexity hidden behind the apparent uniformity of a public irrigation system. I have analyzed the establishment of pekaseh and subaks, their development in relation to WUAs and TUs, and the widely differing conceptualizations of management that are at the basis of these processes. I have focused on three key issues here. First, I have discussed the changes introduced by Balinese farmers in the tertiary infrastructure, and analyzed these changes in the broader tension field of subak and WUA. Second, I have done the same for the ways in which irrigation management is organized. Third, after pointing out that technology and organization of local management are closely intertwined with the normative-legal dimension, I have discussed legal forms of regulation and local processes of creation of law.

The analysis of the history of development and interaction of subaks and WUAs shows that, at the organizational level, the local government enforced a separation between subaks as belonging to the domain of religion, and WUAs as organizations for management. Since this separation, subaks and pekaseh as organizations have dealt with religious-ritual obligations, agricultural planning, and subak tax collection. Subak legal authority, especially pertaining to tax collection and transplanting on land outside the initial subak areas, is contested. Conflicting views exist on the redefinition of pekaseh and subak legal authority over land. However, the subak as a formal organization restricted to the domain of religion leads quite a different life from the subak as an institution, as "regularized patterns of behavior between individuals and groups in society" (Leach et al. 1999). As an institution, persubakan cannot be restricted in scope and separated from manajemen, as I have shown by focusing on the three key dimensions of tertiary irrigation: technology, organization, and legal regulation.

Changes in tertiary water division technology introduced by the Balinese are clearly based on the subak. The Balinese preference for continuous proportional water division technology can be related to more general norms about equitable water division. Analysis of the organizational dimension shows the important role of small farmers' groups within the WUAs in arranging water distribution, canal cleaning, and maintenance. Their relative success in local irrigation management seems related to the introduction of Balinese notions of equity and proportionality in allocating collective labor tasks. Finally, I have shown how these smaller groups are actively creating new forms of local law (F. von Benda-Beckmann et al. 1996; Pradhan and Meinzen-Dick 2003). Main concerns of such regulation are collective labor, fines, loans, and local water distribution. The case of the ethnically mixed TU shows that, once the WUA of this TU became a "Balinese only" type of organization, subak regulations pertaining to the ritual purity of the irrigated fields entered the WUA regulations. If a key characteristic of institutions is that they can structure and regularize human behavior, this case study has identified the subak as an important institution in local irrigation management, and the WUA as a formal organization with little structuring influence on human behavior, except through the incorporation of institutional elements associated with the subak (see Leach et al. 1999; Meinzen-Dick and Pradhan 2001a).

The local management situation discussed here is the unexpected and largely unintended outcome of blueprint approaches to irrigation development. The implicit assumption behind this type of irrigation development—that people will adapt their behavior to the technical, organizational, and legal frameworks of the system—has again proved to be a weak point of departure. Why, then, is this the case? In the introduction to this chapter I pointed to sociotechnical approaches in which the need for a balanced relationship between social and technical dimensions in processes of sociotechnical stabilization is taken into account. The tension between conceptualizations of irrigation and water control that belong to the life-world of the users, on the one hand, and those that are external to it, on the other, has been identified as a major problem in such processes (see Boelens 1998; Diemer and Huibers 1996). As I have shown in this case study, the technical, organizational, and legal dimensions of irrigation introduced through state irrigation development are largely external to the life-worlds of the Balinese water users. Conceptions of irrigation, water control, and water rights internal to Balinese society, reinvented and adapted to a new agroecological setting outside Bali, have emerged in the TUs/WUAs with Balinese farmers. This has led to a redefinition of water rights, broadly conceptualized as bundles of rights and responsibilities pertaining to resource use and control (see Ostrom and Schlager 1996). It is not so clear what the "rules in use" in the Balinese WUAs are. Similarly, the technology and organizational arrangements that are so closely interwoven with the rules and principles of water allocation and division are also contested. In the process, the Balinese have appropriated a more encompassing bundle of rights. From local system users and managers authorized by the state they became agents of (small and gradual) change. In the history of local irrigation development discussed here, the existence of an alternative technical, organizational, and normative repertoire deriving from Balinese subak has been a source of much uncertainty as well as an asset used in shaping the process of sociotechnical stabilization (see Meinzen-Dick and Pradhan 2001a). Wherever possible within the constraints of the TU/WUA complex, farmers used their repertoire of subak rules, norms and principles, technology and organization to transform these TUs and WUAs from externally imposed arrangements into something more akin to the Balinese subak.

NOTES

1. For irrigation and water rights, see F. von Benda-Beckmann et al. 1996; Bruns and Meinzen-Dick 2000; Meinzen-Dick and Pradhan 2001a; Spiertz 2000.

2. See Boelens and Dávila 1998; Boelens and Hoogendam 2002; Bruns and Meinzen-Dick 2000; Meinzen-Dick and Pradhan 2001a; Pradhan et al. 2000; Spiertz 1991, 2000; Spiertz and de Jong 1992.

3. For sociotechnical approaches, see Bijker and Law 1992; Pfaffenberger 1988; for irrigation, see Boelens 1998; Diemer 1990; Mollinga 2003; Vincent 1997, 2001.

4. The elements mentioned can also be analyzed as dimensions of water control. Boelens (1998) discerns technical, sociolegal and political, organizational, and cultural-metaphysical control. See also Mollinga 2003.

5. In Indonesian irrigation policy, systems are classified as "technical" (*teknis*), "semi-technical" (*semi-teknis*), or "simple" (*sederhana*), depending on the degree to which measurement and regulation are possible (see Oad 2001).

6. South Sulawesi covers 83,000 square kilometers with a population of 7,558,400. The main population groups are Bugis (3 million), Makassarese (2 million), Toraja (600,000), and Mandarese (400,000).

7. The turmoil caused by the recent political changes in Indonesia have not left the administrative situation in Sulawesi untouched; Luwu was divided into three new districts: Luwu, North Luwu, and East Luwu. In this paper I simply refer to Luwu District (the pre-1999 situation).

8. The main objective of the colonization program, started in 1905 in southern Sumatra, was the reduction of population density of Java and Bali. One ambition of the program was to spread knowledge and experience with irrigated agriculture by Javanese and Balinese rice farmers to population groups mainly engaging in shifting cultivation. This program was the predecessor of the later Indonesian state-sponsored transmigration program (*transmigrasi*) for resettlement of inhabitants from Java, Bali, and Lombok to islands with a lower population density such as Sumatra, Kalimantan, Sulawesi, and (former) Irian.

9. Indonesia currently has a total irrigated area of about 7.1 million hectares, 5.5 million of which are served by government irrigation systems and 1.6 million are farmer-managed. Between 1969 and 1994 about 1.4 million hectares of new irrigated land were created by constructing new systems, while some 3.4 million hectares of existing systems were rehabilitated, extended, or improved (Vermillion et al. 2000; Oad 2001).

10. The part of the system below the water division gate to the tertiary canal is called a tertiary unit (TU). Farmers owning land are members of the WUA, in Indonesia called P3A (Perkumpulan Petani Pemakai Air). See Geijer 1995; Oad 2001; Vermillion 2000.

11. The war in the Pacific and the Japanese occupation, the independence struggle against the Dutch, and the so-called Darul Islam movement (1950–1965), which had a great impact on Luwu.

12. In the seventies, transmigration was based on a mixed farming system of irrigated rice and rainfed seasonal crops such as maize, soy beans, and peanuts. However, as local conditions were seldom suitable for irrigation development, deviations from this basic pattern often occurred. From the eighties, transmigration was increasingly combined with cultivation of cash crops such as oil palm.

13. Often, negotiations with local elites, promises of future investments for development, or forms of coercion and violence were part of the game. Transmigration in Luwu has also generated conflicts between local populations and settlers. In Kalaena, however, such conflicts have only occurred on a small scale.

14. Ownership rights are circumscribed by regulation from various state and nonstate agencies and institutions. As to the first, landowners should pay land tax and report transfers of land to the Land Registry Agency (BPN). For owners of irrigated fields, membership of the WUA for tertiary irrigation management is obligatory. Regional authorities, the Agricultural Service, and the Irrigation Service decide on seed varieties and inputs to be used, opening and closure periods of the irrigation system, and target periods for field preparation, (trans-)planting and harvesting. As to nonstate institutions, Balinese owners of irrigated fields are also subject to customary forms of regulation deriving from the subak, discussed below.

15. See Barth 1995; Birkelbach 1973; Falvo 2000; FAO 1982; Geertz 1972, 1980; Grader 1960 (1939); Happé 1919, 1935; Horst 1996a, b; Jha 2002; Korn 1924; Lansing 1987, 1991; Lansing and Kremer 1993; Liefrinck 1969; Ravesteijn 1997; Schulte-Nordholt 1986; Spiertz 1991, 1992, 2000; Sutawan 1987; Sutawan et al. 1990.

16. Geertz: "a subak is . . . a differentiated, corporate, self-contained social organization, devoted specifically and exclusively to irrigated farming, mainly . . . of paddy—a kind of 'wet village,' as opposed to the 'dry' one in which people reside" (1972: 27).

17. Little research has been done on the subak outside Bali. A notable and valuable ex-

ception is Vermillion's study of Balinese irrigators in North Sulawesi (Vermillion 1986, 2000).

18. In Bali, subak terminology may vary among settings and regions. Sometimes the head is referred to as pekaseh. The same term is also used for a higher level that encompasses various subaks and its head.

19. This is in contrast to division structures used in public works systems, where water is divided in a direction perpendicular to the flow. Acceptance of the latter method among Balinese farmers is low (Sutawan 1987; see also below).

20. See, for example, Chambers 1980, 1994; Coward and Levine 1989; 1992; Mollinga 2003.

21. The distinction is a clear expression of a widespread normative bias in favor of civil engineering technology. Further, there is the implicit assumption of the primacy of technology. Once the desired technology is in place, it is assumed that the users organized in WUAs will sooner or later direct their behavior toward the norms, rules, and forms of regulation dictated by the technology choice.

22. KK (*kepala keluarga*) literally means "household head." The second group of fifty households is generally referred to as Tampaksiring, the area of origin of the whole group.

23. Examples of such mixed TUs are TU PS3 (Balinese and Toraja farmers) and TUs KLΙki and KLΙka (with Balinese and Javanese farmers); see figure 4.2.

24. The fact that in Balinese tradition a distinction is maintained between the administrative spheres of the "dry village" and the "wet village" may have played a role. In the government administrative sphere, the administrative village head (*kepala desa*) is responsible for the irrigated areas and WUAs, in the Balinese system the pekaseh holds this responsibility.

25. The pekaseh has a board consisting of chairman (*pekaseh*), vice chairman, secretary, and treasurer. The subak boards also consist of chairman (*klian subak*), vice chairman, secretary, and treasurer.

26. Opening and closure dates of the irrigation system are determined at district level by the irrigation committee (*panitia irigasi*), in a meeting called tudang sipulung (Buginese: "sit and discuss together"). Decisions about opening and closure, the scheduling of agricultural activities, and use of agricultural inputs are passed down to the administrative subdistrict and village levels through lower-level tudang sipulung meetings. In the Balinese village-level tudang sipulung meeting, mainly attended by the pekaseh, subak, and WUA staff, ritual-religious decision making has to be matched with government directives, taking into account other factors such as possible bottlenecks in the availability of two-wheeled tractors or (trans-)planting groups.

27. For Bali, see Horst 1996a. See also Mollinga 2003, who analyzes the social dimensions of technology by distinguishing social requirements for use, social construction, and social effects.

28. Compare Horst (1996a) for Bali.

29. The incomplete handing over of TUs, the bad functioning of the system, the restricted rights of WUAs, a continued dependence on "rehabilitation" programs, and the corruption in water tax collection are major disincentives to farmer investments.

30. This is true of many WUAs, whether with a Balinese or any other farmer population.

31. In the subaks, if even a small amount of money cannot be accounted for, the leader offers to resign and pay back the money.

32. This is often not only or even primarily the consequence of socioeconomic differentiation between Balinese farmers but rather of their farming system choices. Some

farmers have sold all or part of their irrigated fields and fully or partly shifted to cocoa cultivation (on rainfed land). Most farmers opt for a combined system of irrigated rice cultivation and cocoa cropping.

33. The Toraja are an ethnic group from the mountainous interior of South Sulawesi. Many Toraja farmers have migrated to lowland Luwu.

5

Anomalous Water Rights and the Politics of Normalization

Collective Water Control and Privatization Policies in the Andean Region

RUTGERD BOELENS AND MARGREET ZWARTEVEEN

Current thinking about water rights in the Andes, as in many other regions of the world, is intimately tied up with the discussion of privatization. For the sake of increasing water use efficiency and productivity, and strongly justified by the proclamation of a lurking water crisis, reforms are proposed or being implemented that promote the transferability and marketability of water, allowing it to be used where its marginal returns are highest. The need for clearly defined and enforceable water rights is recognized primarily because they are a condition for the success of privatization efforts. Water rights define the rules for water allocation and use and provide the means for describing and accounting for committed uses. Market valuation and tradability of water rights make it possible to price water per unit consumed, inducing users to reduce its waste. A strong assumption of the new policies and the thinking on which it is based is that these benefits can only be achieved under a private water property regime, or if water rights are privatized. This chapter focuses on this assumption and critically examines it.

For water policy making, the attractiveness of the neoliberal language and of the rational choice paradigm on which it is based is not difficult to understand. It is particularly well suited to producing propositions that are partly true in relation to each of a diverse range of specific situations (see M. Moore 1991: 16), and fits well with a preference in professional irrigation thinking for large scale standard policy initiatives and design principles for building viable technologies and institutions (see Ostrom 1992; Plusquellec et al. 1994; FAO 1996). The application of instrumental rationality to problems of resource management appears to offer a convenient, scientific way to solve complicated distributional questions. The belief that flows of money and water follow universal natural laws, and that human beings have roughly the same rational utility-maximizing aspirations everywhere, are important sources of consolation and relief for policymakers and legislators who see themselves confronted with increasingly complex and dynamic water situations.

Although presented as new and innovative, current water reform proposals are part of a long tradition of efforts to privatize property regimes in the Andes. Through linking modernity, efficiency, and civilization to privatization, current water proposals are firmly rooted in a centuries-long tradition of Western enlightenment thinking. This chapter begins with tracing the historical roots of the idea that private property rights are normatively superior to collective ones. We show that there are striking parallels between the reasoning of current water reform proposals and those of earlier attempts to "civilize" or "modernize" peasants and indigenous people. All are based on a universal, positivist ideal, and judge existing water use and management systems against this ideal. Existing local water law systems are characterized as anomalies because of their lack of fit with the ideal model. Such labeling has served to justify and continues to justify far-reaching interventions to normalize and discipline existing irrigator collectives, often endangering or marginalizing their members and their livelihoods.

The rest of the chapter draws attention to the disciplining and normalizing processes that occur as a result of current water reforms, and looks at the threats water reforms pose to the water realities and water-based livelihoods of indigenous and peasant water users in the Andes. It presents a brief characterization of local irrigation management institutions as these have existed for decades or centuries in the Andes, a characterization that shows that the logic of their functioning is difficult to express in the instrumental market rationality of the modern water language, neoliberalism. Yet neoliberalist policies and laws increasingly dictate not just the discursive but also the material terms of their existence. Through powerful laws and rules, the neoliberal model of the water world is forcefully turned into reality. Indeed, and in the words of Bourdieu, "what is presented as an economic system governed by the iron laws of a kind of social nature is in reality a political system which can only be set up with the active or passive complicity of the official political powers" (Bourdieu 1998: 86).[1]

The political effects of this difficulty of recognizing and representing long-standing irrigation institutions are huge. When irrigation and water management behavior cannot be understood and expressed in modern water terms, this is likely to be used as proof that it is backward and irrational. Irrigation collectives displaying such behavior are "anomalies" that deserve to wither and fall prey to market forces: there is no legitimate place for them in modern societies.[2] In contrast, those irrigation communities who conform to the new policies and rules are awarded the "good governance" stamp of approval: they are rewarded with support to help turn them into the modern institutions that behave according to sound and rational new institutional and market logic. Neoliberal thinking is epistemologically positivist and thus based on objectification, whereas what is needed to understand peasant and indigenous water management communities is contextualization. Rather than naturalizing political questions of resource distribution and control, a much more explicit recognition of the politics and power in discussions of water reforms is needed. The conceptual tools of legal pluralism, allowing a focus on the specific contents of water rights and laws as sources and outcomes of social struggles and on the norms and rules surrounding the distribution of water, provide a promising entry point to start thinking about water problems in ways that allow recognition of politics and culture as constitutive. Indeed, the struggle over water control is as much a struggle for distributive justice as it is one for discursive and political recognition and legitimacy, and legal pluralism is one potentially attractive alternative to, and critique of, neoliberalism for understanding and engaging in this struggle.

Paving the Way: New Policies with Ancient Roots

According to Webster's, the word "anomalous" has a double meaning: "1. deviating from a general rule or method or from accepted notions of fitness or order, 2. being not what would naturally be expected" (Webster's New Encyclopedic Dictionary 1994: 40). Both meanings apply to the way in which, historically, outside approaches have defined local, collective water control systems in the Andean region—as political and discursive constructions. Like most other norms, principles, concepts, and properties that make up the diverse universe of Andean sociolegal repertoires, they were labeled "anomalous," "abnormal," and "unnatural" even before the region was known and invaded. Long before Pizarro conquered Peru, in 1532, and even before Columbus reached the Americas in 1492, the image of a New World already existed and served as a frame of reference for European philosophers, policy makers, politicians, and others, who continued to intervene in the following centuries. The images of "Indian" populations—including their property relationships and their modes of managing natural resources—provided a perfect reflection of the ideas embodied in European political and philosophical thought. Ancient Greek notions of civilians versus barbarians, and Christian mythology about the Golden Age and the existence of Earthly Paradise where primitive people had remained in a "state of nature," were central in representing Self and Other, and the Americas provided a neat screen for projecting such notions.

Two recurrent themes in most of these projections are closely interrelated: the assumed lack of private property among the New World's inhabitants, and the question whether they could obey a rational, legal system and the divine or natural order. Depending on one's political and philosophical position, the assumed absence of both was either considered as evidence that they were anomalous, brutal savages (*ignobles*) and needed to be mastered and disciplined, or, on the contrary, used as proof of the fact that they were noble humans not yet affected by the process of transgression and degeneration of Western society and its feudal or capitalist exploitative relations of production. Needless to say, the first position was mostly held by those who defended European authoritarian power structures and superiority, whereas the second was adhered to by those philosophers and philanthropists who were critical of Western culture.[3] Rather than being concerned with understanding the characteristics of the New World's societies and identities, Europeans merely used them for better representing and legitimizing power constellations and property structures in Europe itself (cf. Galeano 1986; Lemaire 1986; Wolf 1982).[4]

Around 1510 an ideological debate started about the nature of the Indians and the legitimacy of subduing them violently, even before Christianizing them, during the Spanish conquest. The debate (Are they rational beings? Can they be Christianized? Do they have a soul? Do they have laws?) reached its climax in 1550. Juan Ginés de Sepúlveda defended the ideas of Aristotle's *Politica* and transferred these concepts to the Americas. Indians were thus constructed and seen as naturally born slaves who needed to be the property of a master. For them this state of slavery is not only beneficial but also just and rightful. According to Sepúlveda, who had never been to the Americas, Indians were barbarians who, just like animals, could not control their passions; they were mentally inferior and cruel cannibals. Moreover, Indians were extreme cowards, "thousands and thousands of them fled like women in face of few Spanish soldiers" (Sepúlveda 1996 [1550]: 107).

> Compare then those blessings enjoyed by Spaniards of prudence, genius, magnanimity, temperance, humanity, and religion with those of the little men in whom you will scarcely find even vestiges of humanity, who not only possess no science but who also lack letters and preserve no monument of their history except certain vague and obscure reminiscences of some things on certain paintings. Neither do they have written laws, but barbaric institutions and customs. . . . *They do not even have private property.* . . . How can we doubt that these people—so uncivilized, so barbaric, contaminated with so many impieties and obscenities—have been justly conquered? (Ibid.: 105–113; emphasis added)

Sepúlveda based his claims on the existence of the so-called Natural Law: eternal, omnipresent law that God and nature have embedded in the minds and hearts of civilized, rational humans, particularly in those of wise men of naturally and ethically superior peoples. Following Aristotle, he was of the opinion that Indians (as barbarians) are not among those humans. The basic statement of his *Treaty on the Just Causes of the War against the Indians* was that "the perfect should rule over the imperfect" (ibid.: 19), thus legitimizing violent colonization as beneficial for both Spaniards and Indians. Bartolomé de Las Casas, commonly known as the great defender of the indigenous cause, was the most important opponent in this historic debate. Instead of fundamental inequality among humans and the need to exclude the savages, he stressed unity and the fact that all humans are equal. At least he reasoned that the miserable but naturally human Indians, if guided and protected properly, could become civilized, Christian human beings. Their *potential to become equals* was fundamental in Las Casas's argumentation (Las Casas 1999 [1552]). The fact that they were "deviating from a general rule and from accepted notions of fitness or order"—Christianity, private property regimes, white-patriarchal civilization—did not mean that they had to be excluded or ruled over, as Sepúlveda had argued. On the contrary, they were ready for a process of Foucauldian inclusion, equalization, and *mestizaje* in which anomalies could be disciplined not by the law of the sword but by the law of the heart.

During the centuries following the conquest, "the Indian," like the presumably corresponding indigenous property regimes, became fetishes to be used in Western ideologies and counterideologies concerned with the process of modernization in the Old World itself (Lemaire 1986). In Leviathan, Thomas Hobbes presented the societal order of the Indian peoples as the ultimate state of nature where savage peoples were without a form of state governance or regulation, resulting in a condition of permanent warfare of everyone against everyone. He used this social construct—a deterrent mirror and a precise opposite of what he considered necessary for Europe—to claim that a strong central state order, with a monopoly on violence and lawmaking, was needed. Without it, savagery, unruliness, and nonprotection of properties would occur, as was the case in Indian societies (Hobbes 1985 [1651]; see also Lemaire 1986). In a similar fashion, John Locke (1970 [1690]) constructed an image of the state of nature and projected it onto the New World and its inhabitants to depict them as an inferior state in which inferior users had not effectively and efficiently appropriated the resources. He argued that through individual (rather than collective) labor investments people should be allowed and enabled to claim individual rights to property. In his view, the accumulation of such rights to transform and possess the "unpossessed" former wilderness represented an act of progress. Locke's reasoning neglected common property systems and considered these as nonproperty: individual appropriation actively excluded the collective use and control rights of others.

In a similar way, many other Western philosophers, including for instance Rousseau, Voltaire, Smith, Hegel, Marx, and Engels, discursively constructed America's indigenous societies and property relations primarily with a view to clarifying their own philosophical-political position vis-à-vis progress, modernization, and civilization in Europe. The societies of the New World neatly satisfied the need for a myth of origin, the state of nature, necessary in order to provide European civilized identity with a foundation. According to their political-philosophical position, thus representing the Indian either legitimated the oppression and control of potential savagery in their own society or symbolized the loss of authenticity, the degeneration, and the exploitation within Western society (Lemaire 1986; Wolf 1982). Scholars, politicians, and activists of the region—indigenous or not—inherited many of these traditions when constructing their racist, romanticized, developmentalist, or revolutionary images of the Indian and the Andean, each situated within a corresponding picture of an essentialized "indigenous" property relations framework (see chapter 7).[5]

It is remarkable that throughout the modernist-positivist tradition of Western thought, civilization has generally been associated with private property regimes. Those writers and thinkers critical of civilization and modernity have, as might be predicted, typically preached the abolishment of private rights systems. Rather than showing concern for a thorough understanding and accurate description of the realities and experiences of local populations and their property systems in the New World, descriptions typically served the purpose of better representing the Old World and its thinkers. Indians were assumed not to have private properties, and the New World was thought to have no property systems, since all resources were considered to be openly accessible and "virgin." The massive killings—in Peru alone, the pre-Columbian population of 9 million inhabitants was reduced to 600 thousand in less than a century (Flores Galindo 1988)—helped to preserve this myth. Because of the decimation of the population, natural resources became abundantly available and the continent indeed presented itself as open and bare, a garden for utopian experiments to create civilization on the basis of natural and scientific laws.

Current Water Reforms: New Wine in Old Bottles

In the last two decades, and like elsewhere in the world, processes are in motion in many Andean countries to transfer water management responsibilities to local government authorities, user groups, private enterprises, or combined public-private institutions. Terms such as decentralization, participation, privatization, or management transfer are used to refer to very diverse actions undertaken to turn over government tasks to lower-level management bodies. There is variation in, for instance, which management tasks are decentralized, in who obtains ownership of the infrastructure, and in how rights over water are arranged. Sometimes, water control is completely privatized, whereby, for example, infrastructure and water property rights are turned over to private entities. More often it is just the operation and maintenance tasks of water control systems that are left to the private sector.

When seen in the historical perspective sketched above, the language, argumentation, and debates of current water reform proposals in the Andes ring familiar bells. Though reforms are presented as modern and new, the basis for current privatization attempts was laid centuries ago. Indeed, the current wish to "civilize" (thus privatize and individualize) water control in the Andes is an echo from a distant past, and privatization efforts are a recurrent characteristic of Andean political economic history. Private property regimes were prevalent in the Andes in countries such as Peru and Ecuador long before the enacting of the current water laws (1969 and 1972) that nationalized water property rights. Examples of modernist water management attempts are abundant, and the following one, which describes the implementation of the Choclococha Project in Ica, Peru, is illustrative of many others: "The main reason for not having succeeded in developing irrigation in the Ica Valley up to now, through private or state efforts, is the existence of collective property systems in the pampas of Los Castillos. It is difficult to risk capital investment without having the backing in terms of security that the property rights of these valley lands will be obtained" (Technical Report, Ica Technical Commission, 1936, in Oré 2004: 66). In the Andean region, not just the last decades' neoliberal economists and planners but, throughout the twentieth century, hydraulic engineers in particular have fiercely promoted the destruction of collective land and water ownership. For example, the collectively owned Los Castillos Valley lands in Ica legally belonged to 114 indigenous families which, according to the engineers of the Ica Technical Commission and the Peruvian Water Directorate, was considered to be the *major obstacle* for the proper execution of this irrigation project. The communal territories' ownership characteristics counteracted the free sale and parcelization (*lotización*) of these newly irrigated fields to individual owners. Therefore the (in those days very powerful) engineers first suggested and later firmly pressed the state for enforcing a law that would allow the expropriation of the Pampa de Los Castillos. The landlords of the Ica Valley, eager to appropriate these large pampas historically owned by the indigenous communities, strongly supported the engineers' proposals and, since they were labeled by the engineers as "the ideal owners of the irrigation area," the landlords were installed as the new land and water property owners (Oré 2004: 65–68).

In general, the privatization of water codes in Peru and Ecuador from the eighteenth century onward has supported landlords and other powerful groups to finish after Independence the work of the Spanish colonizers (see Flores Galindo 1988; Gelles 1998; van Kessel 1992). Many studies have documented how privatization led to a massive transfer of water rights from indigenous and communal systems to powerful private-right holders, especially haciendas. Such transfers did not go uncontested, but provoked violent struggles among different stakeholders.[6] To many peasant and indigenous organizations in the Andes, today's water reform proposals are the latest in a centuries-long series of similar attempts to expropriate the resources that form the basis of their livelihoods

and identities. The memories of fierce struggles of their ancestors against hacienda owners and state employees serve to further fuel today's protests against
new water reform proposals that are so similar in content and effect.

When comparing current reforms with older ones, one important difference seems to be that current attempts no longer explicitly appeal to a civilizing
or imperial mission. Instead of deriving legitimacy from religiously inspired accounts of civilization, current water reform proposals derive status and credit-
worthiness by appeals to science and "the universal" or "the global." New
scientific tools and institutional theories have given new impetus to the old
policy model, and defend the importance of putting it in practice. Water policies in the Andes are particularly grounded in the free market ideology of the
Milton Friedman school. In the 1970s and 1980s, Milton Friedman's students
and followers, the so-called Chicago boys, designed Chile's economic policy,
which later was held up as an example to many other countries in Latin
America. In line with this economic policy, a water policy was formulated that
predicated the treatment of water as any other market commodity.[7] The importance of the Chilean water policy model was enormous, particularly after the
1980s. As Trawick (2003: 977) rightly observes: "It is no exaggeration to say that
a single draft law, modeled on the 1981 Water Code of Chile, is now being circulated in the Andean countries, throughout most of Latin America, and throughout much of the 'developing world'—proposals basically written by the World
Bank for the various national governments" (see also World Bank 1995 and
1996).[8]

On closer inspection, current water thinking continues to be as normative
and "civilizing" as it used to be in the colonial and postcolonial eras. Science has
replaced religion, and today's faith in the superiority—and universal applicability—of scientifically developed technologies and institutional models resembles
yesterday's proclamation of the superiority of Western civilization. Indeed, current water thought as it informs policies in the Andes can be seen to be firmly
anchored in the Enlightenment tradition. In this tradition, the "god-trick" is
pervasive: the assumption that one can see everything from nowhere and that
disembodied reason can produce accurate and "objective" accounts of the
world.[9] This god-trick allows the systematic denial of the connections between
power and knowledge, and between the construction of subjectivity and power.
Such denial is ironic in view of the fact that much water knowledge is written
from the perspective of those who are deemed to be in control: planners, administrators, managers, and policy-makers.[10] Produced knowledge aims at helping *them* realize their objectives, and at solving their problems. It enables them
to speak more authoritatively through the disembodied, transcendent voice of
Reason. In this regard, it is illustrative that, while there is debate and disagree-
ment about the most effective water control and management strategy, the very
possibility of effectively controlling and manipulating behavior of people and

flows of water and money is seldom questioned. Theoretical models about how water efficiencies are achieved are hardly ever tested other than through the deductive method. Outcomes or outputs are measured against the expectations of the formal models, but the behavioral and operational assumptions employed are seldom validated. In this way, belief in the model and thus in the effectiveness of planners' control mechanisms is never challenged, nor are the grounds for the validity of water knowledge questioned. Indeed, it is no exaggeration to conclude that the persistence and popularity of neoliberal water policies and of the theoretical models on which these are based among policy makers in the Andean region are linked to their success in generating funds and power rather than to the accuracy and validity of their statements about the determinants of water management performance.

An important belief that fuels new water policies is that the behavior of water users and managers follows incentives that are largely determined in institutions and markets. The outcome of organizational and political processes in water management are seen as the sum of rational decisions made by individuals, based on interests which can be objectively defined and known by outside analysts. In other words, it is thought that, given the proper incentive structures, human beings will display the same water behavior everywhere. This thought is also directly rooted in an epistemological claim that is typical of the Enlightenment tradition, the claim of human universality and homogeneity. This claim has it that all human beings are equal and share a common rationality. Differences between people are fundamentally epiphenomenal, making it possible to make generic statements about human nature, truth, and other imperial universalities. In such a liberal humanist understanding of human beings, people are approached and seen in a methodologically individualist way, as relatively autonomous individuals. This precludes the understanding of people as deeply social creatures, and reduces all differences between people as rooted in differences in character or personality.[11] Indeed, in theory and principle, inside the neoliberal water domain, all actors are equal or need to become equal—at least their differences do not matter for how they interact and relate to each other in the water domain, since the rules of the water game they follow are the same for everyone.

These two characteristics of neoliberal thinking about water—its denial of the connections between power and knowledge and its specific version of liberal humanism (individual rights moralism)—coupled with its almost religious appeal to scientific rationality make it into a strong political tool to justify far-reaching reforms and interventions.[12] These interventions, in turn, further fuel faith in the neoliberal model, since the conditions for the neoliberal model to work as predicted are created. It is no coincidence that the most far-reaching neoliberal water reform policy, claiming individual freedom for all, was experimented with and implemented under the Pinochet regime, one of the most repressive dictatorships the Andean countries have ever known. Only this authoritarian and repressive regime was able to create the necessary conditions for making the model come true, by silencing and coercively controlling water user communities' voices of protest and acts of resistance. Thus the critique launched against neoliberal policy model makers for "trusting in models that they have practically never had the occasion to subject to experimental verification" (Bourdieu 1998: 101), could easily be waved aside, since the Pinochet regime offered the opportunities for experimentation and for creating the conditions for the model to fulfill its own terms of success. In the meantime, the national water law and policy of Chile has been, and continues to be, considered by many one of the world's most successful and effective water governance models. In the eighties and nineties, Peru, Bolivia, and Ecuador, as well as many other Latin American countries, were forced by the World Bank, IMF, and Inter-American Development Bank to adopt neoliberal water legislation, copying the Chilean model. The banks contracted Chilean water experts to promote the model in all neighboring countries, and when, under nationwide popular protests and intensive struggle, especially in peasant and indigenous sectors, the latter could not accept its adoption, they were blackmailed and threatened with not receiving new bank loans.[13]

Objectification or Contextualization?

The three basic ingredients of neoliberal water reform recipes are decentralized decision making, private property rights, and markets.[14] Attention to (private) property rights is primarily justified because markets depend on them. In short, the reasoning is as follows: Water needs to be transferable and marketable so that it can be used in an economically efficient way, producing the highest possible marginal returns. For privatization efforts to succeed, clearly defined and enforceable water rights need to be in place. Water rights are thus a crucial condition for water markets to emerge. In neoliberal thinking, water rights, by defining rules for the allocation and use of water resources, are seen to provide the means for describing and accounting for committed water uses. Water rights would allow water to be priced per unit consumed, inducing users to reduce wasting water. In addition, water rights provide a good basis for allocating maintenance responsibilities among beneficiaries. They also, and importantly, provide security of tenure to users, which in neoliberal thinking is primarily valued because it is seen to establish incentives for investments in infrastructure.

The neoliberal argument rightly points to the importance of establishing and protecting security of water tenure for water policy and management. Yet, and following in the footsteps of many Enlightenment thinkers, neoliberal water thinking has two major flaws. The first lies in the way it automatically links water rights to water markets, as if the two are inseparable. This is not true. Most of the benefits attributed to water markets would be achieved through the provision of security of tenure alone, irrespective of whether water rights are traded or otherwise transferred. In fact, the treatment of water rights by advocates of water markets and privatization of water is rather misleading. The suggestion is created that the lack of (incentives for) transferring or marketing of water is the root cause of current water problems (Seckler 1993: 6), whereas it would be more accurate to say that water management is such a complicated matter precisely because of the difficulties inherent in establishing an effective and enforceable system of water allocation. The second main error is the assumption that tenure security can only be achieved by means of private water rights. This is certainly not true from the perspective of Andean peasant and indigenous water users, whose water security was typically lowest in periods of privatization. As we show below, both flaws of the model directly explain why it cannot realize its major claims: that of increasing water use efficiency and water use productivity. For this, we need to shed light on the friction between the universalistic pretensions of the neoliberal model and the contextual and locally embedded properties of Andean water control systems.

Neoliberal thinking refers to universal and natural truths about how water and money flow, and about how humans behave. Rather than being rooted in local specificity, it preaches that water management should be based on universal and global truths. The neoliberal model in fact actively promotes externalization or delocalization of water rights: water rights should be delinked from the land, the community, or the territory so as to allow for competition and enhance free trade of water to its most productive uses. Yet existing water uses, and forms of distribution and management in peasant and indigenous irrigation systems in the Andes, are typically local, embedded, and context-specific. In the Andes, there are many indigenous and collective water rights and irrigation management forms. These are dynamic institutions that have evolved, and continue to evolve, from long historical processes of collective investments in infrastructure and shared struggle against intruders. They exist because of and through contextuality and historicity, and processes of externalization or delocalization threaten the basis of their existence and survival.

Where the neoliberal discourse sees water rights primarily in the positivist and instrumental sense, as an expression of state law, rights to water in Andean communities (as elsewhere) typically encompass not just a sociolegal dimension but also both a technical and an organizational dimension (see also chapter 4 for examples in Indonesia). The first, the sociolegal dimension, refers to the fact that a water right is an expression of agreement about the legitimacy of a right holder's claim to water. This agreement is intimately linked to social relations of authority and power, and can be based on a variety of grounds and on rules and norms that originate from diverse sociolegal repertories. The technical dimension of a water right relates to the technical means (infrastructure, technology, technical skills) to actually take water from a source and convey it to its destiny. The organizational dimension is about the need to organize and manage not just water turns and the operation of water conveyance infrastructure but also the mobilization of resources and decision-making processes around these issues. Having a right to water, which in the Andes often means being a legitimate and recognized member of the water users' community, is often accompanied by the right-holders' participation in system operation and management and with a number of duties and obligations regarding operational and maintenance responsibilities. When someone fails to comply with these duties, they risk sanctions such as exclusion from one or more water turns, or the payment of fines (see Boelens and Zwarteveen 2003).

As mentioned, most Andean irrigation systems exist and function in conditions of legal pluralism, where rules and principles of different origin and legitimization exist in the same locality. State law often is only one, and not necessarily the most important, source of reference for water-related choices. There may also be a diversity of mechanisms for acquiring water rights. Claims may be based on prior appropriation or stem from acquisition mechanisms based on socioterritoriality. In addition, there are several examples in Andean history of the appropriation of water through the use of armed violence by large landlords. A further acquiring mechanism is based on the fact that many water use communities have, as it were, earned their rights to water through the investments of often tremendous amounts of labor and other resources in the construction of irrigation infrastructure. Such investments in kind to establish water access and control rights are difficult to recognize in neoliberal terms, because they have not passed through the market and because they are not sanctioned by state law.[15] Labor and money investments often also served as the basis for deciding the division of water rights within communities. With the collective construction of infrastructure, collective property and joint rights to use the infrastructure were also established. Individual (or household-level) rights to use water and the infrastructure, and to participate in water-related decision making, therefore exist because of and are interlinked with collective rights of the entire community vis-à-vis other communities. "Private" rights at the individual or household level are thus radically different from the privatized rights as envisaged in neoliberal policies (see also Beccar et al. 2002; Boelens and Doornbos 2001).

It is important that water-related rights and duties are, in many Andean communities, closely linked to all kinds of nonwater-related rights and duties. Water allocation and distribution are closely intertwined with economic and noneconomic institutions and networks of social and political relations. In other words, definitions of rights, of relative claims, of appropriate uses and users are closely embedded not only in specific historical sets of political and economic structures but also in cultural systems of meanings, symbols, and values (Peters 1987, in Cleaver 2000). Transfers of water rights, for instance, often happen in a social context in which gifts and donations function as important mechanisms for maintaining networks of friends and relatives. Also, in some communities, people's sense of community identity is strongly linked to having a shared history of struggling against landlords for water and land rights. Similarly, through years of collective investments in the construction and upkeep of infrastructure, communities have consolidated not only their water rights but also their sense of togetherness and collectivity. The recognition of embeddedness provides an important challenge to neoliberal theorizing and policies, which are importantly based on the assumption of the insulation of the water domain from other domains of life and work. Such theories and policies postulate that people's water behavior is primarily guided by the characteristics (expressed and analyzed as incentive structures) of this domain, and thus that people set aside their nonwater related social identities and powers when dealing with water. These assumptions are unrealistic everywhere, but particularly in Andean water communities in which water is just one of the many resources that people share and just one element in the multi-stranded relationships they have with each other.

Comparing Neoliberal Water Dreams with Realities

As shown above, existing water realities of Andean peasant and indigenous water users are radically different from the universal water reality as assumed and promoted by neoliberal policies. This lack of congruence and fit, as we show in the next section, lies at the basis of many struggles and fights over water. In this section we show, with some examples, that it also explains why neoliberal reforms are not very successful when measured against their own objectives. The most important objectives of reforms are water savings, higher water use efficiencies, more competition over water and lower water service fees, more private water investments in infrastructure and maintenance, less public water spending and higher economic returns on water investments. In addition, water reforms depend on and hope to bring about democratization of water decision making.

A growing number of studies have produced evidence that raises important doubts about whether these objectives are realized, and about whether they can at all be realized through the proposed neoliberal means. For example, Assies (2000), Bustamante (2002), and Perreault (2005) mention the strong increase of water fees after privatization of drinking water service in the Bolivian Andes, in a situation where simultaneously water use efficiency, distribution, and system upkeep fell down. Oré (1998, 2004) and Trawick (1996, 2003) describe the causal link between rights privatization and the decline of water use efficiency, agricultural productivity, and tenure security in irrigation systems in Peru. Hendriks (1998) similarly describes for the case of Chile how water distribution, water use efficiency, and agricultural productivity in common property irrigation systems are worsening under the neoliberal regime. One of his examples refers to the lack of linkage between water rights and land rights. "The Chilean Water Code has no relationship between water use rights for agricultural uses and land ownership. They are considered as commercial goods that are totally independent from each other. Within this context, it is not surprising to find quite a disproportional relationship between farmers' water share property and the agricultural area owned. A recent study in the Valley of Codpa shows that water rights range from 200 to 10,000 m³ per hectare per turn. Farmers at the low end of the range suffer from serious water shortage, while their neighbors enjoy plentiful irrigation water with no need to use it carefully. This over-entitlement for some holders reflects relative irrationality at the system's level in handling and distributing this scarcity" (Hendriks 1998: 305). Decoupling water rights from their territory or community opens the door for scenarios in which local communities are confronted with new, nonlocal water interest sectors and powerful enterprises.

Also at the intrasystem level, water rights privatization and the selling and purchasing of water rights among individuals leads to the rupture of collective schedules. As a result, and contrary to the policy's efficiency objectives, fields are irrigated nonsequentially in terms of space and time, canals run dry between irrigations, and intrasystem water losses strongly increase. It also is time-inefficient, since considerable time of individual families and collectives is lost when water is moved around in the system "at random" (see, for example, Hendriks 1998). As a result, the individual irrigation frequencies decline, prolonging overall watering intervals and drastically reducing the system's production capacity. Many experiences in the Andes also show how situations of nonsequential or unordered collective distribution schedules negatively impact on the possibilities to socially control and monitor water flows so as to prevent water stealing.[16]

Other examples show that making water rights transferable does not necessarily stimulate its allocation to the highest economic value and most productive use. In Chile, companies that try to get hold of water rights do not necessarily get their profits from using or selling water. Speculation by holding surplus usage rights is currently much more profitable, leading to the emergence of private water monopolies (Bauer 1997). The Chilean Water Code does not prevent the emergence of such monopolies, or the hoarding and speculation by powerful enterprises. It is, first of all, not necessary to pay taxes or fees to own water. And second, the right-holder has no obligation to effectively or beneficially use the water to which he or she owns the rights, or to build the works needed to utilize it (CEPAL 1998; Solanes 2002; Dourojeanni and Jouravlev 1999). Hendriks provides some striking examples of water speculation by the hydro-power sector. The three major electricity-generating companies accumulate 78 percent (1,324 m³/s) of the water used for this purpose; they have rights to 73 percent (8,162 m³/s) of the currently unused water; and they have applied for 69 percent (26,753 m³/s) of the total volume pending grants. It is estimated that in the total nationwide level a flow exists of 30,000 cubic meters usable for electric generation. The same tendency of concentrating water rights in the hands of a few commercial companies can be noted with the development of mining activities in the dry northern region (Hendriks 1998: 308). Peasant and indigenous movements actively protest against such water monopolies, and also the current government attempted to modify the water legislation to avoid unproductive uses. Such attempts have met with the resistance of the existing large right-holders and hegemonic power groups, who are reluctant to give up their privileges and actively oppose any changes in the Water Code (Douro-jeanni and Jouravlev 1999).

In most communal water systems in Peru, Bolivia, and Ecuador, the "one person–one-vote" rule applies, implying that each right-holder has one decision-making vote in the users' organization. In contrast, World Bank and Inter-American Development Bank proposals for new water legislation in Peru and Ecuador stipulate that voting rights should be made proportional to the quantity of water use rights each user holds, like shareholders in a joint-stock company. The Chilean Water Code sets the example for these proposals. Hendriks (1998) illustrates how such a redefinition of voting rights may shape the local political economy and power relations. In Belén, Precordillera Comuna de Putre, the great majority of irrigators, smallholders who depend on agriculture for their livelihoods, called for changing the irrigation schedule in order to intensify their agriculture and save water. They wanted to have more frequent irrigation turns with smaller flows, a decision ratified in several community assemblies. But in Belén, a majority of water shares is owned by a small group of wealthy absentee landholders who reside in the city of Arica and make a living out of other economic activities. They only go to the irrigation system when necessary, for example when they have their water turns. Obviously, they have no interest in increasing irrigation frequency, for it would mean more time and travel costs. This group's voting weight and related decision-making power prevents the majority of smallholders who depend on agriculture from improving their irrigation system and economic productivity. As Hendriks (1998: 306) remarks: "when users with abundant water and less need for careful use of available water have more weight in decision-making it affects the rationality of the system's collective operation. This problem of resistance to change, by the people who migrate to the city and own a relatively heavy weight of water shares, is recurrent in many remote locations in the north of Chile." Similar cases are reported in Peru after the neoliberal government of Fujimori changed the regulations of water user associations, concentrating decision-making rights and voting rights in the hands of a powerful minority of large water-right holders (Oré 1998; Vos 2002).

Although, in theory, the privatization of water depends on and strengthens decentralization and user organizations, and grants them greater autonomy and rights' security, the current policy does not foster interuser collaboration and local-level resolution of rights-related conflicts. On the contrary, the policy provokes and generates tensions, and severely undermines existing collective arrangements to deal with and settle conflicts. Intrasystem rights, which formerly were rooted in localized normative systems and strongly embedded in local institutions and social networks, are now eroded through their increased dependence on the market and on state legislation. Rights can and are bought by outsiders, or become concentrated in the hands of a few users. This so-called flexibilization[17] and disembedding of water service and access rights threatens the stability of collective rights' systems and significantly decreases the tenure security they can offer to their members.[18] These members, in turn, are no longer as motivated to personally and collectively invest in system maintenance and operation: "why invest today, if tomorrow my neighbors may have sold their rights to outside parties, which will disrupt the schedule, decrease my own flow, or maybe even cut the water off from my land?" In addition, outside rights-holders generally do not have the same commitment regarding their contribution to operating and maintaining the system, especially if they take the water elsewhere or use it for activities other than irrigation (Boelens and Dávila 1998; Gentes 2002; Hendriks 1998).

One of the fundaments of many collectively managed Andean systems tends to be undermined by the neoliberal approach. As explained earlier, through user investments in generating irrigation infrastructure, property relationships are created among system users, which in turn provide the foundation for collective efforts in operating and maintaining their system. These efforts are considered as an investment to recreate and consolidate rights. Privatization and subsequent market purchase of individual rights forcefully breaks these existing rights-creation and consolidation mechanisms. Embedded individual rights are being replaced by multiple and conflicting private rights at the intrasystem level. Indeed, and as Hendriks concludes his analysis of the effect of Chilean policy on peasant irrigation systems: "the more individual owners of water, the fewer owners of the system." According to Hendriks, in precisely those locations, valleys and oases of the North Chilean desert where the scarcity of water could, in principle, be expected to induce a well-organized and quite solid organization, collective systems of operation and investments have either severely eroded or stopped to exist. Farmers are claiming their individual rights, but collective control is vanishing, and general assemblies and community decision making disappear:

> It is difficult to achieve a quorum for an assembly, even on very important topics. There is little local contribution to maintenance or improvement of the canal network. Little is sanctioned or corrected in relation to robbery of water, because the local organization to complain to is not effective. The social pressure by the other users, when an individual is opposed to certain measures, is ineffective. . . . Evidently, this means that there is not much responsibility shared by users in regard to system operation, maintenance and improvement. It also means that users appeal and complain more to outside agencies [state institutions] to resolve problems, to take responsibility for the maintenance, to invest in improvements, etc. Apparently, the individual water owners are searching to find a system's owner who is disposed to be responsible for the whole system. (Hendriks 1998: 306–307)

While promoting decentralization and user management on paper, neoliberal policies thus lead to the breakdown of common property systems, sometimes to the detriment of water use efficiency and agricultural productivity. Ironically, multiple and internally conflicting private users now resort to the state for materializing their individual water rights, and for arranging system management.

Bauer (1998) describes how the neoliberal model as implemented in Chile has led to enormous challenges and conflicts, not just at the system level but also between multiple-use sectors at the watershed and river basin level. Where, before privatization, conflicts among public power generation companies and indigenous irrigator groups could be solved on the basis of public interest arguments, after the introduction of the neoliberal water policy they had to compete as supposedly equal competitors in the "free market." The proposed multistakeholder platforms as mechanisms for forging solutions were dominated by the more educated and vocal representatives of private companies, while outcomes were easily neglected because they were not legally binding and not backed by public policy. The Water Code stimulated local competition instead of collaboration. Although decentralization was supposed to help reduce state involvement (and government expenditures), the different actors seem to increasingly rely on expensive, legalistic procedures in centralized courts and thus on state bureaucracy for solving their disputes. This well-known Chilean example is the reason why most advocates of water rights markets and privatization "with a human face" in the Andes argue that the model should be accompanied with and embedded in an equitable legal framework. However, where private companies do know how to make use of civil courts and legal frameworks when it comes to defending their private water interests, there appears to be an enormous lack of legal capacity in the Andean countries when public or common water property interests have to be defended. The de facto subjugation of the Indigenous Law to the Water Code and the Mining Code in Chile, illustrated in chapter 7, is one clear example.

All these examples and cases go to show that neoliberal water reforms are based on a number of erroneous assumptions, and on a very limited understanding of what is at stake in actual water allocation practices. New laws and policies tend to destroy or erode existing systems of local water rights in peasant and indigenous communities who had vested those rights through years of labor investments and use. Rather than in state registers, claims of such rights were recorded in the minds and collective agreements of current users, and in the technical layout and organizational setup of irrigation systems. But location-specific and people-bound rights find no hearing since new water access arrangements depend solely on its price in the market and on its legitimization through state laws. For collective irrigator groups, often, neoliberal policies have decreased rather than increased their water tenure security, and have therefore reduced their willingness and motivation to make further investments in water infrastructure, or to use water efficiently and productively.

Disciplining, Normalization, and Resistance

The examples presented above raise doubts about whether neoliberal water policies meet their own expectations, measured against their own goals and indicators for success. These doubts, as proponents might argue, do not need to imply that the policies need revision. For one, there are the whims and fancies of the market to blame. A faulty implementation, caused by poorly functioning government bureaucracies is another likely explanation for disappointing results. Another important and frequently heard explanation is to be found in the backwardness and stubbornness of local water use communities (see also McCay and Jentoft 1998). These traditional communities fail to act "rationally" or "democratically" and thus fail to "fit" the model. Existing ways of managing and using water in many Andean communities are not seen and judged on their own terms, and not even on the basis of water use efficiencies or marginal returns to water, but are evaluated against the universal and ideal model. Worse still, existing norms and agreements appear, in the eyes of neoliberal thinkers, as "anomalies" to the rational frameworks of national and international rights. They tend to be seen as obstacles to efficient and modern water control, obstacles that need to be removed to pave the way for water modernization and for the emergence of the rational water actor. To provide just one illustration, in Chile, when the new Water Code was enforced in 1981, most indigenous communities were left unaware of the need to officially register their century-old customary rights (Solón 2003). Water rights that were not registered and legally formalized were labeled as "unused rights" and allocated to those who did have the presence of mind and the information to present official requests. In this way, much water that indigenous groups had appropriated through prior use, territorial rights, and through investments in infrastructure was reallocated to commercial companies (electricity and mining companies, especially) and bigger landlords (Gentes 2000, 2002; van Kessel 1992). Territory- and community-bound rights were thus considered as an obstacle to the proper functioning of the free market. Chances of indigenous groups to claim or reclaim water rights are minimal, since the allocation of new or surplus water rights is done through auctions. The highest bidder is the one who is rewarded with these rights, and since indigenous groups normally are not in a position to make very high bids, they do not stand a fair chance of having their water claims rewarded (Castro 2002; Dourojeanni and Jouravlev 1999; Gentes 2002; Hendriks 1998). Local communities and actors are only allowed rights to water and water decision making when they accept the terms and conditions as specified by higher levels, those based on universal values and truths. To proponents of neoliberal reforms, the described problems of efficiency and equity described in the previous section are not seen as effects of new neoliberal laws and policies, but are instead analyzed as stemming from the as yet incomplete implementation of the model, and of the as yet imperfect incorporation of existing water use communities in markets and state legal systems. Therefore, and paradoxically, the remedy that is prescribed is to increase free market rules in local communities and give more freeway to outside and private interest groups to improve management, increase efficiency, and enforce water rights. In other words: to take over and further externalize their resources, rules, and authority. In this way, the neoliberal water model becomes indeed a self-fulfilling prophecy.

As the examples have illustrated, although privatization aims at deregulating bureaucratic water management through delegation of decisions to the lowest possible level, actual water reforms in the Andes tend to have opposite consequences for local and indigenous water rights systems. Through the installation of neoliberal rights and regulations, locally embedded collective property systems become disembedded from the community's social relationships and security systems, and existing collective water management arrangements are replaced by outside or market-based rules of the game. From the perspective of water policy makers, the destruction of systems of collective rights are seen as important successes and achievements of the model, particularly in those cases where the impoverished users, who are labeled as the irrational and inefficient, seek to receive the blessings of the model to become healthy again. The excluded are included, and become "potentially equal, normal water users."[19]

Yet not all water users accept the label of potential equals, and increasingly they demand adherence to different standards of equality than the ones the neoliberal model offers as inevitable and natural. There is an increasing number of documented instances of farmer organizations fiercely standing up against privatization efforts and neoliberal water reform programs. This resistance shows that "not fitting" the model is often a conscious choice rather than the result of backwardness, irrationality, or unreasoned stubbornness. As already mentioned, large-scale water conflicts and related social differentiation processes under private water property regimes are by no means new to the Andes. Many communities and indigenous organizations perceive the new water plans as yet another in a sequence of attempts to take away resources that historically belong to them and that form the basis of their livelihoods. In Peru, Bolivia, and Ecuador massive nationwide uprisings have effectively resulted in a standstill of the implementation of the new water policies and laws.

Protests are directed against the model as such and against many of its particular principles, often taking the results of the Chilean experiment as an example. For instance, in order to promote possibilities for free trade in water rights and to allow water to be allocated to its most profitable uses, Chilean neoliberal water policy states that water rights allocation should follow market principles. Chilean legislation, therefore, does not establish access priorities or preferences for particular uses (such as drinking water for human consumption above industrial use), nor does it express norms to protect particular vulnerable groups, the environment or, ultimately, water quality (CEPAL 1998; Dourojeanni and Jouravlev 1999). Peasant and indigenous organizations in the other Andean countries that were to adopt Chile's water legislation have strongly objected to this lack of prioritization in water allocation. For example, CONAIE, the Confederation of Indigenous Nationalities of Ecuador, defended a water allocation principle in their water law proposal that prioritizes water for human and domestic use and for subsistence agriculture above water for commercial agriculture. Commercial agriculture, in turn, was to receive a higher priority than industrial, mining, and power generation activities (CONAIE 1996; see also Pacari 1998). Also, in Bolivia, peasant and indigenous organizations fiercely protested against market allocation principles that would, in their opinion, endanger water access for the economically less powerful (Bustamante 2002; Perreault 2005).

Another widespread act of resistance is raised against the privatization of public or common water rights and bringing them under control of commercial companies for profit-making purposes. An example is the case of the Central Valley of Cochabamba in Bolivia. Here, the main water users of the valley are peasant and indigenous irrigator communities, who for decades have organized access to and distribution of water according to their "uses and customs." They engaged in a major conflict when in 1997 the Cochabamba drinking water company started to drill wells in the Central Valley, affecting their already overextracted ground water resources. In 2000, the valley again became a violent battlefield when indigenous and peasant communities together with urban water users protested against the state's plans to privatize the drinking water sector. The government signed a contract with a large foreign consortium, and enacted a privatization support law that allowed the international company to have exclusive water rights of all waters in the district—including those of smaller systems in the metropolitan area and rights to exploit the aquifers. Another law was rushed through the parliament so that the company could capture new water resources, and even charge water fees for cooperative wells that were to be expropriated. Directly after privatization, the international company considerably raised water fees, without any system improvement. In a strong alliance, urban and rural water users protested: the citizens protested against rising water rates, while the rural municipalities and indigenous communities protested against the new law because it affected their rights and could expose them to new encroachments of their water sources. Violent confrontations with the army were the result. At the end of this "water war," the government had to retract its decision and also commit to amending all the proposed law's articles that the popular alliance objected to (see, for instance, Boelens et al. 2002; Bustamante 2002; Orellana 2001; Laurie et al. 2002; Perrault 2005).

These struggles highlight the contested nature of water rights, and the fact that much, very much, is at stake. Central in the water rights struggle are not only access to and withdrawal of water resources. The formulation of the rules—that is, the content of water right and management rules, and the mechanisms to acquire water rights—are also at stake, as well as the legitimate authority to make decisions and enforce rights. A major fourth element in this privatization battlefield is the struggle over the discourses that establish, impose, or defend particular water rights policies and regimes. What becomes apparent in the analyses of water rights conflicts in the Andes is that rights and struggles about rights and authority not only exemplify the inherently political nature of water but also are closely associated with cultural meanings and identities and with ideals and ideas about what constitutes humanity and development. To understand and interpret these struggles, therefore, they should thus not be seen narrowly as protests against the effects of new water policies, but require a broader historical and social contextualization. Water struggles in the Andes are also struggles for specificity and local autonomy, for the right to self-define the nature of water problems as well as to decide on the direction for solutions. The struggles are a critique of the very rationality of the reforms, and actively question their claims to neutrality and objectivity. They show that policy choices that are justified on the basis of neutrality and efficiency in actual practice work to promote a very clear political agenda. In doing so, they also challenge the Enlightenment epistemology that provides justification to this agenda at its core.

Conclusions

The history of the privatization debate, as we have shown, is directly connected to the way in which "civilized" Enlightenment thinkers have tried to take themselves as the universal norm of humanity by judging other water rights frameworks and hydraulic identities as inferior to their own and, at the theoretical level, by claiming universality of their models and laws. Following this Enlightenment tradition, the neoliberal discourse largely derives its strength and legitimacy from presenting and imposing itself as self-evident and through actively constructing a logic of its own inevitability. In doing this, the neoliberal model not only assumes and desires universal laws but also actively establishes them. Coexistence of a great diversity of rules, rights, and obligations is actively discouraged, since such diversity would obstruct interregional and international transfers and trades, which require a uniform legal framework. Locally particular rules and rights that are critical of the generalization of market rules, transfers, and sales are anomalies that stand in the way of investments and profits. In the Andean region, market policies do not replace bureaucratic policies, as is commonly suggested in decentralization discourses, but they complement each other in disciplining and counteracting local pluralism of water rights repertoires. Recognition of the diversity of water authorities and rules—obstacles to their positivist frameworks—undermines the power and rule-making capacity of both national bureaucrats and powerful market players and forces. State bureaucracies, therefore, are "reformed" to provide and enact legislation that allows markets to emerge. Communities and collective rights systems that do not fit the neoliberal picture are by definition inefficient and backward. Thus, they are either doomed to wither, get subtly (self-)included in the market as those with potential to become equals, or they are forced to join the neoliberal game on unequal terms.

The formal ability to demand and practice rights to water in the neoliberal world is a function of one's ability to enter and bargain in markets and meetings. In neoliberal political thought, and through seeing the water domain as functionally and ontologically isolated from the rest of society, all water actors are assumed to behave as if they were equals. Such assumption is crucial, since markets and meetings only function when all participants can interact as equals. Equalization in the water domain is achieved though uniformity of objectives and rules, through private water rights, and through the adoption of the rational choice paradigm which reduces humans to rational pursuers of economic self-interest. Yet the concept of equality presupposes a frame of reference, a mirror that is typically not made explicit in neoliberal thinking: "equal to what?", "equal to whom?" Clearly, the cultural, political, and normative standards for becoming equal, and thus for normalizing the abnormals, are set by the neoliberal policy model makers. They have used their own preferred self-representation and ideals about humanity and human nature to construct such standards, a process that nevertheless remains hidden from scrutiny behind the thick cloaks of positivist science. Such hiding allows the standards to be presented as unavoidable laws of nature. Actually existing differences, characterized by historically grounded social differentiations and divisions in terms of decision-making power, monetary income, skills, information, and education, which strongly favor private companies and business actors, are discursively neglected, or presented as precisely the gap that can be bridged by the potential equals when joining the market game.

Actually existing water use practices and water rights systems in the Andes are deeply embedded in plural normative systems, social and cultural institutions, political networks, and technological and agroecological environments. The fundamental suggestion of neoliberal policies that water rights can simply be lifted out and isolated from this complex reality and historical organization of control, in order to "bring them to the market," cannot be taken seriously unless the destruction or radical transformation of local livelihoods is accepted. The proposed water reforms, though presented as neutral and scientific, involve quite radical modifications in the social and political structures in which water management is embedded, and in the ways in which water is to be owned, distributed, and managed. If the policies are implemented, such relations are increasingly dictated by extracommunal laws, institutions, and markets. Thus, the proposed water reforms are deeply political, in the sense that they aim to actively create and transform the political and social water world. The policies that are based on new institutional theories establish universal criteria for optimizing water management. Market becomes the metaphor for complex social and ecological dynamics, and people and nature are deemed relevant only in their commoditized form imputed with value useful to the economy. Such universalization can be seen as a process of Foucauldian disciplining. Through prices, very diverse water values can be compared, categorized, measured, and judged and thus transferred and traded. Through reducing motivations for human behavior to self-interested profit maximization, water actors are judged upon their degree of market orientation.

Not surprisingly, therefore, peasant and indigenous communities often have lost their rights and voice as a result of neoliberal regulation and privatization projects. Not just their water rights but also their management rules and identities have been denied and undermined after exposure to a model that simply assumes freedom of expression without actually verifying the conditions of its existence. It is telling that the most far-reaching water privatization policies have been adopted in Chile, under Pinochet. As in no other place, a nationwide neoliberal "water rights laboratory" could be installed in order to experiment and implement the model. Popular resistance and dissent voices were violently silenced, assuring emergence of the conditions that would enable the model to work. In most other Andean countries, protests have partly halted or substantially altered water privatization efforts. So far, however, protests have hardly led to opening and widening the discursive spaces for discussing water, nor have the terms of the debate significantly altered as a result of protests. Neoliberalism has not yet been dethroned as the hegemonic water language. For this to happen, as a first important step, the assumptions of political neutrality and scientific objectivity legitimizing Andean water reforms should be thrown into the dustbin in favor of conceptualizations and narratives that explicitly show the politics of water distribution and the on-the-ground results of water policies, which allow for diversity and historical context-ualization, and that acknowledge subjectivity and situatedness.

In sum, neoliberal policies and the theories underlying them are indeed a serious threat for local water use communities. This threat does not relate to just an abstract academic debate on the most appropriate frameworks and principles for water control and legislation. Although heavily contested, it has the means and power of creating truths and converting itself into reality. As Bourdieu explained, "in the name of a scientific programme of knowledge, converted into a political programme of action, an immense political operation is being pursued, aimed at creating the conditions for realizing and operating of the 'theory': a programme of methodological destruction of collectives" (Bourdieu 1998: 95–96). Yet, the takeover of water rights is not a silent one. On the contrary, peasant movements and indigenous organizations are actively standing up for their rights. Understanding such protests requires a more layered, contextualized, and complex analysis than the one that currently tends to dominate global debates. The current struggles are not, as many observers would have it, a simple battle between public and private water interests; neither is it a conflict between common and private property regimes, the prior associated with tradition and the latter with modernity. Rights, and struggles about rights and authority, not only exemplify the inherently political nature of water and its close association with power relations but in the Andes are also closely associated with cultural meanings and identities. Hence, while the main stake in these struggles to either resist or comply with neoliberal approaches is security of water tenure, the struggles are not just about water. They are also about cultural meanings and ethnicity, about the right to self-define and exist as collectives and individuals, about sameness or otherness, about power and identity.

NOTES

1. As we show below, neoliberal rules and instruments that aim for universal water management solutions are also problematic when measured against their own objectives, that of establishing well-functioning and efficient water allocation and use

mechanisms. But the political and discursive power attached to the model (and the model makers) make it very difficult to demystify these fundamental conceptual inconsistencies.

2. Except, maybe, in special reserves, as is shown in chapters 3 and 7.

3. Observers could also easily change their position. For example, Columbus himself was very positive about the Indians during his first voyages (intelligent, peaceful, friendly, open since not restrained by laws, no greed since they don't have private property), but he changed his views when they did not behave according to his plans; he then saw them as savage, war-minded ignobles who obeyed neither God nor Law and who were lazy since they had no private property (cf. Lemaire 1986).

4. Even Thomas More, who wrote Utopia (1516) before Pizarro reached the Inca Empire, is said to have referred to Andean identity and property relations to produce his counterimage to the power constellations that prevailed in England at that time. Morgan (1946) argues that More was informed by Portuguese Amazon explorers about the existence of the socialist-totalitarian Andean empire, and that he based Utopia largely on the properties of Inca society (for example, common property, labor duties, and collective work parties; central planning, social control, and the importance of labor and agriculture; a collective storehouse system, the extended family structures, and the way of colonizing other peoples; warfare strategies, the legal system, and so on). More fiercely protested against the politics of the enclosures in England and advocated radical abolition of private property regimes, in line with assumed Inca Empire regulations (Lemaire 1986: 112–118).

5. As a consequence, just as the history of the "peoples without history" closely coincides with European history (Wolf 1982), the dynamic Andean "indigenous" identities and property regimes can only be rightly studied in relation to the construction of Western colonial and postcolonial identities and intervention processes.

6. See, for example, Boelens and Dávila 1998; Gelles 2000; Guevara et al. 2002; Mayer 2002; Mitchell and Guillet 1994; Oré 1998, 2005 (forthcoming); Vos 2002.

7. The objective of this new Chilean policy was the creation of a free water market as part of Chile's monetary economy, an objective that was strongly supported by the economically powerful national elites. The water policy proposal meant a radical break with the centralist water bureaucracy that had prevailed in Chile until then.

8. The new model (as well as the discursive destruction of the "old, traditional water rights allocation systems") has been actively promoted and imposed by institutes such as the World Bank: "In most countries water is still regarded as public property. . . . The track record of such administered systems of water allocation has not been impressive. Despite growing water scarcity and the high costs of hydraulic infrastructure, water is typically underpriced and used wastefully, the infrastructure is frequently poorly conceived, built, and operated, and delivery is often unreliable. . . . The results show that a market-based system of allocation is likely to lead to a more efficient outcome in water-scarce countries than are traditional systems of assigning water rights. Such a system has the potential to increase the productivity of water use, improve service delivery, stimulate private investment and economic growth, reduce water conflicts, and free government resources for activities with a public good content or positive externalities. . . . The Bank could assist in such efforts by raising awareness of the potential benefits of tradable water rights and by providing technical assistance to establish such rights. . . . The findings have been presented at professional workshops in water management in Berlin, Paris, and Washington, DC,

and in Bankwide seminars. They also have been presented to senior government officials in Mexico and Peru, members of Peru's congress, a group of nongovernmental
organizations in Peru, and a convention of water user associations in Peru" (World
Bank 1996).

9. The term "god-trick" comes from Donna Haraway; see Haraway (1988). Earlier, the
utilitarian philosopher Jeremy Bentham used the idea of a "god-view" from nowhere
and everywhere in his design of the panoptical prison in the eighteenth century. On
this basis, Foucault (1995) developed his ideas on power, discourse, disciplining, and
normalization.

10. In other words, water knowledge is written "from the center." Chambers referred to
this as the "center-outward, core-periphery" perspective (Chambers et al. 1989: 6). A
powerful characteristic of the neoliberal water policy discourse is that this center is
made invisible (as in the Panopticon), thereby strengthening its disciplining power.

11. In neoliberal thinking, water use and management are typically postulated as activities whose rationale can be directly deduced from, and are limited to, a clearly delim-
ited and relatively insulated water domain. Who you are in this domain is thus seen as
primarily a function of the characteristics of the domain itself, related to the internal
rules of the game and its functional hierarchies, rather than as stemming from any
outside social context or identity.

12. See also Gleick et al. 2002; Goldman 1998; Mollinga 2001; Moore 1989; van der Ploeg
2003; Roth 2003; Zoomers and van der Haar 2000; Zwarteveen 1994a, 1997, 1998.

13. This blackmailing was witnessed in Ecuador, when internal Washington documents
that made new loans conditional on the enactment of a new Chilean-type water law
leaked. For the case of Peru, former World Bank consultant Trawick revealed the same
policy practice (Trawick 1996 and 2003).

14. See Briscoe 1996; Rosegrant and Binswanger 1994; Rosegrant and Gazmuri 1994; Perry
et al. 1997; Ringler et al. 2000.

15. They do not normally, for instance, count as the much wanted private investments in
water infrastructure. Although neoliberalism strongly rewards and actively aims to
promote private investments in water infrastructure and maintenance, investments
of local water rights' collectives in constructing and maintaining irrigation systems
are commonly not recognized and, as we will show, are even destroyed by neoliberal
policies.

16. See, for example, Apollin et al. 1998; Apollin 2002; Boelens 1998; Gerbrandy and
Hoogendam 1998; Trawick 1996, 2003.

17. In another context, Bourdieu (1998: 85) argued that the idea of flexibility is a deliberate "insecurity-inducing strategy" of the neoliberal model. This "flexploitation"—the
rational management of insecurity—is strategically induced by elites in order to impose and control the outcomes of the market process. The above-mentioned
deterritorialization of water rights is an important example. Another powerful example is the soaking off of water rights (regarding both property and its contents)
from collective and community-controlled frameworks, turning them into flexible
rights (and obligations) under the control of individual market competitors.

18. Such examples thoroughly question the equity and social justice arguments of
privatization proponents, such as the World Bank. The bank states, for example, that
"tradable water rights allow the price of water to reflect the value of its alternative
uses, which creates incentives to put it to the most productive use. . . . Secure water
rights are particularly beneficial for smaller farmers, who have been most vulnerable

to reductions in their water allocation over time and who have few other sources of collateral. Tradable water rights, by empowering existing users, help reduce the abuses of administrative allocation and give assurance to poor farmers that their water availability will not be reduced" (World Bank 1996: 11–12).

19. From a remote history, Las Casas's humanist beliefs and inclusive intentions echo through. Yet his inclusive approach, although paternalistic, did not primarily aim to control local populations, their behavior, and their resources.

6

Complexities of Water Governance

Rise and Fall of Groundwater for Urban Use

AMREETA REGMI

Kathmandu, the administrative, economic, and cultural capital of Nepal, is undergoing rapid and radical demographic, social, and economic changes that directly impinge on water service demands and the regulation and planning of water resources. The current population of Kathmandu Valley is estimated to be approximately 1,200,000.[1] The population density in Kathmandu ranges from an average of nine persons per square kilometer to 683 persons or even higher concentrations in the core urban area (the area within the surrounding Ring Road).[2] Outside the core area, the density of population is relatively low. The area with the highest concentration of people is also the area with increasing numbers of hotels and industries, which all compete for water with domestic users. The current water infrastructure is inadequate to serve these increasing domestic and industrial demands. The resulting scarcity of water has made water management into one of the dominant themes pursued by both the intellectual and expert water elite and local water users. Increasingly, water users in both the domestic and commercial sectors have resorted to the use of groundwater, and the use of groundwater extraction technologies has become more and more important both in facilitating and in defining people's access to water.

This chapter examines the complexity surrounding regulation of domestic water supply. To understand and identify the key problems and issues that exist within the water supply system, the chapter first provides background information on water scarcity in Kathmandu and on Nepal's efforts in planned development of urban water resources. The chapter then continues with a description of water sources. It identifies different categories of water users and analyzes the diverse rules and practices of users to access and use water. It shows that new technologies for water extraction increasingly mediate and shape water use practices, configuring new ways of accessing water. The new complexities of increasing demands and new practices and patterns of use and access largely escape attempts by the state to arrange safe water supply, and to regulate water access security. Yet the chapter argues that policies and laws are central in solving current and future water problems. Therefore, in the final part of the chapter a framework for allocation is presented, distinguishing between allocation as a fundamental right, as a discretionary right, as a provisional right, and as a hydraulic right, respectively.

Water Scarcity in Kathmandu

In recent years, pollution of land, air, and water have made Kathmandu's already fragile ecosystem even more vulnerable. Nepal is vulnerable to earthquakes, as a consequence of the tectonic stresses along the Himalayan region. Kathmandu witnessed three major earthquakes in the nineteenth century. In addition to this natural ecological vulnerability, over the past few decades there has been a rapid depletion of natural resources. This is caused by the neglect of the watershed, surrounding forests along the foothills and slopes of the valley; overdraft of groundwater; and the diminishing quality of water in surface sources. Kathmandu's ecosystem and repository of complex sociocultural diversity and practices render the ecology even more complex. Air pollution, previously unheard of in Kathmandu, has become a new reality of environmental degradation. Kathmandu Valley is believed once to have been a lake; and the soil quality is prone to liquefaction. Along with population growth and a rising demand for water, water resource availability and scarcity in the city is also importantly correlated to Kathmandu's ecological peculiarities and social complexities.

Water scarcity is not a new phenomenon for certain sections of Nepalese society. Situated in the upper catchment area of the Bagmati River, Kathmandu has always faced water scarcity; this has clearly worsened over the years. Communities have learned to cope by using multiple sources of water for domestic uses. The existing customary practices and value systems have also made it easier for people to deal with water scarcity. The existence of water scarcity was already visible during the 1960s, when only privileged homes had piped water supply. It was a common practice for such households to have their clothes laundered in communal systems. Members of the elite also used public or communal systems to perform their morning baths and the rituals that normally followed after bathing and cleansing, with the offering of water to the gods. These peculiarities of Kathmandu's ecosystem and social and traditional practices have received little attention from the state and its agencies. Hence, they have largely remained outside the regulatory framework of state plans and strategies for addressing the urban water supply of Kathmandu Valley.

State Efforts

Involvement of the state in planned development of Nepal's urban public water supply and sanitation began during the First National Plan (1956–1961) period. Thereafter, every plan focused on achieving a set target "coverage" of households to provide "access to water." These coverage targets were made and incorporated in the planning documents without considering the complexities of the technical, social, and ecological vagaries that confront the management and governance of water resources. At present, about 61 percent of the total population has access to water, as against a planned target in the Ninth Plan (1997–2002) of achieving 100 percent.

Very recently, the development of national water plans for Nepal has also encouraged water sector reform and strategic development for this sector. The strategy places considerable emphasis on public dialogue in terms of information dissemination and mass media communication seeking to involve civil society and participation of all stakeholders. This strategy was further strengthened during the initiation of the Melamchi Water Supply Project, which helped establish a nongovernmental organization coalition on Kathmandu's urban water supply and sanitation. This urban water coalition comprises of about thirty NGOs, including various activist groups that represent diverse intersectoral water platforms and agendas. The participation of civil society has encouraged focus on planning and decision-making processes. However, it remains unclear how the interests of such groups are translated into actual implementation through policy reform and new legal frameworks, in the interest of intersectoral demand.

The current strategy is guided by the need for an integrated harnessing of water resources. There is a need for policy and legal reform toward the formulation of a regulatory framework that encompasses these various intersectoral issues and actors. One thing is clear: given the great variety of uses and sources of water, an adequate urban ecosystem approach to governance by quantifying water allocation limits is not forthcoming. Meanwhile the community will have to continue coping with increasing water scarcity through the currently available water sources.

Sources of Water

At an initial glance, sources of water supply appear to be diverse. They range from formal piped conveyance systems, communal yard stands, extracting devices, stone spouts, and surface sources, to private and commercial water tankers. A simplistic categorization of these diverse water sources can be made by type of conveyance system: piped and unpiped sources. Typically, piped water that is supplied to the consumers is provided through parastatal institutional arrangements, and unpiped supply through nonstate sources. The state supplies water for domestic and urban uses by using both surface and groundwater sources.[3] The Nepal Water Supply Corporation (NWSC), the parastatal agency responsible for the supply of treated piped water, provides access to 80 percent of households. That leaves 20 percent of the population still dependent on traditional stone spouts, rivers, and other sources, as they do not have access to the NWSC system. Within the category of those households who do have access to the state system, 36 percent are estimated to have fully plumbed connections, 46 percent have access to communally shared yard stands, and 18 percent use public and communal standposts (World Bank/UNDP 2000). In addition, NWSC maintains a fleet of water tankers that provide water, mainly from groundwater sources. This is done during the dry season in particular, the period when releases in the main pipe system decrease.

Although most households do have access to some state-supplied water, the gaps between what the state delivery system supplies and actual demand are significant and increasing. Coverage by the state delivery system, including an industrial consumption of 5 percent, is estimated at only 53 percent of the required volume. The current demand for water is estimated at 193 million liters per day (MLD), whereas the NWSC supplies only 80–100 MLD, depending on seasonal variations. The demand for water is expected to rise to above 213 MLD by the end of 2002. The release and flow in the supply system is also affected by other factors such as leakage, seepage, and stealing of water. For example, there is a high rate of unaccounted water use—as high as 40 percent—and the informal use of water in both domestic and commercial sectors makes it difficult to calculate urban consumer demand. Estimates of the current shortfall in supply vary between 93 MLD (World Bank/UNDP 2000) and 25 MLD (WECS 2000).

Even though 80 percent of households have access to the organized system, currently only one-third of the users have private connections. The population without private connections to piped water supply relies on various water sources, usually a combination of sources. Most of them have access to public or private yard stands or standposts. They, along with others without access to piped water, also rely on the traditional communal stone water spouts (*dhunge dhara*), springs (*kuwa*), wells (*inar*), groundwater pumped by private pumps, and water supplied by private tankers. There are about 103 functional traditional stone spouts within the jurisdiction of the Kathmandu municipality. The poor also rely on streams or rivers, most of which are polluted. Groundwater is increasingly filling much of the deficit experienced by the urban water users through both private pumping and informal water markets.

A water consumption tariff is imposed, monitored, and controlled by NWSC through water meters to measure piped water use. Those households that have not installed water meters pay a minimum monthly tariff. Many households prefer to pay the minimum flat tariff, and some have dismantled their water meters. This tariff, which covers an allocation of 1,000 liters of water, is in fact more expensive than the actual quantity consumed by the household. Yet, many domestic water users reject meters on the basis of the perception that the installation of the water meter obstructs the flow of supply. In addition, water users complain that the meter continues to run even during low flows. There is a perception that there is no accurate correlation between consumption and pricing.

Unregulated private water carriers and bottled water are also becoming major sources of domestic supply, although they are limited to economically powerful consumers. There are about fifty private water tanker services operating in Kathmandu Valley. They charge between NRs 800 and NRs 1,000 per tanker of 9,000 to 12,000 liters of water.[4] Prices fluctuate according to season and availability of water. The industrial consumption of water through the central supply system amounts to only 5 percent of the current supply and does not take into account the water extracted from private tube wells, which is acquired free of cost.[5]

The rise in water markets is largely unregulated and unmonitored. In the commercial sector, water markets have expanded into locations outside the periphery of the municipality where fertile agricultural land is being leased out and operated for selling water. Between 1984 and 1994 alone, the fertile agricultural land in the valley declined from 64 percent to 52 percent, whereas nonagricultural land increased from 5.6 percent to 14.5 percent (HMG/ADB 2000). The water table in the areas, from which water is extracted by private truckers and sold to city consumers, is relatively high. In addition, domestic users, hotels, industries, and state supply systems tap groundwater by using pumping technology, to fulfill much of their demand. Between the state and private access to other surface supply, groundwater has emerged as one of the most valuable sources of water for discretionary use for both domestic and commercial water users.[6]

However, the extent of the water table in areas controlled by these water-extracting devices (WEDs) is not known.[7] In addition to drinking, cooking, and ritualistic needs that are fulfilled through state supply, groundwater fulfills much of the discretionary uses of water. Groundwater is also a major source of water supplied by the state in both Kathmandu and Bhaktapur. Both discretionary and state uses indicate that extraction is quite substantial. Domestic uses such as bathing, washing, watering the garden, recreation, and industrial uses are fulfilled by the use of groundwater and, to a lesser extent, by other traditional water sources. The abstraction from water markets is unknown. A recent compilation of groundwater extraction data for Kathmandu Valley estimates use at about 59 MLD for domestic and private usage.

The state has made several attempts to meet Kathmandu's urban water demand, and future planning has begun. One of the initiatives is the Melamchi Water Supply Project, which was initiated in 1999 with the financial assistance of over US$600 million from various donors. Despite the surrounding controversies in the approval of this megaproject, the interbasin transfer of water from the Melamchi Valley in Sindhupalchowk District to Kathmandu is under way. This project is expected to supply water to 4.3 million people at the rate of 120 liters per day. The project is moving ahead with plans for privatization and full economic pricing. The price per unit of water is expected to be triple what consumers are currently paying. It is unclear how this project will meet much of the industrial demand for water as well as the traditional use of water.

The Renter Population

The social and political changes during the postdemocracy era in Kathmandu have led to a tremendous increase in the number and categories of water users in the valley. The increase in rural-urban migration has incapacitated basic service provision, in addition to posing challenges in regulated water supply delivery. Migrants from other districts continue to enter the valley, looking for better economic opportunities or escaping from districts that have been afflicted by insurgent activities. This group of water users, referred to here as "renter population," is clearly a distinct category of water users as compared to the homeowning users and the commercial users.[8] The renter population is heavily concentrated within the core urban areas and is dispersed among the houseowning population: over 80 percent of the households in the core urban area keep renters, letting out one or more rooms under the same roof.

For this study, the current urban population of Kathmandu was stratified into three distinct groups: first, land and houseowning local residents who entered the valley with the Gorkha rulers when Nepal's small principalities were unified in 1760;[9] second, houseowning immigrants who entered the valley before 1990; third, migrants who entered the valley after the restoration of democracy and have been living as renters.

As mentioned above, not all houses have private connections to the NWSC system. Private and individualized connections are granted by the NWSC only to those households that have a legal title to the house. Although this makes it difficult to estimate water consumption by the renter population, it can be safely assumed that the large number of renters significantly increases water demand and use. Renters and houseowners often share water from the same sources, but the rights of the renters are secondary to those of the houseowners. Though most of the landlords do not charge the renters for water they consume, the latter contribute to electricity charges in instances where boring is used or where water from the NWSC system is pumped to overhead storage tanks. The landlord has the first priority to use the supply from the NWSC system, and the renter's share of water is largely dependent on the quantity allocated by the landlord or the availability of water from public standposts or groundwater supply. The renters rarely enter the premises of neighboring houseowners to request water. They often frequent other renters on the basis of social relationships existing with these people.

Groundwater Use, Access, and Implications

Contrary to the general perception that WEDs are primarily used by the rich and the elite, a large portion of the urban population today depends on at least one kind of pumping device. Simultaneous use of two systems, one to withdraw water from the main pipeline and the other to extract subsurface water, is also quite common. However, the choice of technology and the capacity for extraction depend on how much one can afford to pay for the installation of the system. Thus, deep tube wells are primarily used by NWSC, the big hotels and other commercial enterprises, and government institutions. In contrast, domestic users mainly depend on shallow tube wells and deep wells.

Although, on the face of it, access to groundwater seems open in that rules and laws do not regulate it, in practice physical access to this resource largely depends on the ability to install technology. Thus, the richer households have better access to groundwater because they are able to install more powerful WEDs to extract water from deeper levels. The owner of the pump, and not necessarily the owner of the land, enjoys access to the water the pump delivers. This is evident, for example, where a vacant lot is leased out to commercial water carriers for the sale of water, or when a house is rented out for independent residential purpose where the tenants pay water charges to the state. The poor continue to use the communal systems in the form of either traditional sources or shared public supplies. Use of technology, in particular Rower pumps, by economically weaker sections of society for pumping out water is on the rise.[10]

The Rower pump was introduced in Kathmandu in 1987, when tube wells made out of galvanized iron pipes were gradually being diffused in the urban sector as spill-off from the (rural) irrigation sector. Rower pumps have a simple PVC design, and using them does not entail any electricity costs. Further, these pumps are not expensive, prices ranging between NRs 2,500 and NRs 3,000. In addition, Rower pumps are locally manufactured; spare parts are easily available. The amount of water withdrawn through Rower pumps is not clear. In spite of their popularity, the declining water table in certain areas has made their use less effective. As a result, urban dwellers have also started upgrading from Rower to deeper jet pumps over the past few years.

Another popular device in use is a pump set known as "Nepal number six," which was initially imported from India. This pump is now fabricated in Bhairahawa, a town located in the mid-southern plains bordering on India. The design is very similar to UNICEF's tube well model, and the pump weighs between twenty-eight and thirty kilograms per unit. These are commonly used for public standposts by local donor organizations and municipalities. Private users in the domestic sector prefer the Indian model, which weighs slightly less than twenty kilograms. There are various other extracting devices, mostly made in China and India. The centrifugal pumps use electricity to pull or draw water from bore wells. Jet pumps and submersible pumps reach lower aquifers. Submersible pumps of Indian, American, and Italian makes are used for deep-water extraction and are popular with the water markets. In the domestic sector, jet pumps have become popular over the last few years. This technology does not require any manual structure or installation of hand pumps. Another common practice among users is the use of booster pumps to increase the flow by suction of water from the main pipeline during times of state supply.

Sharing water and networking for organizing access happens regularly but is usually restricted to people who belong to the same water use category. Use of WED technologies seems to have further segregated water use among social groups. For example, affluent households tend to restrict entry of neighbors to their private premises. In many instances, they control access to their water pumps by using padlocks or deploying guards (*chowkidars*). Users of communal and traditional systems continue to refer to deep-rooted traditional rules and practices surrounding the use of water. Examples are carrying ritually pure, not defiled water (*chokho pani*) from a free-flowing source to the house, the first offering of water to the sun-god Surya during sunrise, and ritualistic ablutions in a group while chanting incantations (*mantras*) and morning prayers. All of these are still common phenomena that bind water users together in a communal system. Where a pumping device is used, such activities are uncommon. The technology itself does not encourage such bonds, as the pumps have to be operated by individuals. This restricts the use of hands for other purposes like worshiping, offering, or washing. The use of private WEDs has not only reduced interactions among water users, but it has also led to the fragmentation of water rituals that celebrate the relationship between humans and water. Thus, rules, practices, and perceptions of water users are increasingly mediated by water-extracting devices.

The use of deep-water aquifers for industrial and commercial purposes started well before the 1980s, and has risen exponentially and spread over the domestic sector. Currently, there are no limits set on industrial and commercial water withdrawals. Thus, a large quantity of water is being extracted by this sector, infringing upon the water rights of those in the domestic sector as well as of those who do not own property (Saleth 1994a). Access to groundwater extraction by the powerful is affecting the poor, both in terms of quality and quantity of water. The decrease in the water table, high pumping costs, electricity charges, and installation investments are invisible factors that affect this group. As Meinzen-Dick and Appasamy (2001) have noted, the interface between quality and quantity of water within urban use discounts not only the withdrawal amount but also the return flow and the condition of the water put back into the hydrological system. While local residents report a deterioration in surface supplies through gradual drying of the valley's river system, climate change, and low flows in stone spouts, the quality of water extracted from the ground is also said to have degenerated over the years. Groundwater extracted from Anamnagar, Bishalnagar, Bhatbhateni, Kalimati, and Dillibazar is a murky brown liquid and is clearly unfit even for washing clothes or watering vegetables.

The Bagmati River and its tributaries, which form the main surface water sources, function as unrestricted disposal sites for domestic solid and liquid waste. In addition, human waste, animal carcasses, and industrial discharge let out in these rivers affect the quality of groundwater. The groundwater, both shallow and deep, is said to be contaminated with high concentrations of ammonia, lead, fluoride, iron, and manganese, exceeding WHO standards (JICA 1990). The presence of fecal coliform in water is said to exceed the recommended standard in both rivers and shallow groundwater. Future costs related to health hazards would further rise as new externalities continue to affect the poor, which in turn would affect equity in water rights.

These practices of water users show that unregulated water use is on the increase with, among others, the prevalence of the Rower pump. The use of groundwater by consumers to fulfill their immediate demand at one level contrasts with state attempts to secure water supply and regulate access through various legal processes. State attempts to restore the environmental balance in groundwater use through artificial recharge are under way.

Attempts to Secure Safe Water Supply and Regulate Water Access

Since 1974, various legal acts have been codified and amended to expand state control over water resources. The two primary ministries involved in managing water resources coordinate with the central National Planning Commission. These are the Ministry of Water Resources, which is responsible for utilization, allocation, and monitoring of national water resources, and the Ministry of Housing and Physical Planning, which is responsible at the central level for overall planning and development of water supply and sanitation projects in the country. In 1990, the Nepal Water Supply Corporation was established under an enabling act, which made it responsible for managing water supply in major municipalities, including Kathmandu. As the primary agency involved in urban water supply, NWSC is responsible for planning, implementation, operation, and maintenance of water supply and sanitation. However, under the act, it does not have full statutory authority and can be dissolved by His Majesty's Government with the issue of a direct order.

The state institutions that are directly involved in the management of groundwater fall under the Water and Energy Commission Secretariat. These are the Department of Irrigation and the Groundwater Resources Development

Board, which monitors groundwater exploitation and investigation. In addition, the Department of Hydrology and Meteorology is in charge of the collection of hydrological and climatological data. Among most agencies the focus of groundwater management has primarily remained on the irrigation and rural sectors. The responsibility of authorities in dealing with urban groundwater management is not clearly defined. The NWSC's role in the subbasin of Kathmandu appears to be that of a supplier of water rather than a controller of groundwater. Currently, the Melamchi Water Supply Project is spearheading most of the planning for urban water supply. It is quite likely that NWSC will become redundant in the near future.

Nepal does not have a national water quality standard, and effluent standards have not yet been legally mandated and enforced. The Nepal Environment Policy and Action Plan of 1993 provides guidelines for air and water quality standards and provisions for their enforcement. Similarly, under the 1992 Water Resources Act, the government could frame rules or issue orders specifying standards and quality of water for various uses. The 1998 Environmental Protection Act and the 1999 Environment Protection Regulations focus on several environmental issues, including water pollution. Under the NWSC Act, the municipalities are responsible for the control of wastage, leakage, and pollution of water. Under the Local Self-Governance Act, local institutions are responsible for protecting the environment and maintaining sources of clean water. The provisions in various laws indicate that improvement of groundwater control could arise from the development of acts related to hydrological control with an allocative framework for various uses.

Levels of Authority

Three distinct levels of authority operating within the current urban water structure and practices can be identified. At the primary level, state institutions exist and operate within the codified legal system, promulgated and decreed through various orders and acts. At the secondary level, the agencies of water users operate and function mainly through local and customary norms. At the tertiary level, market-driven forces, constituting industries, the commercial sector, and the water markets perform on the basis of private "provisional" norms based on the economics of demand and supply.

At the primary or state level, the Water Resources Act, introduced in 1992, granted to the state ownership of water above and below the ground.[11] That act ranks the order of priority regarding the use of water resources in a list of eight uses. Drinking and household uses of water take precedence over other (agricultural, industrial) uses. The first Water Cess Act was introduced in 1966. The 1966–1992 period marked a process of redefinition of state control and prioritization of rights to water resources. As a consequence of this process, land and water rights came to be separated as distinct rights.

At the local level, according to customary and religious local laws, water was viewed as a common property resource within the domestic arena of use. The first national code (Muluki Ain) was decreed in Nepal in 1854 as a codified written law. This code was amended in 1963. Very little explicit reference is made to water rights in this code. Customary and religious norms still prevail among domestic water users; use of water for drinking is still considered free of cost. The supply from piped systems is primarily used for drinking purposes. Water extracted from the ground is generally perceived as unsuitable for drinking. This perception is based on notions of purity, physical contamination, and pollution. Modern technology is traditionally perceived by some water users as constricting the free natural flow of water, which is then considered to render water conveyed through pipes as spiritually and naturally impure. The extraction of groundwater underneath one's landholding is perceived as appropriation of individualized private property. According to local norms, the state has no claim to water below the ground in individual landholdings, whereas in statutory law state control extends to formal ownership of all water resources.

Private Control and the 1992 Water Resources Act

At the private level, two specific segments of the 1992 act can be analyzed to examine the development of groundwater regimes. First, section four of the act specifically exempts from license the use of water resources for drinking and other household purposes on an individual or collective basis (which was also stipulated in the 1967 act). In this respect, the state actually supports emerging local laws for individual and private extraction. Second, this act exempts from license utilization "in the prescribed manner, water resources confined within one's own land by the landowner." This code further presents a dichotomy between state ownership of water resources and private control. Ownership in practice is granted to the actual landowner for private extraction. The statement also emphasizes the nexus between land and the water underneath one's landholding. This has major implications for the hydrological environment. Domestic water rights are exercised all year around in various ownership forms: communal, private, individualized, and state.

The 1992 act further emphasizes productive water use either through irrigated agriculture or through hydro development. However, both "consumptive" and "productive" domestic needs, which continue to expand and increase water use in a general context of urbanization, industrialization, conflict, migration, and population growth, are being overlooked. This statement is further verified with section 4.3 of the 1992 act, which states that "any individual or corporate body utilizing water resources must do so in a profitable manner by ensuring that such use does not cause any hardships to others." The word "profitable" can, of course, be interpreted in various ways. With reference to the water table and groundwater, simple hydraulics also explain that individualized and private control rights to groundwater derive from the ability to extract water. Such actions are also validated on the basis of one's individual ownership or "provisional" ownership, in the case of leased property, of the land above the water. The use of extractive technology further means that where users depend on a common aquifer, extraction by one owner reduces the supply and therefore access of the next. "Profitable" also refers to access by the commercial, industrial, and water markets for productive uses, where water is essential to the generation of income and revenue. Therefore, the word "profitable" is effective as long as the demand and supply cycle of water remains renewable. Adaptive institutional frameworks and more stringent regulations may be required to ensure that groundwater resources are not exhausted.

Examining the role of law in this specific context, the development of the Water Resources Act and the sections that relate to water rights appear to apply specifically at the higher level. The use of groundwater technology and booster pumps points out certain vacuums in state law that directly relate to issues of governance and management. Certain segments of the act that relate to private control in fact indicate that it does not include issues of water rights in groundwater use, ecology, drinking water, and the domestic sector in the urban sphere. It can be argued here that the act may not be appropriate for urban groundwater uses and domestic uses. Given its primacy as an overarching statutory mandate, it is surprising that these issues are not addressed in the act. Such urban issues will continue to be important, and even become more important in the future, as will also be the case with ecological and hydrological aspects of water use.

Technology Diffusion and the Water Cess Act

Technological interventions to access groundwater resources have been in use in Nepal since historical times. Traditional stone spouts, which date back to A.D. 500, are still in use in urban areas. These communal systems demonstrate a remarkable engineering feat that enabled society to adapt to urban life.[12] These systems make use of conjunctive surface and groundwater sources. As a result, an ecological balance used to be maintained, with subsurface recharge through rivers, manmade lakes and ponds, wells, and springs. Under both state and local laws, water was considered a "common property" resource, organized through communal systems and, to some extent, through the state system for domestic water use. However, with the introduction of a water delivery system in the form of piped water after 1950, the domestication of water began, reshaping access and use patterns.[13] The piped water supplied by the state was not sufficient for the residents of Kathmandu. Therefore, many continued to use the traditional water systems, which were not recognized by the state as sources of water. It was only with the introduction of the 1997 Local Self-Governance Act that local government bodies began to address traditional sources of domestic water, such as stone spouts, as sources of water.[14]

The impact of the introduction of centralized piped water supply on social subcultures took a major turn only in 1966. During this year the first Water Cess Act was introduced in Nepal. This act, among other things, levied fees on the use of piped water. The act altered traditional water regimes, which treated water as a free-flowing fluid to be acquired free of cost. Water was now brought under formal regulatory control of the state. It further highlighted the economic attributes of water through a state delivery system, introducing individualized services as opposed to free communal access. The introduction of the Water Cess Act created two specific regimes: first, a system of piped water, supplied to individual households, for which charges were levied by the state; second, heterogeneous traditional sources of domestic water for which no charges were levied.

The Water Cess Act applied only to those citizens who were connected to the state piped system. It brought in a gradual change in the perception of the value of water, although, most users influenced by local legal conceptions of water rights still acquired water free of cost. The overlap between the state and local laws illustrates that all laws operate within certain boundaries. It also shows that long-held rights and values are not static but evolve through the influences of technology and markets (Boelens and Doornbos 2001). Gradually, from 1966 onward, legal ownership of water was transferred from the community to the state. As mentioned above, this process culminated in the Water Resources Act of 1992. However, ownership of water in private land (*raikar* land), for example, continued to be vested in the landowner. It was not really clear who owned water sources such as rivers and lakes. However, the state did claim ownership rights to water on or in public or state land (Pradhan 2000). On the one hand, state law reflects the state's claim to the right to control use, to demand licenses, and to levy charges. On the other hand, state law grants a degree of independence to the use of technological options in the case of private land. In this process, WEDs and the Rower pump were options that met the needs of the majority of the people, the latter meeting the needs of the less powerful in particular.

Complexity in Regulating Water in Kathmandu

The use of WEDs in the urban sector challenges the notion that groundwater is a common property regime. With the common property assumption, WEDs become legal as long as groundwater remained an open access resource. In the absence of an appropriate framework, however, groundwater is no longer an open access resource but rather is technology-controlled. The issue of equity depends on the power of technology; norms and values pertaining to water use are also impacted by these forms of access. Regulating water is not just about guiding and defining a tariff structure in accordance with various uses and users. Rather than formal rules and laws, variations in type of technology, access to piped sources, and economic capabilities seem to guide urban water users and groundwater use. Yet both the declines in groundwater levels and concerns over the deteriorating quality of water call for a regulatory allocative framework. This concluding section suggests that governance of water in Kathmandu requires recognition of the diverse and interlinked forms of access and technologies. The regulatory allocative framework proposed here reflects the complexity at the structural-legal policy level, the physical service supply and demand level, and the ecosystem-habitat level. Therefore, the integration of these three levels become important in order to understand water rights at these different levels and dimensions. In short, the proposed allocative framework suggests that the water balance for Kathmandu Valley requires a systemic analysis of use, access, and allocation in terms of prioritizing the quantitative limits of water resources in urban water governance. This proposal can be applied, first, by differentiating user groups; second, by defining urban water and groundwater rights and prioritizing urban water uses; and third, by specifying quantitative limits of water withdrawal.

Three immediate observations emerge from an examination of the groundwater situation and current water use and extracting practices in Kathmandu. First, competition among users and uses, in particular between the domestic and the commercial-industrial ones, contributes to the rapid depletion of groundwater resources and negatively affects the ecological balance. The success of future schemes will largely depend on the ability of the scheme to provide equitable allocation to both domestic and industrial consumers. These considerations will depend on the project's capability of instituting an integrated framework, in which the industrial and commercial sectors abandon the unlimited and uncontrolled use of open and free access to groundwater, and adapt to a formal regulatory system. The water diversion scheme of the Melamchi Water Supply Project also considers a system of licensing, metering, and charging for extractions from the shallow aquifers, if the water users are found to be engaged in commercial activities that extract water. It will be very difficult to distinguish between water use for commercial and domestic uses, in particular when most of the houses are already using some sort of extracting device. The same goes for distinguishing between small and big commercial activities, as some of these enterprises are operated from private homes.

Second, state attempts and the existing framework to secure and supply water to urban domestic users do not provide a clear mandate with reference to urban water rights and issues related to groundwater rights for urban use. The current Urban Water Supply Sector Reforms for Kathmandu Valley include

instituting cost recovery and tariff policy, urban water sector policy development, the formulation of a regulatory framework for private sector management, public awareness, groundwater monitoring, and licensing and charging
for use. This chapter suggests that this comprehensive water resources management under private sector management will also require redefining rights to
water and groundwater use based on prioritization of urban use that distinguishes drinking and discretionary water allocation.

Third, people's perceptions of rights and the contradictions between the
different coexisting regulatory frameworks continue to prevent some sections
of society from benefiting from basic state services. Taking into account existing water use traditions and practices remains a challenge, as does the inclusion of new categories of water users such as the Kathmandu renter population.
This chapter also suggests that specifying quantitative limits on groundwater
withdrawals could potentially enhance the provision of basic services to those
who currently rely fully on traditional systems.

The above observations imply that a judicious combination of allocations
will require an integrative approach that accommodates local practices, state
regulation, and the overlaps between the various water uses and users, and
their water rights. It may be necessary to amend existing laws and even to introduce new laws that specify quantitative limits on the withdrawal of water and
create categories of water allocation for different uses.[15] It is suggested here that
asymmetries be minimized by defining boundaries in allocation of water as fundamental, discretionary, provisional, and hydraulic.

Proposing a Framework for Allocation

In the domestic sector in Greater Kathmandu, water is used for a multiplicity of
purposes, such as drinking, cooking, washing vegetables and clothes, bathing,
performing religious rituals, recreation, and so on. In addition, it is used for
commercial and industrial purposes. Among all domestic uses of water, drinking water has always been accorded high value in Nepalese society. This is revealed from both the fields of statutory official law and the local laws. At the
local level, user perceptions and interpretations of rights and allocation are
closely interlinked with demand. If the desired amount is made available by the
state, then the rights of the users are presumed to be sanctioned. Moreover, a
clear-cut hierarchical structure and sectoral allocation of rights denote distinctions between rights of the government, the market, and the users.[16] The right
of the state is perceived as that of a supplier of water of good quality and sufficient quantity.

There is a need to develop law to encompass these different fields of water
access. In the context of Kathmandu, rights to water, depending on the type and
source of delivery system, are perceived by the users as closely connected with
techniques (technologies) of appropriation of water. Therefore, access to water

is closely interlinked with acquisition of rights to particular sources. These can be categorized as, first, a fundamental right; second, a discretionary right; third, a provisional right. Within the broader patterns of water use, the notion of right is further expanded and hypothesized to include, fourth, allocation of water on ecological grounds in order to maintain a balance between extraction and recharge. Fundamental water rights minimally amount to fulfilling drinking, cooking, and ritualistic purposes. Discretionary water rights fulfill other domestic needs, like washing, bathing, and other uses. Provisional water rights refer to the right of industries, the commercial sector, and water markets to extract groundwater for nondomestic uses or for sale for domestic purposes. Finally, hydraulic rights should regulate water extraction to maintain ecological balance.

ALLOCATION AS A FUNDAMENTAL RIGHT. The demand of water for drinking, cooking, and ritual needs is largely perceived at the local level as "free" water, notwithstanding the tariff paid to the state for using this water. This view can, in part, be attributed to sociocultural influences, where the traditional communal systems operate on the assumption that water is a common property resource. The traditional normative systems continue to exert their influence and overlap with contemporary regulations and practices. The need for drinking water is fulfilled by state supply and, to a lesser extent, by the traditional step wells.[17] Individual allocation for this need cannot be reduced even in times of low supply. Thus, this quantity becomes a precondition and a requisite for human existence; "rights" impinge here upon basic human needs. The quantity of one gagri of water per day for drinking, cooking, and ritualistic needs cuts across various socioeconomic groups.[18] Customary values tend to equate this amount to one's fundamental right to water (Regmi 2001). The preferred supply for this use is through conventional pipeline systems, which are considered clean, easy to use, and hygienic. Therefore, the community expects the state to provide this service and to be willing to pay for it. On the other hand, this water is freely shared with friends and neighbors, and to a large extent still continues to be disassociated from present economic value attachments. At times, this amount is even bartered with groundwater.[19] The use of booster pumps is acknowledged as an inequitable practice, as the suction from the pipeline to one house diminishes supply to the neighboring house. In certain water-scarce areas, communities have come together to prohibit the use of these devices, on the ground that communal wells like stone spouts experience low flows. However, the use of booster pumps is prevalent among urban households. There is no legal restriction on the use of this device.

ALLOCATION AS DISCRETIONARY RIGHT. Access to discretionary use of water includes uses for bathing, washing, and maintaining the domestic periphery. The quantity used varies according to class, caste, gender, plot size, ownership, income level, and household consumption. These needs are primarily fulfilled through traditional systems, public standposts and nonconventional sources, and with WEDs. For discretionary use, water from communal sources as open access is preferred, as this is free of cost and state supply cannot meet these requirements. Groundwater is generally not used for drinking purposes. However, it was found that users belonging to the low-income groups sometimes use this water for drinking in times of scarcity. Some wealthy households install water treatment plants in their backyards, usually not visible to the public, and use its water for cooking. The domestic water users perceive their right to water underneath their property as an ownership right. Parallel to this view, the market use of this resource is seen as usufruct, based on economic grounds, where water is acquired free of cost from natural reserves (excluding the installation and service charges in case of private water carriers). Pumping technology grants rights to control resources underneath individual landholdings, on the basis of private investments made for the installation of the artifact. Thus, private and individualized rights are based not only on ownership of urban property but also on the mode in which water is acquired. Variations in size, capacity, and type of technology used for conveyance also affect the discretionary amount used, with shallow pumps extracting a smaller amount than the deeper pumps.

ALLOCATION AS PROVISIONAL RIGHT. Domestic water users often regard the increasing use of groundwater by industries, the commercial sector, and water markets (private trucks) as expropriation of a common resource. The random and rapid extraction by this sector shows many characteristics of self-regulation. However, it is also provisional, without a statutory legal basis for sanctioning or justifying claims, and with no regulatory framework that coherently segregates and addresses domestic users, market needs, and ecological needs. In sum, there is no existing effective legal framework that controls access to this resource. Market-based adaptations and responses to water scarcity supercede the natural recharge cycle. As a consequence, consumption is being reduced not only on a short-term basis; long-term availability in communal and traditional systems is also affected. Daily water extraction through deep boring by industries, private water sellers, hotels, cement factories, and carpet factories is estimated to be 50 MLD per day.[20] Economics is not just a question of demand but is also tied up with supply and reserves. Ecosystem approaches to water governance also link economics with hydrology. Therefore, such approaches should pay due attention to nonmarket forms of regulation and control.

ALLOCATION AS HYDRAULIC RIGHT. The above three allocations of water use signify that acquisition of water is largely based on the ability to access water. Access is further redefined and shaped by the type of technology used. This often shapes and reshapes practices. These choices of technologies reveal social and economic costs incurred by the users, often obscuring the ecological costs. However, long-term water use practices in Kathmandu reveal that the ecological costs are physical, tangible, volatile, and affect the future. Whereas technology use in the form of WEDs may control the environment, in a reciprocal manner the environment also controls the technology. Reduction in surface aquifers leads the users to replace lower capacity pumps or manual pumps such as Rowers with more sophisticated technology, thereby increasing the power and capacity to tap into deeper and confined water tables. The disjunctive use of surface and groundwater depletes not only the water table but also reduces the surface supply. In a judicious use of water, it becomes necessary to integrate groundwater and surface water sources, both being important in processes of environmental change related to water extraction. These linkages also depend on the nature of the soil type, pervious and impervious layers underneath the soil, and other ecological peculiarities. All have their impact on the recharge cycle. In this context, maintaining the hydrological symmetry focuses on treating both surface and groundwater in a complementary manner, taking into account the formation of the entire subbasin of the Kathmandu Valley in which water is stored. Although this suggestion of allocating water as a hydraulic right in abstract terms may sound ambiguous, emphasis is placed on simply ensuring that the natural reserves are not exhausted; thus focusing on an ecosystem approach to water governance.

NOTES

I would like to thank Linden Vincent and Margreet Zwarteveen for their useful comments and suggestions on an earlier version of this paper.

1. It is estimated that the current population of the core urban area of Kathmandu today stands at 892,555, excluding the floating population (estimated at 500,000). The projection for the Kathmandu core area in 2011 is 1,648,984. The actual population might differ from the projected one, as the growth rates were based on the assumed growth rates applied to the 1981 census. This twenty-year-old growth rate assumes an average per annum population growth rate of 3.5 percent for Greater Kathmandu.

2. Kathmandu municipality consists of thirty-five wards. A recent GIS mapping of Kathmandu Valley, undertaken by the municipality, illustrates the density of population in each of these wards. After construction of the Ring Road in 1977, the area surrounded by the Ring Road is termed Greater Kathmandu. In this paper, the area within the municipal jurisdiction of the Kathmandu municipality and the area surrounded by Ring Road are referred to as the core urban area.

3. The surface water sources depend on a network of river systems, which includes the Bagmati, Bishnumati, Dhobi Khola, Hanumante, and Manohara. The main groundwater sources are the wells of Gokarna, Dhobi Khola, Bansbari, Balkhenkhala, Ring Road, Manohara, Pharping, Gongabu, Mahadev Khola, and twenty-one other small-capacity wells.

4. Exchange rate at the time of the research (2001): one US$ - 76.10 NRs.

5. The "free" cost increases when the scarcity value of water is added to include ecological, economic, and social costs, putting an extra burden on the economically less powerful sections of water users.

6. See Regmi 2001. The minimum fundamental requirement of fifteen liters of water for drinking, cooking, and ritualistic uses per person per day is taken as the basic entitlement to water; uses for other needs are defined as discretionary. When the fundamental right is expanded beyond fifteen liters to forty, seventy, or even higher figures, the discretionary portion of requirements or demand also increases.

7. The term WED for water-extracting device is derived and expanded from the terminology used by T. Shah (1993). This author uses water-extracting mechanisms (WEMs) to include combinations of well types such as open dug wells, filter points, bores, deep tube wells, and water-lifting devices such as the Persian wheel, rahat, chadas, diesel pump, and electric pump. WED is used in the context of this chapter to define the extracting and suctioning nature of a pump.

8. The term "renters" is used here in lieu of tenants, as the term "tenants" in a rural context is usually associated with the leasing of land for productive purposes, whereas in an urban domestic context, the space is rented out with the objective of acquiring a shelter. Renters are usually migrants from other districts of Nepal, mostly rural areas, and also include Indian migrants. The Nepalese renter population is generally made up of low-income earners and daily wage laborers. Precise data on the renter population in the valley is not available. The Ninth Plan of Nepal (2000) estimates that over 24 percent of the urban population are renters. Other studies and the Nepal Living Standard give an estimation of 29 percent, with a total of 64,000 households. Our survey in the urban area estimates that the concentration of renters is much higher within the core area.

9. Up to the middle of the eighteenth century, Nepal was divided into small principalities. Prithvinarayan Shah, then king of Gorkha, conquered and annexed these principalities into one Kingdom of Nepal. He was the first king of Nepal and founder of the present Shah Dynasty. After consolidation of Kathmandu Valley from the Malla rulers, Prithvinarayan Shah made Kathmandu the center of his administration. With the relocation of his dynasty and administration from Gorkha, in the central mid-hills of Nepal, to Kathmandu, the original Gorkha-based social and political elite, an entourage of the new king, also moved to this location.

10. The Rower pump was introduced for the first time in Bangladesh by Intermediate Development Enterprises (IDE) in 1980. It made its debut in Kathmandu in 1987, when tubewells made out of galvanized iron (GI) pipes were gradually being diffused in the urban sector as spill off from the irrigation/rural sector. Rower pumps introduced a simple PVC design with no electricity costs. In addition Rower pumps are locally manufactured, and spare parts are easily available. It is estimated that annual sales in Kathmandu surpass 5,000 units of these pumps (personal communication with Munir Hussein, National PVC Pipe). Because of the declining water table in certain areas, the Rower pumps are no longer effective there.

11. Pradhan (2000) analyzes the history of state intervention in and control over water for irrigation and hydroelectricity. Emphasizing that the 1967 act was important in this regard, he shows that there was a gradual increase in state control over water.

12. These systems demonstrate the culmination of an intricate and dynamic network of traditional water utilization methods that comprised a comprehensive design of water conduits. Such systems were by no means egalitarian. Organization, distribution,

and utilization of these resources were based on hierarchies such as the caste system and on geographical boundaries, incorporating governance through divine, cultural, social, and ecological synergy.

13. See Dixit (1997) for historical changes in water uses. According to Dixit, the domestication of water for private use started forty years after the beginning of the Rana regime in A.D. 1840, when a piped water system was built to provide water to private households. For historical developments of domestic water supply vis-à-vis the involvement of the state before and after 1951, see Sharma (2001). Sharma highlights the rise and decline in state involvement in the domestic water supply sector as being inextricably linked to foreign aid. He provides a historical development of the urban water sector before and after 1951, and emphasizes that diffusion of this technology to the lowest rung of society does not occur in practice.

14. The Kathmandu municipality now has the responsibility for maintaining stone spouts, including public traditional wells and step-wells. Few stone spouts within its jurisdiction have been maintained and repaired and, if so, usually with the assistance of various donors.

15. Moench (1992) argues that without specifying quantitative limits on individual water withdrawals, the groundwater markets and water user groups cannot function effectively. However, he has not differentiated between different uses of water, as is proposed here.

16. There is a clear distinction between rights of the government, the houseowners, renters, and neighbors. Although drinking water is freely shared with neighbors and renters, water for other needs is not. Current practices further illustrate that the right to water also varies according to class, caste, and gender (Regmi 2001). Although the right to drinking water, on the one hand, is emphatically linked to religious and customary norms, the discretionary use for other needs is contingent upon one's ability to pay.

17. Some urban households prefer to use the traditional systems because of the "purity" of water. Water from stone spouts is believed to possess curing and healing powers for certain diseases. Other households use these systems for lack of options, given the water scarcity.

18. A gagri is a traditional brass, copper, or clay vessel used for carrying drinking water. A gagri can contain about fifteen liters of water.

19. Interviews around Maruhiti and Asantol areas, which have been the hardest hit by water scarcity, reveal that owners of traditional wells and those with electric pumping devices trade groundwater with each other. Those without access to groundwater provide drinking water from the state system in exchange for groundwater for other uses. Thus, both parties are able to fulfill their needs, groundwater for discretionary use and municipal water for drinking.

20. Adhikari (2001) states that Hotel Everest extracts 700,000 liters of water per day from a depth of 900 feet; Nepal Dairy Development Corporation extracts 100,800 liters per day from 200 feet, and carpet and cement factories extract over 100,000 liters per day through deep boring. There are about seven five-star hotels aside from other star categories within the metropolitan area. Five-star hotels alone use 4.9 MLD of water extracted from deep aquifers. Other figures estimate that over 50 MLD of groundwater is extracted, three times the annual recharge capacity of 15 MLD (JICA 1990).

7

Special Law

Recognition and Denial of Diversity in Andean Water Control

RUTGERD BOELENS
INGO GENTES
ARMANDO GUEVARA GIL
PATRICIA URTEAGA

In the Andean region, norms and practices of peasant and indigenous communities play a key role in local water management. In irrigation, for example, users' groups and organizations have developed—sometimes over centuries—irrigation management practices that incorporate elements from Andean, colonial, and postcolonial water traditions, and contemporary norms and technologies. Both older irrigation systems and new ones, whether "communal," "state-owned," or "private," feature their own specific practices and norms. Therefore, each irrigation system operates by a different set of rules of play.

At the same time, despite the great diversity of particular sociolegal repertoires, local management does not operate in isolation from the national context. "Peasant," "indigenous," and "local" law is interwoven with official-law norms, rules, and organizational forms. Although local community authorities are often the first level of oversight and coordination to materialize water rights and resolve water conflicts, nonetheless people also turn to public rules and authorities representing official law. The existence of normative plurality in water management systems in Andean countries is not a question but an inarguable fact, grounded in the interaction of different normative repertoires for the regulation of water within a given sociopolitical and physical-technical setting (Beccar et al. 2002).

In order to understand the foundations of water management in Andean communities, therefore, there is a need to recognize this pluralism of water rights repertoires and decipher its empirical manifestations. Apart from this analytical dimension of recognition, there is the question of how to deal with this fact in state law and intervention policies, and how to assure that the governmental judicial system recognizes and validates this social phenomenon. This legal-administrative recognition, then, is different from analytical recognition (Boelens et al. 2002). Generally, it has major political-strategic dimensions. Often, it is based on claims by societal groups whose collective rights and particular norms have been denied. They demand greater social and political power, and legal-judicial recognition of their norms and rights. But, inherently, this very process of legal-administrative and political-strategic recognition can—intentionally or not—result in processes that counteract local claims for more autonomy, respect, and decision-making power.

One recurrent way in which legal-administrative recognition has occurred is through the enactment of special law, the focus of this chapter. In the Andean countries' legal systems, agrarian and community laws create particular legal rights especially applicable to the peasant and indigenous populations. As Vidal observes, the historical development of this special legislation has had its own particular trajectory that reflects the recurring recognition and denial of sociolegal diversity (Vidal 1990). Special legislation is commonly grounded in external, essentialized ideological constructs of both "indigenous identity" and "peasant communities" in the Andes. These stereotyped and ideological concepts converge in formal recognition policies to institutionalize local Andean water users' rights and management norms, freezing dynamic local normative systems, reinforcing the process of subordination to other bodies of law, and strengthening the interests of hegemonic players. Thus, the outcome of this recognition may be the oppression or obliteration of local law, codifying it in isolation from its cultural context and slotting it into larger-scale power structures and strategies.

Within the field of special legislation and water management, we focus on the issue of indigenous and peasant legal systems,[1] since this is one of the fields of legal debate that has become most important in the past decade.[2] First, we turn our attention to the legal-administrative context, which in most Andean countries is centralized in regard to water resource management. Next, we briefly present some historical background on legal pluralism in the Andes, highlighting fundamental features of "recognition policies" since colonial times. In the third section, we analyze the interrelatedness between local rights systems and official legislation, and show how they mutually shape and are shaped by each other. We argue that institutionalizing this mutual relationship through special laws or dual legislation does not resolve the inherently conflictive relations between official law and local normative systems. In the next sections we illustrate this position with the cases of Peru and Chile. In the last section, we reflect on the responses of peasant and indigenous communities in the Andes to the problems of institutionalized legal pluralism.

Legal Recognition of Diversity in the Andes: Indigenous Peoples, Peasant Communities, and the Technocratic Legacy

Legal Centralism in Water Resource Management

In most Andean countries it has historically been, and often remains, the state's exclusive prerogative to make laws, rulings, and procedures, and define and allocate water rights. Similarly, control over enforcement of these laws and sanctioning has generally been considered the monopoly of state institutions and agents. A key feature of these laws is that they deny the existence of diverse management approaches and sociolegal repertoires for regulation of water control (cf. Beccar et al. 2002; Bustamante 2002; Gentes 2002; Peña 2004; Urteaga and Guevara 2002). When national laws are drafted, actual water management practices tend to be ignored. Society is portrayed as a homogenous reality, into which no diversity of rights conceptions could fit (see also chapter 5 in this regard). Many concepts and procedures are copied from laws from other countries, and the myth of social and legal engineering is powerful. This myth assumes that by simply enacting and enforcing official laws, the many-faceted reality of water management in the Andes can be molded and homogenized, to create "modern," "efficient," and "rational" management.

A case in point is Ecuador, where the 1972 Water Law and its regulations do not provide any match with existing local management processes, nor is any authority granted to establish rules or organizations responsive to local diversity. Instead, very detailed, uniform prescriptions are stipulated. For example, administration of state irrigation systems over the last few decades has been governed by a single rigid set of regulations—a blanket version covering management of systems throughout a country characterized by extremely diverse zones (coast, highlands and Amazon region) and an enormous variety of irrigated production systems. In spirit and contents, the legal text attempts to turn users' organizations into administrative dependencies of the state agency (see chapter 4 for similar assumptions in Indonesia). National regulations impose a rigid structure to which irrigators must adapt, installing new, artificial forms of leadership and unsuitable organizational structures (Boelens and Doornbos 2001).

Examples similar to Ecuador's Water Law are quite common in the Andes.[3] The ideological basis is that the official law is omnipresent and cannot take particular features of existing norms into account. A fundamental principle is uniform enforcement throughout national territory, based on the proclaimed liberal equality of all the country's citizens before the law. One ideological function of such an equalizing law (Correas 1994) is to create national identity within an "imagined community" (Anderson 1983), a uniform nation in which all parties share similar interests and have the same "natural" objectives regarding water resource management. Torres-Galarza (1995: 59) observes in this regard that "under the law, each party is shapeless, ambiguous, undetermined and, therefore, the legal value that is protected ignores peoples' identities, so that they can be integrated." In practice, although this image of a natural, objective, and neutral normative framework for all is maintained, this "imagined community" in the Andes is based on the interests of a small minority of powerful societal groups. Traditionally, these groups dominate official structures and discourse on water policy and set the standards for this so-called equality. Even after the latest water-sector reforms, the technocratic, legalistic, male-biased, and ethnocentric fundaments of this tradition have persisted as a weighty factor in irrigation policy making and water management.

This liberal argument of equality under the law results in a myth in legal practice, as manifested, for instance, in the capacity of hegemonic sectors to legally manipulate conflicts over natural resources (Urteaga Crovetto 1998). Still, the ideology of the equality argument effectively counteracts the demands of various ethnic and societal groups for *genuine* recognition of the right to be different. This ideology delegitimizes water management according to autonomous local norms and organizations. Problems of water distribution that are grounded in ethnic identities and social relations thus get reduced to mere questions of inclusion and exclusion. Consequently, it is often concluded that occurring problems are caused by the indigenous and peasant communities' backwardness and lack of access to official legislation, since these population groups are fixed to their own traditional water management systems and also lack modern inputs and education. Official discourse suggests that these people will be included though instruments like legal training courses, improvement of the means of communication, and legal and institutional access (through rural development). Along with their users' organizations, they are considered marginalized and excluded from the general normative system, and consequently from the social benefits of national society. So there is an assumed need for educating the uneducated and for consciousness-raising to include the "excluded."

The Politics of Recognition in Historical Perspective

Andean countries have not always followed this monojuridical, monocultural model. During the first two centuries after the conquest, the legal situation and practice regarding water management and indigenous rights changed frequently and in a complex manner. In some parts of the Andes, the encomienda system entailed a sort of indirect government and a tax model to extract local wealth, while maintaining administration by ethnic groups. However, there are also regions and periods in which most indigenous communities' water rights were usurped directly by Spanish settlers (landlords, miners, and others), denying local management systems and norms for their leftover water rights.

Faced with this situation of extraction and usurpation in addition to massive rights abuse and genocide, the Spanish Crown reacted from early on by enacting official law that contained an ambivalent legal model. It was the result of the contrary positions of metropolitan elites regarding the human condition of indigenous peoples in the Americas (see also chapter 5). They wondered whether the "natives" could be considered human beings, whether they had the capacity and norms to respect and obey "human and divine laws," and sufficient capacity to govern themselves with legitimate authorities. Or should they, because of their "natural inferiority," be governed by special laws emphasizing social segregation and political exclusion. The system established as a result of this polemic was discriminatory but designed to protect Indians from other colonial agencies. Indians were "miserable but human." Ignorant but descendants of and closer to the natural state of Divine Grace, they deserved not to be enslaved but to be cared for. For this purpose, a parallel legal system was set up: the Republic of Indians, complementary to the Republic of Spaniards. This administrative and judicial system was to protect the legal affairs of the Indians. Colonial law was established in paternalistic, clientelist terms, and the indigenous had to operate under both legal systems. In this regard, both juridical plurality and interlegality (Santos 1995) were daily situations of the colonial world. It was certainly exclusive, but not dichotomous (Guevara 1993). Indeed, amid the period of the greatest exploitation and usurpation of indigenous communities' water rights, their "rights, uses, and customs" were also defended by the Laws of the Indies and by decisions of the Crown. Moreover, colonial legislation ordered the Spaniards themselves (in 1536) to follow the modes of distribution and allocation of water historically practiced by the "natives." It formalized a sort of norm of turning to the indigenous custom. However, this was gradually abandoned and omitted from subsequent laws.[4]

Obviously, practice often differed from the law, and there were also many rebellions by colonial entrepreneurs against the "protective" law sent from Spain, since it reduced their capacity to exploit. In the following decades, after the unprecedented starvation of millions of people, Viceroy Francisco de Toledo, in 1570, enacted his well-known ordinances to establish the Reductions: artificial towns in which the indigenous survivors were concentrated in order to make sure of their political and cultural subordination and economic exploitation. Reductions had their own, segregated jurisdiction and authorities, although only to deal with minor conflicts (Yrigoyen Fajardo 1998). Soon after, the land composition process (1594) followed, which consolidated colonial haciendas' rights to reallocated water. Since then, official water distribution was increasingly discriminatory against indigenous communities, forcing them to adapt to outside regulations.

With independence from Spain in the early nineteenth century, this colonial model of expropriation was legitimized on the basis of nation-state law and liberal ideology. In general principle, this law was based on state monopoly over the legitimate use of violence (Correas 1994), and the merging of identities between state and law. Apparently the new model fit in well with traditional feudal relationships in rural areas: the haciendas became much more powerful by the end of the nineteenth century, eliminating or marginalizing indigenous rights and forms of water management. At the national level, an "ideology of equality" was formulated in terms of a major political undertaking of racial mixing (*mestizaje*). It standardized all inhabitants of the nation under the model of the white-mestizo hegemonic groups, with regard to cultural codes, norms, and even physical aspects (Albó 2002; Assies et al. 1998; Baud et al. 1996; Stavenhagen and Iturralde 1990).

Later, largely due to the influence of indigenist currents of thought, this assimilation model was combined with an integration model (Yrigoyen Fajardo 1998).[5] This attempted to grant indigenous communities more rights and integrate them into a market system, to enable them to share in the benefits of "modern" society. Although certain indigenous cultural norms were taken more seriously, even in legislation, this did not affect the ideology and sovereignty of the national government's political administration. The approach of normalizing and equalizing the "inferiors" to fit them into the white-mestizo hegemonic groups' model was combined with a paternalistic and civilizing approach geared to "supporting the backward," recognizing certain traditional norms, folk customs, and individual rights.

Current Changes in Recognition Policies

During the last decade, there has been a major change in the laws of most Andean countries. The constitutions of Colombia, Peru, Bolivia, and Ecuador now formally recognize cultural diversity and legal pluralism. They grant legal validity, to different degrees and in varying breadth, to indigenous peoples' own jurisdictions, to peasant and indigenous communities' own norms and authorities, and to self-governance within their own territories (cf. Guevara et al. 2002; Palacios 2002).[6] Yet, such general changes regarding recognition of diversity are not reflected either in the "powerful" water laws or agrarian laws. Despite the great importance of the many ways of managing water for local economies and societies, they are still denied legal existence. In Bolivia, version 33 of the proposal for a new water law is being discussed but there are no signs of reaching agreement on water rights issues that are fundamental to the peasant and indigenous populations. In Peru, in a similar way, enacting a water law that would respect peasant and indigenous rights and the country's diversity is far from reality. In Chile the hegemonic sectors with water rights monopolies have managed to prevent any legal change that would increase social justice, environmental balance, and political democracy (Dourojeanni and Jouravlev 1999). In Ecuador, the Confederation of Indigenous Nationalities of Ecuador (CONAIE) had led a process to formulate a proposal for a new water law that recognizes Ecuador's diversity in peoples, regions, and water management institutions (CONAIE 1996).[7] However, actualization and operationalization of these rights may well take a long time because of resistance by vested interest groups. According to Nina Pacari, indigenous leader and minister of foreign affairs in Ecuador (in 2003):

> At this time, regarding the Water Law, we have preferred to suspend debate, because an unfavorable correlation of forces in Congress could upset the indigenous peoples' efforts to defend better water distribution. Market and privatization theory prevails, and in this context, [these power groups] would achieve a legal instrument instead that would smooth the way to materializing as soon as possible their profit-seeking, market-driven goals, which would by no means be a contribution to Ecuadorian society. From this standpoint, we feel that it is preferable to keep our proposal on stand-by and continue, for the time being, with the law we have at present. (Personal communication, Pacari 2002)

This last remark seems to be crucial: to what degree do legal changes for recognition and implementation thereof in society have political and social support? How can these new provisions be reproduced beyond the constitution, in "strong" legislation (such as water law), in public administration and procedures, and daily water management practices? And to what degree are new legal changes actually responsive to demands for greater local autonomy and self-governance in water management?

Special Legislation in the Andean Countries

Whereas in other studies on water resource management we have focused on the issue of legal complexity within local systems, in this chapter we pay particular attention to the multiple layers, spheres, or legal orders within positive law, a form of intrasystemic legal pluralism (Guevara 2001). We approach the issue by analyzing the multiple legal orders existing in Peruvian and Chilean legislation and their confrontation with local water management practice in peasant and indigenous communities. The question of dual legislation and special laws is central. In water rights, several laws are generally relevant, such as agrarian law, water law, and environmental law, each with its own particular regulations and prescriptions. In addition, governmental law often establishes other laws that also influence natural resource management. This is the case of special laws to protect, regulate, and legally recognize societal stakeholders such as peasant communities and indigenous peoples. Often their purpose is to formally protect or sanction the management modes and rights of these groups.

Before turning to the cases, it is useful first to analyze some fundamental and inherent problems of this special law, which itself is product of a "forced engagement" between official and local law systems.

Local and Positive Law: "Mutual" Recognition and "Shotgun Marriage"

Despite interaction and overlapping among the different semi-autonomous normative systems for water management, they have very different functions, uses, and characteristics. National government law is formulated to regulate water resource management throughout the country, whereas local normative systems operate within certain localities and water management systems.[8] The origin of governmental law (based on the colonial laws of Spain and the Napoleonic Code, and more recently on liberal codes) also differs greatly from those normative systems, which have originated in indigenous and rural communities. But, as was mentioned, although Andean customs and traditions can inform peasant and indigenous irrigation practices and norms, they can not be considered as the only sources of local norms and law. The latter are basically a set of contemporary norms, geared toward establishing control among the members of a societal group. These norms are dynamic, constantly undergoing reformulation and transformation. In this dynamic process of creation and recreation of water rights within semi-autonomous normative contexts (cf. S. F. Moore 1973), one can identify a multitude of sources of legal rights and spaces for reproducing norms (see also chapters I and II). These spaces are located both within and outside Andean communities and irrigation systems. It often happens that certain rules considered local and Andean are actually official or colonial norms appropriated and internalized, with certain changes, by communities. For this very reason, local law (whether indigenous, peasant, or other) cannot be conceived of as a normative repertoire either preexisting governmental law or autonomous vis-à-vis the state. Local law in the Andes assumes the presence of government law, and defines itself in contrast and relation to it, in terms of concepts and specific contents (Boelens and Doornbos 2001; Guevara 2001).

We can turn this conclusion around, however: an observation that is usually neglected, especially in legalistic, positive-law analyses, is that governmental law also, although differently, grounds its existence and survival in the presence and constitution of multiple local sociolegal repertoires. Several governmental laws have silently acknowledged this fact, when faced with the problem that the law loses legitimacy in practice; official justice is seen as inadequate in many specific cases. Legal rules are general, whereas concrete cases are particular. Positive law, then, is not sufficient for doing justice in particular situations, and the need emerges to move from one body of law to the other. In several cases, customary law has been used, and in other cases this second set of principles has been institutionalized and codified. This has not replaced the positive-law set of rules, but simply complemented and adapted it. In fact, it is ironic that justice (that is, the official legislation model) has often survived thanks to the equity and acceptability of customary laws that were incorporated (Schaffer and Lamb 1981; Boelens 2003). Hence both need each other, base their existence and survival on mutual interaction and recognition, and are engaged in a "shotgun marriage."

Customary laws and practices are sometimes incorporated into national law by decrees that operate, to some degree, as special laws. Here, official legislation includes special norms that are enacted solely for certain societal stakeholders and relationships, often in order to leave the official constitutional norm unmodified. However, this "institutionalized equity" is a contradiction in terms. It almost automatically leads to an ironic situation in which the common-law or customary rules become a general formalized system, which takes away their nature of suitability, acceptability, relevance, and being fair in particular cases (cf. Schaffer and Lamb 1981). Indigenous sociolegal repertoires make sense only in a particular, dynamic context, whereas national law demands stability and continuity. Indeed, there is a danger of freezing customary and indigenous rights systems by incorporating them into relatively static, universal governmental law, in which local principles lose their identity and their capacity for renewal, and become useless (cf. F. von Benda-Beckmann et al. 1998; Roth 2003). Moreover, local rights frameworks may face assimilation and subsequent marginalization when they are legally recognized. And it is not uncommon to see that only those customary rights, peasant rules, or indigenous norms that fit into governmental legislation are officially recognized, thereby muzzling the complex variety of "unruly rules" through legal recognition.

Here, we focus on three interrelated issues that throw into doubt the effectiveness of special law in safeguarding peasant and indigenous water rights. First, we analyze how legislation makes use of simplified and stereotyped constructs that misrepresent peasant and indigenous organizational forms, identities, and natural resource management dynamics. Second, we show how these essentialized constructs are being used politically to freeze, subordinate, or delegitimize (illegalize) the diversity of locally existing sociolegal repertoires. We then continue, third, with showing the ambiguous discourses within dual (plural) national legislation; although, officially, the different bodies of law have equal validity and power and should be internally consistent, in water resource management practice there often is an informal hierarchy among these multiple and contradicting fields of governmental legislation. This is used and extended by powerful actors in order to strategically select the—for them—most convenient legal options (Urteaga Crovetto 1998; Gentes 2000). We use the cases of Peru and Chile to illustrate and discuss these three points.

Water and the Peasant Community: The Case of Peru

On the face of it, the centralized and monojuridical legal system of Peru seems to have changed in the direction of plurality and decentralization through recognizing local and indigenous rights. Peru's 1993 constitution (Art. 2.19) recognizes that all persons are entitled to their ethnic and cultural identity. On the basis of this principle, the state recognizes and protects the nation's ethnic and cultural plurality. Moreover, Quechua, Aymara, and other native languages are, in addition to Spanish, officially recognized in areas where they are predominant (Art. 48). These rights are supported by Article 89, which obliges the state to respect native and peasant cultural identity. The constitution also recognizes the legal existence and corporate status of communities, specifying that they are autonomous in their social, economic, and administrative organization, in community work, and in deciding about their land. In the juridical-administrative structure, the constitution (Art. 149) grants authorities of native and peasant communities the power to exercise judicial functions within their territory, applying their own customary laws, provided that fundamental human rights are not violated. Further, the recent amendment to Chapter 14 on decentralization, regions, and municipalities includes norms to promote the right to political participation (Art. 2.17) of native communities and "original peoples" in setting up regional and municipal councils (Guevara et al. 2002).

In water management, however, these progressive legal principles do not seem to apply. Although ethnographic studies have provided abundant evidence of the fact that Andean communities administer water according to their own dynamics, applying a wide variety of normative repertoires (e.g. Gelles 2000; Guevara 2005; Guillet 1992; Urteaga et al. 2003), national legislation and public policies in Peru deny, ignore, or only barely acknowledge the existence of these rural and indigenous norms. At best, there is a timid legal recognition, subordinated to the white-mestizo nation-state's centralization, homogenization, and modernization policies. For water governance and management, even throughout the privatization era of the 1990s, the paternalistic system remains firmly in place (see also Gelles and Boelens 2003).

In recent decades, prior to the wave of privatization, the governmental norms created not only guidelines for water management but also public institutions to implement these directives, in order to manage water more directly. In 1940, the government created the Central Water Council and established the first official procedures for rural water administration. Community organizations were legally deprived of their responsibility for water supply, which formally came to lie with a "technical administrator" in charge of overseeing a great number of water use systems. This official of the Ministry of Agriculture was to make an inventory of irrigated land with formal rights, assure that irrigation would serve only those lands, and make granting of water rights

conditional on tax payment. At the same time, governmental law called for appointing water distributors for each community, with a salary provided by the
national government (Guevara 2005).

The General Water Law (Decree Law 17,752, 1969), still in force, declared all
water sources to be state property. Though, like Ecuador's water law, it contained certain major improvements over previous laws, and though subsequent
official proposals were made to further distributive justice (del Castillo 1994,
2001), it was completely based on the reality of Peru's coastal region. This political and geographical area has water management systems, needs, and cultures
that are totally different from those of the Andean and Amazon regions. The law
ignored any other form of organization, imposing a single model regardless of
geographical, productive, and sociocultural differences. It codified water user
organizations (irrigators' commissions), and legally imposed their establishment in every community. A technocratic system was enacted to define water
rights and internal distribution in communities: a "rational" and "efficient" distribution based solely on technical criteria such as crop water requirements,
soil types, and micro-climates in each irrigation administration (see chapter 4
for similar enactments in Indonesia). The one-dimensionality of these technical
criteria is alien to Andean social irrigation reality.

The official nomenclature was accepted in most communities (users'
board, irrigators' commission, irrigators' committee, and so on) but not necessarily the contents.[9] Different authors have different opinions about the effects
of this imposition of administrative water management models on Andean
communities. Montoya, for example, maintains that the law undermined existing community structures and norms in Puquio, and that peasants did not realize that they were gradually losing community control over water. He also
claims that this bureaucratized water management reinforced the com-
moditization of water rights and relations, by replacing most community work
by the cash payment of fees. In fact, he identifies this law as one of the most
important factors in the progressive decomposition of community structures
(Montoya 1979). Gelles (1998, 2000), in the analysis of the communities of
Cabanaconde, and Guillet (1992), in the analysis of irrigation in Lari, also look at
state attempts to strengthen control over Andean communities by setting up
local forms of water bureaucracy, and by codifying management norms and
forms. However, they feel that the "success" has only been partial. Many communities have resisted the institutionalization process or adapted it to their
own interests and organizational forms (see also Mayer 2002; Urteaga and
Guevara 2002). Most studies conclude that local elites in the neighborhood of
peasant communities are usually among those who most ferociously push for
formalization of water management in accordance with the governmental
model. The reason is that, unlike most local collective rules and community
rights systems, installation of formal institutions facilitates outsider political

control over water management and local production processes (see also chapter 3 for a comparison with the United States).

The General Water Law makes no mention of peasant and indigenous user rights, but simply prescribes a uniform treatment for all those whom the law calls "users" (Art. 12). Since there are no references to peasant or indigenous communities, these must organize as irrigators' commissions, join the respective users' boards, and apply for official recognition from the technical administrator of the Irrigation District (Art. 60), in order to retain or gain official water rights. This goes side by side with the provisions of another legal instrument that is very important for the Peruvian Andes, the General Law on Peasant Communities (Law 25,656, 1987). This law, as we explain below, codifies a simplified notion of "the community." The two laws, on water and peasant communities, are connected in a way that subtly links existing peasant and indigenous water user communities to both a top-down water administrative framework, and an essentialized legal framework for peasant and indigenous recognition: the irrigators' commission is established as a specialized committee within the codified community. "Organizations constituted within the community, such as irrigators' committees, mothers' clubs, peasant rounds, credit committees, and other similar ones, have the status of Specialized Committees" (Art. 73). Thus, national legislation not only prescribes legal irrigation management forms but also relates them to the elementary form of peasant and indigenous organization, the community. Where the General Water Law denies the existence of this basic institution, the General Law on Peasant Communities seeks to codify and relate it with official water management.

This codification is supposedly based on existing organizational forms. The General Law on Peasant Communities defines "peasant community" (*comunidad campesina*) as a public-interest organization with a legal existence and corporate status, comprising families living in and controlling certain territories, linked by ancestral, social, economic, and cultural relationships, expressed in communal ownership of land, communal work, mutual assistance, democratic governance, and pursuit of multisectoral activities, geared toward their members' full self-realization and that of the country. This definition is closer to the mythology created by the early-twentieth-century indigenists than to realities as experienced by community members (Guevara 2005).

The legal definition of peasant communities and their members determines how the special law is applied. In this regard, the most important legal texts are the 1984 Civil Code, the 1978 Native Communities Law, and the 1987 General Law on Peasant Communities. In the Civil Code, recognition is subject to a series of conditions established by the code's articles: "for communities to exist legally, in addition to registration in the respective roster, they must be officially recognized" (Art. 135). "The Executive Branch shall regulate the status of communities, which officializes their economic and administrative autonomy, as well as the rights and obligations of their members and other norms for their recognition, registration, organization, and operation" (Art. 137). In turn, the General Law on Peasant Communities establishes that, to obtain recognition and official registration of their corporate status, communities must possess their territory, have the other characteristics defined in the law, and the consensus of at least two-thirds of their membership. Additionally, to obtain title to their territory, communities need to present "official evidence" that accredits their claim.[10]

The apparently full recognition that the 1993 constitution establishes for the legal existence and corporate status of peasant communities evidently runs up against the barriers of the Civil Code and the Law of Peasant Communities, which impose the prerequisite of official registration and recognition by administrative agencies. Moreover, although it could be construed that the constitution overrides the lower-ranking laws, in day-to-day legal practice communities can operate with any chance of success only when they have accredited their official registration and recognition, as outlined above for water users' organizations.

In practice, then, recognition of peasant and indigenous communities by the state is a necessary step, since their existence must be proven by a series of legal procedures. Otherwise, they do not exist under the law, and therefore are not entitled to the rights granted by it. Something similar happens with Amazonian indigenous communities that have been legally classified as native communities. Many rural groups, self-defined for decades as peasant or indigenous communities, are involved in lengthy procedures, but have not yet received their official classification notice—sometimes with serious consequences for the defense of their rights to natural resources, and access to loans and public resources.

In the last decade's neoliberal era, this governmental, patronizing guardianship of rural communities has been limited to some degree, but it is clear that this "flexibilization" happens precisely in those domains that weaken the collective capacity of communities to defend their natural resources (see also chapter 5). The reduction of the constitutional guardianship achieves the goal of incorporating communal land and water rights into the market economy. Similarly, although the 1993 constitution recognizes the right of rural and indigenous community authorities to administer justice and natural resources according to their customary laws, the law does not recognize a local right to regulate or exclude third parties that utilize these resources. What has been written with one hand has been erased with the other. Thus, if conflicts arise, there is no effective legislative protection or recognition to enable communities to make use of their local jurisdiction over the resources they control (Urteaga and Guevara 2002).

In general, changes in the General Law on Peasant Communities have not altered the essentialist concept of rural communities under the previous law. The legal change was not made to adapt the concept to the current complex rural reality, but mainly to thrust rural communities into the market, to make it easier to break them up and sell their land. In the specific case of water, market liberalization has not yet happened because the current legislation is public-service–oriented. It is being used by major sectors of rural society, in particular the peasant and indigenous communities, to oppose full privatization of water resources. The numerous draft laws discussed since 1993, with the purpose of making special law fit into the constitutional framework, however, argue that water management must be freed from bureaucratic red tape by expanding local organizations' room for action, and carry the political agenda of (neo)liberalism. Before outlining some central conclusions regarding the politics of recognition of local water rights and management frameworks in Peruvian legislation, we first present some insights in the case of Chilean legislation and recognition policies.

Water and the Indigenous Law: The Case of Chile

In Chile, as in the other Andean countries, legal pluralism results not only from the interaction among the state legal system and multiple local sociolegal repertoires. It also originates in the different spheres of formal legislation itself: laws that, for example in the field of indigenous water management, tend to overlap and sometimes contradict each other. Although this phenomenon of dual legislation is characteristic of all countries with special laws for certain subjects or particular players, in Chile it creates an especially anxious situation. Under its neoliberal water law and policy model, the contradictions among the different bodies of law are enormous.

A clear example of legal-normative conflict is the friction between provisions on water management in the Water Code (or, worse, the Mining Code) as against those of the Indigenous Law (or the Environmental Foundations Law). In their legal conceptions and judicial practice, it is easy to detect which of the fields of social and political power in Chilean society underlying these bodies of law is more powerful. We now present a sketch of the 1981 Water Code and its contents and spirit, and of the 1993 Indigenous Law. We analyze the interaction between the two in concrete field cases.

THE WATER CODE. The 1981 Water Code anchored three principles in Chilean legislation, which we review more extensively below: freedom in ways of utilizing water, the granting of private and tradable water rights free of fee payment obligations, and a limited role for the state and governmental institutions. The military junta's neoliberal ideology markedly influenced the different legal amendments. Profit-seeking sectors of the economy (including mining) were favored, and traditional collective economies were legally circumscribed.

Although formally the state remained owner of all water resources, its judicial powers were sharply curtailed. Conflict resolution was transferred from public to private jurisdiction. Conflicts among water rights holders had to be resolved according to regulations of civil law. Because of the high costs and legalistic tradition connoted by civil lawsuits, indigenous and rural communities generally cannot make use of this law. When they do claim water rights, their attempts are often frustrated.[11] With the enforcement of the Code previous rights were partly assumed as binding and partly regulated. To maintain their rights, communities were forced by the new law to register their local rights in the formal property owners' records. Thus customary water access rights were subordinated to positive law, and most of them were codified on behalf of individual owners.

In the code, water rights are separated from land rights and transformed into a tradable commodity. In practice, acquired water rights, as defined in the law, have the status of private property. To further facilitate the transfer from one type of use to another, legal priorities for water allocation (in the previous 1969 law) were eliminated. This, for instance, allows the transfer of water from subsistence-level irrigation or domestic and community drinking water supply to more profitable uses such as industries (see chapter 11).

When several rights applications for the use of the same water sources are presented simultaneously, the concession may be auctioned off to the highest bidder. Again, the commercial function of water prevails over its social functions and uses. Moreover, the code establishes that once water rights have been delivered, there are no new charges (such as taxes) for holders or obligations that prompt them to use the water effectively or beneficially. Rather than the intended increase in water use efficiency, the law paved the way for, and indirectly even encouraged, intense speculation. It did not establish any financial or legal impediments to monopolization of this liquid gold, especially in arid and semiarid regions. As droughts increase, along with the demand for water by industry and mining, a public resource has become a tradable raw material divided into commodity shares (Gentes 2000).

In general, indigenous water problems were largely ignored in the 1980s. It was only in the 1990s that the public at large realized that indigenous peasants, with only a few exceptions, had no registered water rights. Attempts to apply for new rights were frustrated, either because no water was available in the main watercourses or because water rights had already been allocated to large farmers, agroindustries, and mining and logging companies. In many cases, complete settlements that had previously had natural access to water were now given restricted and irregular access. Direct effects are the abandonment of farming, and emigration to mining zones and coastal cities. The new status of water caused major conflicts within indigenous communities (*ayllu*) and peasant communities, as well. Local water distribution regulations were overlaid by new market practices. For most local people, the current law is not only unclear but also unknown. Some people take advantage of this situation. Thus, water resources join the supply-and-demand circuit, competing on a macro level with major mining companies, while on a micro level there are disputes between water rights–owning private parties and the ayllu inhabitants (cf. Muñoz 1999). Moreover, the individualization of formerly collective rights and management systems has created internal chaos.

THE INDIGENOUS LAW. To counteract the drastic consequences of neoliberal legislation for indigenous peoples, a special law was enacted in 1993, the Indigenous Law (No. 19, 253). Strict codification of indigenous rights is what this law is about. Articles 9–11 grant indigenous peoples and associated institutions legal status, constituting a new private right–holder: the indigenous community. Article 12 also guarantees protection of personal and collective indigenous property, once entered in a governmental register. Therefore, infractions against the provisions of the Indigenous Law can be penalized pursuant to the Criminal Law Code (Art. 467).

The special law recognizes that land is the cornerstone of the existence and culture of indigenous peoples. The Indigenous Land and Water Fund is created to guarantee, among other things, the constitution, regularization, or purchase of water rights or to finance projects to obtain water resources (Art. 20). The law also establishes the Indigenous Development Fund to finance, among others, concessions for fishing and fish farming. Water on indigenous community land, such as rivers, canals, ditches, and springs, are considered goods belonging to and to be used by indigenous communities, without precluding third-party registered rights. It is forbidden to grant new water rights over lakes, ponds, springs, rivers, and other aquifers supplying water to indigenous communities, without guaranteeing a normal water supply to the communities affected.

Although the Indigenous Law has managed to fill some gaps in the Water Code, the effects remain questionable. For example, it continues to be difficult to substantively defend indigenous rights against third parties or to register exclusive indigenous water concessions (cf. Aylwin 1997; Toledo-Llancaqueo 1996). In Chile, specific indigenous rights have always been granted by special laws or decrees, whereas the constitution has maintained silent. In the case of water use, the regulatory framework for indigenous rights is weak. Many indigenous organizations feel that the Indigenous Law is a dead letter: it fails to resolve the countless conflicts regarding territorial and natural resource demands (Gentes 2003).

In concrete terms, the Indigenous Law is grounded in an essentialist concept of "indigenousness" and disregards the dynamic nature of identity, local rights systems, legal pluralism, and cultural diversity. It does not distinguish between the internal characteristics of ethnic groups throughout the country; classic and traditional Andean concepts are applied regarding "the community," and processes that have altered territories, local economies, and household systems are not taken into account (Toledo-Llancaqueo 1996).

Perhaps a more fundamental problem relates to the difficulty of protecting collective community laws in an overall neoliberal framework that destroys collective organization and favors individual and private rights. Government agencies assume that indigenous groups must either fit into the market or count themselves out of the process of globalization. Economically profitable projects often get priority. For example, regarding the building of dams and other large-scale water projects in indigenous territory, there is currently (again) the chance of coercive action by the government. The state is hardening its attitude toward demanding sectors. It enforces national security laws, while also seeking dialogue and negotiation "aside from the official law," granting importance to "family cases" (not collective cases) and compensating indigenous families that have been affected. This undoubtedly contributes to breakups within communities (Gentes 2002). In this context, stronger sectors can interpret and take advantage of dual legislation according to their own political and economic interests.

INTERACTION BETWEEN THE WATER CODE AND THE INDIGENOUS LAW. In the practical legal hierarchy—parallel to the political and economic hierarchies—there are strong and weak laws. The Water Code, neoliberal and business-oriented, is very powerful, even though, in jurisdiction and legal practice, it is usually overridden by the Mining Code. For example, Articles 110 and 111 subordinate water rights to a legal mining concession, authorizing access to both surface and underground water. Since 1993, this multiple legal marginalization of indigenous communities faces contradiction in the Indigenous Law, which stresses special protection of water for indigenous groups. But, at the same time, it establishes that, in any event, this must not interfere with water rights that have already been registered pursuant to the Water Code.

One point of friction with the Indigenous Law is clear immediately: the state is bound to oversee and protect new land and water concessions obtained thanks to the Indigenous Development Fund. However, the state represents various positions (interests in mining, irrigation, logging, and hydropower) that often are in conflict with indigenous rights and recognition, and the Indigenous Law in practice submits to economically demanding laws (Toledo-Llancaqueo 1996). In addition, indigenous resources protected by the government remain dependent on the fund's administration and demands, which are extremely limited. Further, indigenous communities have limited "economic competitiveness": although they may own the formal right to water in their territory for future use in local strategic development, shortage of public funding does not always make this possible (see also chapter 3 for a discussion of the role of public funding in the United States). The transitional provisions of the Water Code stipulate that a use right already registered but unused by the owner may be transferred to a third party if the latter has, for five years, freely, openly and without violence utilized that resource (Arts. 1–2). This mainly benefits large mining companies. They often use water reserves that, theoretically, belong to communities. However, the latter often cannot use the water for technical and financial reasons.

The existence of "dual legislation" (Water Code versus Indigenous Law), along with the complex interpretation of the Water Code, offer an open field for finding legal loopholes to favor dominant sectors. The imbalance of powers and the passive policy of priorities can be illustrated by examples of legal provisions (in case of contradictions, the stronger laws prevail) and the practice of third parties who manipulate collective rights (cf. Gentes 2000).

The state, as owner, shareholder, and grantor of mining concessions, is directly interested in "suitable, convenient mining exploration and exploitation" (Mining Code, Art. 120).[12] The national panorama is completed by international jurisdiction. There is a tendency to establish bilateral and multinational treaties, which bring increasing pressure on local population groups to enable companies to openly tap their water resources.[13] The seriousness of transnationalization of water business is, among others, shown in the proposal of a law to export water from Bolivia (mainly from peasant communities and indigenous territories) to Chile.[14] Many mining companies continue to tap aquifers around the wetlands that are the water source for many indigenous communities in northern Chile. Water rights of indigenous peoples in southern Chile are also encroached upon, especially by forest plantation projects. In their conflicts with hydropower and mining companies, indigenous peoples receive hardly any protection from the Indigenous Law.

There is undoubtedly a major paradox in Chile's neoliberal model: along with neoliberal economists, it is precisely the business sectors that are pushing for strong rights for indigenous and peasant communities. In practice, these become a dead letter, since the objective of these powerful actors is not to defend local rights and indigenous autonomy but to provide a broad catalogue of legal certainties for outside investors in rural areas and indigenous territories. The water rights market and investment in water resources, according to them, cannot operate if there are local and customary rights that are not registered but do entail a certain legal protection. Therefore, they seek ways to motivate all water users to register their rights. On that basis, they drive public policy geared to make users participate in a market system of tradable water rights (Gentes 2002).

Special Law: Essentialized Constructs
and de facto Legal Subordination

In this section we draw some basic conclusions regarding the lack of effectiveness of special law in defending or extending peasant and indigenous water rights. As we have mentioned, we focus on three pitfalls: first, the fact that special legislation tends to create essentialized constructs that do not represent the dynamic character of peasant and indigenous identities and rights frameworks; second, the danger that these simplified constructs, once codified in national regulations, are being converted (consciously or not) into political tools for freezing and subordinating the existing diversity of water rights and local normative frameworks; and, third, the fact that dual national legislation tends to facilitate power plays in which dominant actors use and extend an informal hierarchy among "strong" and "weak" legislative fields and so strategically push for the legal options and outcomes most convenient to them.

Politics of Representation: Social Construction
of "Indigenous" and "Community"

Since the early twentieth century, lawmakers, policy makers, and scholars have used different approaches to analyze and regulate "the indigenous question" and the issue of "peasant communities" in the Andean region. At one extreme are the modernizers, liberals, or progressives, who strive to change the agrarian reality at any cost, including cultural costs. At the other extreme, radical Indianists and proponents of recovering Andean culture and technology postulate a romantic environmentalism that places Andean peoples beyond history and near an autarkic utopia.[15] Such concepts as "Andean," "native," "indigenous," and "peasant" have been, and still are, fragmented through projection of stereotyped images by many currents of thought. These essentialized constructs have often served in official identity politics (for example, to validate segregationist policies, to justify ethnonationalism, or to legitimize biopolitical mestizaje), but they were also used as political and cultural tools of identification by marginalized groups. Rights were, and are, often claimed on the basis of indígena or campesino identity—but what distinguishes this identity is not straightforward. Whereas "peasant" is a socioeconomic category, "indigenous" is used to refer to ethnic and cultural properties in Andean society; but the boundaries are fluid in the Andes and strongly depend on place, time, people, and the political purpose of defining.

Indeed, the linking of identity to (re)distribution automatically pulls ontological and boundary questions about identity into the politics of water control. Differences in conceptualization have inspired varying public policies and agendas. Like the progressive military government in Ecuador, the military reformist government in Peru tried to eradicate the word "Indian" from the official national vocabulary in the seventies. To avoid its racist connotations, it replaced it with "peasant." This led, however, to a denial of their ethnicity and culture (see Gelles 1998, 2000; Guevara et al. 2002; Skar 1997). For the past decade, therefore, the term has been reappropriated and reclaimed by indigenous movements. They also dynamically explore other normative discourses and select those elements that can strengthen their positions and legitimize their demands. In this way they construct new, diverse indigenous and community identities (Baud et al. 1996; Boelens 2003; Guevara 2005; Starn 1992).

In a similar way, the concept of "community" has generated an Andean battlefield of philosophical, political, and legal definition, and continues to do so. Despite the deconstruction of the original community myth by ethnographic studies, which showed the huge differences among societies we call "communities,"[16] positive law making in the Andean countries, in particular the special legislation enacted *for* indigenous and peasant populations, often misses the importance of analyzing Andean cultures and their management forms as dynamic and adaptive to new contexts.[17] In general, the label cannot be taken for granted but constitutes a political and ontological question that must be unraveled in each specific case. The heterogeneity of forms and contents, the variety of local uses of the concept, and the way in which peasant, indigenous, and community identity are linked to struggles for sociocultural recognition and resource distribution produce serious difficulties for research or development projects. This is even worse when drafting national legislation, special laws, or public policies that, by definition, deal with one-dimensional concepts of the phenomena they regulate.

Legal Constructs Based on Naturalized Concepts: Freezing, Subordination, and Illegalization

Stereotypical, objectified representations of "peasant," "indigenous," and "community" converge in legislation, sometimes unconsciously, sometimes clearly as a policy for subordination. As we have illustrated, in response to demands and uprisings by indigenous and peasant groups, and to avoid losing legitimacy in the eyes of a heterogeneous society, there are many cases in which national governments in the Andes have expanded their concept of unique, omnipresent, and overall national law. Thus, by recognizing or protecting specific social groups of society, for which they establish particular norms in special laws, they introduce special legal treatment within the positive law system itself. The flip side of the recognition question is the well-known danger of curtailing local autonomy, chaining these groups to new, strict rules, boxing them into a generalizing state law system. The dynamics and multiple manifestations of local water-rights systems cannot be codified into blanket legal terms without jeopardizing their foundations. They refer to a broad range of diverse living rights systems and cultures that constantly reorganize their rules precisely to reinforce their identity, and their capacity to negotiate and solve problems.

As Wray (1993) observes, legal recognition of rural communities in the Law on Communes and the Legal Decree on Peasant Communities (1937) has greatly harmed people's own forms of organization in Ecuador. "This is not recognition but the imposition of a single form of organization, with characteristics reflecting the criteria and values typical of 'representative democracy' rather than the uses and customs of the community itself." This policy of boxing in local law aims to turn variety into uniformity, and to make "tangible" those norms that do not match formal policy or the official legal system. In the case of Andean water management, this facilitates central control over nonofficial management systems.

Legal recognition and the subsequent freezing of a sociolegal repertoire, on the basis of naturalized norms and identities of "indigenous culture" or "peasant approach to water management" not only has repercussions for those societal groups who are "recognized." It also affects peoples or management systems that do not have this new legal backing. As a direct consequence of nonrecognition, these have to suffer exclusion from certain services and basic rights. The legalization of some is accompanied by the illegalization of others.[18]

It is clear that official recognition policies are not simply responses to the demands of marginalized sectors for greater authority and autonomy. Although this may be the rhetorical argument for legal change, the interest of the water bureaucracy or the neoliberal politicians—although not monolithic and internally divided—is different. Consciously implemented or not, freezing and subordination of sociolegal repertoires through strategies of official recognition contribute to control over a set of dynamic local norms and diverse intangible rights. It also illegalizes those local normative systems that do not fit the uniformity-based control efforts by the state and the market. As such it facilitates and reinforces political control and vertical power of bureaucracy (the powerful "hydrocrats"; see Rap et al. 2004), and helps neoliberal sectors incorporate local groups and organizations into the market system.

Even if peasants and communities do manage to get their autonomy, local authorities, and collective rights recognized in formal legislation and special laws, there are still ways left to curb their advancement. We shall briefly analyze one of them: the strategic use of double legislation and the informal hierarchization of formally equivalent, coherent bodies of law.

Multiple Normative Repertoires within State Legislation: Strategic Selection and Political Hierarchy

In studies on legal pluralism the phenomenon of legal shopping is often analyzed as if it were characteristic only of peasants and indigenous communities and other stakeholders who practice customary or local rights.[19] However, government agencies, water bureaucracy officials, judges, businesses, mining companies, and hydropower plants also apply this strategy. This does not necessarily involve interaction among different sociolegal systems. Dual legislation itself also allows for strategic selection from a range of legal bodies and instruments with, often, quite divergent meanings and purposes.[20]

Practice in the Andes has shown that this selection among bodies of law or legal instruments does not follow a neutral or objective rationale, but is heavily influenced by the power of governmental departments, officials, and societal groups behind water interests. Correas (1994) argues that there is really not a single legal discourse, as it would seem from the expression "the law." In reality, there is a complex of discourses from different sources. According to the prestige or position occupied by the officials, law has different degrees of effective force. The Andean experience with dual or double legislation also shows that different bodies of law and special laws, although formally equivalent and coordinated in a coherent structure, are inserted in a de facto legal hierarchical structure based on unequal powers. For example, as illustrated in the previous section, Chile's Indigenous Law is subordinated in practice to the Water Code and the Mining Code.

The existence of plural legislation also makes it easier for politicians and hydrocrats to handle a two-faced discourse of defending both indigenous rights and rational, efficient use of water. The latter may lead to state-centered, top-down management and to neoliberal policies promoting privatization and water markets.

Obviously, application of official dual law further reinforces legal complexity. The theoretical function of government officials and institutions using official law is to enforce it, not to create it. Nevertheless, official agents apply official law in highly varied social situations, introducing criteria and ways of thinking that go beyond the letter of the law. It is necessary, therefore, to distinguish between the official legal wording of special laws (that is, selection from among formal rules), and the interpretation of norms and directions contained in these legal texts by those using them (Correas 1994).[21] Moreover, only a small part of the many legal norms and decrees is applied in practice. In the Andean countries, interpretation of the law under conditions of multiple legislation—with special laws that are often contradictory—offers plenty of room for officials to "make their own legal pie" (F. von Benda-Beckmann et al. 1998; cf. S. F. Moore 1973). Here, hegemonic stakeholders in the water sector, both within and outside state agencies and formal structures, have great influence in the selection of the law's ingredients. Their influence goes beyond just a selection and interpretation of existing legal instruments. As Max Weber wrote: "it is precisely these groups, with vested interests, who are in the position to distort the intended purpose of a legal norm, to the point of turning it into the opposite" (Weber 1954, in S. F. Moore 1973:721).

Reflection: Local Responses

In the Andes, various water law and policy reform programs are grounded in standardized management norms derived from universal policy models. To facilitate bureaucratic control or to create an efficient market for water rights, it is considered necessary to overcome "backward" local practices. According to this mindset, economic and social efficiency and the well-being of all would increase considerably if all followed the same norms and if general rules could be applied to all players in the same way. Therefore, even when legal changes are made to recognize peasant and indigenous rights legally and politically, legal homogeneity and generality are the basic foundations and higher values that prevail.

Over the last few decades, peasant and indigenous communities have faced a great variety of policies and ideologies: denial of "the Andean community," local norms, and rights by racists and colonials; assimilation of these norms, organizational forms, and identities into the overall process of cultural equalization (*mestizaje*) and integration into the "imagined community" of the national bureaucracy; romanticization by Indianists and cosmovisionists; ideological interpretation in terms of revolutionary movements; and lately philosophical deconstruction by postmodern currents, and political and economic deconstruction by neoliberal policies.

Initially, the Andean peasant and indigenous movements demanded, together with socialist-inspired labor-union organizations, the right to equality. However, integration-oriented thinking based on "normalizing the nonnormal people" has meant that many groups in society are not recognized or do not feel recognized in official legislation, which does not represent their cultural norms and management forms. Therefore, in a second phase, they organized to demand, in addition, the right to be different: to recover and rebuild their identity not as a static tradition of folklore but as a proactive, dynamic construct. In fact, the past decade has been characterized by self-reorganization of Andean and indigenous identity. And it is evident that the identity-oriented political drive is also an effort to reconstruct community and collective life, and to (re)appropriate the resources they lack, among which water is a crucial one.

This political thrust takes place within and among water users' organizations, at the level of local communities. However, another important strategy, especially for the indigenous movement in the last decade, has been to attempt to strengthen national confederations and establish alliances with international forums. This multilevel approach of "protesting and advocating proposals"—*protesta con propuesta*—does not necessarily take place within the arena of official legislation (or if so, only very partially). The struggle to defend, define, and enforce local rights systems and organizational principles may be positioned within the law, outside the law, or head-to-head with the law.

Within the law are the struggles to achieve greater justice in water access and to change current water-rights property structures; to obtain greater autonomy and control for internal water management; and to recognize water rights as collective rights. In many cases, knowing that their sociolegal repertoires are dynamic, and aware of the dangers of subordination and freezing when essentialized normative frameworks are legalized under special laws, people do not demand specific operating rules or rights, but rather legal recognition of their rights regarding access to and control over water. Through access and control (called uses and customs, customary rights, peasant and indigenous rights, and so on) they demand greater autonomy to develop their own management rules. In other cases, they ask for legal recognition of certain general principles that promote greater democracy, transparency, and equity, in the water management process and its results.[22] These principles have to do, for example, with democratic representation at all levels of water resource administration, and defending fairer water distribution and government investment in water resource development. Obviously, this process of demanding a redefinition of positive law also constitutes a process of constructing, reinventing, and transforming local and customary rights frameworks themselves. It is an affirmation and reconstruction of local identities and water cultures. Here, it is important to observe that, often, the legal strategy—including the official legalization of community and self-defined institutions—is part of peasant and indigenous movements' struggle as a mimetic strategy, seeking to take advantage of dominant players' instruments of power and control: "instead of their formalizing our institutions, we will do it ourselves, but in our own way."

Outside (or in the margins of) the law are most rules, norms, and practices that water user collectives apply when they materialize their local water rights. These norms and normative structures are not accepted or denied by the law. The less detailed and codified they are within the official legal framework, and the more autonomy for action they have, the better they elude bureaucratic control. The struggle for recognition is often geared toward establishing the necessary conditions under the law (access to water and autonomy for management), in order to stay out of the way of the law. At the same time, this is a struggle against those recognition policies that seek to tame this variety of "unruly" rules and rights.

Struggles *against* the law are also often grounded in protests against assimilation or integration processes, or when illegal rules are applied as outside institutions and companies attempt to usurp or trample on local water rights. These rules and rights are also applied in day-to-day management of water usage systems. Commonly, these local rules are viewed and labeled illegal by official law. Often, they are expressions of resistance to official laws and to the imposition of outside technological, political, and cultural models.

It is important to realize that, in the Andes, there are many water management forms that are apparently strongly influenced by the official legal system, whereas a deeper analysis shows the contrary. A clear example is the organizational structure of many Andean irrigation systems. They often have the formal structure of irrigators' boards, irrigation councils, or other structures prescribed by national laws. Their hierarchical structure and forms of representation are often identical to official legal stipulations. Nevertheless, the supposed homogeneity and formality of these norms, mainly for external representation and formal protection, harbors a tremendous organizational and normative diversity under its surface: a variety of norms and rights that are different from and even contrary to official legislation. The more formal and visible elements of the organizational and normative system are more accessible through legislation. However, the most powerful elements like networks of contacts, informal norms, social positions, and "water rights in action" can hardly be reached by official legislation. These are precisely the ones that tend to be the most durable and effective.

Consequently, we can observe in the Andes the overlapping existence of different normative frames and organizational forms for water control, as well as diverse strategies for recognition: from drives for official codification to counterhegemonic strategies—under the law, outside the law, and illegal. Local water interests are multifaceted: alongside strategies to (re)appropriate water and the associated facilities, there is a simultaneous struggle to define local rules, rights, and organizational forms to manage water, and to legitimize their own local authorities who are to establish and enforce such rules and rights. This strategic, political struggle for counteridentification also includes the construction by local groups of their own discourses about the meaning of community, Andean and indigenous, and the construction of policies to regulate water accordingly.

NOTES

The first version of this chapter was translated from Spanish by Samuel Dubois, for which the authors wish to express their thanks here.

1. As we further elaborate below, we use the concepts of "indigenous," "peasant," and "community" as contextualized, dynamic constructs. In the Andean region, the relation between the imposed or self-defined class-based definition (*campesino*) and ethnicity-based identification (*indígena*) is complex, and fluid, and strongly depends on who uses which labels in what period, context, or place. For example, *indígena* (or even more *indio, nativo, runa*) is used both as a contemptuous term to racially condemn ethnic peoples, and as a proud, self-conscious designation recently appropriated by the indigenous movement as part of the "first nations" discourse (*pueblos originarios*). Similarly, *campesino* is both a construct imposed on indigenous peoples to deny their cultural identity and a term (often claimed by themselves) to strengthen class-consciousness, political alliances, and so on. In the Andes, place- and territory-bound names are commonly used to refer reflexively to indigenous groups and peoples' identity.

2. Earlier we have sought to understand pluriform rights and local water management in their particular contexts (for example, Boelens and Dávila 1998; Gentes 2003; Urteaga et al. 2003). Here we address this issue from a different vantage point: an analysis of official legislation on rural and indigenous water rights, and the policies of recognition for these local normative systems.

3. Water law and policies in Bolivia, although sharing the same technocratic, legalistic style, are in many ways an exception, because the state has little influence in peasant irrigation, and because of the virtual absence of state-managed systems.

4. Even so, there are still many instances of defending "indigenous" rights on the basis of these historical rights. See, for example, the case of Urcuquí, analyzed by Apollín et al. (1998).

5. Indigenist thought was formulated mainly by nonindigenous (*mestizo*) intellectuals, and emerged in the early twentieth century in response to the subordination of the indigenous and the heartfelt lack of any national identity, which led to a revaluation of indigenous culture. Attitudes toward contemporary indigenous peoples were highly ambivalent, and included romantic, paternalistic, and revolutionary approaches.

6. But it is too early to analyze the true direction and depth of penetration of the latest processes of legislative changes. In civil society and among indigenous and peasant groups, such changes have often failed to materialize (Yrigoyen Fajardo 1998). Communities of irrigators have often been unable to take advantage of the opportunities for self-governance offered by the new constitution's concept of a multicultural and multiethnic state. Another aspect is that constitutional changes have not yet produced changes in the development of regulations that will enable implementation (Assies et al. 1998).

7. CONAIE is the main representative of the country's millions of indigenous families.

8. In the Andean region, the user groups that are more incorporated into market trade systems and the dominant sectors, with greater access to and influence over (re)production of government law, generally are more oriented in their actions toward positive state law.

9. It is actually common for communities to adjust to legal formulas in order to obtain formal rights for access to water and to reinforce their water entitlements, as well as to qualify for loans and public assistance; however, under formalized structures, many local, extralegal forms and norms often persist.

10. Regarding belonging to a community, Article 5 of the General Law on Peasant Communities distinguishes between native and outsider community members. The former were born in the community, are sons or daughters of members or of people integrated into the community. "Integration" can involve establishing a stable couple with a community member or an application by an adult to the General Assembly for membership. Outsider members are adults (or people who otherwise acquire such civil-law capacity), live in the community for over five years, do not belong to any other community, and are registered in the communal roster.

11. Ironically, neoliberal policy reinforced the bureaucratization of water conflict management by frustrating local conflict management among neighbors, within and among different use sectors and watersheds (cf. Bauer 1997; Hendriks 1998).

12. Articles 110 and 111 link the granting of a mining concession with the express, ample right to use the water sources located in area of exploitation. The Water Code also intervenes in this regard (Art. 56), and even goes a step further. It can grant provisional rights in "restricted areas" (Art. 65), which may be turned automatically into

final water use rights after five years of actual use (Art. 67). The separation between surface and groundwater is also eliminated. The political purpose is to clear away bureaucracy in granting concessions for strategic economic sectors. Collective interests are curtailed to individual lawsuits, and here the free market acts as a leitmotiv.

13. For example, the mining treaty between Chile and Argentina (August 1999) has the purpose of "facilitating development by investors from the two countries of their respective mining businesses." The protocol states that "it shall be understood that the parties will allow investors from either country to use all necessary sorts of natural resources to develop mining business, including water resources available in their respective territories, even if these water resources are not shared among both countries."

14. This water exportation project was declared a national priority and passed by Bolivia's Chamber of Deputies in 2001. The law provides for studies, utilization, and sale of water from the Department of Potosí, Bolivia. Although its Article 5 establishes that "for the purposes of selling water resources, current norms regarding environmental preservation, natural resources, environmental and sociocultural impact on indigenous and rural communities shall be strictly observed," the law establishes no guarantees and could entail major problems for the mainly indigenous communities.

15. See Albó 2002; Assies et al. 1998; Gelles and Boelens 2003; Guevara 2004; Salomon 2002; Stavenhagen and Iturralde 1990; Urteaga and Guevara 2002.

16. See, for example, Golte 1992, 2000; Mayer 2002; Mossbrucker 1990; Salomon 2002; Starn 1992.

17. Golte (1992) presents a coherent approach from the standpoint of peasants' political and economic daily reality versus the colonial and postcolonial state. According to him, "community" is a legal concept that originated in colonial legislation and was meant to patronize "Indian commons." This social aggregate had a differentiated political organization and acquired customary rights to land. This concept was taken up by early twentieth-century indigenists to "protect the indigenous race." More important, peasants themselves selectively adopted it when they felt the exceptions granted under the separate system would be in their interest. Throughout history, they often adopted certain legal norms and forms of political organization. This does not mean that "communities" are or can be considered the same in their basic characteristics of actual social, political, and economic organization (Golte 1992). It comes as no surprise that Skar found in the Peruvian highlands that *mistis* (*mestizos*, that is, nonindigenous people) had manipulated the community recognition law to establish "their pseudo-community under state protection" and that "ironically, although the law was made to benefit indigenous communities, newly established communities were often neither communities nor indigenous." He reports that the population of one recognized community "was mainly black, while others were apparently of Chinese descent" (1997: 111). Social groups use official law to serve their own interests, beyond official dictates.

18. Regarding the issue of illegalization: it seems essential to mention the paradox that the decade in which the greatest wave of official recognition of indigenous and customary rights emerged in Latin America was the same in which the neoliberal model has been implemented. Many have explained this by saying that this contradiction arises due to the resistance of grassroots sectors against the hegemonic, standardizing model, whether state- or market-centered. The more strongly the neoliberal model is imposed, the greater the resistance, and the more changes are achieved in the legal and policy arena. However, others have pointed to the great support pro-

vided by multilateral institutions and financial lending agencies to the cause of "multiculturality" and "recognition of diversity." In fact, there is a convergence of interests between the neoliberal model and certain multicultural currents (see Hale 2002). This congruence is especially strong in the case of recognition of currents that demand "cultural" rights to one's own language or costume, to rituals and customs, but which do not affect the state's political sovereignty or the process of market exchange among individual property rights holders. This liberal ideology defends recognition of the freedom of individuals to define their own cultures and identities. Recognition contains clear ideological and political contents, which are grounded in the position of those groups that have decision-making power (cf. van der Ploeg 1998). Also, paradoxically, in the neoliberal age of state downsizing, decentralization of water administration is often seized upon by central governments both to lighten their responsibilities and strengthen their legitimacy and control at the local level. For example (see Conaghan et al. 1990), the Bolivian government has explicitly stated that the core purpose of decentralization is to reestablish state authority. Watershed management legislation in Peru is another example of how the state uses the new participatory discourse to strengthen its control (cf. Boelens et al. 2002).

19. Whenever possible, communities attempt to solve conflicts and problems through their own (hybrid) sociolegal repertoires. However, studies have shown how water users within local normative systems also use outside forces and norms, or threaten to do so, when confronted by other stakeholders in their social arena. Water users strategically use the existence of legal plurality for their own specific interests. Legal shopping ("forum shopping," F. von Benda-Beckmann et al. 1998) is an integral part of Andean community life. In water rights issues, it is not limited to a choice of opportune access and control rights. Legal shopping also extends to the field of strategic selection of behavioral norms, identities, and political discourses ("discourse shopping"), in order to strengthen and legitimize specific water control positions (Boelens and Zwarteveen 2003).

20. A recent WALIR Program mission examined not only the wide variety of legal decrees on water resources in Ecuador but also the major legal contradictions and confusions they are causing (Hendriks et al. 2003). In Bolivia, similarly, water is regulated under a panoply of national laws and decrees, issued for different sectors (mining, agriculture, water supply, industry, and so on) which often contradict each other and in practice rank hierarchically (cf. Bustamante 2002).

21. Further, mediation of official law through various stakeholders in practice—thus the way it is inserted in actual societal relations—is a third important factor explaining why "law in action" appears to be quite different from the letter of the law (cf. F. von Benda-Beckmann et al. 1998; Boelens and Zwarteveen 2003)

22. This demand for "codification" by rural and indigenous sections of society generally involves more the regulating of governance forms and procedures (management processes, jurisdiction of authorities, and decision-making structures) than substantive, precise operating rules (Hoekema 2004). Significantly, within local water management systems, these substantive rules and rights are generally defined very precisely, as a prerequisite for proper operation of such systems (Beccar et al. 2002).

8

A Win-Some Lose-All Game

Social Differentiation and Politics of Groundwater Markets in North Gujarat

ANJAL PRAKASH

VISHWA BALLABH

Agriculture in India has gone through enormous changes since the Green Revolution. Based on external inputs such as fertilizers, pesticides, high-yielding variety seeds (HYVs) and irrigation, Green Revolution technology became popular in many states of India. Large surface irrigation schemes were initiated in the sixties, and subsidy for HYVs and fertilizers was provided with the aim of making India self-sufficient in food production. However, the new technology also demanded more control over irrigation, which canal systems were unable to provide. Well irrigation was seen as an alternative to the bureaucratically controlled canal systems and this perception led to increased groundwater irrigation in many locations. Today, groundwater accounts for more than 50 percent of total irrigation in India. As a result of intensive groundwater-based farming, problems of large-scale overdevelopment of aquifers have emerged. Gujarat, a western state of India, is a case in point. In this state, groundwater supports more than 77 percent of total irrigation requirements.

Due to this increased dependence on groundwater for irrigation purposes, many parts of Gujarat have changed from water-abundant areas into water-scarce areas in only four decades. Groundwater overdraft, coupled with increasing scarcity and pollution of surface water supplies, has resulted in groundwater "mining" in many parts of Gujarat. As a consequence, an increasing number of areas are now categorized as overexploited. The latest figures released by the government show that, whereas in 1984 88 percent of the subdistricts were under the "white," or safely exploited, category, this has decreased to about 51 percent in 1997.[1] The number of overexploited subdistricts has increased from just one in 1984 to thirty-one in 1997. Salinity intrusion into the groundwater is another problem caused by excessive withdrawal of groundwater, especially in areas close to the seashore or in marshy areas like Kutch and coastal Saurashtra.

The number of subdistricts affected by salinity has increased from one in 1984 to seven in 1997. In 1997, only 52 percent of the subdistricts in Gujarat have groundwater that is considered safe (Hirway 2000). These figures show an extremely grim picture of groundwater utilization and its development in Gujarat.

Along with water scarcity, Gujarat has also experienced a spurt in water markets. These markets developed mostly in alluvial regions of central and north Gujarat that were suitable for sinking deep tube wells. The emergence of water markets has given rise to debates over their nature and way of functioning. A group of academics and policy makers advocate the need for dense and competitive markets on the grounds of efficiency, transaction costs, accessibility, and equity in resource distribution. Using the concept of property rights, they argue that tradable rights to groundwater will increase the efficiency of water use (see Chambers et al. 1989; Kolavalli and Chicoine 1987; Rosegrant and Binswanger 1994; Shah 1993; Tsur and Dinar 1997). Another group opposes these ideas, arguing that water markets, dominated by resource-rich upper-caste farmers, lead to the violation of rights of poor and marginalized farmers.[2] They argue that transactions in groundwater markets are based on the politics of powerful well owners, and therefore reflect the economic and class relationships that are detrimental to the poor and marginalized sections of the village population (see Janakarajan 1992, 1993; Saleth 1994a; Shah and Ballabh 1995; Singh 1994). Whether the argument is in favor of or against water markets, it is clear that the functioning of groundwater markets is very much situation-dependent (Dubash 2002).

Through an intensive village case study in Mehsana District in Gujarat (see figure 8.1), the present chapter tries to capture some of the key issues in the debate. It shows how a class of people flourished even in a situation of extreme water scarcity. These people are resourceful farmers who invested in deep tube wells and hence could access and sell surplus water. Small and marginal farmers lost the race of chasing the water table and became buyers of water. The groundwater markets flourished in the nineties, thus increasing access to irrigation for the people. However, control over water is largely concentrated in the hands of sellers. Further, it also created differential rights over groundwater for buyers and sellers. In India, access to groundwater is directly linked with land rights. However, in its attempts to regulate groundwater extraction, the government responded by controlling institutional finance, spacing, licensing, and electricity pricing rather than directly striving for an equitable system of land and water rights. These measures could not stand up to the powerful farmers who lobbied for nonimplementation of the regulations. As it largely ignored sociopolitical realities, government regulation did not produce the desired result.

This chapter focuses on the relationship between legal regulation and social relations through the politics of groundwater markets in north Gujarat. It

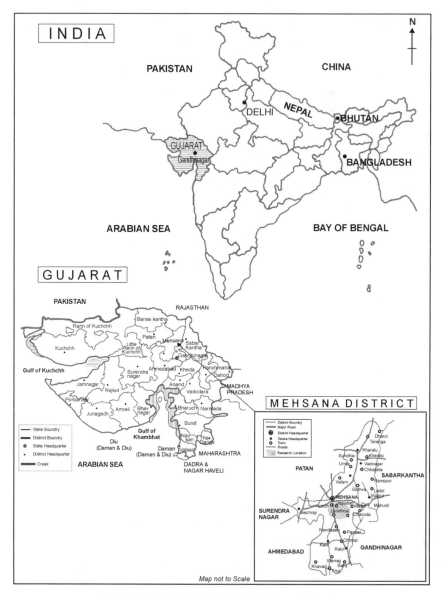

FIGURE 8.1. India, Gujarat, and Mehsana District.

captures the tensions between formal legal attempts to regulate groundwater
use and the sociopolitical structures in which access to groundwater is shaped
locally. The following section outlines the prevalent social relations of production in the village that shape and determine access to groundwater. The subsequent two sections analyze the formal legal attempts at national and state level
to regulate groundwater extraction, in the context of locally existing socio-

political systems and relationships, as well as why these have failed to work on the ground. The last section sums up the major concerns of the chapter.

The Social Relations of Production in Sangpura

Sangura is located in one of the over-exploited local administrative divisions (*taluka*) of Mehsana District in northern Gujarat.[3] Gujarat is considered to be one of the more progressive, developed, and industrialized states of India.[4] Around 70 percent of Gujarat's total geographic area falls in a drought-prone arid or semi-arid region (Patel 1997). Surface water is largely concentrated in the southern areas. Therefore, most water needs of Gujarat have to be met by groundwater resources. Of irrigated agriculture, 80 percent is dependent on groundwater. This is in addition to the numerous industrial and domestic needs of the growing population. Sangpura does not differ from the broader state pattern of increasing groundwater scarcity. All water needs of Sangpura are met through groundwater, a resource that has shown increasing signs of overdevelopment in recent years.

In 2001, Sangpura was inhabited by 628 households. Two major caste groups—Patel and Thakore—make up two-thirds of the village population. Other major caste groups are Prajapati (potter caste; seventy households), Parmar (cobbler caste; sixty households), Vaghari (vegetable vendor caste; twenty-five households), and Darbar (former feudal lords; twelve households).[5] Of these castes, the Patels are known as skilled agriculturalists.[6] Patels have organized themselves through caste and kinship institutions, and early on started some of the informal credit cooperatives that provided loans among members of their caste through self-help groups. Before Independence (in 1947), they took advantage of the loans given for shallow wells by the Gaekwad state.[7] They started growing cash crops such as sugarcane and cotton in the early fifties. The mechanization of dug wells also earned them money through the sale of water on a limited scale.[8] In the 1960s, Patels generated enough surpluses from agriculture to advance consumption loans to people of other castes, such as Thakores. The condition of such loans was that the Patel would cultivate Thakore land as long as the loan amount was not repaid. In most cases, repayment did not happen, and the land remained with the Patel moneylender. When the dug wells dried up in the early eighties, Patels were the first to invest in deep tube wells. They were followed by the Prajapatis, who followed a similar development. Thakores, on the other hand, did not organize themselves in a similar way, due to their inability to access credit through the market. This is often attributed to their lack of resources, as explained below. This became advantageous for the Patels, who dominated the sociopolitical arena.

The Prajapatis were less well organized than the Patels, but otherwise on an equal footing with them. Though their traditional occupation was pottery, there are two basic divisions among them. While one group took up pottery as profession, another group was engaged in agriculture. Though initially they had little land in the village, Prajapatis became landowners by diversifying their occupation. Apart from engaging in agriculture, they took up the profession of brick making, which was close to their traditional occupation. Brick making exposed them to urban areas, where demand was increasing as a consequence of expansion in and around Ahmedabad and Mehsana. This also opened up job opportunities in the textile mills of Ahmedabad. Back home, they became close to the caste of the Patels, who taught them the skills needed for commercial agriculture. They bought shares in tube wells and joined the Patels in reaping the advantages of the agricultural boom and the water markets. Apart from benefiting from increased income in agriculture and surplus created through working in the textile mills of Ahmedabad, they were also employed in the diamond polishing industries in Mehsana and Surat. Working in industry also helped to generate resources for the external inputs required for the new technology. The nonresidents supported many mechanized pumps that were purchased in the beginning. This made life easier for those who stayed back in the village; while agricultural production was increasing, there were fewer people to be supported.

In pre-Independence India, Sangpura, along with other villages in the region, was ruled by the Gaekwad of Baroda. In those days Darbars were feudal lords under the so-called ryotwari system, while the Thakores were padi (footmen, soldiers) employed by the Baroda State Army.[9] Being in the army, they also looked after the revenue collection and served as watchmen (*chaukidars*) of land and property. The Thakore role as chaukidars enabled them to appropriate part of the landed property that was considered fallow. The population pressure on land was not so high as to create social tensions. Hence, they could appropriate land without much opposition from other communities. Soon after independence and with the end of the British Raj, the services of Thakores were terminated, and the power associated with their position was slowly lost. But while the agriculturalist Patels took advantage of their skills in the booming agriculture sector, the Thakores could not do so, as they had not acquired the necessary skills. Both the Patels and the Prajapatis started engaging in irrigated agriculture, while Thakores did not do so and started losing their land to Patels and Prajapatis as a consequence of debts related to consumption and other loans.

In the 1970s, dug wells were drying up and farmers were losing access to water. In the early eighties, when tube wells replaced dug wells, the Patels and Prajapatis had the initial advantage of owning more of them than the Thakores, although in Sangpura and surrounding villages, Thakores and Patels had previously been more or less on a par. Thakores claimed to be the descendants of Rajput rulers, and adopted their habits. Being a service class, they did not adapt to the new changes in agriculture. It is sometimes said that Thakores made merry—engaging in drinking, gambling, and eating meat like the Rajputs.[10] In a largely vegetarian society, Thakores were thus considered polluted and were stigmatized in public. In less than four decades, the structures of power changed and Thakores were pushed down to one of the lowest sociopolitical strata, due largely to their lack of capacities to maintain and generate economic resources.

Agricultural Development and Water Scarcity

Before 1960, the water level in the village was around three to four meters below the surface, and there were only two cropping seasons: monsoon and winter. The main monsoon crops were sugarcane, paddy, and chili, and the main winter crops were fenugreek (*methi*), pearl millet (*bajri*), gram (*chana*), indigenous cotton, cumin (*jeeru*), and fennel (*variyali*). There were no summer crops, and even the winter crops grew mainly by capturing subsoil moisture, with little irrigation. What irrigation existed was carried out through open dug wells using draught power, and constituted only 30 percent of the total cultivated area of Sangpura. Agriculture was described as *sookhi evam sasti kheti* (dry and inexpensive agriculture). Milk production took place on a small scale; the milk was mostly utilized for household consumption.

In the early sixties, mechanized pumps were introduced in the village for the first time. By this time, the groundwater level had reached between six and nine meters. The machines were powered by crude oil engines. In this way, irrigation in Sangpura contributed to about 60 percent of the total cultivated area. The remaining 40 percent was irrigated by capturing subsoil water, collected through small bunds and field ponds. The use of irrigation, combined with new HYVs, began giving higher yields. Thus, the new technology contributed considerably to the expansion of irrigated agriculture.

Many developments took place in the village after Gujarat was separated from Maharashtra state in 1960. The most important among these was the establishment of a milk cooperative by a Mehsana-based dairy cooperative in 1965. With the milk cooperative, a ready market was created in the village. This initiated a radical economic transformation for most of the people. Farmers could then invest the capital generated through the milk cooperative in productivity-enhancing measures for agriculture. In this period, only a few Patel households were living in brick houses, while most people lived in mud houses. "Water scarcity" was not in the village vocabulary, as many parts of the village used to be flooded for months after the monsoon, when villagers grew sugarcane. People had enough water for drinking and irrigation. In this same period, the Primary Agricultural Cooperative Society was introduced, providing oil, kerosene, and agricultural credit to the farmers.

Sangpura was electrified in 1970. Patels and Prajapatis were the first to get ten electricity connections for household consumption. Improved varieties of cotton and millet were introduced around the same time, and first adopted by landowners who possessed open dug wells. The water level in the open wells had declined to between eighteen and twenty-four meters, as a consequence of the use of mechanized irrigation. Gradually, HYVs replaced all indigenous varieties of crops. Only indigenous wheat (*tukri ghau*) survived and is still popular among the farmers because it needs less water, is less sensitive to pest attacks, and has almost the same level of yield as the hybrid variety. On the upper reaches of Sabarmati River, the Dharoi multipurpose irrigation dam was built in 1960. By 1970 the water flow in the river had been severely affected. The farmers realized that water in the river, the only source of surface water in the region, was decreasing every year and this had affected the water recharge of the surrounding villages. The water level in Sangpura's wells began to sink deeper and deeper.

As the water level declined further and reached a point beyond the capacity of diesel engines, the diesel engine was fully replaced by the electric motor. Electricity supply for irrigation was round the clock. By 1985, the water level had fallen to around forty-seven meters. This was the time when tube wells, powered with an electric motor, started to be installed in the village (although the first tube well had been installed back in 1974). This number slowly increased to twelve by the end of 1985. Half of this number was installed in 1984–1985. By the end of 2002, the figure further rose to thirty-four, excluding one owned by Gujarat Water Resources Development Corporation (GWRDC).[11] The increased number of tube wells further stimulated the demand for electricity. In an attempt to restrict electricity use, supply was reduced from twenty-four to sixteen hours per day. The credit cooperative provided advance crop loans to the farmers, and the milk cooperative provided its members with ready cash twice a month. Farmers remember the 1975–1985 period as the golden age of agriculture. They had bumper crops and could get incomes from both agriculture and dairy production. Part of the golden age was achieved by the advances in agriculture caused by the introduction of HYV seeds and increasing control over irrigation.

Another part of the irrigation history is the emergence and growth of water markets during these years. Under the flat-rate tariff system, there were eighteen hours of electricity supply per day. Most tube wells sunk in these periods yielded more water than the shareholders required. This gave rise to water markets, as there was plenty of surplus water that could be sold at a good price. There was also a demand for water, because there were very few tube-well owners among the total number of cultivators or landowners. These water sales were fully rational from the shareholders' perspective. The shareholders of the tube wells made tremendous profits. Their own irrigation was, in fact, subsidized by their water sales to smallholders. Most water sellers were resourceful upper-caste farmers, while buyers were mostly smaller and lower-caste farmers who became totally dependent on the sellers. Thus, a disproportionate distribution of productive resources like land and access to water through tube wells across various groups in society yielded uneven socioeconomic relationships.

The growth in agricultural production was limited mainly to the Patels, Prajapatis, and a few Thakores and Harijans whose income multiplied. They built concrete houses and changed their lifestyles. Thakores had land, but were less successful than Patels and Prajapatis.

As the water level continued to decline, access to irrigation became increasingly problematic, while the ownership of tube wells became concentrated among a few resourceful farmers. Their profits from agriculture and the water market helped them to diversify from agriculture through investments in education and occupations in the nearby industrial areas. Some farmers migrated to the United States, setting a trend that has become a major source of cash remittances today.

However, in the nineties the situation started to change, with the water level falling to about a hundred meters and electricity supply reductions to twelve hours a day, with flat rate charges based on horsepower. The land had been overcultivated, and farmers often tried to sustain the level of production by increasing external inputs such as inorganic fertilizers and pesticides. In spite of excessive use of fertilizer and pesticides, the high level of production of earlier days could not be sustained; even crop failure became increasingly common. Under the influence of this development and the rising costs of irrigation, farmers realized that agriculture was no longer as profitable as before. Due to the increasing demand for electricity, the government decided to provide electricity in day and night shifts in rotation. This caused new inconveniences for the farmers. Under this new regime, the water buyers were given night slots while the sellers enjoyed day irrigation.

By this time, many tube wells were more than fifteen years old and started to fail. In order to access irrigation, the wells needed to be renovated for a minimum cost of 200,000 rupees per well. Indebtedness among farmers became high, as they took loans for investing in, or buying shares for, the new tube wells. The hourly charges for water sale were increased to cover the expenses. Until then, the shared tube wells had been making profits up to Rs. 100,000 per year by selling water to the nonmembers. This share was reduced for those who could not afford to pay for reinvestment in the tube well. In 2000, the electricity supply was further reduced to eight hours per day, leading to a significant decrease in water sales. Shared wells were not able to supply water to the shareholders, so water sales were curtailed. This led to a further decrease of profits for the shareholders. To an increasing extent, the land of water buyers remained fallow. To cover this land, two new tube wells were installed in 2000–2001. Major shareholders were, again, the Patel farmers. By the end of 2002, the water level had fallen to 130 meters. To access water at this level, many engines had to be upgraded to higher power. If the 1975–1985 period had been the golden years of agriculture, the nineties became dark years characterized by declining productivity, increased input costs, and crop failures.

A pertinent question here is the response of the state to this growing scarcity. Though there have been a number of water laws instituted at both the national and state levels, the implications of them were hardly visible in Sangpura. The only change felt locally was the secular decline in the supply of electricity for agriculture, which has decreased from twenty-four hours per day in the eighties to a mere eight hours per day in 2003. In the next section, we will look at some of the regulatory mechanisms exercised by the state, and discuss their effectiveness in checking the decline in the water table.

"Water beneath the Land is Mine": Loopholes in Groundwater Law

What determines the right over groundwater for the people in Sangpura? Ask the question and one gets an additional question as reply: "Isn't the water beneath my land mine?" In this section, we examine the basis of this reply, while looking at the formal legal and institutional framework and interventions that determine access to groundwater. The implications of these are also discussed, while answering the question: What does legal regulation of groundwater resources mean for the people of Sangpura?

The constitution of India treats water resources as a state subject. The national government enters only in the case of interstate river water. List two of the seventh schedule of the constitution, which deals with subjects on which states have jurisdiction, says: "Water, that is to say, water supplies, irrigation and canals, drainage and embankments, water storage and water power are subjected to the provisions of Entry 56 of List I." Entry 56 of List I (union list) reads: "regulation and development of inter-state rivers and river valleys, to the extent to which such regulations and development are under the control of Union, is declared by the Parliament by law to be expedient in the public interest" (Government of India 1999: 200). Within the constitution of the state, the right to water is governed by various laws and policies. In the case of groundwater, the most important law is the Easements Act of 1882, implemented by the British government. The act refers to the right of every owner of land abutting on a natural stream, lake, or pond, to use and consume its water for domestic and irrigation purposes (see chapter 6 for similar laws in Nepal). It gives a right to every owner of the land to collect and dispose of all water under the land within his or her own limits. However, this right is always subjected to the overriding power of the state to regulate the resource (ibid.: 211). The consequence of this legal framework is that only landowners can own groundwater. Landless individuals and tribals (who may have group or community rights over land but not private ownership) are left out. The legal framework also implies that rich landlords can be waterlords, and indulge in openly selling as much water as they wish (Singh 1994). This law establishes permits allowing affluent farmers with high pumping capacity and deeper tube wells to have easier access to the resource than others. This situation, coupled to a lack of capacity of the state to effectively regulate groundwater use, has resulted in excessive withdrawals in many areas.

In 1970, the Government of India introduced the Groundwater Model Bill, a legislation-based approach to control the use of groundwater. Since water is a state subject, the bill brought by the central government had to be endorsed by the state. To this day, very few state governments have enacted it. In 1992, a revised version of the bill was introduced, but it was enacted in only a few states. Gujarat, where the groundwater depletion problem was very visible, has succeeded in implementing it. However, it is applied only to a limited number of districts that are considered overexploited.[12] Even in these districts the act was never implemented in spirit, due to the existence of a powerful farmers' lobby that opposed any such regulatory measures. Indirect approaches to the regulation of the use of groundwater were taken through limiting institutional credit, manipulating electricity pricing mechanisms, and controlling electricity connections. These approaches made little impact and have proven impossible to implement. Well-to-do farmers were generally able to bypass regulations and obtain credit or access to electricity connections. They often already had wells and, if power charges were increased, they were able to afford them or make further investments for a more efficient use of water, such as the introduction of underground pipes instead of open channels to carry water to the field. As Moench argues, most regulatory instruments that could reduce rates of groundwater extraction in overdeveloped areas are likely to disproportionately affect the poor (Moench undated: 15–22).

Responding to public interest litigation against the over–exploitation of groundwater resources, the Supreme Court of India directed the Ministry of Environment and Forests to constitute the Central Ground Water Board (CGWB) as an authority and to exercise its power under section five of the Environmental (Protection) Act, 1986, to regulate the overexploitation of groundwater resources. The Supreme Court also directed the establishment of the State Ground Water Authority, and interacted at state level to make provisions for administrative regulation at various levels, such as panchayats (local councils) and village communities. The CGWB drafted Environment Protection Rules for Development and Protection of Ground Water. These included legal and institutional aspects and were circulated to all states for their comments before notification. The circulation and enactment of these bills and rules raise the specter of a vast bureaucratic machinery administering use of groundwater through licensing and supervision, with little tangible effects on actual use. Presently, owners of the land have absolute freedom in accessing groundwater. Few wish to trade this freedom for bureaucratically administered licensing regimes. In view of these difficulties, no state has shown any inclination to adopt the proposal (Government of India 1999: 213).

At present, groundwater accounts for around 50 percent of irrigated agriculture in India. At the field level, the use of groundwater is in the hands of those who can afford to invest in wells and tube wells. Those who cannot invest in tube wells and pump sets can access it through groundwater markets. This type of access depends upon geographical conditions, type of economy, and institutional and policy arrangements that vary across India. Due to this variance, different forms of markets, from monopolistic to highly competitive ones, have been reported (see Dubash 2002; Shah 1993; Shah and Ballabh 1997). Two common types of transactions can be distinguished: cash-based and kind-based. In the cash-based system, a fixed amount is charged per hour on the basis of the size and capacity of the pump to withdraw water. Under this condition, water access is recognized at two levels. The first level includes water sellers, who also have the right to irrigate their field. Hence, their rights as owners of the land and the water accessing device prevail over use of the resource by water buyers. The water buyers have subordinate access, as they get water only after the owners' water right is fully met. In times of scarcity, the water buyers are hit hardest, as their right to buy water is curtailed first. In a kind-based system, crop-sharing arrangements dominate, with one-fifth to one-half of the total crop production in the area that receives irrigation paid to the water sellers.

How does this analysis help in understanding the case of Sangpura? We return to the question that was posed to the farmer, and the answer that depicts the actual situation on ground. The groundwater right is tied up with that of landholding. It is further actualized only by means of productive resources. Formal legal attempts were made to counter the depletion of aquifers. An "overexploited aquifer perspective" was used to check what is called "mining" of groundwater resources. Sangpura comes under the "dark overexploited" zone as classified by the government. By notification, no construction of new tube wells is allowed, and existing wells should fulfill certain requirements pertaining to well depth and spacing. However, these notifications have no effect on the ground. Many new tube wells are dug all the time to chase the water table in Mehsana, and Sangpura is no exception to this. Those who construct these wells do not take permission from the government, nor do they pay heed to the technical requirements specified in the law.

The reasons for the nonimplementation of regulations are many. Foremost among them is the farmers' lobby of the Patel caste. It constitutes the strongest political pressure group in state politics. This was the largest group in Sangpura engaged in water sales, and hence no regulation had any impact on their interests. The use of political clout has thus prevented the effective implementation and enforcement of regulation on the ground.

Until now, the people of Sangpura have witnessed only indirect forms of regulation through a decrease in electricity supply and a cut in institutional finance for digging tube wells. Many attempts were made to convert the present flat electricity rate into a pro-rata tariff, but this has not worked until now. The electricity charges have also been raised, but every time the political leadership was compelled to disallow the decision taken by departments like the Gujarat Electricity Board. At present, there is a tussle between the government and the farmers' body over the electricity price issue. Recently, the price was hiked by the electricity board, which resulted in farmers refusing to pay. A strong agitation by various farmers' groups has been reported, followed by negotiations. However, until the time of writing this chapter, a solution acceptable to both farmers and government has not come about.[13] As to the cutback in institutional finance, the rich farmers have never been dependent on the state, and could rely on other sources of finance based on social networks and private credit cooperatives.

In the next section, we show the level of differentiation through ownership and control over the two most productive resources in Sangpura: water and land. We will also show how it has led to powerful minorities winning over a large majority.

Access to Irrigation and Social Differentiation in Sangpura

Mahendrabhai Patel owns ten bighas of land and a 20 percent share in a tube well in Sangpura.[14] Nine other partners share this tube well. Together, they irrigated ninety bighas of land at the time of its construction in 1986. Out of these ninety bighas of irrigated land, the water for forty bighas used to be sold to buyers. With a groundwater table depth of thirty-five meters, a thirty-five horsepower electric engine, and sixteen hours of electricity supply per day, the tube well used to yield a profit of more than 50,000 rupees per year. The profit used to be distributed among the shareholders, on the basis of their individual shares. The land was very fertile; with HYV seeds and timely irrigation, a significant profit could be derived from it. In 1990, when electricity supply was reduced to twelve hours a day, the tube well command area was reduced to seventy bighas. Subsequently, when the electricity supply was further reduced to ten hours a day, the groundwater level had declined to about eighty-eight meters. To sustain a similar level of water supply, the capacity of the electric pump was increased to fifty-one horsepower. The command area of Mahendrabhai's tube well was further reduced to fifty bighas, cutting out totally the sale of water, as the shareholders of the well themselves could barely irrigate their land. This cessation of water sales significantly reduced profits; as now Mahendrabhai had to pay for the irrigation charges for his crops, whereas formerly the price of irrigation was largely covered by the profit generated by his share in the tube well. In addition, land productivity had gone down drastically, due to more than three decades of overcultivation; hence crop failure and reduced agricultural production became a common feature.

All these problems made Mahendrabhai take a very important decision. While visiting a relative's house in a neighboring village, he heard about going to the United States, where many of his distant relatives had migrated. He could see a perceptible change in their lifestyle, and he was impressed by the idea. Long-distance migration thus became a strategy for becoming financially independent and diversifying from stagnating agriculture, the profitability of which was going down steadily. Mahendrabhai contacted his relative and the agent who arranges visas for the United States. After five months of struggle and constant follow-ups, he reached Chicago illegally, after having paid around Rs. 800,000 to the agent in October 1992. The money was borrowed from different sources at a 24 percent rate of interest per year. Mahendrabhai now works in a motel near Chicago owned by one of his distant relatives. In 2002 he earned six dollars an hour. He works for sixteen hours a day and repaid the entire loan in the first two years of his stay in the United States. His two sons, daughter, wife, and aging parents stayed behind. His elder son has finished an apprenticeship course in engineering, while the younger one is planning to attend college. His daughter married a wealthy business family in Mehsana. Mahendrabhai's sons are not interested in agriculture now, and therefore eight out of ten bighas of land have been given out in sharecropping. The remaining two bighas of land are used by the family for growing fodder crops for feeding the buffaloes. The family now keeps five buffaloes instead of the two they had in 1990; the milk is sold at the village dairy cooperative. This brings in an income of more than 10,000 rupees per month. Mahendrabhai was the first person in his village to migrate to the United States. He was followed by ninety-nine others in the next ten years. Apart from repaying his loan and marrying his daughter into a wealthy family, he invested in another tube well, of which he owns a 30 percent share. The new tube well has been dug to a depth of about 200 meters, while the water level has now reached a depth of 120 meters. The capacity of the electric pump is seventy-two horsepower; it irrigates forty-five bighas of land. The shareholders sell water for seven bighas, while the rest is used by the shareholders for their own land.

Lakhaji Thakore cultivated four out of Mahendrabhai's eight bighas of land in a sharecropping contract. Lakhaji owns 1.5 bighas on the westernmost side of the village. He used to irrigate the land by buying water from a neighboring tube well. However, for five years he was refused water for irrigating his land as the water was not sufficient even for the shareholders, and the command area of the well has been considerably reduced. Since then, Lakhaji and his wife have been cultivating land through sharecropping contracts. He has an aging mother and two sons who are married. His sons are working as daily wage laborers in and around the village, while the daughters-in-law work on the land. Under the contract, the total agricultural production is divided equally into three parts, one for each of the three major inputs: land, labor, and water. Two-thirds of the net production goes to Mahendrabhai, as he owns the land and also has a share in the tube well that supplies irrigation water to the field.[15] Sharecropping hardly meets the needs of Lakhaji's family, as the productivity of land has been going down year by year. Lakhabhai wishes to have a share in one of the tube wells, but that seems a far-fetched dream. As he puts it: "if we could afford a share in a tube well, shouldn't we be working on our own land? What do we get in sharecropping? Only some grains for the household and weeds as fodder for the buffalo." Since their own land is not irrigated, they can only grow pulses if there is a good monsoon season. To feed the family, they have to grow irrigated crops such as pearl millet and wheat. That rationalizes the decision to take land on a sharecropping basis.

The above case of two farmers illustrates the situation in Sangpura. On the one hand, the family of Mahendrabhai enjoys a socially and economically powerful position in the village, and has enough resources to diversify. On the other hand, Lakhaji is trapped in agriculture characterized by decreasing productivity, ever-increasing irrigation prices, crop failure, and hard work without much return. As his case shows, having a piece of land does not guarantee access to groundwater. Although both Mahendrabhai and Lakhaji hold land in the village, the latter is denied access to water while the other can freely use it. The point is that access and rights to groundwater are directly related to an individual's access to other resources, of which land is one important element. The question here is: What are the mechanisms that induce such a level of differentiation?

In Sangpura, agriculture and animal husbandry are the two main economic activities. In a way, these two are intertwined, one feeding on another and vice versa. Historically, access and control over land and water determined the pattern of agriculture and generation of surplus. This surplus was invested in animal husbandry, which generated profits through the milk cooperative system. The introduction of new agricultural technology, development of groundwater irrigation, and establishment of a milk cooperative happened almost simultaneously. The development of groundwater irrigation happened in the private sector, but was informally linked with the partly state-funded cooperative sector, including primary agricultural and milk cooperatives. The primary agricultural cooperative society provided institutional credit to farmers, whereas the milk cooperative gave a village-based selling point for milk. Institutional credit boosted investments in agriculture through HYV seeds, irrigation, and other

inputs. Agricultural produce and residues were well utilized for animal husbandry, creating a loop between them. Did this development follow a distinct
path, favoring some and excluding others? We will examine this through the
distribution of land and access to groundwater resources in Sangpura.

Patterns of Landownership

In rural India, land is still the most valuable asset and indicator of wealth. Land
resources in Sangpura are very unequally distributed, as is shown by data from
Sangpura's 2002 land revenue register. Though Patels constitute around 32 percent of the total number of households, they possess 54 percent of the agricultural land in the village. Thakores, who constitute approximately 36 percent of
the total number of households, have only 21 percent of the land. Prajapatis, who
represent 12 percent of the households, have 14 percent of the village land. Almost 50 percent of the households (315 out of 628 households) are landless; out
of these, 11 percent fall below the poverty line.[16]

Further, the landownership classes (marginal, small, medium, and large
farmers) and their caste associations show another distinct picture.[17] Patels lead
in each land class except the class of landless, which is dominated by Thakores.
Most Patels are small or medium farmers. Only nine households have more than
five hectares. In fact, only 14 percent of the land belongs to large farmers; the
larger part (around 75 percent) belongs to small and medium farmers. This is
largely due to land fragmentation and division among families over the years.
Thakores are worst off: they form the largest caste group (225 households) but
hold only 21 percent of the agricultural land. Most of them are marginal or small
farmers. They are followed by Harijans and Vagharis, who form approximately
10 and 4 percent of the population, respectively, but together hold only 4 percent of the land. Around 19 percent of the Thakores, 26 percent of the Harijans,
and 36 percent of the Vagharis fall into the category of households below the
poverty line.

The large populations of landless and poor families of Thakores and
Harijans form the main agricultural labor force in the village. While Thakores
specialize in agricultural labor, Vagharis lease horticultural plots on a yearly
basis, mainly from Patel and Prajapati farmers who possess orchards of lemon
and guava. The analysis shows that the stratification based on caste closely follows the landownership hierarchy in Sangpura. Landholding is skewed toward
Patels; Prajapatis are also in a comfortable position, while Thakores and other
lower-caste groups have very little land. Thus, it can be concluded that the land
class and caste structures in Sangpura have much in common.

Access to Irrigation in Sangpura

It is a fact that land in Sangpura is a crucial economic resource. However, access
to groundwater determines its productive capacity and the owner's or

cultivator's ability to generate surplus. Therefore, this is another very crucial factor in the groundwater-dependent economy of Sangpura. In Sangpura, thirty-four private tube wells were functioning by the end of 2002. Most of these wells are jointly owned between households, and only four are individually owned. Before focusing upon the issue of access to irrigation, we explain the way irrigation cooperatives are organized in the village.

THE ORGANIZATION OF TUBE WELL COOPERATIVES. The tube well cooperatives are organized on the basis of shares in the well. The shares are generally bought at the time of construction. The total cost of installing a tube well is calculated and then a decision is taken on percentages of shares. The cost excludes the cost of the underground pipeline the shareholder has to invest in, which is based on the distance between the tube well and the field. Investment in a share has two advantages: first, shares ensure the right to certain hours of irrigation, based on the percentage of the share. The tube well generates profit by the selling of water to nonshareholders. The owners of shares get a dividend at the end of every financial year. Shareholders have to invest in repair and maintenance in proportion to their share. Most tube well owners keep reserve funds for incidental expenses, accounted for in the yearly profit-and-loss account. Shares in tube wells follow the patrilineal inheritance right that is passed on to the male heirs after the death of the shareholder. In our discussion of access to irrigation, two categories of people are included: the shareholders and the water buyers.

THE SHAREHOLDERS. We divide the tube wells into three broad capacity classes of thirty to forty-five, forty-five to sixty, and sixty to seventy-five horsepower. An examination of the percentage of shares owned by caste reveals that the Patels have 65 percent of total tube well shares, though they constitute around 32 percent of the village population. Thakores, around 36 percent of village households, own only 15 percent of the tube well shares. The Prajapatis, 11 percent of the village population, hold 13 percent of the shares, while the Harijans, approximately 10 percent of the village population, hold only 2 percent of the total number of shares. The majority of tube wells are in the forty-five to sixty horsepower class (41 percent), while the others are almost equally divided into the other classes. Castes like the Darbar, Harijans, and Vagharis possess shares in only lower-capacity tube wells. Patels, the largest group of well shareholders, are at the top in each tube well class (57 percent in the thirty to forty-five horsepower class, 65 percent in the forty-five to sixty horsepower class, and 74 percent in the sixty to seventy-five horsepower class). Most of them fall in the medium-capacity class. The prototype of shares closely follows the patterns of landholding and irrigation: 66 percent of the total land under irrigation (through tube well shareholders) belongs to Patels, 15 percent to Prajapatis, and only 10 percent to Thakores. It also shows that Patels tend to own higher-capacity tube wells: 57 percent own shares in tube wells between forty-five and seventy horse-power.

THE WATER BUYERS. Until the late nineties, water buyers constituted a large group in the village. From 2001, there has been a drastic reduction in the supply of electricity, so the number of water buyers has decreased. This is mainly because the reduction in the total amount of water pumped from a particular tube well has to fulfill the water needs of the shareholders first. Though selling water is a profitable business, it will not be done at the cost of the amount of water available for the owners. Analysis of the water buyers in the village reveals that the total numbers of buyers has decreased from 173 in 1999–2000 to 104 in 2001–2002. The total area of land irrigated through buying water was also reduced from 124 hectares to a mere 49 hectares in 2001–2002. Thakores, who are the largest water-buyer group in the village, were hardest hit by this development, as the total area of land irrigated with water bought from tube well cooperatives decreased from 45 to 20 hectares in 2001–2002.

The process was detrimental to the buyers. Marginal farmers, who largely formed the water buyers' group, were converted into sharecroppers. Sharecropping started to pick up in late nineties, when the water market started shrinking and water buyers were gradually losing their economic opportunities in agriculture. Since two-thirds of crop production goes to the owners of land and water rights, this situation favored upper class, which appropriated surplus in this process. The wealthier farmers also had relatives in the United States who sent money back home; hence they were economically independent of agriculture. Thanks to these factors, their bargaining power increased under the sharecropping arrangements, whereas there was no real economic alternative for the lower classes.

A Win-Some Lose-All Game

In Sangpura, as we have seen, irrigation interacted with the basic inequality in landownership, benefiting the landed farmers. Government intervention through legislation largely concentrated on indirect forms of regulation such as cutting the supply of electricity and controlling institutional finance. The choice for regulation through electricity cuts was largely a consequence of the inability of the government to increase the price for electricity use in agriculture, due to political pressures and demands for sustaining the interests of the large farmers' lobby. With the shrinking of groundwater markets due to the power cuts and the drawdown of the aquifer, the command areas of wells shrank. The first priority in access to irrigation water went to the owners, while the buyers of water were mostly pushed out of the market. Controlling institutional finance did not hamper the growth of tube wells, as large farmers could obtain money from other sources. It only affected the late entrants in tube-well business, who were mostly small farmers who could generate some resources and tried to have a tube well of their own. They did not have the resources to make ever greater investments as the groundwater receded. On the other hand, the upper-class farmers, mainly Patels, who migrated to the United States from the early nineties, sent money back home. The money generated in the United States made the upper-class farmers independent of the agricultural production system. Thanks to their new source of income, they were in a position to take more risks. They continued investing in agriculture in general and tube wells in particular. This also increased their bargaining power in the day-to-day management of agriculture, and made them powerful enough to control the groundwater-based agrarian economy. Middle-level farmers who had invested in tube wells earlier did not have the financial means to participate in new tube wells.

For the underclass, the changed scenario resulted in new institutional arrangements of sharecropping, whereby the sharecropper received only one-third of the net production. For the upper class, the sharecropping system was cheaper than the use of hired labor. Apart from generating more surplus through the sale of water, it saved landowning farmers from the transaction costs of supervising and managing the laborers. Here, the charge of water was deducted from the total production, which was always higher than the actual cost of water per hour in the water market. Yet, the underclass did take up land under the new sharecropping arrangements, as most of them were out of the water markets and needed work to survive. People in this class remained dependent on farming for their household food security.

Water Laws, Water Markets, and Social Differentiation

The case study of Sangpura presented in this chapter points toward a complex web of regulation, market relations, and social relationships that, together, provide opportunities for one class of people to control and redefine the course of production relations in a situation of water scarcity. This social differentiation clearly creates a division between those having and those not having the opportunity to escape the agrarian trap, the political clout to defy regulation, and the power to shift the social and economic burden of water pricing. It also emphasizes the dynamic linkages between the physical nature of groundwater as a resource and the larger socioeconomic, political, and institutional context within which its use is regulated.

Two major generalizations can be made here from a water-rights perspective. First, the case shows the loopholes in formal groundwater legislation that does not capture the socioeconomic realities and ways in which water rights are actualized. In the existing legal framework, the rights are in a private regime, groundwater belonging to the person who owns the land from which it is accessed. In this framework, landowners have all rights while the landless are left out. It also gives power to rich property owners to become waterlords and indulge in water sales (Singh 1994). Yet having land rights in itself does not ensure access to water in areas like Sangpura. Ownership of the means of production is much more important in ensuring the right to be exercised than control of land alone. The cases of Mahendrabhai and Lakhaji clearly illustrate this point. The absence of clear-cut water rights initially led to a spurt in the groundwater market. Later, it was tied up with the land rental market through sharecropping arrangements. This specific definition of groundwater as property made it possible for resourceful farmers to acquire tradable rights defined by Saleth (1994a) as extra-legal. This is the more so in view of the severe scarcity of water, especially in areas where increasing multisectoral demands create pressure on the available sources of water. This is not only the case in water-scarce areas but even in areas that are historically known as water-abundant.[18]

Second, transactions in groundwater markets are socially contested and embedded in the way society or communities have historically been organized. The relationship between irrigation development and social differentiation has been widely debated and polarized. Many believed that irrigation development has, by definition, a positive impact on productivity; it can generate year-round employment through intensification of agriculture, and could therefore be used as a weapon against rural poverty (Chambers 1988; Shah 1993). However, the Sangpura case suggests that the outcome is quite different. It shows how water markets have only built upon the inequality in resource allocation. The caste-based system of hierarchy and unequal access to resources such as land and water reflected the prevalent production relations that were reinforced through water markets. Similar situations have been documented by Meinzen-Dick (2000) for tube well irrigation and water markets in Pakistan. As in Sangpura, in Pakistan the control over groundwater is for those who can afford to invest in the wells. This unreliability of access limits agricultural productivity for those who depend upon water from other people's wells. In the southern Indian state of Tamilnadu, a similar development has been observed by Janakarajan (1992, 1997). He points out that the unequal trading relationship that prevails between sellers and buyers results in the exploitation of buyers not only through price mechanisms but also through nonprice mechanisms.[19] His analyses show that the "transaction" in groundwater markets leaves little room for buyers to negotiate. This leads to an involuntary involvement of resource-poor farmers who have no other choice but to cling to the exploitative structures that perpetuate inequity in resource allocation and access.

The proponents of water markets advance two basic arguments. First, there is a plea for reallocation of water to the highest-valued uses, considering that groundwater is a scarce resource. It is argued that water markets allocate the resource to the most valued use (Rosegrant and Binswanger 1994: 1,616). Here, water is allocated to the sector with the highest marginal benefit; a useful means of achieving efficient water allocation is to put a right price tag on it (Tsur and Dinar 1997). It is argued that, under the "efficient" water market system, competitive water sellers would bring down the cost per unit of water. Hence, water would be available at a more competitive price. Further, the water sellers would cut the water price to a level close to the average cost of pumping. This would generate a larger irrigation surplus and more livelihoods for the resource-poor and landless. Referring to the "efficiency" arguments, Shah (1993) argues for using a flat rate in charging electricity for pumping, as that would create competitive markets. In the competitive water market, the forces of demand and supply determine prices and the highest bidder gets water. It is assumed that the price paid for the resource reflects the value of the resource to a person. From the case of Sangpura we have seen that this argument ignores the implications of the existing distribution of income, in which the price at which water is bought does not reflect the use value of the resource. Further, market allocations of groundwater generate externalities such as a declining water table. These externalities are not reflected in market transactions, which are poor indicators of value of commodities for which property rights are not concisely defined (Brajer et al. 1989). Many also believe that water markets are responsible for depleting aquifers, due to competition among farmers in overexploiting an open access resource and creating negative equity impacts (Bhatia 1992; Janakarajan 1993; Saleth 1994a). In the process, resource-poor and marginal farmers are losing access to groundwater and find it hard to cope with the declining water table.

The second argument pertains to groundwater markets as an appropriate way to increase control over resources and reduce constraints related to irrigation water supply (Rinaudo et al. 1997). Water markets are considered equitable because the sale of water in the open market has benefited many farmers who would otherwise not have had access to the resource. It is also argued that buyers are minimizing risk by not investing in modern water extracting mechanisms (Shah 1993). As we have seen in Sangpura, access of farmers to groundwater increased due to water markets in the early stages of their development. Given the high cost of developing new water sources, resource-poor farmers were at a distinct disadvantage in their ability to compete. However, it is also true that the water buyers have been almost totally dependent on the sellers and that a new class of waterlords is emerging, which has benefited from access to and sale of water, as well as from accumulation of surplus generated from it.[20] A similar process is documented by Dubash (2002), who observes that the groundwater markets have resulted in a reorganization of well ownership and the deepening of commodity relations through local politics, economic functions, and class power. The increasing accessibility argument does not hold in Sangpura, as we have seen that the groundwater markets are no longer expanding, and are even shrinking, and have reached a dead point. This does not primarily affect the sellers, as they still enjoy access and have diversified from agriculture through the surplus generated in the process.

In conclusion, the Sangpura case shows that currently existing forms of legislation and resource regulation policies do not address the issues of equity in resource distribution and groundwater depletion. By exerting their social and political power and influence, the resource-rich and powerful class has been able to bypass regulation more than anyone else. Apart from that, regulation of groundwater resources is inherently difficult to enforce in a consistent manner. As a consequence, legal regulation of groundwater resources in India turns out to be highly inequitable in practice. The fate of the model bill for groundwater regulation in India and Gujarat proves the case. Many experts reject such hierarchic and prescriptive top-down models in favor of approaches that involve an open, nonlinear and ongoing process of social dialogue (Moench 1999). It remains to be seen, however, whether such dialogue stands a chance of success under the current sociopolitical conditions of class, caste, and power differences that form the daily reality of life in Sangpura and many other Indian villages. Approaches to resource regulation and management that do not take seriously into account these realities will only perpetuate or even worsen the existing conditions of inequality and overexploitation of groundwater resources.

NOTES

1. According to the Central Groundwater Board of the Government of India, the overexploited subdistricts are areas in which the level of groundwater extraction is more than 100 percent of the annual recharge. Dark subdistricts are areas in which the level of extraction is between 85 and 100 percent of annual groundwater recharge. Grey areas have between 65 and 85 percent extraction; white areas have less than 65 percent.
2. The Hindu caste system in India and other parts of South Asia is crucial in determining access to the means of production and control over resources, institutions, and forms of surplus extraction (Chakravarti 2001). We reject Dumont's understanding of caste as "discrete systems where political and economic aspects are relatively secondary and isolated" (Dumont 1998: 21–32, 235). For a detailed critique, see Gupta 1991; Das 1982.
3. Sangpura is a pseudonym for the village in Mehsana District, Gujarat, in which we did research on the social, political, and legal dimensions of groundwater use. A taluka or block is an administrative division at the subdistrict level.
4. Gujarat is the fourth most urbanized state, with 37 percent of its total population living in urban areas (the national urbanization rate is 28 percent; Hirway 2000). According to the 2001 census, 70 percent of Gujarat's population is literate, as against 65 percent nationally. Of its villages, 97 percent are linked by concrete roads, and all villages in which this is feasible have been electrified. Gujarat is one of the most industrialized states of India, concentrating especially on chemicals, fertilizers, textiles, and dairy products (Wood 1997).

5. Though we mention the major professional characteristics associated with the castes, these and other characteristics tend to be phrased in generalizing terms; it is important to avoid too essentialist an approach to, and conceptualization of caste.

6. The name Patel has been derived from *patidar*, "people who own land." The term *patidar* has now become extinct (Vyas 1998: 279).

7. The Gaekwads of Maharashtra invaded the plains of Gujarat near the end of the Mughal Empire in the early eighteenth century. During the 1723–1730 period, they challenged the Mughals and established their claim in today's Mehsana District and other parts of Gujarat. During the British period, this area came under direct rule of the Gaekwad of Baroda in the first decade of the nineteenth century, and remained such until 1949, when Baroda state was merged into Bombay state. In 1956, the states were reorganized, and a bigger bilingual state of Bombay was formed. In 1960, Bombay state was split up into the separate states of Gujarat and Maharashtra. Since then, Mehsana has been part of Gujarat state (Government of Gujaret 1991).

8. Water was sold during those days on a crop-sharing basis rather than a per-hour basis. The rationale was that, land productivity being much higher in those days than it is now, there was not much risk involved in selling water on the basis of crop sharing. Gradually, when crop failure became rampant, the hourly charge for water was institutionalized.

9. The ryotwari system for tax revenue administration and collection was based on a full survey and assessment of all cultivable land. This distinguishes it from the zamindari system, which was based on revenue collection through (local elite) intermediaries, a form of indirect collection (see Patel 1969).

10. Thakores are nonvegetarians. In Gujarat and elsewhere, there is a stigma attached to being nonvegetarian. It is mostly related to the notion of being impure.

11. The GWRDC was established in 1975 as a state-owned company responsible for establishing and managing irrigation tube wells with support from the state government. Between 1975 and 1994, the GWRDC set up 2,800 public tube wells. The primary objective of the program was to increase the area under irrigation by utilizing the groundwater. However, the public tube well program ran into problems caused by huge losses, and the government decided to transfer the management responsibilities of the defunct tube wells to the farmers' organization, in order to reduce the financial burden on the state and to improve utilization of the wells (Shah et al. 1994). The GWRDC tube well at Sangpura was not transferred to the farmers' organization, and is still managed by the corporation.

12. "After some prodding from the central government, the Bombay Irrigation Act (governing Gujarat) was amended in 1976 to regulate new deep tube wells and the use of water in existing tube wells. As a result of a series of legislative delays, the amendment only entered into force in 1988, and currently applies to nine districts" (Dubash 2002: 70).

13. On the basis of the Gujarat Electricity Regulatory Commission's award dated October 10, 2000, the Gujarat government hiked the tariff of electricity used in agriculture from June 2003. There are an estimated 600,000 farm connections in the state, owners of which pay for electricity according to the contracted load of their motors. The rates for electric motors of less than 7.5 horsepower capacity increased from Rs. 350 to over Rs. 1,100 per year; those for motors of more than 7.5 horsepower capacity rose from Rs. 500 to Rs. 1,260 per year. Many believe that the government has acted under pressure from the Asian Development Bank to do away with subsidies in the farm sector. After this it was decided to cut subsidies to the Gujarat Electricity Board, worth

Rs. 11.56 billion. Around 57 percent of this is shouldered by the agriculture sector alone. The Gujarat government spends Rs. 1,700 crores (one crore equals ten million rupees) every year on subsidies to farmers. Soon after the declaration of this tariff hike, strong agitation was mounted by farmers' organizations. They stopped paying electricity bills and, in some cases, did not allow the electricity department officials to enter the village to demand payment or sever connections due to nonpayment. The government used force to suppress violent agitations. However, as the general election was around the corner in 2004, the government offered a 25 to 33 percent reduction in the power tariff. The new tariff was not accepted by the farmers' organizations, which continued their resistance. In February 2004, one of the organizations (BKS) compromised with the government and called off its strike after a decision further lowering the tariff. However, other organizations are continuing their agitation, saying there was a great betrayal by BKS, caused by their closeness with the ruling BJP party. In the general election of 2004, the ruling BJP received a major setback. It lost twelve of the twenty-six parliament seats, including Mehsana.

14. The names of individuals have been changed to protect their identity. One bigha is equal to 0.23 hectare.

15. Sharecropping arrangements vary in the village, but the most popular form involves division of the net production in three equal parts for land, labor, and water for irrigation.

16. Poverty-line criteria in India are defined by official standards developed by the Planning Commission from the 1970s onward.

17. The land-based classification of farmers is: marginal (less than one hectare), small (one to three hectares), medium (three to five hectares), and large farmers (five hectares and above).

18. In Bangladesh, for example, conflicts are emerging between groundwater users in the context of declining water tables during the dry season. Despite seemingly abundant water, the increasing use of deep water table extracting technologies for irrigation takes water away from shallow hand pumps used for domestic water supply. This causes a seasonal water crisis affecting millions of people who depend upon hand pumps. Because groundwater rights are not defined, nobody knows how to deal with the growing problem. As well-endowed farmers with tube wells draw down groundwater, while nonirrigating households usually depend upon shallow hand pumps for domestic water, control over groundwater becomes an issue of access to improved technology (Sadeque 2000). See also chapter 6 for a similar situation in Kathmandu.

19. Janakarajan (1992) studies the interlinked land lease and credit markets in a village in Tamilnadu, and highlights the manner in which differential access to groundwater resources can be instrumental in precipitating an exploitative interlocking of water, labor, and credit markets. According to him, an exploitative triangular relationship is established between trader, water seller, and water purchaser. He observes that the water market favors the traders and sellers; often, landlords are also waterlords.

20. Prahladachar studies innovations in the use and management of groundwater in the hard-rock regions of India. He indicates that, because of their advantageous resource position and bureaucratic-political influence, owners of large farms have disproportionately appropriated the gains of lift irrigation. He calls for innovative institutional arrangements to improve access to water for small farmers, especially in the water-scarce hard-rock regions (Prahladachar 1994).

9

Redressing Racial Inequities through Water Law in South Africa

Interaction and Contest among Legal Frameworks

BARBARA VAN KOPPEN

NITISH JHA

In the apartheid era prior to 1991, South Africa was a country torn by formal racial divisions. Under a comprehensive official policy of racial segregation, and in an attempt to create a society of whites only, the government of South Africa broke off its association with the British Commonwealth and created a white republic in 1961.[1] Simultaneously, in an attempt to confront the reality of a black majority within its borders, the republican government instituted a program of "separate development" through which it carved out a number of black states inside its own boundaries.

Comprising no more than 13.5 percent of the country's area, these ten arbitrarily created administrative territories—called *Bantustans* or Homelands—were allegedly the original areas of settlement of what the state had identified as the country's nine main African ethnic groups. Within these territories, several of which were highly fragmented, black Africans could aspire to self-rule (Ross 1999: 135).[2] In reality, these areas—whose nominal autonomy went unrecognized internationally—served merely as dumping grounds for blacks who were deemed in excess of numbers acceptable within the white republic. They acted as dormitories from where black men commuted to work in white South Africa while the women, most of whom stayed behind, were relegated to the roles of procreators of a future labor force and of caretakers for the sick and elderly (Omer-Cooper 1994). Moreover, these areas became economically very weak, as forced removals led to huge population densities that often far exceeded the carrying capacity of the land (Ross 1999). The new multiracial government of South Africa, which was elected to power in 1994, continues to be confronted by these institutions that had been put in place by its predecessor.

Under apartheid, the open embodiment of racism in law carried over into the water sector, as well. As a result, control over water in contemporary South Africa can be understood as the interaction and contest among three formal legal systems, besides several informal ones. The three formal systems are: the apartheid-era laws, enforced in the white republic; the former Homelands laws; and the postapartheid laws. Although superceded by the laws of democratic South Africa, in certain respects the two legal systems of the apartheid era continue a de facto existence.

During the apartheid era, the white government, large-scale farmers, and mining, forestry, and tourist companies have influenced the establishment of well-defined formal laws and well-organized institutions based on riparian rights. This ensured their permanent access to the country's scarce water resources. In contrast, even though most Homelands formally recognized the Water Act of 1956, which also prevailed in the white areas, water was one of the subjects falling under the jurisdiction of the Homeland governments, who partially relegated control over water to local chiefs and tribal councils. The National Water Act of 1998, formulated during and immediately after the political changes that led to the democratic election of the new government, broke radically with previous policy. At least in principle, the act shifted the locus of formal water control from riparian title holders, consisting largely of the white minority, to the nation's new government, in particular the minister of water affairs and forestry, who was deemed the custodian of the nation's water resources. The act is not only widely recognized in policy circles as the most comprehensive water law in the world but also specifies, more clearly than any other comparable document, that water is essentially a tool to move society towards social and environmental justice and poverty eradication. Its stated aim is redressing race and gender inequities inherited from the past.

The first years of implementation of the National Water Act highlight how most of the former white powers, who are generally high-volume water users with vested economic interests, attempt to define and use the new legal instruments for their continued de facto control over water. By contrast, the Department of Water Affairs and Forestry (DWAF), in the spirit of the act, seeks to regulate water use and water control by these high-volume users and to enforce better sharing of water and water-related benefits with the historically disadvantaged and mostly poor black population.

At the same time, in its direct interaction with the poor, DWAF promotes water development for domestic and productive purposes. It also fosters empowerment of poor men and women, and a stronger voice for them in decision making over water, both within communities and in interactions between poor communities and high-volume users. In doing so, DWAF seeks to be reconciled with the previous formal law in the ex-Homelands, which exclusively vested local resource management authority in the traditional chiefs. However, the new constitution and the National Water Act recognize the primacy—especially for the provision of domestic water supply—of the new, democratically elected local governments, which are frequently at loggerheads with the traditional chiefs (Republic of South Africa 1998b: 56, 58). Nevertheless, the de facto influence of traditional rulers continues.[3] Thus, DWAF's objectives must be realized at the interface of, on the one hand, the National Water Act and, on the other, the de facto continuing water laws that governed both the former white Republic of South Africa and the former Homelands.

This chapter analyzes these interactions and contests between the three legal systems in further detail. It highlights the impact of legal pluralism on attempts to realize the societal and developmental aims mentioned above. As background information, in section two a brief picture is provided of the links between water and poverty in South Africa. In the third section we discuss the historical roots of the two formal legal systems of the apartheid era. The next section focuses on the formulation process and contents of the National Water Act of 1998. The interactions between these three legal systems during implementation are illustrated for two important aspects of the National Water Act. First, we discuss DWAF's current interpretation of the concept of "basic human needs" at the new interface between DWAF and the historically disadvantaged communities. A second aspect is DWAF's approach in establishing catchment management agencies (CMAs). This highlights how the vested powers seek to use the new law to their own advantage, and DWAF's responses to this. We elaborate upon the case of the CMA of the Olifants River Basin, a water-stressed basin that has been designated as the second pilot basin for CMA establishment in South Africa (see figure 9.1). In the final section we conclude that the act itself potentially provides for radical changes, but that the ultimate achievement of these aims depends largely upon DWAF's interpretation of the act in further regulating the control over water of the high-volume users, and in crafting new partnerships with the black population, building upon local water tenure arrangements from the old era.

Poverty and Water in South Africa

As a legacy of the apartheid regime, poverty is widespread and inequities are huge in South Africa. Almost 50 percent of South Africa's population is income-poor, spending less than 353 rand (US$55) per adult equivalent per month.[4] More than one-quarter of the population, or ten to twelve million people, are without clean water. South Africa ranks as low as thirty-one among all forty-eight sub-Saharan African countries in terms of the performance of its rural water supply sector. Unemployment rates in 1999 were 52 percent for African women between fifteen and sixty-five years, and 37 percent among men in the same age group (Statistics South Africa 1999). Of the poor, 70 percent live in rural areas. The income distribution in South Africa is among the most unequal of all countries in the world. The distribution of land resources is also highly skewed, with 13 percent of the population—who are mostly whites—owning 87 percent of the available land (Cousins 2000; Lahiff 1999). Inequities in access to water may be even wider, as fragmentary evidence shows. As much as 95 percent of water for irrigation is used by large-scale farmers, while smallholders only have access to the remaining 5 percent (de Lange 1998). In the Mhlatuze Basin in KwaZulu Natal Province, a mere 10 percent of the population has access to more than 97 percent of available water resources. Only a very small part of the benefits from the bulk of the water that this minority uses trickles down into poorer sections of society (Steyl et al. 2000).

The linkages between water and poverty are multiple. Poverty is defined as a state and process of multidimensional deprivation, affecting economic, health-related, psychological, sociocultural, legal, and political facets of well-being (World Bank 2000/2001). Water deprivation is intrinsic to poverty. Lack of access to safe and nearby drinking water and proneness to waterborne diseases are widely recognized as dimensions of poverty. Although water is essential for crop cultivation, livestock, fisheries, small industries, and other components of rural people's diversified livelihood strategies, poor people often lack the assets and technologies to harness water to these ends. Even though the scale of their enterprises is typically small, the poor even lack access to the small quantities of water that could considerably increase enterprise productivity and reduce their vulnerability to droughts and climatic changes. Moreover, if there is competition over water—whether within communities or between communities and external high-volume users, from local to basin level—the poor are easily ousted by more powerful, high-volume users. Marginalization of the poor from the public governance structures through which these conflicts can be mediated reinforces their exclusion.

The close relations between water and poverty also imply that water resources development, management, and control can contribute to the eradication of poverty if it boosts water availability and control among the poor, and more equal sharing of the benefits from water with the wealthy water users. This would improve the well-being of the poor in terms of health, income, assets, resilience against adversities, and sociopolitical and legal inclusion in governance structures. In general, it would ensure them a greater say over their own lives. Therefore, under the National Water Act, DWAF endeavors to give the poor of South Africa a greater control over water resources. It bears repeating that, in South Africa's water sector, the fault line between rich and poor closely mirrors that between white and black users.

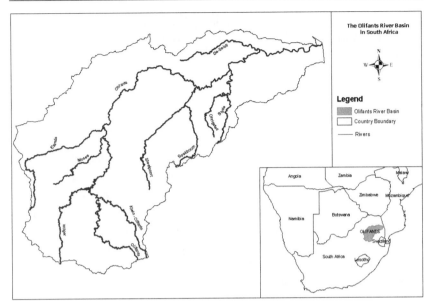

FIGURE 9.1. The Olifants River Basin in South Africa.

Pluralistic Water Law under the Apartheid Regime

Apartheid Government Law

In order to be better able to appreciate current changes, we give a sketch of the two separate legal systems in existence before 1994. Jurisdiction over water followed the geographical segregation of the apartheid regime. The Department of Water Affairs and Forestry served the former white Republic of South Africa. Here, water rights were primarily vested in riparian right holders. Commercial farmers, an important constituency of the apartheid government, were well served by DWAF through highly subsidized schemes and dam development. Gradually, however, DWAF started shifting its focus to other important water users, such as power generation and industries. It also intensified water quality management. By the mid-1980s, the first river basin studies were undertaken, in collaboration with consulting firms that had accumulated expertise for the area in which they were active. The first ideas for catchment management agencies originate from that period (DWAF 1986; J. van Rooijen, personal communication 2001).

Among the water users in the white Republic of South Africa, a considerable degree of self-management had crystallized. Democratically elected irrigation boards managed large-scale irrigation schemes, and their representatives participated effectively in national farmer organizations. Portions of rivers in which farmers had built weirs were governed collectively. Large-scale water users also started to organize at basin level. For example, in 1992, the Olifants River Forum was initiated to promote better coordination between mines and a national park downstream of the Olifants River and the upstream mines, industries, and the country's largest electricity generation company—all in common pursuit of a healthy river.

Homelands Law

In the former Homelands, formal water authority was vested in the Homeland governments, which were represented at the community level by tribal chiefs and councils.[5] Generally, laws applicable in the Republic of South Africa stayed in force for a specific territory when it became a national state or self-governing territory, until amended or repealed by a competent authority. For water control, the Water Act No. 54 of 1956 and other relevant water acts in force in a specific territory at the time of independence of a national state or self-governing territory became the water law for that state or territory. Except for the territory known as the Republic of Bophuthatswana, there were only some small differences between the provisions of the water law applicable in the territories of the different national states and self-governing territories. However, implementation through tribal structures fundamentally differed from implementation of the same act in the white areas. As documentation and analysis of the implementation of formal legal systems has been extremely limited, only broad and impressionistic remarks can be made here. Generally, these governments undertook some rural drinking water supply schemes. Within rural communities, chiefs and their headmen were the main contact persons for the Homeland government and any other outsiders intervening in issues concerning water supply facilities. Specific tasks, such as the operation and maintenance of water supply systems, were usually delegated to members of the tribal council, who then formed the relevant committees.

Most Homeland governments also initiated state-subsidized irrigation schemes in collaboration with development corporations (parastatal organizations investing in rural development). These schemes were usually the only effort to improve agricultural development and, for that matter, access to irrigation water in the Homelands. These endeavors were dominated entirely by outside agencies, with neither any formal power for the local chiefs and councils nor any voice of the farmers themselves, the majority of whom were women. Formal ownership and management of land and water in these irrigation schemes and sometimes also the management of farming and water management operations, credit provision, and marketing remained with these parastatals. Formal water rights for irrigation schemes were also in the hands of governments or agencies. However, chiefs played important de facto roles in land reallocation. The domination of the state and of parastatals in these irrigation schemes became particularly evident when the new government suddenly withdrew support in the late 1990s, as a result of which most of these irrigation schemes collapsed in whole or in part.[6]

Mines intending to operate in territories of specific chiefs also approached them for permission. Even where Homeland governments gave them formal permission, none of the concomitant responsibilities were adhered to. The mines, which considered both land and water resources in the Homelands as open access resources, took this as a carte blanche for polluting such resources without taking on the commitment to clean up.

Informal Law or Local Water Tenure

Although most questions about the actual implementation of formal water law in the ex-Homelands are yet to be answered, even more study is required to understand the informal arrangements within black rural communities that governed water development and management. As the authority of chiefs typically concerned all resources of the community, the ultimate say over water infrastructure development, such as small reservoirs for use by humans and livestock, water allocation, and water pollution issues also fell to the chief and the tribal council. Anecdotal evidence describes how chiefs set and enforced rules to solve problems of water pollution, or convened meetings to resolve conflicts between users of water for domestic purposes and irrigators. These practices and norms were embedded in a particular cosmology that regarded water as a powerful resource.[7] This comprehensive set of sociopolitical arrangements of rules and norms as well as practices of water use and control that prevail in poor rural communities can be called local water tenure, analogous to the much more common concept of local land tenure, which often derived from the same sources of authority (cf. Cousins 2000).

Every outsider taking a conventional sectoral approach to water issues has overlooked the fact that local water tenure is intrinsically integrated. In poor rural communities, the same water source is often used simultaneously for (unpiped) drinking water, other domestic uses, and a diverse range of productive purposes. Sanitation and waste management often directly affect other water sources, as well. Water development with government aid, for example, for one group of villagers easily detracts from the welfare of other users and may jeopardize the fulfillment of people's basic needs. In short, water tenure in rural communities is conceived of—if only in practice—as integrated water resources management.

The National Water Act of 1998

Context

The transformation of the above-mentioned legal systems was a fundamental part of the political events arising out of the end to the apartheid era in 1994 (de

Lange 2004). Under the leadership of the then minister of water affairs and forestry, a process was launched to incorporate public views nationwide and to
harness global knowledge for the formulation of the National Water Act, which
was finally promulgated in 1998. These globally recognized, so-called best principles for integrated water management include the integration of surface and
groundwater management, the gradual decentralization of water management
to the lowest appropriate level, self-financing of water management by user
groups, public participation and community involvement, the preservation of
water for ecological purposes, and the shift from administrative to hydrological
basin boundaries for water management, ultimately to be implemented by
catchment management agencies.

In promulgating the new law, the government abolished the former system
of permanent riparian rights and took over the water management authority as
the custodian of the nation's water resources. With the abolition of the Homelands, DWAF's jurisdiction became countrywide. As custodian, the government
guarantees water provision for uses stipulated in the National Water Reserve,
which encompasses a basic human need component and an ecological component. For any other use, the government authorizes water use without any guarantee, although international obligations and strategically important uses are
prioritized. Authorizations take the form of either licenses, general authorizations or, for minor uses, permissions under the so-called Schedule One.[8] The act
also introduces water demand management and efficient water use in order to
reduce people's water use and free up water for others.

Since 1994, DWAF has also become responsible for rural water supply. Although former Homeland governments had experience with rural water supply,
including reticulation, this was a new task for DWAF. Until then it had only supplied bulk water to municipal water boards in the white areas, which then took
care of reticulation. Since 2003, the democratically elected local governments are
expected to take up the responsibilities of providing water services nationwide.
As water supply services had a high political priority for the new government, a
special Water Services Act was already promulgated in 1997 (RSA 1997).

South Africa's new local government plays a new role not only in domestic
water supply in the ex-Homelands but also in other aspects of integrated water
resources management. Constitutionally, the local government is already responsible for water supply reticulation, sanitation and storm water management (RSA 1998b: 58). A step that has been taken more recently is to include
water for agricultural uses in the mandate of local governments. Indeed, water
for small-scale agriculture is now being considered in the integrated rural development plans of those local governments that are targeted by the president's
new Integrated Sustainable Rural Development Strategy of 2001. The formal role
of local governments in the new catchment management agencies is stipulated in

the act, but its precise meaning and actual implementation are yet to crystallize.

The capacities of the nascent local governments are still fragile. After two rounds of national elections since 1994 and stabilized administrative boundaries since 2000, this democratically elected, party-bound layer of government is still finding its feet, especially in poor rural areas where no such structure previously existed. Depending on the area in question, this governance body continues to be challenged either by the traditional, black authority structures or the former white municipality leaders, both of whom have remained, in fact, more powerful. These new governance layers concur with or contest, first, local water tenure arrangements embedded in the traditional power structures; second, attempts of the formerly vested white powers to continue their own de facto control of water; third, DWAF's own responses. The question how they do so is probably the most critical to answer, if the goals of the act—to redress the inequities from the past—are to be achieved.

Contents of the National Water Act

A closer look at the contents of the National Water Act (RSA 1998b) highlights components that are most relevant for the question of how the act could possibly transform society and what may thwart its stated objectives.

REDRESS OF INEQUITIES OF THE PAST BASED ON RACE AND GENDER. The basic human right to sufficient food and water is firmly rooted in section twenty-seven of the new Constitution of South Africa (RSA 1994), and subsequently enshrined in the National Water Act. Throughout the act, the principle of "redress of racial and gender inequities from the past" is mentioned as a main criterion for South Africa's new integrated water resources management.

BASIC HUMAN WATER NEEDS. The National Water Act stipulates that the government must allocate a reserve for basic human consumption needs before any other use. A similar priority allocation is made for the ecological reserve.

DEMOGRAPHIC REPRESENTATION. According to the National Water Act, governance bodies should be representative in terms of including sections of the population that were not previously represented in governance forums, especially blacks and women. The Minister of water affairs and forestry has far-reaching powers to ensure demographic representation in new legal governance structures like CMAs.

COOPERATIVE GOVERNANCE. A general government policy in South Africa, which is crucial for rectifying race and gender inequities through water law, is the emphasis on strong horizontal and vertical "cooperative governance." This entails, first, cooperative governance within government agencies. In this case, it concerns coordination between the various divisions within DWAF: Water Supply, Water Quality, Groundwater, Catchment Management Agencies, Resource Planning, Modeling, and so on. Such integrated water service delivery is especially important in rural areas where the same water sources are used for multiple purposes, and uses by the one often directly affect uses by others. More coordination and synergy among the various divisions of DWAF would improve service delivery, and better ensure that the still unmet domestic and productive water needs of the poorest are taken into consideration.

Second, the South African constitution requires cooperative governance *among* the various government agencies. This is crucial to aid the poor through water development and management for productive uses. High-volume users have already succeeded in establishing large-scale and profitable enterprises. They obtained access, often in the past and with considerable state support, to the range of production factors that makes a water-related enterprise profitable. In contrast, poor people tend to lack access to the inputs, skills, technologies, and markets that render a water-related enterprise more profitable, or else they pay relatively more for these inputs and services. Moreover, water reforms without, for example, effective land reform will have only a limited impact. Poverty is multidimensional and warrants an integrated approach.[9]

Another major issue in cooperative governance for water management and control, from the local to basin level, is the role of the local government already mentioned above.

COMPULSORY LICENSING FOR WATER REALLOCATION. The legal tool in the National Water Act that allows reallocation of water from high-volume users to poor water users is termed compulsory licensing. DWAF can call for compulsory licensing where and when needed. A project of compulsory licensing concerns all water users in a specific area. It cancels all existing licenses and replaces these on the basis of a new allocation schedule. Redressing race and gender inequities from the past is a key criterion for such a reallocation. This is the case, even if the reductions result "in severe prejudice to the economic viability of an undertaking in respect of which the water was beneficially used." Normally in such a situation, a person may claim compensation for any financial loss suffered in consequence through the Water Tribunal (National Water Act, sections 22.6–7 and 43 to 48).[10] The inclusion of this clause weakens the possibility of reallocating water. Fortunately, there is a safeguard built into the act that exempts the government from payment of this compensation if it is to:

- provide for the reserve;
- rectify an over-allocation of water use from the resource in question; or

- rectify an unfair or disproportionate water use.

It is vital that this safeguard be implemented effectively.

Although the above-mentioned elements of the act potentially foster the transformation of South African society toward greater equity, the status quo of the apartheid era remains unaltered through two important factors: first, through the recognition of existing lawful use. The National Water Act recognizes all existing lawful water use in the two years preceding promulgation of the act as lawful. Hence, it also accepts the inequities prevailing at that time. The second factor is the composition of the civil service: Nationwide, there were no retrenchments in the government administrative services in the new dispensation. This means that the new approach to water resources management is being implemented by many of the officials responsible for executing the previous, inequitable legislation (staff awareness and support are, of course, crucial conditions for implementation and enforcement; see also chapter 2 for similar conditions in Nepal).

The compromises between changing and maintaining the status quo undoubtedly contributed to what is perhaps the most remarkable achievement of the formulation of the National Water Act, which is that most of the highly diverse stakeholders in this "rainbow nation" endorse and "took ownership" of the law.

Implementing the Protection of Basic Human Water Needs

An issue that illustrates the challenge of finding a compromise between the pro-poor formal law of South Africa and local water tenure is the protection of poor people's basic human water needs. The National Water Act interprets "basic human water needs" guaranteed in the National Water Reserve as needs only for domestic purposes. The government took the policy decision to guarantee domestic water provision for twenty-five liters per person per day and committed itself to the provision of the infrastructure required to bring this quantity of water sufficiently near to poor people's homes. In 2000, the government further committed itself to ensure that these minimum quantities of domestic water supply, which equal 6,000 liters per household per month, were to be delivered for free. Larger quantities are to be charged according to stepped tariffs. The government's commitment to the development of infrastructure and the organization of delivery of free basic water is of major importance. DWAF is engaged in massive efforts to achieve a minimum state of welfare that is still a distant ideal for millions of poor black South Africans.

Water for productive purposes, to help poor women and men to improve the harvests of their homestead gardens or fields, their poultry and livestock enterprises, or small crafts, is not covered in the National Water Reserve. Even Schedule One, which stipulates small water uses that are permissible under any condition without need for registration, authorization, or payment—even in the river (sub)basins declared to be "water-stressed"—is not clear on whether such uses for basic income needs are permitted. "Schedule One water uses" concern water for reasonable domestic use, livestock other than feedlots, and small gardening, not for commercial purposes. However, farming and gardening by poor farmers are often market-oriented for at least part of the harvest, and are expected to become even more so in the near future. One of those who drafted the National Water Act now realizes that small-scale but market-oriented productive water uses by the poor were overlooked during the drafting process. With hindsight, she would have paid more attention to possible options for including such uses in the National Water Reserve (R. Stein, Wits University, personal communication). As changing the law is highly complicated, the pragmatic approach that the Department of Water Affairs is currently taking is to articulate publicly, for example in the minister's budget speech in 2003, that small-scale productive uses of water by historically disadvantaged individuals for food security are authorized and even encouraged under Schedule One, without any further obligation.

DWAF has also started implementing the tool of compulsory licensing as an integral part of water allocation in general. Currently, a policy for water allocation is being drafted that specifies the abstract overarching principle in the National Water Act of "redress of inequities from the past" into more concrete water allocation measures to be taken in both highly water-stressed basins such as the Inkomati and Olifants basins and elsewhere in South Africa. For stressed basins, options and potential financial and legal implications of taking water away from the haves and giving it to the have-nots are thoroughly studied and debated. Although contested by the vested powers, DWAF aims at implementing such reform without compensation. It is also increasingly realized that taking "existing lawful use" as the starting point of formal water rights reallocation not only recognizes the current existing inequities in water use but also favors those who have written documents, such as permits recognized under the apartheid law in the white areas. These provide much stronger proof of existing lawful water use than what the inhabitants of the ex-Homelands can verify (see also chapter 7 for the Andes). A solution may be to just declare all current actual water use in the former Homelands as legal. However, more study and policy debate on other options and implications are required. For both water-stressed and nonstressed situations, the focus has extended beyond legislation, and now also includes the practically required cross-sectoral support to the poor in accessing water through small-scale infrastructure development and in using water more productively through collaboration with, for example, the Department of Agriculture.

Implementing Catchment Management Agencies

CMAs in the National Water Act

A second illustration of the interactions between the old and new formal legal systems in South Africa, which is already being implemented, is the establishment of catchment management agencies. In compliance with the National Water Act, the minister of water affairs and forestry has started the process of establishing CMAs in the nineteen water management areas of South Africa. Gradually, he will assign to these new governance structures considerable water resource management powers currently held by DWAF. The CMA is supposed to compile the Catchment Management Strategy and, ultimately, also to carry out functions such as water resources planning in the catchment, registration, water charge collection, water authorization, and licensing (including compulsory licensing). Public participation in the establishment process and fair representation in the future governing board and activities of the CMAs are legally required. In the governing board, the interests of water users, potential water users, local and provincial governments, and environmental interest groups will be represented. CMAs are to become self-financing.

This change from a centralized management approach based on command and control from the nation's capital to a decentralized participatory model based on cooperative governance and coordination through CMAs is a major step (Muller 2001). Parallel to the process of establishing CMAs in the water management areas, DWAF itself is being reorganized. The remaining national functions of DWAF are being defined, and preparations have started to restructure DWAF regional offices into technical support structures of the CMAs in the new water management areas. As long as CMAs are still being established and maturing, DWAF continues to carry out all functions not yet taken up by the CMAs themselves. Implementation of other elements of the National Water Act that are essential for CMAs is also underway. Since 2002, for example, charges for water resources management according to registered water use are being levied. Ultimately, CMAs are to be self-financing from the income of these charges. In 2002, the first draft of the National Water Resources Strategy was published. This national strategy sets the framework within which the CMAs have to function. In extensive rounds of public consultation throughout South Africa, more than two thousand formal reactions have been received, which are all considered during the finalization of the strategy.

To illustrate the establishment process of a CMA, in the remaining part of the chapter we present the case of the highly water-stressed Olifants Basin, the nation's second pilot basin for this process. The Olifants River has its source in Gauteng province and passes through Mpumalanga and Limpopo provinces into the Kruger National Park, before entering Mozambique and joining the Limpopo River. More than three million people live in this water-stressed basin.

The majority of them are poor. Many of the poor live in the congested former Homelands. The process of CMA establishment is driven by the DWAF Regional Office in Mpumalanga (Ligthelm 2001). The establishment of the CMA proposal in the Olifants Basin illustrates the angles and approaches of the various parties: the white power groups and their vested interests, the historically disadvantaged groups, and DWAF.

Formulation of a Technical Proposal for CMA Establishment

The process of establishing the CMA in the Olifants Basin (DWAF 2003) highlights the processes through which those who dominated water control during the apartheid era basically consolidate their power.[11] Attempts were made to ensure legitimacy by nominally including historically disadvantaged individuals. An earlier attempt to even reinforce control was rejected by DWAF. The aforementioned Olifants River Forum, comprising the white-dominated mines, tourist industry, the public sector electricity supply company and industries throughout the Olifants River Basin, proposed that it would constitute the CMA and then take the process from there. This was suggested as soon as the new governance structures of CMAs were adopted in the deliberations over the National Water Act. However, DWAF rejected this proposal as it wanted the future CMA to be inclusive from the start.

DWAF launched the process of establishing a CMA in the Olifants Basin in mid-1999 by appointing technical consultants who, in the past decade, had accumulated technical knowledge of this basin. These consultants had also begun quantifying the ecological reserve for this basin. As stipulated in their terms of reference, the main purpose was to submit a formal proposal for a CMA to the minister and assist DWAF in establishing representative catchment management structures. Two rounds of public meetings were held in five places in the basin, in order to inform and consult people who would be affected. Written invitations for these public meetings were sent not only to all contacts of DWAF and the consultants but also to new local governments, tribal authorities, traditional healers, and so on. Although new contacts between DWAF and rural communities were established in this way, this happened in an unsystematic way. Local governments, just established at the start of the process, had no special role. This oversight of local government officials continued in later phases, even though they had become much better consolidated by then.

The first round of public meetings, in which 655 people participated, consisted primarily of providing information about the concepts of basin-level management and CMAs with public participation. After the first round of open consultations, DWAF and the consultants decided to add a second round in order to publicize the ideas they had developed for the future structure of the CMA. In the second round, the emphasis was also on information provision. In all public meetings, the main language was English, with translators only pro-

viding summarized translations in local languages on request. The consultants
were the main authors of a first-draft, incomplete proposal that was finalized by
mid-2000. This was made up largely of technical information and water use
projections that had essentially already been available before the process of establishing CMAs started. In this draft, it was admitted that no attention had
been paid to poverty issues.

Although the historically disadvantaged rural communities were certainly
interested in establishing contacts with DWAF, often for the first time in history, they were also quite critical of DWAF and the consultants. Frustration that
English was the main language; suspicion about the dominance of, again, white
consultants as perceived process drivers and the ones earning high salaries
from a process that is generally seen as very expensive; negative feelings after
the consultants' explanation of the ecological reserve, "as if they find fish more
important than our lives"; complaints about a lack of time for proper preparation and discussion, and inadequate explanations of what the issues really are—
these were drawbacks of the process as perceived by black participants. They
were, in particular, dissatisfied about the way in which the drinking water supply issue was handled. Invariably, participants raised their pressing problems in
this regard during the meetings. However, for these and similar problems, the
DWAF officials and the consultants referred people to other divisions within
DWAF, explaining that the CMA was one of the many parallel processes in which
DWAF interacts with the public and, thereby, tries to avoid interdivision dupli-
cation of tasks.

The first round of public consultations was also used to invite volunteers
from the historically disadvantaged communities to take their place in a so-
called Stakeholder Reference Group. This Stakeholder Reference Group, consisting in part of the former contacts of the consultants and DWAF, discussed the
CMA proposal in greater depth. However, while the white participants of the
Stakeholder Reference Group were well organized and reported back to those
they represented, the black participants were invited in an ad hoc manner,
without being required to represent a constituency or report back to it. So black
participants of the Stakeholder Reference Group were unable to give mandated
perspectives, and regretted that there was no opportunity to interact with a
constituency and ensure an input mandated by them. After a long delay, in February 2002, a final meeting with the Stakeholder Reference Group was held.
However, even at this meeting, the participation of stakeholders was little more
than nominal. Problems from the previous meetings had not been properly addressed. Moreover, the wishes of many poor stakeholders for a more integrated
approach to water management by the CMA were peremptorily disregarded.

The process also ended up disappointing the self-organized high-volume
water users and others who had worked closely with DWAF before 1994, but for
different reasons. Their hope that a reliance on formerly collected technical

expertise and the new public space for catchment management would easily enable them to continue exerting a strong de facto voice in water management is at least partly vanishing. A similar trend could be seen in the adjacent Inkomati Basin, which was the first pilot project where a similar approach of formulating a proposal, led by technical consultants, had been adopted. In the Inkomati, an active proponent of the National Water Act and strong defender of the interests of large farmers since the formulation of the act, acknowledged that the public (read "white") participation expected through CMAs had been a major motive for initially endorsing the act. However, later she felt that the expectations raised had not come true (P. Waalewijn, personal communication, 2001).

Bottom-up Institution-Building for River Basin Management

A problem that the DWAF regional office identified early on in the above-mentioned process of CMA establishment was that small-scale irrigators risked being overlooked. Whereas large farmers were well organized and represented in the CMA process, the many small irrigators were typically unorganized and had no avenue through which to voice their interests. Therefore, a parallel process of consultations in the former Homelands of the Olifants Basin was initiated just after the first round of public meetings. This was a bottom-up reconnaissance of small-scale water users' needs, and of their suggestions for ways to ensure their effective voice through, for example, small-scale water users' forums. The lead implementer of the process was a black community development activist. Local governments and NGOs facilitated the logistics of the meetings. Her network of contacts throughout the basin originated from her rural development activities during and after the antiapartheid struggle.

Nine day-long workshops were held in the local language with a total of 365 participants attending. These generated overviews of the problems participants experienced with regard to water, including drinking water—often given top priority—but also rain-fed and irrigated agriculture, and disputes with large-scale users on water allocation. The debates also encompassed issues indirectly related to productive water use such as the lack of markets, inputs, and training for both irrigated and rain-fed agriculture, and frustrations about the slow pace of land reform. Concrete suggestions to organize and cross-subsidize multi-tiered small-scale water users' forums for effective representation in the future CMA governing board and committees were made. Moreover, broad technical support and exchange through the CMA were proposed to address development issues less directly related to water. The report on these workshops (Khumbane et al. 2001) was included in the final technical proposal compiled by the consultant.

The consultant's approach proposes bottom-up institution-building for river basin management as an instrument for fundamentally redressing social inequities from the past, in which water is one of the factors. Cooperative governance is also an intrinsic part. A first component of this approach is to stimulate poor people, especially women, to use more water more productively, for example through water harvesting for homestead gardening and tree cultivation for food security. Second, if needed, she mediates between communities and DWAF to solve disputes about issues like excessive groundwater abstraction by mines, which dries up boreholes for domestic water supply in neighboring communities. Wherever high-volume water users already recognize the need to improve social justice in their localities, the facilitator harnesses this willingness into an encompassing process of dialogue between nonpoor and poor about better sharing of water, water-related benefits, and other benefits.

As mentioned, there was a lag between the second and third meetings of the Stakeholder Reference Group in the Olifants Basin. The reason was that the Mpumalanga Regional Office and the consultants preferred to wait for the final response of the national Department of Water Affairs and Forestry to the first formal proposal for the Inkomati Basin. Earlier, DWAF had commented on the lack of sufficiently inclusive public participation and the lack of attention to poverty issues, which necessitated considerable revision of the Inkomati proposal. A final decision has yet to be taken. This is also the case for the composition of the new governing board for the Inkomati CMA. The minister is likely to use his powers to ensure a more representative composition than exists in the team leading the process until today. A major task that the national Department of Water Affairs and Forestry envisages is to further specify performance requirements that can serve as checks and balances for the new CMAs.

Conclusions

Although the process of establishing a CMA in the Olifants River Basin at the interface of the former formal water laws and the new National Water Act has only just been initiated, some conclusions can tentatively be drawn. First, the contest at the interface of the different legal systems in crafting new river basin management institutions at the lowest tiers takes the form of dialogues on issues directly and indirectly related to water, among parties disparate in terms of wealth and power. These inequities exist between communities and high-volume users, but also within communities. The roles of DWAF and other actors are to level the playing field by stimulating information provision, social facilitation, dispute resolution, and capacity building. It has become clear that technical experts lack such skills and, hence, cannot effectively lead the establishment of CMAs. Their narrow focus on water as a "neutral" natural resource misses the social and political forces that drive the distribution of water and water-related benefits, and hence the opportunities to redress current inequities.

At the interface between DWAF and high-volume users, DWAF has effective legal tools to regulate water use by these users, such as individual registration, licensing, and demand management. A specific issue in establishing CMAs is preventing high-volume water users from "cherry picking" water management tasks. Their ability to immediately take over (and finance!) important water management tasks is strong. But the risk is real that they would mainly capture the tasks and positions in water management that would most benefit them, such as water authorization, licensing and compulsory licensing, and fee setting and collection, while leaving to DWAF the more complicated tasks in the public interest, like combating pollution and ensuring the redress of inequities.

At the interface of the National Water Act and water control in the former Homelands, on the other hand, blends of both legal frameworks are probably most effective in combating water deprivation. Even though there is currently little organized knowledge on implementation of the water legislation before and after 1998, much can probably be learned from a community's own integrated approach to accommodating multiple water uses and needs.

The institutional fragmentation of DWAF into various divisions—in effect, an abrogation of the principle of cooperative governance—may be effective for better-off areas, where domestic water supply is well catered to. However, in poor rural areas, domestic water needs are still largely unmet and the various water sources are used for multiple ends, so a more integrated service delivery is required.

A second domain where it is important to consider the institutional legacy of the past regards the managerial roles that DWAF vests in the local government, especially in former Homelands. These roles need to be somehow compatible with the roles of the traditional authorities. The challenge is, evidently, to empower the poorest members of the village vis-à-vis these traditional authorities, but also to ensure accountability by and transparency of local governments. One option is that villagers themselves be entitled to choose their own management form.[12] In both domains, cooperative governance within DWAF, and among DWAF and other agencies through the new CMA structures from local to basin level, could play a crucial role both in fostering the required integrated approach and in ensuring an effective local government.

Finally, blends between local law and the National Water Act may be fruitful because legal tools that are useful in regulating high-volume users are not necessarily appropriate and could even be counterproductive if they are applied in the same way to the millions of very small-scale users (Shah et al. 2001). A better understanding of local notions of registration of use, legitimacy of use, allocation principles, dispute resolution mechanisms, and collective community rights vis-à-vis outsiders according to local law could inform policy makers to specify new regulations that more effectively empower poor people. In all domains, only DWAF's strong, effective steering role in crafting CMAs that build upon local law can lead to inclusive, bottom-up river basin organizations that contribute to achieving "Enough for All Forever."

NOTES

I. Although this date does not mark the beginning of the various segregationist policies pursued by the white state, the unilateral declaration of a republic does herald the removal of what it perceived as a last check to the execution of its policies. As far back as 1913, it had created African reserves under the Native (Black) Land Act, which not only stipulated that blacks could own land only within specifically demarcated territories but also denied them access to even sharecropping arrangements in areas outside these reserves. In 1948, racist policies got a boost with the election of the exclusively Afrikaner National Party. Forced removals of blacks from so-called white areas to the reserves, later termed Homelands, started only after 1961 (Ross 1999).

2. In fact, four of the ten Homelands achieved "independence" from the Republic of South Africa, while the others were considered as being on the path to such self-determination when liberation from white rule was achieved.

3. This is over and above the fact that, subject to certain restrictions, traditional leaders may also participate constitutionally in local governments (RSA 1998a: 56). However, the extent of overlap between their mandate in customary matters and the issues that fall within their jurisdiction as ex-officio members of local government councils is not known.

4. In 2004, one US $ equals 6.4 rand.

5. These repressive governments were, for the most part, puppet states of the white Republic of South Africa. With its backing, they dismantled the structures of traditional chiefdoms as they had existed for centuries and replaced them with their minions who were hardly accountable to the local communities they were in charge of administering (Ross 1999). Therefore, as chiefs became salaried government officials, staying in office at the whim of a government that was beholden to the white South African state, they also risked losing their legitimacy to rule in the eyes of their followers. This nexus between Homelands governments and the apartheid state explains some of the animosity people feel toward chiefs even today. It may also explain the attempts made by the post-1994 governments to replace the authority of the chiefs with that of newly instituted local government councils, which consist mainly of elected representatives.

6. Until now, the government has done little to reinstall farm support systems and to accord farmers formal title to water and land. In some cases, large-scale farmers, white or sometimes black, have used this legal impasse to occupy the collapsed schemes and start cultivating, using the idle irrigation infrastructure and extracting water without any payment. In one such case, a white farmer took over a large tract of land in the Flag Boshielo (former Arabie) scheme in the Olifants Basin by paying a substantial bribe to the local chief and petty amounts as "land rent" (but only for the first year) to the farmers that had previously occupied the land. In order to cultivate the land, this farmer brings along his own laborers but also creates some unskilled agricultural employment for laborers from the area. This minimal gain divides the local population and blocks any attempts at effective protest against his modus operandi. The provincial government sued the farmer in a court case over the land issue. But though two years have passed, the case has seen no progress. Meanwhile, DWAF, too, has been lax about levying the necessary water charges.

7. One such belief concerns the Mother River Serpent. She is claimed to own the water and live in water bodies, such as dams, streams, or groundwater. Above all, the Mother River Serpent needs to be kept content. Polluting water or drilling modern bore holes are said to anger her and cause her to move away, leaving chaos—in the form of tornados or heavy flooding—in her wake, which in turn adversely affects the existing water body or water course. Traditional healers and prophets are said to stay in deep waters for long periods, to communicate with her and acquire powerful knowledge. Some of these traditional healers and "rainmakers" were renowned for their knowledge about the weather and seasons, and were consulted about the right time to start cultivation. Further, some springs were considered sacred places that could not be accessed by ordinary people.

8. Licenses are granted for a maximum limit of forty years, but can be revised every five years. Pre-1994 permits are gradually being changed into licenses, provided water is available or can be exchanged with others who are willing to give up part or all of their allotment. All who want to engage in new water uses have to apply for licenses, which are only issued under similar conditions. Requests for licenses by historically disadvantaged water users receive priority. "Stream flow reduction activities" by large-scale forestry estates are also being licensed.

9. An example of improved collaboration between the Department of Water Affairs and Forestry and the National and provincial Departments of Agriculture is the drafting of a new national policy to mainstream the marginalized through agricultural water use, using an integrated approach that also encompasses access to land, markets, credits, skill development, and so on. Links are being established with the Integrated Rural Development Program—established by presidential decree—which is to be implemented through the local government.

10. De Lange (2004: 55) analyzes the process of formulation of the Water Act, mentioning that "initially, the Minister was opposed to any form of compensation for reduced or lost water allocations. However, in meetings with the Minister and through the press, the agricultural sector pointed out that this would be unconstitutional, a position that was confirmed by constitutional lawyers advising the Minister."

11. The latest version of the CMA proposal is of April 2003. It currently awaits submission to the minister. Information in this paper is based on this proposal, and also on the review of the public participation processes by IWMI (unpublished).

12. Empowering villagers to choose their own management forms is also proposed for communal land tenure (Cousins 2000).

10

Routes to Water Rights

BRYAN BRUNS

As water becomes increasingly contested, water users are increasingly affected by the actions of strangers with whom they have few other links besides sharing the use of a common resource. The success of attempts to resolve conflicts and coordinate collective action in water use depends, among other things, on the ability to find efficient solutions to problems of collective action. If reaching agreement is time-consuming and difficult, and agreements difficult or impossible to enforce, then water allocation is unlikely to be effective, or to occur only through the unilateral imposition of state authority rather than arising from agreement among users. Changes in water resources management are more likely to succeed if new institutional arrangements are efficient in terms of the information, time, expenses, and other resources required. This chapter explores some aspects of how the transactions costs of institutions for water management might be optimized through better understanding of, and working with, legal pluralism in water governance.

Developing Water Rights

Clearer recognition of water rights in one form or another is required for all three major approaches currently advocated for improving water allocation institutions (Meinzen-Dick and Rosegrant 1997): first, clarifying agency allocations through more explicit contractual arrangements, for example, through service agreements for provision of bulk water supplies to irrigators' organizations; second, promoting markets for transferable water rights; third, facilitating development of self-governance institutions (organizations, forums, platforms, and so on) through which users and their representatives can manage water as common property. In irrigation reform, water rights have been acknowledged as important for enabling better governance, including management transfer to local organizations (Burchi and Betlen 2001; Vermillion 1995). However, with the partial exception of Mexico, relatively little policy attention has been paid to how water rights can be integrated into irrigation reforms.

Water rights and water governance can take many different forms. In their attention to rights in various forms, however, whether explicit in shares, turns, licenses, and so on, or implicit in distribution practices, approaches emphasizing the development of water rights can be contrasted with approaches that look at water allocation purely as a technical engineering exercise, as a means of maximizing economic productivity from a societal perspective, or as mainly a zero-sum political struggle over entitlements to assets. Instead, this chapter focuses on the development of rules for water allocation as a process of governance involving stakeholders who have mixed motives to both compete and cooperate concerning water, and constitute rules of the game regarding legitimate claims to water. Such rules furthermore take on a life of their own, with emergent properties that are not simply the solution to a technical or economic calculus nor merely an automatic reflection of the constellation of political and economic power (on the challenge of fostering locally appropriate forms of control and management, see also chapter 9).

Water users' desire for security and interest in retaining access make changes in allocation likely to be a contested process, whereas the benefits from coordination and differences in needs provide strong inducements to cooperation. The difficulties of developing suitable institutions may be so large as to make it not worthwhile, especially if suitable infrastructure and other technical capacity is not available and opportunities for gains from trade in water are low. However, even when there are few potential gains from trade or these cannot be achieved, water users are still likely to be interested in ways to increase the reliability of their access to water.

Legal Pluralism

In looking at how water tenure institutions might be improved, this chapter builds on the insight that, for water governance as well as in other domains, a diverse combination of state and local laws, norms, and other forms of social ordering may perform much better than overreliance on centralized state law, in terms of criteria such as effectiveness, equity, and efficiency. Guillet (1998) has argued that reliance on local institutions to handle most allocation and conflict resolution has characterized the evolution of water rights institutions in Spain. More generally, Ellickson (1991) analyzed gaps between official legal doctrines and local practice, emphasizing the practical and theoretical advantages of relying on local knowledge and self-organization to optimize transaction costs and improve institutional performance. Government regulation that reflects and reinforces local norms and self-governance is likely to be far more successful than attempts to impose state rules at variance with local ideas and practices (Cooter 1997). Put more simply, attempting to impose state law in ways that seek to erase or ignore local law is a recipe for failure.

Analysts of legal pluralism have emphasized that for water, as in other domains, local laws (norms, customs) are not only important and interact with state law but also are diverse, dynamic, contested, and heavily influenced by local power relations (see for example, F. Benda-Beckmann et al. 1996; F. Benda-Beckmann and K. Benda-Beckmann 2001; Spiertz 2000; Spiertz and Wiber 1996). Misguided attempts to crudely codify local law not only risk misunderstanding complexity and freezing a dynamic process but may also reinforce inequities and create new vulnerabilities to abuse by those better able to manipulate legal and bureaucratic systems (see chapter 7 on such a dynamic in the Andes). The challenge is to understand how state intervention may interact with the complexity of local law and find routes through which it may be possible to reach better outcomes.

This is a challenge not only for bureaucratic agencies, technical experts, and academic scholars but also for water users, local leaders, and other stakeholders concerned with how water is used, as they seek to craft institutions to solve the problems they face. Institutional performance matters for irrigators seeking to improve water allocation within an individual irrigation system, and for all stakeholders involved in governance of an entire river basin, but not in the same way for both groups. Policies in irrigation and water resources management now commonly call for increased participation by stakeholders and empowering water users in water governance.

Studies of legal pluralism offer insights about the perspectives and strategies of different actors, and how differences in knowledge, power, wealth, and other resources influence disputes and other social action. Such understanding may be useful for all those who seek to develop better institutions for water management. Ideas about how to better promote water rights may be of particular interest to those concerned with empowering disadvantaged people to protect and improve their access to water.

Optimizing Transaction Costs

Transaction costs are composed of the time and other resources required to reach and implement agreements (Coase 1990; North 1990; Williamson 1996). Thus, for example, water users may seek to resolve conflicts and coordinate collective action in using water from a stream or other water resource. An agency charged with administering an irrigation system may seek to formulate and implement rules regarding how water should be distributed. Theorists of new institutional economics have highlighted how institutional changes, for example a legal framework of contracts and courts, can facilitate transactions among strangers. The advantages of enabling strangers to bind themselves to enforceable commitments are not limited to commercial trades but also apply to the challenges of creating institutions for self-governance of resources such as water.

Where the scope and scale of water conflicts extend well beyond the domain of existing community-based institutions, the challenge for those involved is to craft suitable arrangements for governance. Much research on community-based natural resource management emphasizes the independent capacity of self-governance (Ostrom 1990, 1992, 1999) and the dangers of disrupting local institutions. In dealing with problems of a wider scope and scale, however, there is the need to go beyond existing local institutions.

This chapter is particularly concerned with the possibilities for institutional change that include a continuing role for self-governance among stakeholders. Rather than simply imposing agency administration or atomized markets, institutions could be crafted that work with and enhance existing local ideas and practices, while also responding to wider concerns about equity, environment, and other issues. Although much discourse on water management is still dominated by a top-down technocratic perspective, there is increasing concern to involve stakeholders and pursue democratic processes for improving resource governance, creating more space for initiatives by resource users and those acting on their behalf.

In comparing alternative institutional arrangements, transactions costs are an important characteristic. However, it should be noted that efficiency is only one of many criteria that may be used in assessing the performance of institutions. From the perspectives of various participants, efficiency in lowering transactions costs may well be outweighed by considerations of effectiveness, equity, and other objectives.

Institutional performance matters not only from the perspective of government and overall social welfare but also from the perspective of water users interested in taking part in collective action to manage water resources, and those who might take part in transactions to transfer water between uses. This is not to say that everyone necessarily wants changes in institutions, or wants the same changes. Those who benefit from the status quo may well prefer conditions that let them protect and sustain their current access to water over institutions that would facilitate efforts to redistribute water in pursuit of goals of equity, environmental conservation, or economic productivity.

Organization of the Chapter

This chapter looks at opportunities to optimize the transaction costs of developing water rights, in contexts where legal pluralism is an important part of how water is currently governed. It is particularly concerned with reallocation, and the potential for reallocation to occur through voluntary transactions among water users. The first section after this introduction presents examples of water conflicts in Southeast Asia that illustrate how legal and institutional complexity poses challenges for improving water management. The second section reviews a variety of strategies that can be employed to reduce the transaction costs of developing water rights systems. The third section discusses how the transaction costs of coordinating water management tend to rise as the scope and scale of competition for water increases, while transformations in water allocation institutions may increase or decrease transaction costs along different trajectories. The chapter concludes by emphasizing how better acceptance and understanding of legal complexity, the existence of a dynamic variety of institutions interacting to regulate access to water, offers one way of helping to make water management more effective, efficient, and equitable.

Water Conflicts in Southeast Asia

This section presents a series of cases that illustrate some of the challenges involved in trying to improve water allocation institutions in Southeast Asia. The cases cover water distribution among irrigators within a single scheme in western Laos; competition between farmers and factories in Bandung, West Java; basin scale coordination in the Brantas Basin of East Java; groundwater pumping in the highlands of southern Vietnam; and conflicts between upland and lowland water users in northern Thailand. The cases reflect sites with which the author has some familiarity, and were chosen to help portray some but by no means all the sorts of variation present in water allocation institutions in the region. The presentation draws on published literature as well as the author's experience as a consultant in water management. As discussed later in the chapter, the cases can be arrayed in terms of the scale of coordination needed to manage water and the scope of heterogeneity between multiple uses of water, with increasing scale and scope tending to raise the transaction costs of collective action in water allocation.

Irrigation Rehabilitation and Expansion

Rehabilitation of the Nam Tan irrigation scheme, located in the Laotian province of Sayaboury, restored service to downstream parts of the scheme that had received little or no supply for many years (UNCDF 1998, see also Coward 1980 for discussion of the scheme in an earlier period). State intervention was aimed at increasing rice production, as part of a national program for pursuing rice self-sufficiency. Statutory rules about water allocation were not a significant factor, but project plans and practices—project law—deliberately sought to give all farmers within the irrigation perimeter direct access to water from newly built or improved quaternary canals. This contrasted with the field-to-field flows that had prevailed in many areas, as well as the various reductions in areas served and other accommodations farmers had made as the capacity of the canal system declined due to neglect and lack of financial and technical resources. Rehabilitation extended water delivery to many areas that, before rehabilitation, had been poorly served, or not served at all. Rights to water derived from access to land within the irrigation perimeter.

For the rehabilitation project, project staff organized small groups of farmers to participate in planning and implementing rehabilitation of tertiary areas. This approach drew on many of the methods for participatory irrigation development earlier carried out in the Philippines (Korten and Siy 1988). Building on the organization of small farmer groups, a water users' association (WUA) was formed to coordinate among the fourteen villages, almost two thousand hectares and some two thousand households served by the system. As rehabilitation proceeded, one of the first achievements of the association in terms of water management came in response to inadequate rainfall during the 1998 rainy season. The association arranged careful rotation among different units in order to distribute available supplies, a process that had become possible using newly rehabilitated canals and gates. The allocation principle was primarily the project-sponsored objective of evenly spreading water over the irrigated land within the perimeter (rather than allocation according to water shares, historic use, household, or any other basis).

Water allocation in the Nam Tan scheme primarily concerned one use, irrigation, within a relatively limited area and among a relatively homogenous set of users. Rice farming was usually undertaken by households as a joint enterprise, usually under the direction of male household heads. The male household heads usually represented the household in community governance activities, such as meetings and other activities that established a WUA, devised rules, dealt with disputes, mobilized resources, distributed water, and maintained the irrigation system. Most participants in the meetings were male, though women did attend and were vocal at times. Conceptions about membership often did not make a clear distinction between households and individuals. Children and younger married couples living in a parental household usually take part in rice cultivation as a household enterprise, but often also engage independently in enterprises such as raising small livestock and cultivating nonrice crops in the dry season. Some water is for household use and home gardens. The area includes ethnic minority people, some of whom had lived in the upstream watershed area until they were required to move as part of government measures intended to protect the watershed. However neither multiple use of water nor ethnic diversity yet plays a major role in water allocation. Upstream of the Nam Tan weir there is little irrigation, while downstream the Nam Tan joins a larger river, with few pressures so far to coordinate water use along the river.

As in many irrigation schemes, water rights were not explicitly framed in terms of shares or written licenses, but were implicit in the infrastructure, rules, and procedures used to deliver water. These were transformed by how the rules and their application changed as a result of project intervention. Rehabilitation of the canal network and construction of field channels to each farmer's plots altered the physical infrastructure, allowing new options. At the same time, project activities emphasized a norm of allocation according to area, which was applied by the newly established association. Repairs to the canals and control structures augmented the water that could be supplied to the system. Installation of field channels and new distribution arrangements were intended to deliver water in similar amounts to all irrigated land, rather than allowing those upstream to deprive those further down along canals and in other parts of the system. New distribution rules were proposed by the project and ratified by WUAs. Major control structures continued to be operated by technicians, according to the new rules, while WUAs took on responsibility for implementing and monitoring distribution within their areas. With relatively limited scale and scope of water use, the water users' association provided a forum for negotiating access to water during seasonal shortages in the wet season and during dry season cultivation, without necessarily requiring any further formalization of water rights.

Competition between Farmers and Factories

Textile factories take water from canals and fields in the Ciwalengke irrigation scheme, located south of the city of Bandung in West Java, Indonesia (Avianto 1996; Kurnia et al. 2000). Factories had obtained permits for abstracting water from the provincial government, issued under authority held by the provincial governor according to national laws and regulations. According to calculations by the provincial government agencies, there should have been enough water for both factories and irrigation. However, factories often installed additional unauthorized intakes, or attached pumps to intake pipes through which water was supposed to flow by gravity. Many fields located further down along irrigation canals experienced water shortages and farmers began to leave some fields fallow. In some cases factories agreed with neighboring farmers to pay for access to water the farmers would otherwise have used for irrigation. However, formal water law did not permit such transactions.

In some cases, factories provided assistance in materials, facilities, and money to communities located in the head end of the scheme, perhaps intended as compensation for use of water by the factories. Farmers located in the tail end of the scheme complained that such arrangements were unfair, but lacked effective ways to voice objections to arrangements that they felt disadvantaged them. In addition to conflicts over water quantity, wastewater from factories seasonally polluted canals and groundwater. Farmers whose fields were hurt by water shortages or pollution had mixed feelings about the problem, since many of their adult children worked in the factories.

The provincial irrigation agency allocated particular volumes of flow for irrigation. The mining agency (which was responsible for regulating groundwater) had approved water use permits that were then issued under the governor's authority. However, the institutional framework did not provide much security for either kind of access; that is, those affected by problems had no effective way to ensure that abstraction was kept within the permitted limits. There was no effective procedure for investigating complaints and enforcing licensing restrictions. The political and economic power of the factories, and the failure of earlier protests, made irrigators reluctant to challenge the factories. In the case of waste disposal, factories had frequently evaded inspection and enforcement by stopping discharges during periods when senior officials were visiting the area, while discharging at night and after the spotlight of official attention was gone.

The institutional framework for water rights did not provide a way for mutually agreeable trades to be made, nor did it ensure that the impacts on others of water abstractions and transfers between uses would be given due consideration. Overall figures indicated that adequate water should have been available within the scheme for all uses. In the event of shortage, farmers were willing to give up water in return for compensation. However the prevailing institutional arrangements made it hard for such agreements to be reached and enforced. Since trading of water rights was not permitted under the law, such agreements would not be legally enforceable. That situation was further complicated by ambiguities, inconsistencies, and lack of coordination between different government agencies concerning how permits were issued and enforced. Indonesia's national government and the province of West Java were both in the process of revising water laws and regulations, though it was not clear to what extent the new framework would recognize water use rights that would enable or assist users to regulate and reallocate water among themselves, to obtain greater security in their access to water and to enable transfers.

In Ciwalengke the competing demands of farmers and factories expanded the scope of issues involved, although within a relatively limited scale. Many of the factory workers came from outside the area, but enough came from local households to create cross-cutting interests concerning water management. This case illustrates some of the differences between official policies and regulations concerning water allocation and the realities of local practice. The structure of local interests and incentives was not a simple conflict between two major types of uses, but instead included multiple interests on the part of households whose livelihoods depended on both farming and factory labor, and selective cooperation between some factories and farmers.

Local law was evolving through transactions that demonstrated the potential for water transfers that might benefit both farmers and industries. However, the formal legal framework did not enable, let alone facilitate, such arrangements. At the local level, agreements between factories and neighboring farmers appeared to be accepted as legitimate. By contrast, the fairness of selective deals between factories and some groups of upstream water users was questioned by those with fields downstream. Excessive abstraction by factories, using pumps and nonpermitted intakes, was criticized as illegitimate in terms of both local norms and state rules, but enforcement institutions were largely absent or ineffective.

Growing Urban Demands

Surabaya, Indonesia's second largest city, lies at the downstream end of the Brantas River basin. During the dry season the potential demand for urban water, irrigation, and other needs exceeds the available supply, creating challenges for water management in the basin (Rodgers et al. 2001; Sunaryo 2001). The government-owned Jasa Tirta I Corporation has managed some major storage reservoirs and provides other services to manage water in the basin. It works under the direction of the national government minister responsible for water resources (previously the minister of public works, currently the minister for settlements and regional infrastructure), acting in cooperation with the minister of finance. Within Indonesia's unitary state, the provincial government has the authority to issue water licenses and regulate water resources. Most urban water utilities and some factories have water abstraction permits, while irrigation diversions are not formally licensed.

Irrigators in upstream areas in the basin enjoy a location advantage and face few effective restrictions on how much water they divert, sometimes growing a third crop of rice during the dry season, while those lower down in the basin suffer from severe water shortage and must leave fields fallow. In some sections of the basin, the government water resources agency sometimes instructs upstream irrigation systems to stop taking water for one day a week in order to help replenish storage reservoirs in the midstream area. There are anecdotal reports that at the local level, those controlling access to springs and other upstream sources sometimes "sell" water to those a bit further downstream, only releasing flows once they have been paid, even though such transactions are legally prohibited and regarded as illegitimate by irrigation officials.

In lowland schemes, farmers irrigate second and third crops of rice or less water-demanding crops such as soy beans, corn, and peanuts. Profits are low. The higher market value of water in urban uses, and potential for diversification into horticulture and for other household enterprises outside of agriculture, suggest the possibility for voluntarily transferring water rights, if suitable laws and organizations were available. The physical structure of the basin would make intersectoral transfers possible, particularly if it is a matter of reducing abstractions upstream and allowing water to flow downstream. There may also be opportunities to coordinate and reallocate surface and groundwater sources, such as shifting groundwater currently used for irrigation to urban water supply and replacing it with alternative sources of surface water for irrigation, which is less sensitive to water quality. The presence of some reservoir storage capacity in the basin, and existence of an agency managing most of those reservoirs and other major structures, also mean that some technical potential does exist for reallocation among uses and locations.

At present, the main tool of the government to reallocate water lies in control over cropping patterns in large government-managed schemes, farmers in which may be given reduced allocations and told to grow nonrice crops, often with little opportunity for consultation, and no compensation. National policies and government regulations issued in 2000 and 2001 stated that governance authority over these schemes and secondary units within them would be transferred to WUA federations and that, as part of this process, water rights should be clarified. Stakeholders are supposed to be included in provincial and basin water management committees.

The Surabaya basin highlights the problems involved in a much larger scale of water management, ranging from small irrigation schemes in upper watersheds to large lowland schemes. The scope of issues is complicated by growing urban and industrial use. In some cases, local institutions have allowed the creation of local rights to the point where access to water is sometimes "sold," even though this is illegitimate in terms of state regulations regarding water. The potential exists for mutual gains in water transactions, both at the local and basin scale, but the institutional framework for such transactions is absent from the formal legal system, while informal local institutions only operate at a limited scale.

Expansion of Private Pumping

During the 1990s, coffee growing expanded rapidly in Dak Lak and neighboring provinces in the southern highlands of Vietnam. Farmers, mostly ethnic Vietnamese moving in from outside the highlands, cleared land to plant coffee and irrigated coffee trees with water pumped from ponds, streams, and wells (Ahmad 2000, Andersen 2001). Over time, groundwater tables dropped and dry season stream flows were reduced. Declining international prices for coffee threatened the profitability of coffee cultivation, although the history of past price fluctuations encouraged continued planting of coffee on the basis of speculative hopes that prices would rise again.

Vietnam's 1998 Water Law and subsequent legislation created a new framework for regulating groundwater extraction and surface water diversion. Laws and implementing rules formally required licenses for almost all groundwater extraction. However, in practice licensing all existing and new wells would have been extremely difficult or impossible, and has so far not been implemented (chapter 8 describes a similar situation in Gujarat).

Declining groundwater levels created a cause for alarm. However, available hydrological data and capacity for monitoring and analysis were too limited even to determine where groundwater was being extracted within levels of safe yield, albeit perhaps at the expense of users elsewhere, and where it was being inefficiently "mined" with increased costs for pumping and for deepening wells that made all users worse off. Effective collective action to address the problem would need to include not only those served by canal irrigation systems but also state farms and dispersed smallholders irrigating coffee trees using groundwater. A Danish-funded water project supported initial efforts to involve users in participatory management of irrigation and watersheds. However, with the exception of a few specific irrigation schemes, such efforts were still in a formative stage.

Water management in this area involved a wide scale, and competition between older gravity schemes, mainly those of rice farmers and coffee growers pumping directly from surface and groundwater sources. Urban use was also growing and competing for surface and groundwater supplies in some areas. The population of the area included both indigenous ethnic minority groups and a rapidly growing population of ethnic Vietnamese (Kinh) settlers, adding to the cultural complexity of the situation. As one indicator of some of the issues present in the area, in 2001 ethnic minority groups in Dak Lak and neighboring provinces engaged in major protests. A key issue was their loss of rights to land and livelihoods. Although not directly focused on water conflicts, the protests did take place in a context shaped by increasing competition concerning access to natural resources essential for rural livelihoods. Water was a crucial input for the agricultural practices by all the different groups.

In terms of institutions that influence access to water, there was a gap between ambitious regulations that imply comprehensive registration and regulation of water abstraction and the realities of dispersed water abstraction, particularly for groundwater, which was especially hard to monitor. The transaction costs of actually inventorying existing uses would be high, and effective monitoring and enforcement concerning quantities abstracted even more difficult. Rapid acquisition of rights to land, either individual land rights or subsidiary rights as tenants of state farms, and accompanying de facto open access to water by settlers, was creating growing scarcity.

Highlands and Lowlands

Lowland irrigators in the Chom Tong District of northern Thailand have blocked roads, petitioned authorities, and made a variety of other protests against water use and pollution by vegetable growers in the highlands upstream of their villages (Tankimyong et al. 2002). Ethnic differences between lowland Thais and other ethnic groups, mostly living in the highlands, complicated perceptions and interactions. Irrigated cultivation in highland areas had been backed by various government projects as an alternative to opium cultivation. During the dry season, water for cabbages and other crops was diverted from streams in upper watershed areas. Lowlanders' water use had not been static, either, as increasing areas have been planted with lychees and other fruit orchards, perennial trees for which investments were at risk if water is not available. Water from canals and wells was pumped to supply fruit trees. Groundwater levels had been declining. Water was only one point of contention, as cultivation in highland areas had also been entangled in polarized debates about formalizing land use rights for those living and farming in mountainous areas designated as forest reserves, watershed conservation areas, and parks. These issues were highlighted in controversies over a possible Community Forest Law, including a draft bill debated by Thailand's parliament in 2001.

Government projects, politicians, nongovernment organizations, and other outsiders became embroiled in the conflicts, pursuing their own goals and seeking to support local actors, justified in terms of a range of concerns such as poverty, national security, conservation of upland catchments, justice for ethnic minorities, habitat conservation, and controlling water pollution. Numerous attempts were made to mediate conflicts but it proved difficult to reach workable agreements. Upstream irrigators had frequently been able to use their locational advantages to take additional amounts of water, leaving those downstream to suffer the consequences. However, in other cases downstream users were able to get government agencies to restrict land use, resettle upland communities, or otherwise influence water diversion by those upstream.

The issues were largely framed in terms of competition for irrigation and domestic water use within specific small subbasins formed by tributaries of the Mae Ping River. Those debates were not closely linked to the larger scale relationships between water use in northern Thailand and the growing water demands of the Bangkok metropolis and overall water management within the Greater Chao Phraya Basin. Efforts had begun to promote the development of subbasin committees, but the composition and roles of such bodies were still being explored.

IN THE CASES DISCUSSED ABOVE, formal water rights, such as licenses and permits, have hardly played a role. Even where urban or industrial use was licensed, the ability to monitor and enforce use in accordance with license conditions was limited. Government agencies controlled some irrigation schemes and claimed authority to regulate water, but had very limited capacity to monitor and enforce allocation. The main users of water, irrigators, had long-standing access, mostly for irrigation schemes managed by government agencies, but agricultural access to water was usually not formalized in permits or licenses. Water rights in state law were often vague and contested. The conditions that would enable easy enforcement of agency mandates were absent, as were technical services such as those needed to assess consumptive use and sustainable groundwater yields, as well as courts or other authoritative forums to resolve conflicts. Local institutions for allocating and reallocating water were evolving ahead of formal law, but important aspects of access to water were increasingly contested at the local level and at wider scales. The cases showed legal pluralism in the multiplicity of sources of claims to water, as well as substantial ambiguity and dynamism in water allocation institutions. Local institutions could not be easily ignored or overridden. Attempts to clarify water rights needed to deal with the diversity of challenges created by such conditions.

Facilitating the Evolution of Water Rights

A range of methods is available for making the establishment of new water rights more feasible and successful. Most of the approaches for facilitating the development of water rights discussed below have already been discussed by various authors (for example, Easter et al. 1998; Rosegrant and Binswanger 1994; Velasco 2001). It is useful to review them here in terms of how they may help optimize transaction costs and facilitate water management in contexts of legal pluralism. These may be part of a tool kit for addressing situations such as those described in the previous section, helping those engaged in crafting new institutions.

Much discussion of developing water rights institutions tends to focus on the perspective of experts and government agencies. However, the strategies discussed below are also relevant to water users who may undertake initiatives to defend or expand their access to water, and others, such as NGOs and academics, who may seek to help them defend their interests.

Acknowledge Existing Rights

Sometimes state law simply disregards local rights, authorizing only those rights already incorporated in state law, while ignoring or overriding local institutions that regulate claims to water, and acting as if water allocation started with a blank slate, easily written and rewritten. In other cases, concerns about clarifying rights prompt efforts to document, register, and otherwise formalize water rights according to state law and bureaucratic procedures. In practice, existing water use creates a system of implicit or de facto water rights. Such rights are often unwritten, arranged through institutions that do not rely on the impersonal routines of formal bureaucracy, and may well be embodied in operational practices rather than consciously designed to allocate quantities of water.

Rather than having to assign rights from scratch, the pattern of existing use provides a framework that can facilitate the efficient development of a more formalized water rights system. Conversely, failing to recognize or protect existing rights, for example by only allocating water in proportion to land, may increase gaps between state and local law. One illustration of building on existing patterns is that, where rights are nominally allocated in volumetric terms, during periods of shortage water may be shared in proportion to the volumetric allocations, with proportional principles being much more similar to customary local practices. In developing suitable means for formalizing local rights, existing access can be protected, while still setting limitations and procedural requirements concerning the extent to which those rights can be transferred, and how to resolve conflicts when existing claims exceed available supplies.

It should be noted that acknowledging local water rights institutions need not be predicated on an assumption that such rights constitute a fully integrated, consistent, and consensus-based system. The allocation institutions may well be based on principles that are conflicting, with inconsistencies that become more visible as water becomes scarcer (as in Gujarat; see chapter 8). There is sometimes a tendency to idealize local knowledge and practices, rather than recognize the extent to which they may be incomplete, inconsistent, and incoherent. By virtue of their role in regulating access to a finite shared resource, there are physical linkages and constraints in how water flows and is diverted. Perceptions about claims and their validity are influenced by the patterns of where water actually flows. Nor need there be an assumption that such local practices are inherently equitable, particularly given the prevalence of many forms of inequality, and the often widely differing views regarding equity. Even within formal law systems, conflicts exist between different laws and regulations (see chapters 3 and 7). These may persist until some particular case or issue draws the attention of a legislature or court to the need to provide greater consistency.

Acceptance of traditional water rights, even when these have not been formally registered, has been a key principle underlying river management in Japan (IDI 1997: Article 87; Sanbongi 2001). Existing users were not forced to register merely to defend their access. Instead, the law established the principle that they have legal standing to protect their interests when necessary. The River Laws of 1896 and 1964 provided a formal basis in state law, through which agencies and courts could take account of existing rights. It is worth noting that this is the case even though in general the development of Japanese law was deliberately designed to rely on civil law, not common law principles. The provisions of the River Law mainly focus on actions by bureaucratic administrators, not judges. The principle of being "deemed to have obtained permission" illustrates one way of reducing conflicts between state and local law without forcing local rules to explicitly conform to the criteria and formulations of state law.[1]

Such state acceptance of existing use need not require immediate registration, formalization, comprehensive inventorying of uses, or other deliberate interventions to recognize rights. Rights can still come into play in the event of disputes or other conflicts, for example in response to plans for water resource development. Such an approach of accepting existing rights, without insisting on any comprehensive formal registration, can maintain the legitimacy of existing users, while drastically reducing the transaction costs involved in regulating water allocation. This may sound like an obvious approach, but the examples of Indonesia and Vietnam discussed above illustrate the problems that may arise where such existing use is not acknowledged (see also chapter 5, for the Andes). In the case of Thailand, existing use by communal irrigation systems is at least arguably recognized by the People's Irrigation Act of 1939, but other water allocation for irrigation does not have as clear a basis for accepting water rights. Such an approach need not mean either that local rights are always uncritically accepted or that any possibility of state intervention to promote greater equity in water allocation and reallocation is given up. It only means that this is done in ways that acknowledge, and interact with, local institutions rather than just acting to ignore or erase them.

Promote Subsidiarity

The subsidiarity principle emphasizes that problems should be dealt with at the lowest suitable level. Water is managed at multiple scales and levels. Rules regarding access to water are constituted and enforced through a variety of local institutions. Many aspects of water rights, for example transactions among irrigators within a single irrigation scheme, may well be left to local social institutions rather than having to be processed through a formal water rights registry or other state procedures (see chapters 3 and 4). Similarly, local organizations may well be able to handle most conflicts. Thus, there is no need to assume that all disputes must be dealt with through agency or court procedures. This approach can draw on the strengths of local institutions and local social capital, in order to lower transaction costs.

A commonly recognized example is the potential for a water users' association to hold water rights, either in its own right as common property or acting on behalf of its members. Under such an arrangement, outsiders need not get involved on a regular basis in dealing with tens, hundreds, or even thousands of individual farmers. Instead, they can deal with one organization that aggregates the interests of its members. Individuals may still have legal rights and be able to seek recourse if they feel their rights have been infringed upon by the organization, but this can be the exception rather than the rule. By not insisting on initial imposition of state rules within schemes, while still allowing recourse to these rules in the event of disputes, transaction costs may be reduced while still obtaining the advantages of local institutions and of potential state intervention to promote equity and other goals (see chapter 11).

Allow Gradual Formalization

It is not necessary that all rights be immediately inventoried and formally registered. Instead, this can be a gradual and stepwise process, one stream or subbasin at a time. The need for this may arise as water resource development projects, conflicts among users, and other factors encourage users to organize themselves, voice their concerns in the media and other forums, and seek formal registration to clarify and protect their claims. One claim may generate a cascade of claims along a particular stream or basin, as others along the same stream seek to defend their rights, but still not impel the immediate demarcation of rights within other subbasins and basins.

Discussion of developing water rights often seems to assume that all rights must be formalized, and that in countries with long histories of formal water rights all rights are already registered. However, even in countries with well-established legal institutions to regulate water rights, such as Spain, Chile, or parts of the western United States (such as New Mexico), it turns out that many, and even the majority of water rights are not formally registered. Guillet (1998) shows that many of the water rights in Spain are not formalized, despite its long history of state regulation of such rights. A similar situation exists in Chile, where many water users did or do not have registered rights, either in the earlier periods of the nineteenth and twentieth centuries or in the past few decades (Brehm and Quiroz 1995). Some basins in New Mexico are in the process of having rights formally adjudicated to clearly determine rights. However, the adjudication process has taken decades, and it is not clear when it may finish (NNMLS 2000 and personal communication). Fully adjudicating rights in a basin is a complex, information-intensive, and time-consuming process. As long as informal mechanisms are sufficient, there is no need to impose formalization from outside. Allowing a gradual, selective process of registration, and accepting that many rights will be unregistered, dramatically reduces the transaction costs involved in establishing and operating a water rights system.

Develop Forums for Resolving Conflicts

In many cases, courts may be unavailable or ineffective. Where the number of disputes that disputants take to outside authorities is relatively small, ad hoc arrangements by water agencies or local administrative and political officials may suffice. Beyond this, it is possible to develop forums along streams, in subbasins, and in basins, which can help mediate conflicts. Agency officials may be given limited judicial powers, or special water courts might be developed whose judges have better technical understanding and familiarity with the special issues involved in water conflicts.

Such forums need not require that rights be formally registered. In addition to resolving specific disputes, such forums may have a wider impact than previous ad hoc dispute management by local authorities and others, if such institutions help establish precedents that guide others, influencing processes of self-organization and mutual adjustment. Even without full formalization, the precedents established by such bodies can influence many others, parallel to the way court rulings guide the resolution of many cases settled "in the shadow of the law" (Mnookin and Kornhauser 1979). Formation of forums need not wait for, or depend on, formalization of rights.

Simplify Calculations

Various simplifying rules can make rights easier to understand and manage. Proportional shares may be both consistent with local principles and more flexible in adjusting to varying flows than rights defined in terms of absolute quantities. In deciding what portion of diversions are consumed and so might be transferable, standard rates for consumptive use may be set using average figures, thus avoiding the need for detailed calculations as to what proportion of current flows is actually lost or returned (Theobani 1998). Conversely, Schleyer and Rosegrant (1996) point out that under arid conditions, in which return flows are less important and traditionally regarded as not representing any secure right, such as in parts of Chile, irrigators can simply be assigned rights to the full amounts diverted, again reducing the need for complicated calculations. Use of such simplifying rules may seem obvious, but often is forgotten in discussions about water allocation in terms of detailed engineering calculations and the complexities of consumptive use, return flows, and lag times. At the same time, such rules point toward ways to make water allocation based on water rights workable even in the face of severe limitations in hydrological data and technical capacity. Again, this is relevant not just for government agencies but also for users organizing ways to coordinate their actions.

Prepare for Sparse Transactions

As Young (1986) and others have pointed out, water trades, especially permanent transfers, may be relatively rare. Temporary transfers within a single scheme and season can usually proceed with little formality, even to the point of enabling relatively efficient spot markets. Water is bulky. Transfers are limited by the available network of rivers and canals. Physical, financial, and transaction costs may be relatively high, particularly for permanent transfers across long distances. Urban water supply expansion occurs only sporadically. Therefore large investments in developing formal registries, building capacity to scrutinize potential third party impacts, and other costly measures, may not be justified by the potential level of transfers. Colby (2000) stresses that markets for water and other rights associated with resource flows can develop and offer substantial gains in the long run. Initial transactions tend to encounter opposition and relatively high transaction costs, however, proceeding not like simple trades but instead resembling complex negotiations.

Enable Institutions to Adapt

In combination, the strategic principles outlined above show how it may be more efficient to allow institutions for water transactions to evolve, as users and those who would like to make transfers seek to clarify and defend their access to water. Institutions can then be developed efficiently in accordance with demand, rather than pushing premature institutional development that burdens water transactions with unnecessary overhead. Acknowledging existing rights and allowing transfers need not mean that rights are immediately registered and quantified, nor that extensive trading results immediately or even in the longer term.

Enabling water transfers need not imply that huge initial investments must be made in the institutions to allow trading. Recognizing that transactions may be sparse and allowing institutions for transfers and trading to evolve in response to demand from rights holders can thus further reduce costs and enhance the feasibility of an adaptive approach to water management. The principles outlined above could support the feasibility of a gradual, evolutionary approach to developing water allocation institutions, optimizing transaction costs through better integration of state law with existing norms, internal regulations of common property organizations, and other forms of local law.

Scope, Scale, and Transaction Costs

In general, increases in scale and scope of conflict over water can be expected to increase the transaction costs of managing water. Geographic scale and scope of multiple use are distinct dimensions, capable of varying independently. The ways in which institutions may change do not necessarily follow a single path, for example of increasing transactions cost, but instead may follow different paths under different circumstances. Scale concerns the number of users and geographic areas involved. Coordination across longer distance tends to increase transaction costs even when uses are relatively homogenous, as for example between different groups of irrigators. Interaction between different kinds of uses and users expands scope. This may both bring new concerns, such as water quality, and create new opportunities for mutually beneficial agreements, building on the differences in interests.

Transaction costs may take many forms, from time spent traveling to and attending meetings, to money spent paying agents to monitor water use, to legal fees. Transaction costs may come from procedures mandated by government (as in the case of requirements for environmental impact assessments and public consultation), as well as under the influence of the increasing capability and willingness of different stakeholders to pursue their interest in available forums, including courts and the media. Transaction costs may rise as the opportunity cost of time increases, while on the other hand changes in information and communication technologies may tend to reduce costs.

Strengthening and formalizing water rights is one possible response to increasing competition over water. Institutional changes to formalize rights may help efficiently solve problems and optimize overall transaction costs of water management. However, initial investments, with substantial transaction costs, may be necessary to put in place new arrangements that ultimately may be more efficient. Changes in institutions may emerge as a response to increasing scale and scope of competition over water and the rising value of water in competing uses, but may also be driven by other processes, such as the expansion of bureaucratic agencies or an increasing reliance on laws and courts. Institutions and transaction costs may follow various trajectories over time.

Transaction costs may tend to keep on rising as water users spend increasing amounts of their time and other resources in trying to acquire water and protect their access against competitors. Transaction costs of acquiring and protecting access to water may rise slowly or steeply over time. This could take the form of an escalating "arms race" where each person's efforts cause others to work harder, with most or all ending up as net losers. Increasing transaction costs of monitoring, guarding, and litigating could diminish, or even extinguish, the value of existing access to water, even if users were nominally allocated the same volumes. Thus, transaction costs could rise to the point where they induce some users to stop using water or to seek other sources. Institutional changes, such as those discussed in this chapter, are often undertaken in response to the increasing time, effort, and other resources required to secure access to water.

An institutional change could reduce transaction costs. New institutional arrangements may make it possible to gradually reduce, or even jump or "tunnel through" to a new arrangement with much lower transactions costs, for example where water distribution is handed over to a trusted third party. A simple example would be shifting from having each irrigator draw water from canals into their own field to having a single common irrigator distribute water. This might reduce not only time spent traveling to and from fields but also time spent monitoring whether others were taking too much water. The general argument for institutional reform is that it can lead to such changes, whether at a local scale within a single irrigation system or within a large river basin. This could be the case whether such changes are crafted through self-governance among users or promoted by government action.

In other cases, substantial resources and time may be needed to devise and implement new arrangements. These may be subject to much testing and tension before working more efficiently. Establishing new institutions is likely to be costly, especially if new arrangements must be formulated and then accepted by a diverse range of stakeholders. Thus, transaction costs may initially rise, but then later drop over time as new institutions are accepted and begin to operate more smoothly. A major question for many proposed reforms is whether the initial costs may be so high as to make change very costly, perhaps to the point where change is impossible, or not worth the effort. Institutional changes may not always lower transaction costs, and the amount of impact may vary. Users may be willing to invest more time and expense in protecting their access to water if their use of water is sufficiently valuable. Minimizing transaction costs is rarely an overt goal, but rather a form of efficiency subject to achieving some other objective, so that even after an institutional change, transaction costs may still be higher than before.

In general, increases in scope and scale of competition could be expected to induce institutional innovations that allow water transfers. However, as North (1990), Olson (2000), and others have stressed, the paths by which changes actually occur are strongly influenced by the structure of interests, organizations, and property rights. Among other things, these factors help explain why potentially beneficial changes may not occur, if they are blocked by those who would lose out, or if property rights are not strong enough to allow potential beneficiaries to capture the gains from changes.

In some cases the cultures and values of the different groups involved may be so different, so incommensurable, that the time and effort needed to reach agreement would be extremely high or infinite, making solutions very difficult or out of reach (Blatter and Ingram 2001; Espeland 1998). In other cases rivalry, distrust, and strategic manipulation may greatly raise the threshold of costs needed to reach agreements.

Within particular localities, transaction costs for allocating water may be lowered by shared understandings and practices concerning water and by the ways in which management of water is embedded in other relationships. Where groups competing for water do not share common practices or conceptions concerning water, its use and allocation, the transaction costs of resolving conflict may be high. Crafting new agreements may require extensive efforts to interpret different understandings and translate them into mutually agreeable arrangements.

Unwise attempts to impose uniform external definitions, based on government authority or market pressures, may either evoke rigid resistance, paralyzing the potential to constitute new solutions, or shatter the social capital that has facilitated local water allocation. It may breed confusion, conflict, and disruption. Poorly designed or premature institutional changes create risks of having rights taken over by those with better skills, knowledge, and political connections, perhaps regressively redistributing rights. A key implication is, again, that formalization is not always necessary or inevitable, but may be seen as a choice, one of several ways to address water conflicts. An understanding of legal complexity can help to clarify the extent to which conflicts are pursued through different forums, and how efficient alternative arrangements may be developed in terms of various criteria.

Transaction costs capture some, but certainly not all, of the important factors affecting water management. A major incentive to solve conflicts over water comes from the potential gains to the parties, particularly from more reliable access to a secure quantity and quality of water. However, stakeholders may also be influenced by values concerning entitlements to water (either currently or as part of what they consider a better justified allocation), by sacred beliefs concerning particular water sources, and by other ideas, some of which they are unwilling or unable to negotiate. Gains in status by being taken seriously as a stakeholder may facilitate resolution of conflicts. Conversely, resentments about being disrespected or taken advantage of may make it difficult or impossible to even begin discussing possible agreements.

Routes to the Future

In this chapter I have pointed out some of the ways in which facilitating the evolution of institutions for water allocation may offer ways of equitably increasing water productivity with lower transaction costs and risks than the alternatives of strengthening direct allocation by government agencies, universally formalizing all rights, or establishing fully commoditized water markets. I have used examples from Southeast Asia to illustrate the legal complexity of water conflicts. These conditions make it difficult to achieve better water management solely through agency-controlled allocation or commoditized water marketing. Evolutionary strategies can reduce the costs of establishing new institutions, and facilitate voluntary transactions to allocate and reallocate rights to water. A better understanding of legal complexity, of the many ways in which rights are constructed, redefined, and pursued, can be useful in identifying ways to make institutional development of water rights more feasible and successful.

NOTES

This chapter builds on earlier work with Ruth Meinzen-Dick on negotiated approaches to improving water allocation institutions (Bruns and Meinzen-Dick 1997, 2000, 2001). It also draws on water rights research by Mark Rosegrant and his colleagues, as noted in the citations and references. Views expressed in the chapter do not represent any organizations or persons with whom the author has been or is affiliated. The author retains responsibility for errors and omissions. The author wishes to express his thanks to Professor Keiji Sanbongi and to Yukihiro Mizutani for information regarding Japan's River Law.

1. Japan's River Law (Law 167 of 1964, as amended in July 1997), in chapter VI on Miscelleous Provisions (Transitory Measures) Article 87, states that (IDI 1997; Sanbongi 2001):

> A person who, on the basis of the competency and as of the day of the designation of a *class A river, class B river, river zone, river conservancy zone, projected river zone, spatial river conservancy zone or projected spatial river zone* is doing an act for which permission according to the provisions of this Law must be obtained or setting up a structure for which permission according to the provisions of this Law

must be obtained shall be deemed to have obtained the permission according to this Law concerning the act or the setting up of the structure on the same condition as before. The same shall apply to a person who, on the basis of the competency and as of the day of the enforcement of a Government Ordinance referred to in Article 25, Article 27 Paragraph 1, Article 55 Paragraph 1, Article 57 Paragraph 1, Article 58–4 Paragraph 1 or Article 58–6 Paragraph 1 or a Government Ordinance to amend or abolish such a Government Ordinance, is doing an act or setting up a structure for which it becomes necessary to obtain new permission as a result of the enforcement of the Government Ordinance.

Concerning (Article 23) Permission for River Water Use, Article 88 on Notification by De Facto Permittees states that "Upon the designation referred to in the preceding article, those who are designated by Government Ordinance out of the persons who, according to the provision of the article, are deemed to have obtained the permission referred to in Article 23 through 27 shall notify the *river administrator* of the necessary matters as may be provided for in detail by Government Ordinance."

11

Analyzing Water Rights, Multiple Uses, and Intersectoral Water Transfers

RUTH MEINZEN-DICK

RAJENDRA PRADHAN

Demand for water continues to grow worldwide. At the same time, developed water resources are almost fully utilized in many places, and the financial, environmental, and political costs of developing new water control systems are rising. The combination of rising demand and limited supplies is creating scarcity and competition between water uses, as well as users. In this resulting competition, irrigation, the largest sector of water use in most countries, is often at a disadvantage because the other sectors have more economic or political power. There is increasing pressure to transfer existing water supplies from agriculture to other water uses, especially urban and industrial uses. However, transferring water from agricultural use to municipal and industrial uses affects not only agricultural but also other rural uses, including rural domestic use, homestead gardens, livestock, and fishing.

Most discussions and evaluations of such transfers have focused on technical or economic efficiency. Much less attention has been given to equity implications, and the consequences for farmers and other groups in the rural areas. Yet, because water is a vital resource for rural livelihoods and identities, the consequences for rural areas are likely to be profound. What consequences such water transfers will have is likely to depend on the overall economic context, the process by which transfers take place, the nature and extent of recognition of water rights, and the relative power of the different parties. The economic context shapes the extent to which rural populations are dependent on irrigation or other water-related enterprises for their livelihoods, or are able to find other sources of income. The transfer process—whether transfers happen by administrative fiat, market purchases, other types of collective negotiation, or by illegal means—affects who is involved in decision making and who is likely to receive any compensation. The question of what rights are recognized—by whom and with reference to which law, norm, or cultural value—plays a pivotal role in determining the equity of outcomes, not only because it determines who can participate in decision making and who is eligible for compensation but also because perceptions of rights and fairness lie at the heart of the concept of equity. The power of different stakeholders interacts with all these factors. Those who are powerful may be able to shape the transfer mechanisms to suit their own interests, but some negotiation processes can provide somewhat greater leverage for marginalized groups by at least ensuring they have a seat at the table. Finally, power is intricately linked to water rights. Those with power are likely to be able to secure and defend their water rights, while those with water rights that are recognized have some bargaining power, even if they are otherwise less economically or politically powerful.

The consequences of intersectoral water transfers have been studied, to some extent, in the western United States and other industrialized countries, but have received very little attention in developing countries. The experiences of industrialized countries can raise some critical issues, but may not be appropriate indicators of what will happen as a result of intersectoral water transfers in Asia and other developing countries, because in the latter the pace of urbanization and industrialization processes is dramatically compressed. As a result, neither infrastructure nor institutions in developing countries have as much chance to evolve to meet the challenges. In particular, the state legal infrastructure and processes for transferring water are relatively well established in Europe and the United States. As a result, most transfers have taken place through regulated channels, whether through the state or the market. But in most developing countries, particularly in South Asia, water transfers take place through a variety of mechanisms, often simultaneously, with little overall enforceable regulation. Moreover, the economic, political, and cultural contexts differ dramatically between industrialized and developing countries, with profound implications for the processes and outcomes of water transfers.

For understanding both the mechanisms for water transfers and the range of water rights held by different stakeholders, it is important to go beyond conventional approaches that look only at government laws and administrative processes, and to employ the perspective of legal pluralism. The concept of legal pluralism recognizes that there are many overlapping legal frameworks, including state and customary law, but also religious law and project law, forming mixes of local law. Furthermore, water rights are not a unitary item, but can include diverse bundles of rights, including use rights, decision-making rights, and income-earning rights over water. The nature of the bundles and the types of law applicable may differ, depending on both the source of water and the use.

This chapter outlines an approach for identifying claimants and water rights based on state as well as nonstate laws in contexts of intersectoral water transfers. We begin with a review of the concepts of legal pluralism and water rights, and then explore how rights and law change in the context of intersectoral transfers. Particular attention is paid to power differences among claimants and the need to identify "invisible" uses and claims on water resources, particularly those that are important for women and other marginalized groups.[1] Illustrations are drawn from the international literature and a comparative study of water transfers in India, Nepal, and Sri Lanka.

Legal Pluralism and Water Rights

Legal Pluralism

Many social scientists understand law more broadly than just the acts, rules, administrative orders, court decisions, and so on enacted or made by the various state organs. Any "social field" such as a village, an ethnic community, an association, or a state can generate and enforce rules or normative and cognitive repertoires.[2] It is thus possible to have various kinds of law such as state law, religious law, customary law, project law, and organizational law. The coexistence and interaction of multiple legal orders within a social setting or domain of social life is called legal pluralism.[3] These different legal orders are not isolated from one another, but interact, influence each other, and are "mutually constitutive" (Guillet 1998; see also Spiertz 1992). How exactly these different legal orders interact and influence each other in specific contexts depends on social and power relationships between the "bearers" of different laws.

These different legal orders may be sharply distinguished in some contexts as, for example, in the courts. However, they are less sharply distinguished in the everyday life of people in local communities. At the local level we find a mixture based on tradition, new forms of self-regulation, elements of old and new state laws, donor laws, religious laws, and so on. This whole mixture of norms and rules that are expressed and used at the local level is called local law (F. von Benda-Beckmann et al. 1997). It is important to note that local law as well as customary law may be plural in the sense that they are constructed and manifested differently in different levels and contexts (F. and K. von Benda-Beckmann. 1999; Spiertz 2000; Spiertz and de Jong 1992).

The coexistence of multiple laws does not mean that all laws are equally powerful and relevant. In some contexts, state law is usually more powerful and is used by state officials, for example, in allocating water from rivers and reservoirs for nonagricultural uses. State law can also be used by powerful outsiders to claim resources in ways that are not recognized as legitimate locally. It can be used by the weaker sections of a community, backed by external agencies, to claim rights denied to them by the powerful.[4] However, the invocation of state law does not necessarily mean that it is accepted by all or can be actually implemented.[5] In situations of legal pluralism, individuals can make use of more than one law or versions of one law to rationalize and legitimize their decisions or their behavior, a process known as forum shopping (K. von Benda-Beckmann 1984). Which law is accepted and enforced depends on power and social relationships between the different claimants. As groups interact more with outsiders, such as factory owners, who may not share the same community, religion, or other social field, and hence do not recognize the legitimacy of the same laws and enforcement institutions, there may be a tendency to move toward state law and government enforcement or even international law and international agencies, as in the case of rights of "indigenous peoples" (see also chapters 3 and 7).

Water Rights

The term "water rights" is often understood narrowly to mean a use right to a share of water (Teerink and Nakashima 1993) or a system of water allocation (Brewer et al. 1997; Uphoff 1986).[6] For scholars who use either the common property or legal anthropological perspectives, water rights, like property rights in general, are better understood not as a single right but as "bundles of rights" that include several types and levels of rights. These are often grouped into two broad categories: use rights of access and withdrawal, and decision-making rights to regulate and control water uses and users (F. von Benda-Beckmann et al. 1997; Schlager and Ostrom 1992).[7] To these may be added the rights to earn income from a resource, which Roman legal traditions have referred to as usufruct rights (see also Alchian and Demsetz 1972; Eggertsson 1990). Rights to earn income from a resource (even without using it directly) can be separate from use and management of the resource. Examples are government departments that collect revenue from water users, or individuals or communities that collect a charge from others who use water—a factor that is increasingly important in the context of water transfers.

These bundles of rights may be held by a single right holder or dispersed among several rights holders. In most farmer-managed irrigation systems, for example, male landowners have both use as well as decision-making rights over water in the system, whereas women, even if they own land, and tenants may have only use rights.[8] The state may claim the ultimate right to regulate all natural resources within its territory, even water "owned" by individuals. But there are also other decision-making authorities, such as traditional village chiefs, priests, and management committee members of water users' associations, which derive their legitimacy from a variety of legal orders such as customary or religious law. Decision-making authorities enjoy considerable rights to regulate and control the quantity, timing, and types of uses of water in different sources. Decision-making rights affect other rights in bundles of water rights.[9]

Thus, the concept of water rights does not refer to a single and unitary right but to bundles of rights that vary across property regimes, legal orders, and cultures (meanings and values of water). The configurations of bundles of rights to water may even differ within the same law or culture across different property regimes, sources of water, and uses of water. The bundles of rights to water in a water source such as a river often differ from rights to water once it is appropriated and conveyed by infrastructures. Similarly, there often are different bundles of rights to water for different uses, such as religious or domestic uses, and the more economic uses of water. The bundles of rights to water are not static but complex, dynamic, flexible, and subject to change because of ecological, livelihood, knowledge and social and political uncertainties, which make it necessary for the claimants, old and new, frequently to negotiate among themselves to establish their water rights (see also F. and K. von Benda-Beckmann 2000; Bruns and Meinzen-Dick 2000).

Following Wiber's (1992) approach to property rights in general, in this chapter we define water rights as claims to use, derive income from, or control water by individuals or groups that are recognized as legitimate by a larger collectivity than the claimants and that are protected through a form of law. Individuals or groups assert claims of various kinds over resources such as rights to use the resource, derive income from it, rights to control use and make rules regarding resource use and users, as well as rights to transfer these rights to others.[10] It is not sufficient to assert claims to the resource. Unless claims are accepted by a larger collectivity than the claimants themselves, they are not considered legitimate. This becomes clear when there are conflicting claims. The relevant legitimizing institution often varies. Depending on the context it may be a users' group, an ethnic community, a village council, or a state agency. These legitimizing institutions often compete, offer alternative legitimacies, and are based on different laws (state, customary, local, religious, and so on). They provide different definitions of bundles of water rights and rights holders as well as the procedures and conditions by which the rights holders establish, maintain, transfer, and lose rights. Claims accepted and validated as legitimate by one collectivity or law may not necessarily be recognized and accepted as valid by another collectivity or law. Conversely, individuals can call upon a plurality of laws and institutions in their discourse and negotiation concerning water rights. Which law or amalgamation of different laws is applied in specific cases and claims depends on the power and social relationships between the claimants.

In addition to looking at the types of rights and sources from which they derive, it is important to consider the strength or robustness of those rights, that is, the degree to which they can be defended (see Place et al. 1993; Roth et al. 1994). This is especially important in the case of water resources, because the available supply, as well as the demand, tends to fluctuate from year to year or even from season to season. Stronger water rights will apply even during periods of scarcity, whereas weaker rights may be denied when water is scarce.

Laws concerning water rights do not reflect actual practice or configuration of water rights relationships. It is therefore important to differentiate between categorical rights and concretized rights, corresponding to general rights in principle and the specific rights relationships between actual rights holders with respect to an actual resource (F. von Benda-Beckmann 2001; F. and K. von Benda-Beckmann 2000). Although both categorical and concrete water rights are contingent upon a variety of legal and nonlegal elements, it is at the level of actual social relationships that other types of rights and social relationships, such as rights to land, gender and ethnic relationships, and caste status, become significant. In this respect, power relationships are very important, as they often determine the distribution and actualization of rights. The processes of acquiring and maintaining rights, and the processes by which categorical rights are transformed into concrete rights are as important as the rules that are used to justify claims (F. von Benda-Beckmann et al. 1997; F. and K. von Benda-Beckmann 2000).

We also need to distinguish between categorical or concretized water rights on the one hand, and access to water on the other (which may be based on rights, but also on power, the use of force and so on). In addition to (use) rights holders, other claimants may have physical access to water and withdraw water either by stealing water or with explicit or implicit permission of the rights holders. People who steal water may be said to have access to water, whereas people whose claims to use rights are not accepted by the rights holders but who are nevertheless allowed to use or withdraw water may be said to have tolerated access to water, but not rights. It is not always clear whether a person may be said to have rights or tolerated access, especially if there are disputes over this issue. And what may be considered tolerated access according to one law may be considered rights according to another. Nevertheless it is useful to make this distinction because those who have tolerated access are usually not allowed to participate in decision making or meet obligations that would help them establish their rights (Pradhan and Pradhan 2000; Sodemba and Pradhan 2000; see also Meinzen-Dick and Bakker 2001).

Claims to Water and Processes of Water Transfer

Claims to Different Water Bodies or Sources of Water

Multiple claimants assert different kinds of claims to different water bodies or sources of water. The claimants, the types of claims they assert, and the law they use to justify their claims vary depending on the sources of the water (rivers, groundwater, or water that is captured or extracted and conveyed in canals or pipes), water use (irrigation, domestic use, fishing, and so on), and property regime (common, public, private, open access). Natural bodies of surface water (river, lakes, and so on) and those constructed and managed by the government (reservoirs, irrigation systems, drinking water systems) are, in general, public property, regulated by state laws. The state claims rights of ownership, control, or income generation over these waters on the basis of state law. However, others may also have rights over such water bodies or sources of water—such as control or management rights delegated to them, use rights—based on state law, customary law, or local law. Natural bodies of water may be considered common property and not public properties by some communities. Streams in territories occupied by indigenous peoples are an example of this. Farmers may claim rights to appropriate river water on the basis of prior appropriation law or traditional (customary) use; devotees may claim rights to bathe in the river on the basis of religious rights and traditional use; fishermen claim rights to fish in the river on the basis of their traditional livelihood. All these users consider rivers either as public or common property, over which they may not have decision-making rights but certainly have use rights and rights to generate income. On the basis of national or international environmental rights, environmentalists may claim rights to prevent others from withdrawing or polluting the river (which they may consider common or public property or even a global commons).

The state may not recognize or accept all these claims as being legitimate. It may, for example, demand that farmers acquire permits to withdraw water from rivers. The farmers may not recognize the right of the state to regulate water withdrawal from rivers. On the other hand, though devotees may accept the rights of the state to regulate water withdrawals from the river, they may claim rights to bathe in a (ritually) pure river based on religious rights. Such religious rights are often not recognized by the state, environmentalists, and drinking water suppliers, who may accept rights to clean but not necessarily ritually pure water.

Although multiple uses of water from natural water sources are recognized and provided for by the state and nonstate claimants, this is often not the case for irrigation systems. In agency-managed irrigation systems, state law, irrigation managers, and the irrigators would recognize two types of claims and claimants: first, rights of the agency to make decisions concerning allocation and distribution of water and the conditions required for use rights to irrigation water, as well as the right to collect payment from water users; second, rights of landowners in the command area to a proportion of water allocated to them by the agency for irrigation purposes. In some cases, the agency may also allot water to users for nonirrigation purposes, such as for textile factories in the Philippines. Or, as in the case of the Sunsari-Morang Irrigation Project in Nepal, project law allows the villagers, even those without land rights in the command area, to use water in the main and branch canals for nonirrigation purposes such as bathing, washing clothes, and providing water for livestock. In most cases, however, state and project laws do not recognize nonirrigation use rights of the villagers to water in the canal. Simultaneously, in agency-managed systems local laws tend to be functional as well, and these legitimize control and use rights not only for irrigation but for a variety of purposes, including domestic water supply, livestock, fishing, and other enterprises. The holder of these rights, which are vital assets for the welfare and livelihood of rural communities, often belong to weaker socioeconomic groups (such as pastoralists or fishers) or rural women.

In farmer-managed irrigation systems, the farmers with rights to irrigation—and more specifically the managing committee members—collectively hold decision-making rights. Sometimes traditional village leaders or village councils may hold these decision-making rights. All landowning irrigators, men and women, may have categorical decision-making rights. However, women may not be able to concretize their rights because of time constraints, lack of confidence in the public sphere, gender ideology, or customary law that limits the rights of women. Do the rights holders of farmer-managed irrigation systems recognize the claims of villagers for nonirrigation uses of water in their canals? The literature on farmer-managed irrigation systems is silent on this issue. In Nepal, water in farmer-managed irrigation systems, especially in the hills, is probably not used regularly for nonirrigation purposes. However, even if water is used for washing clothes, bathing, and feeding livestock, as in the Chhatis Mauja irrigation system located in the southern plains of Nepal, it is likely that users have tolerated access but not use rights to the water. Claims for nonirrigation use rights of water in farmer-managed irrigation systems may not be accepted as legitimate by male irrigators, whereas they may be fully accepted by female irrigators or women who do not irrigate. An exception is probably made for drinking-water purposes. Hindu and Islamic law, and possibly local laws as well, grant rights to people to quench their thirst from any source of water. But it is not always sure whether this law is accepted for all cases, or whether such rights have to be negotiated in order to be concretized.[11]

Claims to groundwater pose even more complex problems. In most countries, the state claims rights to regulate use of groundwater, but at the same time there is often a strong conception, both in local and in state law, that groundwater belongs to the owner of the overlying land. This accords seemingly strong private ownership of groundwater located under the surface of private land.[12] However, both state and private claims of rights over groundwater often carry little meaning in practice, because they are difficult to enforce. Unlike surface water, where both the availability of the resource and its use are relatively easy to observe, it is much more difficult to get accurate information on how much groundwater is available, who is using how much of it, and how this affects others. Landowners may be relatively free to extract water from under their own land. However, this pumping can also draw water from under neighbors' land. Hence, well owners have an incentive to pump as much as possible, depending only on pumping costs, because they cannot be assured that the water they do not pump will still be available later. This leads to a "tragedy of open access," even for a seemingly private-property groundwater resource. Technology and capital limit the amount of water that can be pumped; it is often the richer landowners who can invest in powerful pumps to extract water from deep bores (see also chapters 6 and 8 on such practices in Kathmandu and Gujarat).

Water Rights in Different Types of Transfer Processes

We now turn to the question of how rights and law change in the context of intersectoral transfers, paying particular attention to gender, caste, and class differences. Changes in rights and law are related to transfer processes, property regimes, and bundles of rights as well as social and political relationships between the claimants to the water that is being transferred. Earlier we identified three main types of property regimes: public, private, and common property. Water under one of these three property regimes is transferred mainly by three processes: administrative reallocation, market-based reallocation, and collective negotiation. To these we could add a fourth process: forced transfer based neither on administrative reallocation nor on market allocation or negotiation. Each transfer of water may involve several processes, such as reallocation and negotiation. Municipalities and industries may take recourse to several of these processes to acquire water.

ADMINISTRATIVE REALLOCATION. Administrative reallocation of water often occurs from large bodies of water such as rivers, lakes, and reservoirs, as well as from large irrigation systems managed by state agencies. The state, as an expression of its sovereignty, claims ultimate rights to regulate water (and all other natural resources as well as the population) within its territory (Beitz 1991; F. von Benda-Beckmann 1997). This right is often backed by state law that vests ownership rights of water in the state. The state and, more specifically, different agencies of the state, use this law to justify their rights to regulate and reallocate water for the benefit of the "wider public." Not surprisingly, in many countries these tend to be primarily the more powerful sections or agents in society such as municipalities and factories (see examples from the Andes and South Africa in chapters 7 and 9). Formal hearings are rarely held, though farmers may protest the transfers through their political representatives or through other forms of agitation.

In administrative reallocation, the state may recognize use and some decision-making rights of the prior users (usually irrigators), but consider their rights secondary to the rights of the state. The state may accord priority to domestic and sometimes even industrial uses, over irrigation, especially in times of scarcity. Unless the rights of users to earn income from water are recognized by the state, compensation for giving up water is usually not included. Thus, for example, in the upper Bagmati Basin of Kathmandu Valley in Nepal, several state agencies divert water from the river to supply drinking water to Kathmandu and a few distant villages, as well as to generate electricity, without taking into consideration the rights of the farmers who have been drawing their irrigation water from the river for a long time (Dixit 1997). The farmers were neither consulted about nor compensated for the diversion of water for nonirrigation purposes. Even if the state does recognize the rights of the farmers to use water for irrigation, and to be compensated for giving up their water, rights to other rural, nonirrigation uses are often not recognized. The "invisibility" of such uses and rights, at least from the perspective of the state and municipal and industrial users, can have serious livelihood consequences, in particular for women and other marginal groups, if water is transferred out of agriculture.

As local law generally also accords high priority to drinking water, farmers often accept transfers of water for domestic use. However, notions of fairness play a major role here. If farm households perceive that municipalities will be receiving a higher level of water service than is available to their rural areas, protests may arise, either through appeals to the government or through sabotage of the pipes transferring water. The example of the Bhavani Basin in Tamil Nadu, India, shows that such protests can be quite effective. When the government proposed to transfer water from an irrigation dam to supply Coimbatore city, rural communities located between the dam and the city protested that they did not have piped drinking water systems. In response to these protests, the government extended the system to provide treated domestic water to hundreds of villages.

According to local law, administrative reallocation for industrial use is generally less acceptable than transfers for domestic use. The decrease of water quality due to effluents factories discharge back into waterways often causes more protests than the decline in water quantity. Both state and local law have had little to say about rights to water quality.[13] However, as municipal and industrial effluents are increasingly discharged into waterways, local groups are more likely to assert claims to clean water. For example, the Bhavani River Joint Protection League has used fasts, protests, and court cases to assert rights to a clean river, often using a combination of state law, religious discourse about rivers, environmental concerns for fish, and appeals to human emotions regarding health and aesthetics.

MARKET-BASED REALLOCATION. In market-based reallocation, water is either sold directly to buyers for nonagricultural or agricultural uses, or land is leased or sold to individuals or factories who then either abstract groundwater beneath the land or use the share of water allotted to the land from irrigation systems.

The operation of water markets with compensation for those who give up water presupposes fairly strong recognition of private water rights, including rights to earn income from water.

The western United States and Chile have both used a variety of market or semimarket mechanisms in which individual farmers lease their water use rights to other users or even permanently sell their use and decision-making rights (Howe 1998; Howitt 1998; NNMLS 2000; Rosegrant and Ringler 1998; Villarejo 1997). State recognition of private water rights, and especially water rights that are separable from land, have facilitated such market transfers, but also facilitate state regulation of these transfers (Easter et al. 1998; Scott and Coustalin 1995). In California, seasonal transfers have been conducted since 1991 through a state drought water bank, which arranges purchases from individual farmers for transfer to other users, usually as temporary leases of water rights (Howitt 1998). Arizona, Utah, and New Mexico conduct transfers through the state engineers' office, which determines technical characteristics of all proposed transfers and conducts hearings on third-party effects. Nevertheless, Northern New Mexico Legal Services (NNMLS 2000) has shown that small farmers from acequias (traditional farmer-managed irrigation systems) have difficulty in actualizing and defending their rights, even though they held the most senior rights in the state, because they are socially marginalized and thus less powerful (see also chapters 5 and 7 for similar problems in the Andes). Colorado uses water courts, which have much higher transaction costs, for both those who propose the transfer and those who might want to protest it. As a result, small water users with legitimate protests are often excluded (Howe 1998). Furthermore, only "beneficial use" rights, and not public uses, are considered. Therefore, there is little recourse for those who are affected by the transfers through reduced return flows, reduced recreational or environmental water uses, or loss of livelihoods.

In many countries, state law neither gives official legitimacy to water markets nor officially prohibits the sale of water, especially groundwater.[14] There may be local law, valid between buyers and sellers of water but not accepted by farmers who do not, or are not able to, sell water, especially the small farmers who are affected by heavy water extraction.

In the Bhavani Basin of Tamil Nadu, Palanisami (1994) found that farmers who could sell their well water to tankers supplying urban domestic and industrial uses viewed the transfers favorably because they were able to earn greater profits than they could have done in farming, or were even able to sell surplus water and still continue their agricultural production. Industrialists own most of the tankers that supply water for industrial uses. Many of them also own deep bore wells or finance the construction of such wells (Janakarajan 1999). However, such sales have accelerated the overextraction of groundwater and led to a lowering of the water table in the region. Agricultural wells have gone dry, and farmers are not only no longer able to grow water-intensive garden crops but also face difficulties even in meeting their drinking water needs. The farmers who have not been able to sell water have protested against the sale of groundwater in the rural areas for municipal and industrial uses. Women have joined in these protests because of the special difficulties they face in providing water for domestic needs. The government does not seem to have been effective in controlling such markets in groundwater, nor in dealing with third party effects of the transfers involved (similar problems in Kathmandu and Gujarat are described in chapters 6 and 8).

Water markets can be considered a "semi-autonomous social field," able to generate and enforce its own rules but also subject to influences from the wider social and political system (S. F. Moore 1973). Because in much of Asia the state neither regulates nor prohibits the sale of water, water markets operate in accordance with their own law but in the shadow of state law, which claims the ultimate right of regulation and ownership of water. The law that is generated by the market recognizes rights of the landowners to extract and sell groundwater under their land for any use. Market law is blind to preexisting rights of others to water for agricultural, domestic, or other uses. However, the sellers of water, who are also part of other social fields (such as village, family, caste), could, but not necessarily will, be influenced by norms originating in these fields that may induce them to limit the volume of extraction. Market law could also be influenced by state law to regulate water extraction. But influencing market law requires interactions between these social fields, for example by agitation, protest, negotiation, and state intervention. In Pakistan, family connections, religious values, local power relations, and social norms affect the functioning of groundwater markets within the agricultural sector, particularly because the spatial range between buyer and seller is limited to a local area (Meinzen-Dick 2000). However, if water is being sold out of the local area and the agricultural sector, local social fields (such as norms related to kinship) are likely to have less influence over the operation of water markets.

COLLECTIVE NEGOTIATION. Another process of reallocation of water is by collective negotiation, either between users and the state or between the users themselves.[15] In the first case, the parties to the negotiation are the state (or the concerned state agencies), the agricultural users (irrigators) who are usually the prior users, and the municipal and industrial users. When the state is represented among the negotiating parties, state law is often invoked. This gives the state a strong position to claim its rights to regulate water uses. The state, however, must also have the will and technical capacity to assert its rights. Political and economic considerations, more than the question of water rights, are important in such negotiations. Saravanan and Appasamy's (1999) historical study of the conflicts between domestic and industrial supply in the Bhavani and

Noyyal basins in Tamil Nadu illustrates how farmers, if they are strongly united and protest vehemently, may for a time prevent reallocation of water from agriculture into other sectors and uses or decrease the amount of water reallocated in this way.

It is not uncommon for the users of water for different purposes to enter into negotiation to transfer water out of agriculture, often for monetary or other considerations. Negotiation between buyers and sellers precedes market reallocation. As inducement to transfer water out of agriculture, farmers may be promised jobs in factories established in rural areas.

Collectively negotiated approaches can expand the range of options, particularly seeking win-win solutions. In California, for example, some municipalities have secured additional water for drought years by paying farmers to either install water conservation devices or to increase groundwater recharge in wet years. The city receives the additional water saved or stored. A tankers' association, supplying middle-class residents in Kathmandu, has negotiated with a Village Development Committee (local government) to purchase water from a stream near the community. But, unlike water purchases from individuals, in this case the funds go to the Village Development Committee for investment in other community assets.

In the case of negotiated reallocation of water, it is possible in theory that the rights of nonirrigation rural uses of water, such as for livestock, fisheries, or kitchen gardens, are taken into consideration because a plurality of laws can be called upon during negotiation to justify a wide variety of claims. However, this is rare because rights and uses for nonirrigation rural uses are invisible to the state, market, and even irrigators themselves.

OTHER MEANS OF WATER TRANSFER. Although it is useful to construct ideal types of administrative, market, and negotiated transfers, many empirical cases involve a combination of these reallocation processes, as well as illegal means such as stealing water from canals, extracting groundwater behind high enclosures, or even using force to divert water from rivers. Kurnia et al. (2000) show how textile factories in West Java have obtained water through a variety of means. The first, through administrative allocation, is sanctioned by state law. The factories have received government-allocated permits to draw water from the irrigation system or groundwater. The second is through buying or renting land or individual irrigation turns from local farmers. This is not sanctioned in state law, but local law generally accepts it as legitimate. Although the water is not supposed to be separable from the land, farmers in the system acknowledge that the owners of fields have a right to a certain turn of water, even for nonagricultural purposes. Factories also negotiate with upstream farmers and give them benefits (for example, help in rebuilding a drainage structure) so that they will not object to the extra water that factories take, while the downstream farmers get less water. This approach compensates some farmers but not those who bear the greatest burden. Finally, factories acquire extra water by adding extra inlets, putting pumps on the pipes so that they draw more water than normally allowed, or taking water out of turn. These means of transferring water are not sanctioned by either state or local law, but continue by virtue of the power of the factories. Although the farmers in this case have the strongest water rights in both local and state law, they are generally not able to effectively defend those rights because of the greater economic and political power of the factory owners.

Consequences of Intersectoral Water Transfers

The consequences of water transfers from agriculture to other sectors have mostly been evaluated from an economic perspective in the United States, but even their broader livelihood and community outcomes have emerged as important issues (Villarejo 1997). As water is sold and land taken out of agricultural production, not only are local agricultural service businesses and labor affected but property values also go down. This affects the rural tax base, and hence public services, including schools. Even the loss of recreational uses and aesthetic values can have significant impact on employment, land values, and tax revenues where tourism is a significant industry in rural areas. The negative economic consequences of water transfers can be quantified and compensated with monetary or other economic measures. What is harder to measure, much less compensate for, is loss of social and cultural values. In New Mexico, members of one acequia (small irrigation system) filed a court case to block water transfers to a ski resort on the grounds that they would disrupt the cultural core of the acequia community, which had been built around mutual cooperation to maintain the acequia. This case won an injunction blocking the sale of water, but the case was finally overturned in the appeals court (Howe 1998).[16]

The repercussions of transferring water out of agriculture and rural livelihoods are also very apparent in Asia. In both West Java and the Bhavani Basin, increasing industrial water use has had serious negative consequences on agricultural production and fishing because of greater water scarcity, pollution, and temperature increases due to factory discharges. However, where the industrial development actually takes place in the rural areas, the employment and incomes generated benefited local people (see also the case discussed by Bruns in chapter 10).

Thus, we need to be careful not to assume a unitary and fictive "farmer" or user. All farmers do not necessarily have the same interests, and the consequences of water transfer are not the same for all farm households, or even for all individuals within the households. A few, especially the larger farmers, may in fact benefit substantially by selling water or from the increase in the value of land. As rural households diversify their livelihood strategies to include more nonfarm activities and migration to towns, interests in water for different uses become more complex.

The range of transfer mechanisms and consequences in Asia indicates the need for a more coherent approach to understanding intersectoral water transfers, to go beyond the conventional analyses that are limited to formal, regulated transfer mechanisms, with recognition only of water rights based on state law.[17]

Conclusions

Perceptions of fairness and equity are fundamentally about acknowledgment of rights. Applying a more inclusive and pluralistic legal perspective in water transfer processes can lead to more equitable and hence more acceptable water transfers. Recognizing and understanding all water users and a broader set of claims is critical for strengthening the bargaining power of the poor and less powerful groups, or even giving them a seat at the table at all. Without this, water transfers risk reducing the asset base of the poor even further, or encountering opposition from those who have to give up water.

Moving from simple administrative or market transfers to more inclusive negotiation processes could further enhance the equity and acceptability of transfers. The result is, first, more likely to be seen as equitable because it includes all who have an interest in the water. When these people take part in the process they are more likely to accept the outcomes. Negotiated transfers can also identify creative means for benefit sharing. If water is to be transferred because nonagricultural uses are of higher value, then rural water users should be able to share in those gains from trade. On the other hand, if the apparent increase in value of water is due to an underestimation of the value of water use in rural areas, then recognizing a broader spectrum of water users will give a more accurate picture of the benefits of water for rural livelihoods.

Until recently, legal pluralism has largely been an academic field, with understandable concerns regarding compromises and distortions that have occurred when government agencies become involved in identifying customary law and rights. However, in the case of water policy, and particularly in contexts of water transfers, legal pluralism is too important to be restricted to academic circles. Gaining recognition for water rights derived from local law is critical for protecting poor people's access to water resources and strengthening their bargaining power in negotiations over water. To implement this is likely to require the willingness of government agencies and international donors to recognize local law, as well as for scholars and researchers in the field of legal pluralism to engage in policy-oriented and applied research. In view of the stakes involved in water transfers, this investment seems fully justified.

NOTES

This is a revised version of a paper presented at the XIIIth International Congress of the Commission on Folk Law and Legal Pluralism, 7–10 April 2002, Chiang Mai, Thailand. The authors wish to acknowledge K. Palanisami and Kusum Athukorala for collaboration in the study of water transfers, and Dik Roth, Margreet Zwarteveen, and Rutgerd Boelens for helpful comments on the paper.

1. This builds upon research using a gender perspective on irrigation systems, which has helped to make visible the role of women as users and rights holders of irrigation water (see Merrey and Baviskar 1998; Zwarteveen 1994a, 1997; Zwarteveen and Meinzen-Dick 2001).

2. See S. F. Moore 1973. Moore uses the term "semi-autonomous social field" to indicate that the social field is not wholly autonomous but partly open to influence from other social fields.

3. For legal pluralism, see F. von Benda-Beckmann 1997; F. von Benda-Beckmann et al. 1996, 1997; Griffiths 1986; Merry 1988; Spiertz 2000.

4. See Pradhan et al. 1997 for cases of farmer-managed irrigation systems. Law thus is a resource in agrarian struggles between the state and local communities, and between different sections of local communities (see F. Benda-Beckmann and M. van der Velde 1992).

5. See K. von Benda-Beckmann (1985) for the reasons and difficulties of implementing court decisions in the social fields where the disputes originated. See Pradhan and Pradhan (2000) for an example of a Supreme Court decision relating to a water dispute not implemented in the village. See also chapters 2, 4, and 7.

6. Bruns and Meinzen-Dick (2000) identify three approaches to water rights studies: legal (state law), institutional (as in irrigation studies and including many ethnographic studies), and common property; see also Pradhan and Brewer 1998.

7. These two types of rights are similar to, but do not correspond exactly to, distinctions of public and private rights (F. and K. von Benda-Beckmann 1999; F. von Benda-Beckmann 2001). For a critique of the common property approach from a legal pluralism perspective, see F. von Benda-Beckmann 2001.

8. See Zwarteveen and Meinzen-Dick (2001) on the consequences of a lack of decision-making rights for women with regard to irrigation.

9. See Adhikari and Pradhan (2000) for an example of how decision-making rights affect the sharing and timing of water received by different rights holders.

10. Each of these rights is constituted by a complex or bundle of rights. For example, there are different kinds of use rights: full and independent use rights, dependent use rights, rights for a particular season or crop, and so on.

11. Research may reveal that, though the largely male irrigators may not accept the claims of women and the landless for nonirrigation use rights of canal water, these claimants may use the canal for washing, fishing, feeding livestock, and so on, basing their claims on other local or customary laws. Irrigators may allow them to use the canal for nonirrigation purposes, especially when the demand for irrigation is low. This gives them tolerated access from their perspective, whereas the nonirrigation users may claim that it is their right to use the water. Thus, a plurality of local and customary laws may be involved (see Spiertz 1992).

12. Groundwater below public or communal land is considered public/government or communal property, over which the state or community has ownership and other rights.

13. Religious law has had more to say about water quality, but this has generally referred to ritual purity (for example, flowing water or contamination by low castes) rather than the biological or chemical content of the water.

14. Easter et al. (1998) distinguish between formal water markets, where transfers are protected through state law, and informal markets where there are no provisions or regulation by the state. However, many of these informal markets may have very formalized rules governing transfers, even if they operate outside the ambit of state law.

15. Although market transactions also involve negotiation, in this context we refer to negotiate with and between groups rather than individual well owners.

16. Community identity values of water may feature prominently in local law (see, for example, Ingram and Brown 1998), but are often difficult to establish in state law.

17. For an outline of such a framework, see Meinzen-Dick and Pradhan 2002.

12

Water Rights and Legal Pluralism

Beyond Analysis and Recognition

MARGREET ZWARTEVEEN

DIK ROTH

RUTGERD BOELENS

One important reason to embark upon the effort to compile this book was to bridge the felt gap between the analysis of water rights and the assumptions and practices of intervention. On the one hand, academic anthropologists criticize water professionals for overly simplifying the water world and for not recognizing its socioeconomic, cultural, and legal diversity. On the other, more intervention-oriented water professionals find detailed analyses of the existence of plural legal situations of little direct use for designing water management systems and policies. All chapters in this book combine, to a greater or lesser extent, academic curiosity with a commitment to change, thus providing testimony that legal pluralism is no longer a mere hobbyhorse of legal anthropologists. Even if not all the contributing authors explicitly engage with questions of change, all of them somehow relate to wider policy debates. Some chapters are clearly written from a wider concern with a law-related social or developmental problem, and engage in a critical analysis of the existence of plural legal conditions, without searching for ready-made solutions. Thus, the analyses by Bhushan Udas and Zwarteveen (chapter 2), Getches (chapter 3), and Roth (chapter 4) contribute to deepening the understanding of the role of law and lawmaking in different settings. In contrast, van Koppen and Jha (chapter 9), Bruns (chapter 10), and Meinzen-Dick and Pradhan (chapter 11) more directly address those who are in a position to implement or devise policies and laws. Van Koppen and Jha describe legally plural conditions in South Africa in the context of governmental efforts to create and implement socially more equitable water distribution policies and laws. Bruns's chapter can be read as an attempt by a concerned social scientist to come to terms with the gaps and tensions between neoinstitutionalist and sociolegal approaches to water problems by using the concept of transaction costs. In a similar manner, Meinzen-Dick and Pradhan embed their social concerns about equitable and just water allocation mechanisms in clear water policy terms and contexts.

In this concluding chapter on legal pluralism and water control, we want to further address the question of the implications of insights about legal pluralism for water policy making and interventions. As we noted in the first chapter, translating academic insights about the coexistence of various legal and normative water frameworks into neat policy recipes carries with it the risk that legal pluralism may become yet another tool in support of basically centralist social engineering. This risk of simplification is intrinsic to the tension between scientific analysis for the sake of improving understanding and research work with an interventionist focus. Analyses belonging to the first group increasingly acknowledge complexity and contingency, and have come to accept the limits of manageability as a fact of life and as a basic starting point of further analysis. Such acceptance becomes more difficult for policymakers and higher-level water managers, whose legitimacy depends on their own and others' trust in their regulating and managing powers, and in getting their plans to bring about progress and systematic improvements accepted. To make policies and laws, a degree of simplification is unavoidable. How simplifications come about, however, is not a given. Many chapters illustrate how specific legal and policy abstractions work to render specific interests or groups more visible than others, how the scope for planned change is often exaggerated, and how routes to alternative solutions are banned from (and at the same time also by) public and professional discourse.

Acknowledgment of the existence of plural legal and normative conditions entails making sense of complex interactions between various normative and legal frameworks that are not easily amenable to forms of technical, social, and legal regulation. Roth (chapter 4), for instance, shows how the norms, rules, and practices associated with the subak are difficult to marry with those associated with state-initiated WUAs. Indeed, the process of gaining acceptance and legitimacy for centrally devised rules and rights is likely to be full of tensions, often pitting the different parties against each other in long-winded negotiations and struggles. These take place within and through wider power differences that may either work against or in favor of legal intentions. Getches (chapter 3) provides clear examples of the limited value of formal legal recognition and protection of the water security of Indians in the United States, if these are not backed up with political and economic power. In their analysis of legal regulation of groundwater use, Prakash and Ballabh (chapter 8) show how the political and economic clout of those with best access to groundwater (and who are most culpable of depleting the resource) make it difficult for the state government to undertake any meaningful legal action. Similarly, the chapter by Bhushan Udas and Zwarteveen (chapter 2), and the one by van Koppen and Jha (chapter 9), suggest that well-intended laws and policies can, by themselves, achieve little in terms of social justice in societies that are characterized by histories of deeply embedded social inequities. What all these chapters suggest is not only that modesty is required as regards the problem-solving capacities of intervening agencies but also that any intervention needs to take into account the "power and politics" of water distribution and control at both local and supralocal levels.

We use the remaining part of this concluding chapter to propose some further points of reflection about translating understanding of legally plural situations to policies, laws, and interventions. In general, the public interest issues that are highest on official water policy agendas are those related to efficiency: using less water more productively is the ultimate objective of most policies and laws. Without disputing the importance of this objective, our reflections here are primarily guided by our desire to increase the visibility and discursive legitimacy of concerns about equity and social justice on water agendas. We start, in the next section, with emphasizing the contested nature of water. Water is politics, and one important implication is that academic reflections cannot objectively or neutrally guide policy making. Powers and ideologies also matter, and require explicit analytical attention.

This insight runs as a red thread through the rest of the chapter, and underlies our plea for embedding any analysis of water rights and laws in a broader analysis of resource access and control. It is not just law and rights in a narrow sense that matter in structuring possibilities of water capture, but also technology, organizations, culture, economy, and ecology (see also Donahue and Johnston 1998). Thus, some form of interdisciplinarity is required. An analysis of law, of the legal and normative dimensions of water, needs to be complemented and interwoven with analyses of other dimensions. We continue the chapter with discussing the idea of recognition as the key to understanding how legally plural conditions become accepted and part of policies and laws. Who recognizes, and what is recognized? We start with distinguishing between cultural recognition, the recognition of social and cultural diversity in ways of managing and controlling water, and material recognition or redistribution, which more directly relates to the question of how water is allocated and distributed. In our opinion, recognition of plural legal conditions should not be limited to the first, the acceptance of cultural plurality and diversity, but should also deal with the second, a fair distribution of water and other resources. One cannot assume the actual manifestation of linkages between the two, as some national water laws do, but these linkages require investigation. We end the chapter arguing that responsibilities of recognition do not lie just with those with formal powers of legislation and policy making. Recognition is shaped by a process of dialogue and social struggle, in which many actors with different perspectives, interests, and powers are involved.

Water Rights and Power

A critical and thorough reading of the chapters in this book suggests that translating academic understandings of legal pluralist situations into new water policies, institutions, or interventions is a deeply political activity. We use this last
chapter to reiterate and emphasize this important point: there is no neutral or
objective wisdom or knowledge about water laws and rights, or about legal pluralism in water. Some (groups of) people are better situated than others to secure access to water, to control water resources, and to determine water
discourses. The groundwater cases of chapters 6 and 8 most vividly illustrate
that having access to and control over water is, in turn, an important source of
power and influence. Conflicts, fights, and struggles over water reflect its importance in people's livelihoods, in generating wealth, and in codetermining influence and status. At any location and in any point in time, existing repertoires of
water rights and laws are expressions of, and dialectically constitute, social and
economic relationships between people. Therefore, proposed changes in such
laws and rights always also entail changes in these socioeconomic relationships.
We distinguish four main ways in which questions of water laws and rights are
political and contested (see also Boelens and Zwarteveen 2003).

Water rights are, first of all, contested because they deal with decisions
about the distribution and allocation of a very important resource. Who has
access to water, and on what grounds? Is access to water (to be) based on identity claims, as in the case of native Indians in the United States or in the new
South African water law? Or is it (to be) determined by markets, as in Chile? Or
on land rights and access to expensive pumping technologies, as is the de facto
situation in Gujarat and Kathmandu? As these latter two examples illustrate,
how water is distributed, and how access to water is negotiated and obtained, is
not just the result of the interplay of norms, rules, and laws from different origins and with different degrees of legitimacy but is also influenced by economic
and political power. Since water is a finite resource, the allocation of a larger
share to one individual or group implies that others will get less. Redefinition of
water laws and rights always causes some groups of people or noneconomic
interests such as the environment to lose, to the advantage of others.

Second, it is not just access to water that is contested. Conflicts and disagreements also and importantly occur over the contents of rules, norms, and
laws that determine water distribution and allocation. What is fair, and what is
just? Should all available water be proportionally distributed over all possible
users and uses, or are there grounds to prioritize or privilege some users and
uses over others? What criteria for allocation to adopt: those based on need,
those based on efficiency, or a combination of the two? Is water a commodity, a
basic need, or a human right (see F. and K. von Benda-Beckmann 2003)? What

are the obligations attached to a water right, and which sanctions apply if these are not fulfilled? How can objectives of fair distribution be matched with objectives of conservation or productive efficiency? Answers to such questions cannot be unilaterally construed as reflecting economic interests and power positions, as some political scientists would have it. Nor can they just be seen to follow technical efficiency imperatives, as seems to be the idea of many engineers. They also reflect history and cultural values and ideas, and embody locally cherished and known ways and traditions of dealing with water.

A third way in which water rights are contested relates to struggles over who decides about questions of water distribution. Who is entitled to participate in water law making, whose opinions and norms are listened to and accommodated? Whose definitions, priorities, and interests prevail? Decision-making spaces are often exclusive in the sense that some people are allowed to enter and participate in them and others are not. Exclusion may be direct, based on caste, gender, or ethnicity. Often it is less direct and, for instance, hidden in membership criteria that are formulated in ways that make some water users qualify as members, but not others. As various chapters in the book show, being allowed to enter the formally designated decision-making domain is, in itself, not enough to guarantee one's ability to voice opinions and influence the nature and direction of decisions. Who is allowed to speak, whose opinions are taken seriously, and who is able to exert influence? These are determined as much by social relations of power and dependency as by cultural norms that associate certain styles of speech and forms of behavior with knowledge and authority and others with ignorance, and that prescribe different forms of behavior to different social groups of people. Language and education are the more easily recognized qualifiers of participation. Gender is one important axis around which attribution of powers of speech and norms of behavior often occurs. The example of Nepali women in chapter 2 is one of many to provide testimony of this. But race and ethnicity also powerfully shape the way people (ought to) behave and how their behavior is interpreted. Often, public decision making itself is an activity that serves to symbolically differentiate the powerful from the powerless. Historically entrenched markers of behavior that have served for generations to delineate and express this differentiation are not easily undone through legal changes. This is one of the many challenges South Africa is now facing with its new water law, and it is also a challenge for Andean countries attempting to recognize and attribute legal powers to peasant and indigenous communities.

A fourth and last important area of contestation lies in the discourses used to articulate water problems and solutions. What are the accepted languages and practices for framing and shaping water laws, and what are the preferred ways of conceptualizing water problems? How do different regimes of representation characterize the relations among actors, the social and technical environment, and water access and control; and how do they devise or promote institutions, techniques, strategic artifacts, and practices to materialize their views and objectives? As the chapter by Boelens and Zwarteveen illustrates, there are important linkages between the way in which problems and solutions are defined and conceptualized, and the political agendas they promote. Specific conceptual languages and discourses stress certain elements and not others, classify water problems in a certain way, infer process and causal mechanisms, and bring with them normative ideas about what should be happening. Each discourse gives an interpretation of the waterscape in accordance with its technical, cultural, and normative contents, and some representations of water realities serve some groups, interests, or purposes, better than others. The neoliberal water discourse, for instance, is well suited for articulating and expressing water problems in terms of market efficiency, competition, and productivity, and reflects a culture and values of individual autonomy and economic rationality. It is a discourse that paints an entirely different picture of water realities than the one used by some indigenous movements, who prefer to use terms that stress reciprocity and the need for collective action. The language, concepts, and discourses used to articulate and define questions of water distribution are also, and importantly, part of the cultural and professional baggage of the ones using them. Any understanding of water problems is based on representations, and always implies a set of assumptions and (implicit) social and political choices that are mediated through sets of discursive practices. Hence, the dynamics of water politics, including water rights and laws, cannot be understood without also scrutinizing the power relationships, discourses, and discursive practices that guide perceptions of problems, and proposed solutions.

Water is, indeed, about power and interests. Therefore, representing water rights situations and describing situations of legal pluralism in relation to water resources cannot be done in a vacuum or from a politically and socially neutral or objective position. All talking, thinking, and acting about water rights and water laws is itself a deeply political activity that presumes a situational and political perspective of the knower (talker, thinker). This point needs emphasizing, since much water thinking and language is characterized by a denial of this situatedness and power (cf. Donahue and Johnston 1998). Rooted in epistemological positivism, and because of a continued belief in enlightenment and modernity, much water knowledge speaks "as if" from nowhere, from a value-free and godlike position. It is constructed from the perspective of someone without interests and background, someone who benevolently represents the universal good—or some version of this, as when speaking on behalf of national interests—and the universal truth. Insights derived from analyses that take into account legal pluralism, when systematically thought through, necessarily imply the active rejection of such a position, and the acknowledgment that all knowledge is constructed, contextualized, concept-laden, and fallible. What one thinks, what one sees, what is thought to matter, and what counts as knowledge or as truth are all deeply dependent on one's position in the battlefield of knowledge and policy making.

The different chapters of this book show how most authors, indeed, identify with and hope to influence water struggles. A diverse cast of authors appears—policy advisors, consultants, development workers, international scientists, activists—each bringing their own experience, culture, and understanding of the social construction of law and water problems. Differences between the chapters cannot just be attributed to differences in the physical and social realities described but also reflect differences between the authors in their ideas about water issues and problems, and about how water should or could best be used.[1] They often also reflect with whom the authors (most) identify and whom they hope to impress, convince, or enroll in their projects. Do authors identify with (a specific group of) users, with managers, or do they instead assume the role of "social auditors" (cf. Moench et al. 1999: xi–xii). Authors, for instance, differ in how much hope they have vested in state powers and authorities for deciding on and implementing water allocation. Is the state to be trusted to protect the water security of those who lack voice and resources to protect their own water interests? Who and what is recognized as power, as politics, as means to defend and protect water interests and guide water allocation? Those authors who are more skeptical about the regulatory powers of the state and who question its willingness to bring about or protect water justice and equity are more likely to be interested in other forms of power and in other sources of law and legitimacy.

One's position may also crucially depend on context. The new water law in South Africa, designed by the ANC government and explicitly aiming at redressing inequities (see chapter 9), is bound to receive a more sympathetic treatment among those interested in a fair water distribution than the recently proposed water laws in the Andes, which are based on the Chilean Water Code. The latter have their roots in neoliberal views of Chicago-trained economists, and primarily aim at raising the productivity of water, while disregarding social priorities (see chapters 5 and 7). Basically, such context-dependent views are political positions about crucial issues like the developmental character of the state, its legitimacy, accountability, and the quality of its institutions.

The differences between the chapters open a window to a perplexing world of contested and plural understandings, and raise important further questions about the linkages between power, perspective, and knowledge. They underscore the awareness that any attempt to think about water rights and laws needs to take into account the context in which knowledge is created, as well as the situatedness of the knowers. Policy formulation and lawmaking are, likewise, interpretative activities in which different—and often contradictory—claims as to what is the problem and its causes and solutions are to be judged, compared, combined, and acted upon. The act of translating academic insights about legal pluralism to policies and interventions, therefore, is crucially based on the exercise of trying to show the politics and political implications of any proposed form of legal regulation. It is also a political activity that stands or falls with the articulation of a clear vision about the desired future situation and that has explicit ideas about the nature and direction of changes to be made in order to get there.

Beyond the Legal

Roberts (1998: 97) has called legal pluralism "a lawyerly way of looking at the social world." Law, he states, "is now . . . graciously embracing others in its discourse, seeking to tell those others what they are" (Roberts 1998: 98). A casual reading of the book may indeed convey the impression that law and rights are the overarching determinants of water distribution and allocation. This is a wrong impression; water realities cannot be understood as a mere struggle between laws or normative systems. There are many other important dimensions of water realities that cannot be simply interpreted as manifestations of law. Technology is one such dimension shaping water control possibilities, as are economics and agroecological conditions. Like legal anthropologists, water analysts from different disciplines often make the mistake of attributing major weight to those determinants of social change they happen to know and understand best. Engineers, for instance, tend to focus on designs and infrastructure, and are preoccupied with technical control. Economists and neo-institutionalist scholars emphasize the financial and economic dimensions of water, whereas thinkers and activists in the empowerment school stress politics and collective action. Different agendas for water development likewise tend to be informed and colored by the disciplinary approach chosen.

We argue that technology and infrastructure, prices and markets, property rights and institutions, and politics and power are interlinked in complex ways. An irrigation system, for example, is a composite water control setup, combining and interrelating physical elements (water sources and flows, the places where water is applied, and the hydraulic infrastructure to catch, conduct, and distribute it), normative elements (rules, rights, and obligations related with access to water and other necessary resources), organizational elements (human organization needed to govern, operate, and maintain the system) and agroproductive elements (soil, crops, technology, capital, labor force) (Beccar et al. 2002). Whatever one's development agenda, analysis and policies should not be narrowly limited to one set of dimensions, but should consider and understand all dimensions simultaneously and in interaction. This cannot be achieved by just "adding on" the different bodies of thought. These all bear clear traces of their disciplinary origins and use incompatible languages, resulting in nonmatching types of information and in documents and projects that are subdivided in separate disciplinary chapters or sections. Instead of the "mix and stir" approach, what is needed is a form of interdisciplinarity that builds on the conceptual and methodological integration of physical-technical and social sciences, including sociolegal perspectives. Such interdisciplinarity refers to the simultaneous analysis of the technical-ecological and social aspects of water realities, as different but interrelated dimensions of it (see Boelens and Hoogendam 2002; Moench 1999; Mollinga 2003; Roth 2003; Uphoff 1986; Vincent 1997).

The different chapters and cases in the book provide a strong ground to further elaborate on possible ways for meaningfully incorporating insights about the plurality and coexistence of legal systems into such an interdisciplinary approach to water. For one, they clearly show that water control systems are complex sociotechnical realities that cannot be reduced to one basic essence or set of essentialities. The chapters by Roth (chapter 4), Prakash and Ballabh (chapter 8), van Koppen and Jha (chapter 9), and Bruns (chapter 10) show that a comprehensive understanding of irrigation and water management requires addressing the physical, normative, organizational, and agroproductive elements simultaneously, and not in isolation or consecutively. Social relations between irrigators are partly shaped by, but are also reflected in, infrastructure, norms, and institutions. Technical designs have "built-in" social norms that shape how the system can (or should) be operated and maintained, the kind and degree of central control that is required, and the mechanisms for accessing and distributing water. In using the infrastructure, as chapter 4 most clearly illustrates, users often also change it so as to better match it to their needs, customs, and norms. This is one way in which "the legal" shapes and influences the design of technology.

A second, and related, important building block of a strong interdisciplinary approach to water is the insight that what a water right is cannot be ontologically separated from the context in which it is expressed or operationalized. The book's chapters illustrate that there exists a variety of (often hybrid) definitions of water rights and of uses of the concept of water rights. This clearly suggests that the meaning and functions of such rights cannot be simply assumed. The precise contents of a right (for example, consumptive use rights, nonconsumptive access rights, usufruct and income-earning rights, control and decision-making rights), the duties linked to these authorizations, the conditions and mechanisms for acquiring rights, the operational rules attached to rights, the legitimacy and enforcement capacity pertaining to certain rights— all these only come to the fore and receive their meaning in the actual context in which they apply. The sociolegal can thus not be easily isolated as one distinct domain or area of analysis and intervention, but needs to be seen as an element of several dimensions that mutually constitute each other. Water distribution practices and norms are expressed simultaneously in infrastructure and technology choices, in written or verbal agreements between involved parties, and in organizational arrangements devised for operating the infrastructure, distributing water, and mobilizing resources for maintenance.

These three—technology, norms, and organizations—are an integral part of social, political, and cultural environments; they are embedded in social relations of power and form part of cultural expressions of identity and community, hierarchy, and authority (Boelens and Zwarteveen 2003; Roth 2003). This embeddedness of rights sheds light on, for instance, the distribution of decision-making powers in water control, and shows how the rules, rights, and duties attached to water are part of larger cultural frameworks of meaning, symbols, and values. Water rights, then, do not just refer to the relationship between users and the resource but primarily express social relationships between users, as well as between users and other interest groups.

Recognition and Redistribution

How can recognition of plural legal and normative systems lead to better policies, laws, designs, management institutions, and irrigation projects? Policy recommendations all too often are limited to a plea for greater attention to, and more recognition of, plural legal conditions. Whether recognition indeed means improvement, however, is a question the answer to which depends on understanding social and ecological change and their dynamic interactions. It requires an analysis of the role of different groups within society, of the state, and of why individuals and groups behave the way they do. Recognition implies that there is a recognizing party, a party being recognized, and a relation between the two parties that is hierarchical. Understanding this hierarchy, and assessing its legitimacy from the perspective of various positions and actors, is crucial in assessing and devising attempts at recognition of different legal systems. Recognition of legally plural conditions implies the recognition of difference and diversity. It would entail recognition (and acceptance) of "the other" by state law, or by those representing some kind of public interest.

Two broad questions are at stake in thinking about and acting on the existence of legally plural conditions in water.[2] The first is a question of recognition, or of acknowledging and respecting various forms of dealing with, organizing around, and talking about water. This has to do with diversity, identity, and culture, and relates primarily to forms of injustice that deny or discriminate against particular socially and culturally embedded rules and practices of water management and control. Remedies to such injustice could involve the inclusion or acceptance of hitherto disregarded or forbidden ways to treat, distribute, or talk about water, or it could involve the transformation of societal patterns of representation, interpretation, and communication in ways that recognize and accept cultural diversity of modes of water control. Granting autonomy to groups of people of water-user communities to devise and apply their own water rules addresses a form of cultural recognition, as does the acceptance and recognition of women as legitimate water actors.

The second question deals with socioeconomic injustice and involves the reallocation of water, or of water-related powers and rights. It may be concerned with redirecting public water investments, or with subjecting such investments to more democratic forms of decision making. Or it may deal with reallocating available water resources. Such remedies to socioeconomic injustice can be grouped under the generic term "redistribution." Socioeconomic injustice is rooted in the political and economic structure of society. Cultural recognition and redistribution are related and influence each other in complex ways. Both are intimately tied up with questions of power and hegemony. The chapter about groundwater in Gujarat by Bhallabh and Prakash most clearly shows these interconnections, in this case between caste and access to water.

Most current water policies deal, at least to some extent, with the first question, but fundamentally neglect the second. There is a growing willingness to accept difference and diversity, and to acknowledge that different people have different ways to deal with, use, and manage water. Water distribution policies and laws, as several chapters in the book show, are often and increasingly based on identity claims, and struggles for water redistribution are often treated as struggles for cultural recognition. In the chapter by Getches, specific water rights are connected to the identity of native Americans. In the chapter by Bhushan Udas and Zwarteveen, gender is a recognized claim to decision-making rights to irrigation water. In South Africa, water allocation is guided by both ethnicity (or color) and gender-based considerations. These examples illustrate that the social scientific idiom of legal pluralism can easily be married to the new political imagery characteristic of the "postsocialist" age, an imagery that favors notions of identity, difference, and cultural domination over those of socioeconomic approaches, such as interest, exploitation, and redistribution.

Basing claims for water on identity means that socioeconomic justice (a fair distribution of water and water-related resources) is based on cultural criteria, on identity claims. This can be seen as an acknowledgment of the fact that socioeconomic injustice and cultural injustice are usually interrelated in such a way as to reinforce each other dialectically. Material economic institutions often have a constitutive, irreducibly cultural dimension: signification and norms pervade them. Conversely, even the most discursive cultural practices have a constitutive, irreducibly economic dimension: they are underpinned by material conditions. As the chapters on the Andes most clearly show, cultural norms that are unfairly biased against the indigenes are institutionalized in the state and the economy, and serve to justify their lesser access to water. Meanwhile,

their economic disadvantage impedes equal participation in the making of water allocation rules and laws, and in actual water distribution decisions. The
result is a downward spiral of economic and cultural subordination.

Yet, despite the entanglement between socioeconomic and cultural justice,
we argue here that there is merit in distinguishing them. A first important reason is that cultural inequalities cannot be simply mapped onto socioeconomic
inequalities. The linkages between the two are not one-to-one, but much more
complex and multistranded. Second, the remedies to address the two kinds of
injustices are different, and sometimes even conflicting. Claims for recognition
often take the form of calling attention to, if not performatively creating, the
putative specificity of some group and then of affirming its value. Chapter 7
clearly illustrates the dangers when this struggle for self-determination and self-
regulation gets incorporated by state agencies and in national laws. In Peru and
Ecuador, the essentialized constructions of indigenous identity that have become codified in special laws do not match with actually existing, dynamic,
identities. In contrast, redistribution claims often call for abolishing economic
arrangements that underpin group specificity. Instead of calling for the right to
be different, these call for the right to be equal.

Distinguishing the two allows asking questions about the relation between
claims for recognition and claims for redistribution, and about the interfer-
ences that arise when both kinds of claims are made simultaneously. It also
draws attention to the politics involved in claiming rights for specific groups, or
in views of redressing historical injustices and inequities. Translating insights
about legal pluralism into policies and laws requires a critical view of recognition, one that acknowledges that it has a cultural as well as a material element.
Justice requires both redistribution and recognition, and the examination of
the relation between the two is what characterizes good scholarship and policy
making. This requires conceptualizing cultural recognition and social equality
in forms that support rather than undermine one another. And it requires clarifying the political dilemmas that arise when trying to combat both injustices
simultaneously. Under what circumstances can cultural recognition help support redistribution? And when is it more likely to undermine it? Which of the
many varieties of identity politics are in synergy with struggles for social equality? And which tend to interfere with the latter?

Negotiated Change and Institutional Pluralism

Different chapters in the book show how rules and rights established by legislators and intervening agents are mediated by different users' groups with their
own ideologies, power bases, and interests (see also Long and Van der Ploeg
1989; F. von Benda-Beckmann et al. 1998). Users plan their own water-develop-
ment strategies, and may resist and at the same time try to take over planned

intervention processes (cf. Gelles 2000; Jackson 1998; van der Ploeg and Long 1994). Such insights serve to moderate expectations about what rights and rules, by themselves, can achieve. Normative instruments are turned into societal practice through the forces and relationships of society. Rules are disputed and modified in formal and informal negotiation forums (Chambliss and Zatz 1993; S. F. Moore 1973, 1978).

In our view, however, modesty about what can be achieved through policy and legal changes is not the same as defeatism or a laissez-faire attitude. Laws and policies can and do make a difference, and are important in codetermining control over water and respective positions of power, either strengthening or challenging the status quo. Though support processes cannot plan irrigation and water management development or the new constellation of powers in a mechanistic and linear sense, they can support local "political action for water control." Identification of interest groups, analysis of problems, needs, and potential assets of least favored groups, interactive action research, facilitation of networks and horizontal linkages (alliance-building capacity), facilitation of negotiation forums accessible to the least powerful groups, preparing them (demand- and proposal-making capacity), and institutional backing in these platforms—all are important elements in such strategies of empowerment.

In understanding and supporting such struggles for water control, it is important to realize that making both law and policy does not simply involve acts by higher-level decision makers, the "patriarchal rationalists who synthesize available information and make informed, objective decisions within the constraints imposed by an external unruly world" (Moench et al. 1999: x). Water rights are dynamic and locally specific. Day-to-day water use and management practices are the result of ongoing processes of negotiation and bargaining between different actors, often with different powers and rights. The definition and enforcement of water rights, by implication, are not the exclusive domain of rational engineers and planners who have the right credentials in terms of expertise and authority for making "technical" choices. On the contrary, they are part of wider political, economic, and social processes in which different actors are involved. In Nepal, as Bhushan Udas and Zwarteveen have shown, water policies come about in meetings between donor agencies and government staff when they discuss the conditionalities of projects and loans. In Gujarat, well-to-do and high-caste farmer groups form an effective lobby against state government plans to better regulate and control groundwater extraction (chapter 8). In South Africa's former Homelands, traditional authorities and chiefs continue to exercise control on water allocation practices, even though formal authorities now rest with municipalities (chapter 9). The different chapters also highlight the wide variety of actors whose individual or collective decisions influence water use patterns.

Rather than looking at policies as texts and regulations that originate from the expert center to be implemented by the water-using population, it is more useful to look at the formulation and implementation of water laws and policies as complex processes of formal and less formal, legal and illegal, open and hidden interaction and negotiation between interest groups with different agendas and different abilities and means to voice their concerns (Long and van der Ploeg 1989; Thomas and Grindle 1990). Reforms, including those that deal with the recognition of a plurality of legal orders, cannot be understood or dealt with when assuming a hierarchic, "rationalist" planning model and institutional monism. It requires, instead, acknowledging and promoting the view of legal and institutional changes as more or less open, nonlinear, and ongoing processes of social dialogue, debate, negotiation, and struggle. Doing this raises its own questions and dilemmas concerning representation, voice, and other differences of power and culture that render mutual understanding and dialogue difficult. A process-focused and pluralist institutional approach brings with it a shift from understanding water realities only in the terms used by the experts and measured against their normative planning ideals to one that is expressed in the terms and frames of reference of those who experience them. It implies, in other words, the treatment and analysis of all people (and not just experts or those with formal powers) as knowledgeable and capable actors, allowing for serious consideration of their actions, skills, concerns, and perspectives.

An important conclusion of this chapter, as well as of the entire book, is that it is not possible to list precisely the ingredients of processes of local empowerment, rule making, and rights building in a universalized and decontextualized form. Changes in water control always entail dynamic relationships that form, reproduce, and transform themselves through specific activities in people's daily lives in specific contexts. Strategies of empowerment, resistance, and users' appropriation of water control that challenge existing water control positions and definitions are only successful when initiated and headed by those who demand more control—groups of water users. Through struggle and well-organized representation at negotiating platforms, they can define and negotiate their water rules and obtain, defend, and enforce their water rights, and influence the formulation of the rules of play. In terms of recognition, this calls for building dynamic strategies, jointly devised with users, including those with the least negotiation power, the ones who are "absent," and those who are made invisible by vested interest groups, new policy discourses, or by current water law and policies practices.

NOTES

I. See also Giyawali (2001), who argues that science is a three-legged stool of government, market, and egalitarian interests. Analysts who are members of hierarchical executive organizations will generally define problems and solutions in ways that reflect the executive capabilities and interests of their organization. Individualists and organizations functioning in a market context will, similarly, tend to define issues and potential solutions in ways that reflect their capabilities and interests. Market organizations do not, generally produce products that cannot be sold. Analysts working for market organizations will, as a result, generally be amenable to produce specific marketable products. Finally, egalitarian organizations also tend to produce analyses that reflect their constituents' interests and perspectives, whether they focus on specific environmental issues or on the needs of minorities or other communities.

2. This distinction is based on Fraser (1997; 2000).

REFERENCES

Adhikari, A. 2001. Dhunge dhara ko samrakchan, upatyakako khanepani aapurtiko upaya, Nepal, Rashtriya Pakshik. *Grand Design ko Goti* I (19): 10–12. Kathmandu: Kantipur Publications.

Adhikari, M., and R. Pradhan. 2000. Water rights, law and authority: Changing water rights in the Bhamke Khola Basin. In *Water, land and law: Changing rights to land and water in Nepal*, ed. R. Pradhan, F. von Benda-Beckmann, and K. von Benda-Beckmann, 71–100. Kathmandu: FREEDEAL; Wageningen: Wageningen University; Rotterdam: Erasmus University Rotterdam.

Agrawal, A., 1995. Dismantling the divide between indigenous and scientific knowledge. In *Development and Change* 26: 413–439.

Agrawal, A., and C. C. Gibson. 1999. Enchantment and disenchantment: The role of community in natural resource conservation. *World Development* 27 (4): 629–649.

———. *Communities and the environment: Ethnicity, gender, and the state in community-based conservation.* New Brunswick: Rutgers University Press.

Ahmad, A. 2000. An institutional analysis of changes in land use pattern and water scarcity in Dak Lak Province, Vietnam. Paper presented at the Nordic Conference on Institutions, Livelihoods and the Environment: Change and Response in Mainland Southeast Asia. Copenhagen.

Albó, X. 2002. *Iguales aunque diferentes.* La Paz: Centro 'de Investigación y Promoción del Campesinado.

Alchian, A., and H. Demsetz. 1972. Production, information costs, and economic organization. *American Economic Review* 62 (S): 777–795.

Andersen, L. S. 2001. Denmark—Vietnam water sector program support. In *Wastewater reuse in agriculture in Vietnam: Water management, environment and human health aspects.* Proceedings of a workshop held in Hanoi, Vietnam, 14 March 2001. Ed. L. Raschid-Sally, W. v. d. Hoek, and M. Ranawaka. IWMI Working Paper 30. Colombo: International Water Management Institute.

Anderson, B. 1983. *Imagined communities: Reflections on the origin and spread of nationalism.* London: Verso.

Apollin, F. 2002. Re-negotiation of water rights in the ancient irrigation system of Urcuquí, Ecuador. In *Water rights and empowerment,* ed. R. Boelens and P. Hoogendam, 202–216. Assen, The Netherlands: Van Gorcum.

Apollin, F., P. Núñez, and T. Ruf. 1998. The historical development of equity in irrigation, Urcuquí, Ecuador. In *Searching for equity,* ed. R. Boelens and G. Dávila, 402–422. Assen, The Netherlands: Van Gorcum.

Assies, W. 2000. David fights Goliath in Cochabamba: Water rights, neoliberalism and the renovation of social protest in Bolivia. Draft. Zamora, Michoacán: Colegio de Michoacán, Rural Studies Institute.

Assies, W., G. van der Haar, and A. Hoekema, eds. 1998. *The challenge of diversity: Indigenous peoples and reform of the state in Latin America*. Amsterdam: Thela Thesis Publishers.

Avianto, T. W. 1996. Potret alokasi air untuk industri, pertanian dan domestik: Studi kasus di daerah irigasi Ciwalengke dan Sungai Cisangkuy. Bandung, Indonesia: Padjadjaran University Center for Development Dynamics.

Aylwin, J. 1997. Derecho consuetudinario indígena en el derecho internacional, comparado y en la legislación Chilena. In *Actas del segundo congreso Chileno de antropología*, Volume I, 189–197. Valdivia: Programa de Derechos Indígenas.

Barnett, T. 1981. Evaluating the Gezira scheme: Black box or Pandora's box? In *Rural development in tropical Africa*, ed. J. Heyer, P. Roberts, and G. Williams, 306–324. New York: St. Martin's.

Barth, F. 1995. *Balinese worlds*. Chicago: University of Chicago Press.

Baud, M., K. Konings, G. Oostindie, A. Ouweneel, and P. Silva. 1996. *Etnicidad como estrategia en América Latina y el Caribe*. Quito: Abya Yala.

Bauer, C. J. 1997. Bringing water markets down to earth: The political economy of water rights in Chile, 1976–95. *World Development* 25 (5): 639–656.

———. 1998. Slippery property rights: Multiple water uses and the neoliberal model in Chile, 1981–1995. *Natural Resources Journal* 38: 110–155.

Beccar, L., R. Boelens, and P. Hoogendam. 2002. Water rights and collective action in community irrigation. In *Water Rights and empowerment*, ed. R. Boelens and P. Hoogendam, 1–21. Assen, The Netherlands: Van Gorcum.

Beitz, C. R. 1991. Sovereignty and morality in international affairs. In *Political Theory Today*, ed. D. Held, 236–254. Oxford: Polity Press.

Benda-Beckmann, F. von. 1993. Scapegoat and magic charm: Law in development theory and practice. In *An anthropological critique of development*, ed. M. Hobart, 116–133. London: Routledge.

———. 1997. Citizens, strangers and indigenous peoples: Conceptual politics and legal pluralism. In *Law and Anthropology*, ed. F. von Benda-Beckmann, K. von Benda-Beckmann, and A. Hoekema, 1–42. The Hague: Martinus Nijhof.

———. 2001. Between free riders and free raiders: Property rights and soil degradation in context. In *Economic policy and sustainable land use: Recent advances in quantitative analysis for developing countries*, ed. N. Heerink, H. van Keulen, and M. Kuiper, 193–216. Heidelberg: Physica Verlag / Axel Springer Verlag.

———. 2002. Who is afraid of legal pluralism? *Journal of Legal Pluralism* 47: 1–46.

Benda-Beckmann, F. von, and K. von Benda-Beckman. 1999. A functional analysis of property rights with special reference to Indonesia. In *Property rights and economic development: Land and natural resources in Southeast Asia and Oceania*, ed. T. van Meijl and F. von Benda-Beckmann, 15–56. London: Kegan Paul International.

———. 2000. Gender and the multiple contingencies of water rights in Nepal. In *Water, land and law: Changing rights to land and water in Nepal*, ed. R. Pradhan, F. von Benda-Beckmann, and K. von Benda-Beckmann, 17–38. Kathmandu: FREEDEAL; Wageningen: Wageningen University; Rotterdam: Erasmus University Rotterdam.

———. 2001. Recognizing water rights. In *Overcoming water scarcity and quality constraints: 2020*, ed. R. S. Meinzen-Dick and M. Rosegrant. Focus 9, October 2001. Washington, D.C.: International Food Policy Research Institute, at http://www.ifpri.org/2020/focus/focus09.htm.

———. 2003. Water, human rights and legal pluralism. *Water Nepal* 9/10 (1/2): 63–76.

Benda-Beckmann, F. von, K. von Benda-Beckmann, and H.L.J. Spiertz. 1996. Water rights and policy. In *The role of law in natural resource management*, ed. H.L.J. Spiertz and M. G. Wiber, 77–99. The Hague: VUGA.

———. 1997. Local law and customary practices in the study of water rights. In *Water rights, conflict and policy*, ed. R. Pradhan, F. von Benda-Beckmann, K. von Benda-Beckmann, H.L.J. Spiertz, S. S. Khadka, and K. Azharul Haq, 221–242. Colombo: International Irrigation Management Institute.

———. 1998. Equity and legal pluralism: Taking customary law into account in natural resource policies. In *Searching for equity*, ed. R. Boelens and G. Dávila, 57–69. Assen, The Netherlands: Van Gorcum.

Benda-Beckmann, F. von, and M. van der Velde, ed. 1992. *Law as a resource in agrarian struggles*. Wageningen Sociologische Studies 33. Wageningen, The Netherlands: PUDOC.

Benda-Beckmann, K. von. 1981. Forum shopping and shopping forums: Dispute processing in a Minangkabau village. *Journal of Legal Pluralism* 19: 117–159.

———. 1984. *The broken staircase to consensus: Village justice and state courts in Minangkabau*. Dordrecht, The Netherlands: Foris.

———. 1985. The social significance of Minangkabau State court decisions. *Journal of Legal Pluralism* 23: 1–68.

Benda-Beckmann, K. von, M. de Bruijn, H. van Dijk, G. Hesseling, B. van Koppen, and L. Res. 1997. *Rights of women to the natural resources land and water*. Women and Development Working Paper 2. The Hague: Netherlands Development Assistance/Ministry of Foreign Affairs.

Bhatia, B. 1992. *Lush fields and parched throats: Political economy of groundwater in Gujarat.* Working Paper. Helsinki: World Institute for Development Economics Research.

Bhattachan, K. B. 2001. Sociological perspectives on gender issues in changing Nepalese society. In *Gender and Democracy in Nepal*, ed. L. K. Manandhar and K. B. Bhattachan, 76–97. Kathmanda: Women Studies Program, Tribhuvan University, and Germany: Friedrich Ebert-Stiftung.

Bijker, W. E., and J. Law, eds. 1992. *Shaping technology / building society: Studies in sociotechnical change*. Cambridge: MIT Press.

Birkelbach, A. W. 1973. The subak association. *Indonesia* 16: 153–169.

Blatter, J., and H. Ingram. 2001. *Reflections on water: New approaches to transboundary conflicts and cooperation*. Cambridge: MIT Press.

Boelens, R. 1998. Collective management and social construction of peasant irrigation systems: A conceptual introduction. In *Searching for equity. Conceptions of justice and equity in peasant irrigation*, ed. R. Boelens and G. Dávila, 81–99. Assen, The Netherlands: Van Gorcum.

———. 2003. Local rights and legal recognition: The struggle for indigenous water rights and the cultural politics of participation. Paper presented at the Third World Water Forum, 16–23 March 2003, Kyoto.

Boelens, R., and G. Dávila, eds. 1998. *Searching for equity: Conceptions of justice and equity in peasant irrigation*. Assen, The Netherlands: Van Gorcum.

Boelens, R., and B. Doornbos. 2001. The battlefield of water rights: Rule making amidst conflicting normative frameworks in the Ecuadorian highlands. *Human Organization* 60 (4): 343–355.

Boelens, R., A. Dourojeanni, A. Durán, and P. Hoogendam. 2002. Water rights and watersheds.: Managing multiple water uses and strengthening stakeholder platforms. In *Water rights and empowerment,* ed. R. Boelens and P. Hoogendam, 110–143. Assen: Van Gorcum.

Boelens, R., and P. Hoogendam, eds. 2002. *Water rights and empowerment.* Assen, The Netherlands: Van Gorcum.

Boelens, R., D. Roth, and M. Zwarteveen. 2002. Legal complexity and irrigation water control: Analysis, recognition and beyond. Paper for the XIIIth International Congress on Folk Law and Legal Pluralism, 7–10 April 2002, Chiang Mai, Thailand.

Boelens, R., and M. Zwarteveen. 2002. Gender dimensions of water control in Andean irrigation. In *Water Rights and Empowerment,* ed. R. Boelens and P. Hoogendam, 75–109. Assen, The Netherlands: Van Gorcum.

———. 2003. Water, gender and "Andeanity": Conflict or harmony? Gender dimensions of water rights in diverging regimes of representation. In *Imaging the Andes,* ed. T. Salman and A. Zoomers. Amsterdam: Aksant / CEDLA.

Bolin, I. 1990. Upsetting the power balance: Cooperation, competition and conflict along and Andean irrigation system. *Human Organization* 49 (2): 140–148.

Booth, A. 1977a. Irrigation in Indonesia, part I. *Bulletin of Indonesian Economic Studies* 13 (2): 33–74.

———. 1977b. Irrigation in Indonesia, part II. *Bulletin of Indonesian Economic Studies* 13 (3): 45–77.

Bourdieu, P. 1977. *Outline of a theory of practice.* Cambridge: Cambridge University Press.

———. 1998. *Acts of resistance against the tyranny of the market.* New York: New Press.

Brajer, V., A. L. Church, R. Cummings, and P. Farah. 1989. The strengths and weaknesses of water markets as they affect water scarcity and sovereignty interests of the West. *Natural Resource Journal* 29: 490–509.

Brans, E.H.P., E. J. de Haan, and A. Nollkaemper. 1997. *The scarcity of water: Emerging legal and policy responses.* London: Kluwer.

Brehm, M. R., and J. Quiroz. 1995. *The market for water rights in Chile.* Technical Paper 285. Washington, D.C.: World Bank.

Brewer, J. D., R. Sakthivadivel, and K. V. Raju. 1997. *Water distribution rules and water distribution performance: A case study in the Tambraparani irrigation system.* Research Report no. 12. Colombo: International Irrigation Management Institute.

Briscoe, J. 1996. Water as an economic good: The idea and what it means in practice. In *Transactions of the 16th Congress on Irrigation and Drainage–Volume 1E.* New Delhi: International Commission on Irrigation and Drainage.

Bromley, D. W. 1992. *Making the commons work: Theory, practice and policy.* San Francisco: Institute of Contemporary Studies.

Bruns, B. 1992. Just enough organization: Water users associations and episodic mobilization. *Visi: Irigasi Indonesia* 6: 33–41.

———. 2004. From voice to empowerment: Rerouting irrigation reform in Indonesia. In *The politics of irrigation reform: Contested policy formulation and implementation in Asia, Africa and Latin America,* ed. P. P. Mollinga and A. Bolding, 145–165. Aldershot, England: Ashgate.

Bruns, B., and R. Meinzen-Dick. 1997. Renegotiating water rights: Directions for improving public participation in South and Southeast Asia. Paper presented at the 1997 conference of the International Association for Public Participation, 7–10 September 1997, Toronto.

———, eds. 2000. *Negotiating water rights.* London: Intermediate Technology Publications.

———. 2001. Water rights and legal pluralism: Four contexts for negotiation. *Natural Resources Forum* 25 (1): 1–10.

Burchi, S., and I. Betlen. 2001. *Irrigation management transfer: Legal issues, introductory note for theme 3, legal issues.* International email conference irrigation management transfer, at http://www.fao.org./landandwater/aglw/waterinstitutions/thenote3.htm.

Burton, L. 1991. *American Indian water rights and the limits of law.* Lawrence: University Press of Kansas.

Bustamante, R. 2002. *Legislación del agua en Bolivia.* Cochabamba: WALIR–CEPAL and Wageningen University.

Castillo, L. del. 1994. Lo bueno, lo malo y lo feo de la legislación de aguas. *Debate Agrario* 18: 1–20.

———. 2001. *El largo camino hacia una ley de aguas.* http://www.agualtiplano.net.

Castro, M. 2002. Local norms and competition for water in Aymara and Atacama communities, northern Chile. In *Water rights and empowerment,* ed. R. Boelens and P. Hoogendam, 187–201. Assen: Van Gorcum.

CBS (Centre Bureau of Statistics). 1999. *Women in Nepal: Some statistical facts.* Kathmandu: National Planning Commission, Centre Bureau of Statistics, His Majesty's Government of Nepal.

CEPAL. 1998. *Ordenamiento político-institucional para la gestión del agua.* Santiago de Chile: CEPAL.

Chakravarti, A. 2001. *Social power and everyday class relations: Agrarian transformation in north Bihar.* New Delhi: Sage.

Chambers, R. 1980. Basic concepts in the organization of irrigation. In *Irrigation and agricultural development in Asia: Perspectives from the social sciences,* ed. E. W. Coward Jr., 28–50. Ithaca: Cornell University Press.

———. 1988. *Managing canal irrigation: Practical analysis from South Asia.* Cambridge: Cambridge University Press.

———. 1994. Irrigation against rural poverty. In *Socio-economic dimensions and irrigation,* ed. R. K. Gurjar, 50–83. Jaipur: Printwell.

Chambers, R., N. C. Saxena, and T. Shah. 1989. *To the hands of the poor: Water and trees.* New Delhi: Oxford and IBH Publishing.

Chambliss, W. J., and M. S. Zatz, eds. 1993. *Making law: The state, the law and structural contradictions.* Bloomington: Indiana University Press.

Cleaver, F. 2000. Moral ecological rationality, institutions and the management of common property resources. *Development and Change* 31 (2): 361–383.

Coase, R. H. 1990. *The firm, the market and the law.* Chicago: University of Chicago Press.

Colby, B. G. 2000. Cap-and-trade policy challenges: A tale of three markets. *Land Economics* 76 (4): 638–658.

Collins, R. B. 1985. The future discourse of the Winters doctrine. *University Colorado Law Review* 56: 481.

Conaghan, C. M., J. M. Malloy, and L. A. Abugattas. 1990. Business and the "boys": the politics of neoliberalism in the Central Andes. *Latin American Research Review* 25 (2): 3–30.

CONAIE (Confederation of Indigenous Nationalities of Ecuador). 1996. *Propuesta ley de aguas.* Quito: CONAIE.

Cooter, R. D. 1997. The rule of state law and the rule-of-law state: Economic analysis of the legal foundations of development. In *Annual World Bank conference on development economics,* 191–237. Washington, D.C.: World Bank.

Correas, O. 1994. La teoría general del derecho y el derecho alternativo: "El otro derecho." *ILSA Journal* (Mexico City) 15: 61–74.

Cosgrove, W. J., and F. R. Rijsberman. 2000. *World water vision: Making water everybody's business*. London: Earthscan.

Cotterrell, R. 1992. *The sociology of law: An introduction*. London: Butterworths.

Cousins, B. 2000. Introduction: Does land and agrarian reform have a future and, if so, who will benefit? In *At the crossroads: Land and agrarian reform in South Africa into the 21st century*, ed. Ben Cousins. Proceedings of a conference held at Alpha Training Center, Broederstroom, Pretoria, 26–28 July 1999. Cape Town: Program for Land and Agrarian Studies, School of Government, University of the Western Cape and the National Land Committee.

Coward Jr., E. W., ed. 1980. *Irrigation and agricultural development in Asia: Perspectives from the social sciences*. Ithaca: Cornell University Press.

———. 1986. State and locality in Asian irrigation development: The property factor. In *Irrigation management in developing countries: currrent issues and approaches*, ed. K. C. Nobe and R. K. Sampath, 491–508. Boulder: Westview.

Coward Jr., E. W., and G. Levine, 1989. *Equity considerations in the modernization of irrigation systems*. ODI / IIMI irrigation management network paper 89/2b, December 1989. London/Colombo: ODI / IIMI.

CRID (Central Regional Irrigation Directorate), Government of Nepal. 2001. *An introduction and progress report year 2000–2001*. Kathmandu: Ministry of Water Resources of His Majesty's Government of Nepal, Department of Irrigation.

Crook, R. C. 2001. Introduction: Law and development. *IDS Bulletin* 32 (1): 1–7.

Crook, R. C. and P. P. Houtzager. 2001. Making law matter: Rules, rights and security in the lives of the poor. *IDS Bulletin* 32 (1).

Das, V. 1982. *Structure and cognition: Aspects of Hindu caste and ritual*. Bombay: Oxford University Press.

de Lange, M. 1998. Irrigation policy draft 4.1. Unpublished discussion document.

———. 2004. Water policy and law review process in South Africa with a focus on the agricultural sector. In *The politics of irrigation reform: Contested policy formulation and implementation in Asia, Africa and Latin America*, ed. P. P. Mollinga and A. Bolding, 11–56. Aldershot, England: Ashgate.

DWAF (Department of Water Affairs and Forestry). 1986. *Management of water resources of the Republic of South Africa*. Pretoria: Department of Water Affairs and Forestry.

———. 2003. Proposal for the establishment of a catchment management agency for the Olifants Water Management Area. Nelspruit, South Africa: DWAF Mpumalanga.

Diemer, G. 1990. *Irrigatie in Afrika: Boeren en ingenieurs, techniek en kultuur*. Amsterdam: Thesis Publishers.

Diemer, G., and F. Huibers, ed. 1996. *Crops, people and irrigation: Water allocation practices of farmers and engineers*. London: Intermediate Technology Publications.

Diemer, G., and J. Slabbers, ed. 1992. *Irrigators and engineers: Essays in honour of Lucas Horst*. Amsterdam: Thesis Publishers.

DIO (District Irrigation Office), Government of Nepal. 1997. *Tukucha Nala irrigation project: Feasibility assessment report*. Second irrigation sector project. Kathmandu: MOWR, Central Regional Irrigation Directorate, Department of Irrigation.

Dixit, A. 1997. Inter-sectoral water allocation: A case study in upper Bagmati Basin. In *Water rights, conflict and policy*, ed. R. Pradhan, F. von Benda-Beckmann, K. von Benda-Beckmann, H.L.J. Spiertz, S. S. Khadka, and K. Azharul Haq, 195–220. Colombo: International Irrigation Management Institute.

———. 2000. Water as an agent of social and economic change in Nepal. In *Water for food and rural development: Approaches and initiatives in South Asia*, ed. P. P. Mollinga, 197–227. New Delhi: Sage.

DOI (Department of Irrigation), Kingdom of Nepal. 2001. Introduction of Department of Irrigation. Kathmandu: MOWR / DOI.

Donahue, J. M., and B. R. Johnston. 1998. *Water, culture and power*. Washington, D.C.: Island Press.

Dourojeanni, A., and A. Jouravlev. 1999. *El código de aguas en Chile: Entre la ideología y la realidad*. Serie recursos naturales e infraestructura (3). Santiago de Chile: CEPAL.

Dubash, N. K. 2002. *Tubewell capitalism: Groundwater development and agrarian change in Gujarat*. New Delhi: Oxford University Press.

Dumont, Louis. 1998 (1970). *Homo hierarchicus: The caste system and its implications*. New Delhi: Oxford University Press.

Easter, K. W., M. W. Rosegrant, and A. Dinar, eds. 1998. *Markets for water: Potential and performance*. Boston: Kluwer Academic Publishers.

Eggertsson, T. 1990. *Economic behavior and institutions*. Cambridge: Cambridge University Press.

Ellickson, R. C. 1991. *Order without law: How neighbors settle disputes*. Cambridge: Harvard University Press.

Esman, M. J., and N. Uphoff. 1984. *Local organizations, intermediaries in rural development*. Ithaca: Cornell University Press.

Espeland, W. N. 1998. *The struggle for water: Politics, rationality, and identity in the American southwest*. Chicago: University of Chicago Press.

Falvo, D. J. 2000. On modeling Balinese water temple networks as complex adaptive systems. *Human Ecology* 28 (4): 641–649.

FAO (Food and Agricultural Organization), United Nations. 1982. *Farmers' participation and organization for irrigation water management*. International Support Programme for Farm Water Management, Land and Water Development Division. Rome: FAO.

———. 1996. *Transfer of irrigation management services: Guidelines*. FAO Irrigation and Drainage Papers 58. Rome: FAO.

Ferguson, J. 1990. *The anti-politics machine: Development, depoliticization, and bureaucratic power in Lesotho*. Cambridge: Cambridge University Press.

Flores Galindo, A. 1988. *Buscando un Inca: Identidad y utopia en los Andes*. Lima: Editorial Horizonte.

Foucault, M. 1995 (1977). *Discipline and punish: The birth of the prison*. New York: Vintage Books.

Fraser, N. 1997. From redistribution to recognition? Dilemmas of justice in a "postsocialist" age. In *Justice interruptus: Critical reflections on the "postsocialist" condition*, 11–39. New York: Routledge.

———. 2000. Rethinking recognition. *New Left Review* 3: 107–120.

Friedmann, J. 1992. *Empowerment: The politics of alternative development*. Cambridge: Blackwell.

Galeano, E. 1986. *Memoria del fuego I, II, III*. Madrid: Siglo Veintiuno Editores.

Geertz, C. 1972. The wet and the dry: Traditional irrigation in Bali and Morocco. *Human Ecology* 1 (1): 23–29.

———. 1980. Organization of the Balinese subak. In *Irrigation and agricultural development in Asia: Perspectives from the social sciences*, ed. E. W. Coward Jr., 70–90. Ithaca: Cornell University Press.

Geijer, J.C.M.A., ed. 1995. *Irrigation management transfer in Asia*. Papers from the expert consultation on irrigation management transfer in Asia. Bangkok: Food and Agriculture Organization of the United Nations / International Irrigation Management Institute.

Gelles, P. H. 1994. Channels of power, fields of contention: The politics of irrigation and land recovery in an Andean peasant community. In *Irrigation at high altitudes: The social organization of water control systems in the Andes*, ed. W. Mitchell and D. Guillet, 233–273. Washington, D.C.: Society for Latin American Anthropology and American Anthropological Association.

———. 1998. Competing cultural logics: State and "indigenous" models in conflict. In *Searching for Equity*, ed. R. Boelens and G. Dávila, 256–267. Assen, The Netherlands: Van Gorcum.

———. 2000. *Water and power in highland Peru: The cultural politics of irrigation and development*. New Brunswick: Rutgers University Press.

Gelles, P. H., and R. Boelens. 2003. Water, community and identity: The politics of cultural and agricultural production in the Andes. In *Imaging the Andes: Shifting margins of a marginal world*, ed. T. Salman and A. Zoomers, 123–144. Amsterdam: Aksant, CEDLA.

Gentes, I. 2000. Culturas étnicas en conflicto: El código de aguas y las comunidades indígenas en el Norte Grande/Chile. *Revista Américas* 4 (16): 7–49.

———. 2002. *Estudio de la legislación oficial Chilena y del derecho indígena a los recursos hídricos.* Santiago de Chile: WALIR–CEPAL and Wageningen University.

———. 2003. *Estudio sobre marcos normativos indígenas y consuetudinarios referente a la gestión del agua en Chile.* Santiago de Chile: WALIR–CEPAL and Wageningen University.

Gerbrandy, G., and P. Hoogendam. 1998. *Aguas y acequias.* Cochabamba: PEIRAV–Plural Editores.

Getches, D. H., C. F. Wilkinson, and R. A. Williams Jr. 1998. *Cases and materials on federal Indian law.* St. Paul, Minn.: West Publishing.

Giddens, A. 1984. *The constitution of society: Outline of the theory of structuration.* Cambridge: Polity Press.

Giyawali, D. 2001. *Water in Nepal.* Kathmandu: Himal Books.

Gleick, P. H., G. Wolff, E. L. Chalecki, and R. Reyes. 2002. *The new economy of water: The risks and benefits of globalization and privatization of fresh water.* Oakland, Cal.: Pacific Institute for Studies in Development, Environment and Security.

Goldman, M. 1998. Introduction: The political resurgence of the commons. In *Privatizing nature: Political struggles for the global commons*, ed. M. Goldman. London: Pluto Press (in association with TNI).

Golte, J. 1992. El problema con las "comunidades." *Debate Agrario* 14: 17–22.

———. Economía, ecología, redes: Campo y ciudad en los análisis antropológicos. In *No hay país más diverso*, ed. Carlos Iván Degregori, 204–234. Lima: Instituto de Estudios Pekuanos.

Government of Gujarat. 1991. *District census handbook: Mehsana district.* Ahmedabad: Directorate of Census Operation.

Govermnent of India. 1999. *Integrated water resources development: A plan for action, report of the National Commission for Integrated Water Resources Development.* New Delhi: Ministry of Water Resources.

Grader, C. J. 1960 (1939). The irrigation system in the region of Jembrana. In *Bali: Studies in life, thought, and ritual*, ed. J. L. Swellengrebel, 267–288. The Hague: W. van Hoeve.

Griffiths, J. 1986. What is legal pluralism? *Journal of Legal Pluralism* 24: 1–11.

Guevara, G.J.A. 1993. *Propiedad agraria y derecho colonial: Los documentos de la hacienda Santotis, Cuzco (1543–1822).* Lima: Pontífica Universidad Católica del Perú.

———. 2001. Notas sobre las causas estructurales de la pluralidad legal en el Perú. In *Antropología y derecho: Rutas de encuentro y reflexión*, 7–27. Iquitos: Defensoría del Pueblo, Red Latinaamericana de Antropología Jurídica-Perú.

———. 2005. La legislación oficial de aguas frente a los derechos campesinos e indígenas en el Perú. In *Water and Cultural Diversity*. Paris: WALIR–UNESCO.

Guevara, G.J.A., J. Armando, I. Vera, P. Urteaga, and G. Zambrano. 2002. Estudio de la legislación oficial Peruana sobre la gestión indígena de los recursos hídricos. In *WALIR Studies* 2: 101–131. Wageningen: Wageningen University and CEPAL.

Guillet, D. 1992. *Covering ground: Communal water management and the state in the Peruvian highlands*. Ann Arbor: University of Michigan Press.

———. 1998. Rethinking legal pluralism: Local law and state law in the evolution of water property rights in northwestern Spain. *Comparative Studies in Society and History* 40 (1): 42–70.

Gupta, D., ed. 1991. *Social stratification*. New Delhi: Oxford University Press.

Gupta, J. 2004. (Inter)national water law and governance: paradigm lost or gained? Inaugural address. Delft: Unesco-Institute for Hydraulic Engineering/Institute for Water Education.

Hale, C. R. 2002. Does multiculturalism menace? Governance, cultural rights and the politics of identity in Guatemala. *Journal of Latin America Studies* 34 (3): 485–524.

Happé, P.L.E. 1919. Een beschouwing over het Zuid-Balische soebak-wezen en zijn verwording in verband met de vorming van waterschappen in Nederlands-Indië. *Indische Gids* 41: 183–200.

———. 1935. Waterbeheer en waterschappen. *De Ingenieur in Nederlandsch-Indië* 2 (11), VI: 135–140.

Haraway, J. D. 1991. Situated knowledges: The science question in feminism and the privilege of partial perspective. In *Simians, cyborgs and women: The reinvention of nature, 183–202*. London: Free Association Books.

Hardin, G. 1968. The tragedy of the commons. *Science* 162: 1,243–1,247.

Hendriks, J. 1998. Water as private property: Notes on the case of Chile. In *Searching for Equity*, ed. R. Boelens and G. Dávila, 297–310. Assen, The Netherlands: Van Gorcum.

———. 2002. Water rights and strengthening users' organisations: The art of negotiating. In *Water rights and empowerment*, ed. R. Boelens and P. Hoogendam, 52–74. Assen, The Netherlands: Van Gorcum.

Hendriks, J., R. Mejía, H. Olázaval, L. Cremers, M. Ooijevaar, and P. Palacios. 2003. *Análisis de la situación del riego en la República del Ecuador*. Mission Report. Quito: WALIR.

Hirway, I. 2000. Dynamics of development in Gujarat: Some issues. *Economic and Political Weekly* 35: 3106–3120.

HMG/ADB (His Majesty's Government of Nepal/Asian Development Bank). 2000. *Project management consultancy for Melamchi water supply project*. Draft report for urban planning sector. Kathmandu: Nippon Koei Co Ltd in association with TAEC Consult and NESS Ltd.

HMG/MWR (His Majesty's Government, Ministry of Water Resources). 1992, 1996. Irrigation policy 1992. First Amendment 1996. Singhadarbar, Kathmandu (Shinchai Neeti 2049, Pratham Sansodhan 2053, in Nepali).

His Majesty's Government of Nepal, Ministry of Law, Justice and Governance. 1992, 1993, 2000. *Water resource act, 1992. Water resource regulation, 1993. Irrigation regulation, 2000*. Kanun Kitab Management Committee. Kathmandu (2058. Jalsrot Ain 2049, Jalsrot Niyamawali 2050, Shichai Niyamawali 2056, in Nepali).

Hobbes, T. 1985 (1651). *Leviathan*. Meppel, The Netherlands: Boom.

Hoebink, P., D. Haude, and F. van der Velden. 1999. *Doorlopers en breuklijnen: Van globalisering, emancipatie en verzet.* Assen, The Netherlands: Van Gorcum.

Hoekema, A. 2004. *A new beginning of law among indigenous peoples. Some observations from anthropology of law.* Amsterdam: School of Law, University of Amsterdam.

Hoogendam, P. 1995. Water rights: Interaction in a normative domain. Mimeographed paper. Ahmedabad: Indian Institute of Management; Wageningen, The Netherlands: Dept. of Irrigation and Water Engineering, Wageningen University.

Hooker, M. B. 1975. *Legal pluralism: An introduction to colonial and neo-colonial laws.* Oxford: Clarendon.

Horst, L. 1996a. Intervention in irrigation water division in Bali, Indonesia: A case of farmers' circumvention of modern technology. In *Crops, people and irrigation. Water allocation practices of farmers and engineers,* ed. G. Diemer and F. Huibers, 34–52. London: Intermediate Technology Publications.

———. 1996b. *Irrigation water division technology in Indonesia: A case of ambivalent development.* Wageningen Agricultural University, Department of Soil and Water Conservation, and International Institute for Land Reclamation and Improvement (ILRI). Liquid Gold paper 2. Wageningen: ILRI.

Houtzager, P. P. 2001. We make the law and the law makes us. In *Making law matter: Rules, rights and security in the lives of the poor,* ed. R. C. Crook and P. P. Houtzager. *IDS Bulletin* 32 (1): 8–18.

Howe, C. W. 1998. Water markets in Colorado: Past performance and needed changes. In *Markets for water: Potential and performance,* ed. K. W. Easter, M. W. Rosegrant, and A. Dinar, 65–76. Boston: Kluwer Academic Publishers.

Howitt, R. E. 1998. Spot prices, option prices, and water markets: An analysis of emerging markets in California. In *Markets for water: Potential and performance,* ed. K. W. Easter, M. W. Rosegrant, and A. Dinar, 119–140. Boston: Kluwer Academic Publishers.

Hunt, R., and E. Hunt. 1976. Canal irrigation and local social organization. *Current Anthropology* 17 (3): 389–398.

IDI (Infrastructure Development Institute). 1997. *The river law.* River Bureau, Ministry of Construction, Infrastructure Development Institute. Tokyo: Infrastructure Development Institute.

IIMI (International Irrigation Management Institute). 1987. *Public Intervention in Farmer-Managed Irrigation Systems.* Digana Village, Sri Lanka: International Irrigation Management Institute.

Ingram, H., and F. L. Brown. 1998. Commodity and community water values: Experiences from the U.S. southwest. In *Searching for equity: Conceptions of justice and equity in peasant irrigation,* ed. R. Boelens and G. Davila, 114–120. Assen, The Netherlands: Van Gorcum.

Jackson, C. 1998. Gender, irrigation and environment: Arguing for agency. *Agriculture and Human Values* 15 (4): 313–324.

Janakarajan, S. 1992. Interlinked transactions and the market for water in the agrarian economy of a Tamil Nadu village. In *Themes in development economics: Essays in honour of Malcom Adiseshiah,* ed. S. Subramanian, 151–201. New Delhi: Oxford University Press.

———. 1993. *Trading in groundwater: A source of power and accumulation.* Paper presented at the International Conference on Water Management: India's Groundwater Challenge, 14–16 December 1993. Ahmedabad: VIKSAT.

———. 1997. The survival of the fittest—Conflict over the use of groundwater: Some evidence from Tamil Nadu, south India. Paper presented at the Indo-Dutch Programme on Alternatives in Development Seminar, Amersfoort, The Netherlands, 11–17 October 1997.

———. 1999. Conflicts over the invisible resource in Tamil Nadu: Is there a way out? In *Rethinking the mosaic: Investigations into local water management*, ed. M. Moench, E. Caspari, and A. Dixit, 123–159. Kathmandu: Nepal Water Conservation Foundation: Institute for Social and Environmental Transition.

Jha, N. 2002. The bifurcate subak: The social organisation of a Balinese irrigation community. Ph.D. dissertation, Brandeis University.

JICA (Japanese International Cooperation Agency). 1990. *Groundwater management project in the Kathmandu Valley*. Main report, Nepal Water Supply Corporation.

Karki Singh, S. 2000. Property rights of women in the perspective of gender equality in Nepalese Law. Ph.D. dissertation, Faculty of Law, University of Delhi.

Kessel, J. van. 1992. *Holocausto al progreso: Los Aymarás de Tarapacá*. La Paz: Hisbol.

Khanal, Puspa Raj. 2003. *Engineering participation: The process and outcomes of irrigation management transfer in the Terai of Nepal*. New Delhi: Orient Longman.

Khumbane, T., M. de Lange, and I. Sibuyi. 2001. A Proposal for establishing small-scale water users forums for the Olifants River catchment. Proposal and report on workshops reflecting the feelings and needs of smallholder irrigation farmers and other small-scale water users in the greater part of the Olifants River basin.

Kolavalli, S., and D. L. Chicoine. 1987. Groundwater markets in Gujarat. Ahmedabad: Indian Institute of Management. Mimeographed paper.

Kome, A. 2002. La copropiedad de la tierra, el derecho de uso de agua y el derecho de asociación en las organizaciones de usuarios del norte del Perú. In *Perú: Problema agrario en debate*, ed. M. Pulgar, E. Vidal, E. Zegarra, and J. Urrutia. Lima: SEPIA.

Koppen, B. van. 1998. *More jobs per drop: Targeting irrigation to poor women and men*. Amsterdam: Royal Tropical Institute.

Korn, V. E. 1924. *Het Adatrecht van Bali*. The Hague: De Ster.

Korten, F. F. and R. Y. Siy Jr. 1988. *Transforming a bureaucracy: The experience of the Philippine National Irrigation Administration*. West Hartford, Conn.: Kumarian.

Kurnia, G., T. W. Avianto, and B. R. Bruns. 2000. Farmers, factories and the dynamics of water allocation in West Java. In *Negotiating Water Rights*, ed. B. R. Bruns and R. S. Meinzen-Dick, 292–314. London: Intermediate Technology Publications.

Lahiff, E. P. 1999. *Land tenure on the Arabie-Olifants irrigation scheme*. South Africa Working Paper no. 2. Colombo: International Water Management Institute.

Lam, W. F., M. Lee, and E. Ostrom. 1993. *An institutional analysis of irrigation performance in Nepal*. Workshop in Political Theory and Policy Analysis. Bloomington: Indiana University.

Lansing, J. S. 1987. Balinese "water temples" and the management of irrigation. *American Anthropologist* 89: 326–341.

———. 1991. *Priests and programmers: Technologies of power in the engineered landscape of Bali*. Princeton: Princeton University Press.

Lansing, J. S. and J. N. Kremer. 1993. Emergent properties of Balinese water temple networks: Coadaptations on a rugged fitness landscape. *American Anthropologist* 95 (1): 97–114.

Las Casas, B. de. 1999 (1552). *Brevísima relación de la destruición de las Indias*. Madrid: Editorial Castalia.

Laurie, N., R. Andolina, and S. Radcliffe. 2002. New exclusions: The consequences of multicultural legislation for water policies in Bolivia. In *Multiculturalism in Latin America: Indigenous rights, diversity and democracy*, ed. R. Sieder, 252–277. London: Palgrave.

Leach, M., R. Mearns, and I. Scoones. 1997. Challenges to community-based sustainable development: Dynamics, entitlements, institutions. *IDS Bulletin* 28 (4): 4–14.

——. 1999. Environmental entitlements: Dynamics and institutions in community-based natural resource management. *World Development* 27 (2): 225–247.

Lemaire, T. 1986. *De Indiaan in ons bewustzijn: De ontmoeting van de oude met de nieuwe wereld.* Baarn, The Netherlands: Ambo.

Liefrinck, S. A. 1969. Rice cultivation in northern Bali. In *Bali: Further Studies in Life, thought and ritual*, ed. J. L. Swellengrebel, 3–73. The Hague: W. van Hoeve.

Ligthelm, M. 2001. Olifants water management area: Catchment management agency establishment. In *Intersectoral management of river basins: Proceedings of an international workshop on integrated water management in water-stressed river basins in developing countries: strategies for poverty alleviation and agricultural growth*, Loskop Dam, South Africa 16–21 October 2000, ed. C. L. Abernethy, 23–44. Colombo: International Water Management Institute and German Foundation for International Development.

Locke, J. 1970 (1690). *Two treatises on government.* Cambridge: Cambridge University Press.

Long, N., and J. D. van der Ploeg. 1989. Demythologizing planned intervention: An actor perspective. *Sociologia Ruralis* 29 (3/4): 226–249.

Lynch, B. D. 1993. *The bureaucratic tradition and women's invisibility in irrigation.* Proceedings of the 24th Chacmool Conference, 333–342. Alberta: Archeological Association, University of Calgary.

Maass, A., and R. Anderson. 1978. *And the desert shall rejoice: Conflict, growth, and justice in arid environments.* Cambridge: MIT Press.

Mayer, E. 2002. *The articulated peasant: Household economies in the Andes.* Boulder: Westview.

McCay, B. J., and S. Jentoft. 1998. Market or community failure? Critical perspectives on common property research. *Human Organization* 57 (1): 21–29.

McCool, D. 1987. *Command of the waters: Iron triangles, federal water development, and Indian water.* Berkeley: University of California Press.

Mehta, L., M. Leach, P. Newell, I. Scoones, K. Sivaramakrishnan, and S. A. Way. 1999. *Exploring understandings of institutions and uncertainty: New directions in natural resource management.* Discussion Paper 372. Brighton: Environment Group, Institute of Development Studies, University of Sussex.

Meinzen-Dick, R. S. 2000. Public, private, and shared water: Groundwater markets and access in Pakistan. In *Negotiating water rights*, ed. B. R. Bruns and R. S. Meinzen-Dick, 245–268. London: Intermediate Technology Publications.

Meinzen-Dick, R. and P. P. Appasamy. 2001. Urbanization and intersectoral competition for water. Paper prepared for the water and population working group, environmental change and security project, Woodrow Wilson Center, Washington, D.C.

Meinzen-Dick, R. S., and M. Bakker. 2001. Water rights and multiple water uses: Issues and examples from Kirindi Oya, Sri Lanka. *Irrigation and Drainage Systems* 15 (2): 129–148.

Meinzen-Dick, R. and B. R. Bruns. 2000. Negotiating water rights: Introduction. In *Negotiating Water Rights*, ed. B. R. Bruns and R. Meinzen-Dick, 23–55. London: Intermediate Technology Publications.

Meinzen-Dick, R. S., M. S. Mendoza, L. Sadoulet, G. Abiad-Shields, and A. Subramanian. 1997. Sustainable water users' associations: Lessons from a literature review. In *User organizations for sustainable water services*, ed. A. Subramanian, N. V. Jaganathan, and R. S. Meinzen-Dick, 7–87. World Bank Technical Paper No. 354. Washington, D.C.: World Bank.

Meinzen-Dick, R. S., and R. Pradhan. 2001a. Implications of legal pluralism for natural resource management. *IDS Bulletin* 32 (4): 10–17.

———. 2001b. Legal pluralism and dynamic property rights. CAPRI Working Paper no. 22. Washington, D.C.: Consultative Group on International Agricultural Research System-Wide Program on Collective Action and Property Rights. http://www.capri.cgiar.org/pdf/capriwp22.pdf.

———. 2002. Recognizing multiple water uses in intersectoral water transfers. Paper presented at the workshop on Asian Irrigation in transition—responding to the challenges ahead. Bangkok, Thailand.

Meinzen-Dick, R. S., and M. W. Rosegrant. 1997. Alternative allocation mechanisms for intersectoral water management. In *Strategies for intersectoral water management in developing countries: Challenges and consequences for agriculture*, ed. J. Richter, P. Wolff, H. Franzen, and F. Heim. Feldalfing, Germany: Deutsche Stiftung für Internationale Entwicklung.

Meinzen-Dick, R. S., and M. Zwarteveen. 1998. Gendered participation in water management: Issues and illustrations from water users' associations in South Asia. *Agriculture and Human Values* 15: 337–345.

Meinzen-Dick, R. S., M. S. Mendoza, L. Sadoulet, G. Abiad-Shields, and A. Subramanian. 1997. Sustainable water users' associations: Lessons from a literature review. In *User organizations for sustainable water services*, ed. A. Subramanian, N. V. Jaganathan, and R. S. Meinzen-Dick, 7–87. World Bank Technical Paper no. 354. Washington, D.C.: World Bank.

Merrey, D. J. 1996. *Institutional design principles for accountability in large irrigation systems*. IWMI Research Report 8. Colombo: International Water Management Institute.

Merrey, D. J., and S. Baviskar, ed. 1998. *Gender analysis and reform of irrigation management: Concepts, cases and gaps in knowledge*. Proceedings of the workshop on gender and water. Colombo: International Irrigation Management Institute.

Merry, S. E. 1988. Legal Pluralism. *Law and Society Review* 22 (5): 869–896.

———. 1992. Anthropology, law, and transnational processes. *Annual Review of Anthropology* 21: 357–379.

Mitchell, W. P., and D. Guillet. 1994. *Irrigation at high altitudes: The social organization of water control systems in the Andes*. Washington D.C.: Society for Latin American Anthropology and American Anthropological Association.

Mnookin, R., and L. Kornhauser. 1979. Bargaining in the shadow of the law: The case of divorce. *Yale Law Journal* 88: 950–997.

Moench, M. 1992. *Debating the options: Groundwater management in the face of scarcity; Collaborative groundwater project*. Ahmedabad: VIKSAT / Pacific Institute Collaborative Research.

———. 1999. Addressing constraints in complex systems: Meeting the water management needs of South Asia in the 21st century. In *Rethinking the mosaic: Investigations into local water management*, ed. M. Moench, E. Caspari, and A. Dixit, 1–55. Kathmandu: Nepal Water Conservation Foundation and Boulder: Institute for Social and Environmental Transition.

———. Undated. *Debating the options: Groundwater management in the face of scarcity—Gujarat, India*. VIKSAT—Pacific Institute Collaborative Research. Ahmedabad: VIKSAT.

Moench, M., E. Caspari, and A. Dixit, eds. 1999. *Rethinking the mosaic: Investigations into local water management*. Kathmandu: Nepal Water Conservation Foundation and Boulder: Institute for Social and Environmental Transition.

Mollinga, P. P. 2001. Water and politics: Levels, rational choice and south Indian canal irrigation. *Futures* 33: 733–752.

——. 2003. *On the waterfront: Water distribution, technology and agrarian change in a south Indian canal irrigation system.* New Delhi: Orient Longman.

Mollinga, P. P., and A. Bolding. 2004. *The politics of irrigation reform: Contested policy formulation and implementation in Asia, Africa and Latin America.* Aldershot, England: Ashgate.

Montoya, R. 1979. *Producción parcelaria y universo ideológico en Puquio.* Lima: Mosca Azul Editores.

Moore, M. 1989. The fruits and fallacies of neoliberalism: The case of irrigation policy. *World Development* 17 (11): 1,733–1,750.

——. 1991. Rent-seeking and market surrogates: The case of irrigation policy. In *States or markets? Neo-liberalism and the development policy debate*, ed. C. Colclough and J. Manor, 297–305. IDS Development Studies Series. Oxford: Clarendon Press.

Moore, S. F. 1973. Law and social change: The semi-autonomous social field as an appropriate field of study. *Law and Society Review* 7: 719–746.

——. 1978. *Law as process: An anthropological approach.* Londen: Routledge and Kegan Paul.

——. 2001. Certainties undone: Fifty turbulent years of legal anthropology, 1949–1999. *Journal of the Royal Anthropological Institute* 7: 95–116.

More, T. 1975 (1516). *Utopia.* Harmondsworth: Penguin Classics.

Morgan, A. E. 1946. *Nowhere was somewhere: How history makes utopias and how utopias make history.* Chapel Hill: University of North Carolina Press.

Moser, C. 1989. Gender Planning in the Third World: Meeting practical and strategic needs. *World Development* 17 (11): 1,799–1,825

Mossbrucker, H. 1990. *La economía campesina y el concepto "comunidad" un enfoque crítico.* Lima: IEP.

Mosse, D. 1997. The symbolic making of a common property resource: History, ecology and locality in a tank-irrigated landscape in south India. *Development and Change* 28: 467–504.

Muller, M. 2001. How national water policy is helping to achieve South Africa's development vision. In *Intersectoral management of river basins: Proceedings of an international workshop on integrated water management in water-stressed river basins in developing countries: strategies for poverty alleviation and agricultural growth*, Loskop Dam, South Africa 16–21 October 2000, ed. C. L. Abernethy, 3–13. Colombo: International Water Management Institute and German Foundation for International Development.

Muñoz, Bernardo. 1999. *Derechos de propiedad y pueblos indígenas en Chile.* Serie Desarrollo Productivo, no. 60. Santiago: CEPAL.

Nelson, N., and S. Wright. 1995. *Power and participatory development: Theory and practice.* London: IT Publications.

Nijman, C. 1993. A management perspective on the performance of the irrigation subsector. Ph.D. dissertation, Wageningen University.

NNMLS (Northern New Mexico Legal Services). 2000. Stream adjudications, acequias, and water rights in northern New Mexico. In *Negotiating water rights*, ed. B. R. Bruns and R. S. Meinzen-Dick, 337–352. London: Intermediate Technology Publications.

Nobe, K. C., and R. K. Sampath. 1986. *Irrigation management in developing countries: Current issues and approaches.* Studies in water policy and management 8. Boulder: Westview.

North, D. C. 1990. *Institutions, institutional change and economic performance.* New York: Cambridge University Press.

Nuñez-Palomino, P. G. 1995. Law and peasant communities in Peru. Ph.D. dissertation, Wageningen University.

Oad, R. 2001. Policy reforms for sustainable irrigation management—A case study of Indonesia. *Irrigation and Drainage* 50: 279–294.

Olson, M. 2000. *Power and prosperity: Outgrowing communist and capitalist dictatorships.* New York: Basic Books.

Omer-Cooper, J. D. 1994. *History of southern Africa.* Second edition. London: James Currey, and Portsmouth, N. H.: Heinemann.

Oré, M. T. 1998. From agrarian reform to privatization of land and water: The case of the Peruvian coast. In *Searching for equity*, ed. R. Boelens and G. Dávila, 268–278. Assen, The Netherlands:: Van Gorcum.

———. 2005 (forthcoming). *La organización social del riego en un valle de la costa Peruana— el Canal Achirana.* Lima: PUCP / WALIR / ITDG.

Orellana, R. 2001. Agua que no has de beber, no la vendas. . . . déjala correr. Privatización y mercantilización de derechos de agua a través del proyecto de ley del recurso agua. *Artículo Primero* 5 (3): 1–35. Santa Cruz: CEJIS.

Ostrom, E. 1990. *Governing the commons: The evolution of institutions for collective action.* Cambridge: Cambridge University Press.

———. 1992. *Crafting institutions for self-governing irrigation systems.* San Francisco: Institute for Contemporary Studies Press.

———. 1997. Investing in capital, institutions, and incentives. In *Institutions and economic development: Growth and governance in less-developed and post-socialist countries.* Baltimore: John Hopkins University Press.

———. 1999. Coping with tragedies of the commons. *Annual Review of Political Science* 1999 (2): 493–535.

Ostrom, E., and E. Schlager. 1996. The formation of property rights. In *Rights to nature: Ecological, economic, cultural, and political principles of institutions for the environment*, ed. S. S. Hanna, C. Folke, and K. G. Mäler, 127–156. Washington, D.C.: Island Press.

Pacari, N. 1998. Ecuadorian water legislation and policy analyzed from the indigenous-peasant point of view. In *Searching for equity*, ed. R. Boelens and G. Dávila, 279–287. Assen, The Netherlands: Van Gorcum.

Palacios, P. 2002. *Estudio nacional de la legislación oficial y los marcos normativos consuetudinarios referente a la gestón indígena de los recursos hídricos.* Quito: WALIR—CEPAL and Wageningen University.

Palanisami, K. 1994. *Evolution of agricultural and urban water markets in Tamil Nadu, India.* Arlington, Va.: Irrigation Support Project for Asia and the Near East (ISPAN), United States Agency for International Development.

Patel, G. D. 1969. *The land revenue settlements and the British rule in India.* Thesis Publication Series 7. Ahmedabad: Gujarat University.

Patel, P. P. 1997. *Ecoregions of Gujarat.* Vadodara: Gujarat Ecology Commission.

Peña, Francisco, ed. 2004. *Los pueblos indígenas y el agua: Desafios del siglo XXI.* El Colegio de San Luis, WALIR, IMTA. Mexico D.F.: Obranegra Editores.

Perreault, T. 2005 (forthcoming). State restructuring and the scale politics of rural water governance in Bolivia. In *Environment and Planning A.*

Perry, C. J., M. Rock, and D. Seckler. 1997. *Water as an economic good: A solution or a problem?* IWMI Research Report 14. Colombo: International Water Management Institute.

Petrella, R. 1999. *Water als bron van macht: Een manifest.* Leuven: Van Halewyck.

Pfaffenberger, B. 1988. Fetished objects and humanised nature: Towards an anthropology of technology. *Man* (N.S.) 23: 236–252.

Place, F., M. Roth, and P. Hazell. 1994. Land tenure security and agricultural performance in Africa: Overview of research methodology. In *Searching for land tenure security in Africa*, ed. J. W. Bruce and S. Migot-Adholla. Washington, D.C.: World Bank.

Planning Commission New Delhi. 2001. *Economic Survey of Delhi 2001–2002.* http://www.delhiplanning.nic.in/ecosurvey.htm.

Ploeg, J. D. van der. 1998. Peasants and power. In *Searching for equity*, ed. R. Boelens and G. Dávila, 39–45. Assen, The Netherlands: Van Gorcum.

———. 2003. *The virtual farmer.* Assen, The Netherlands: Van Gorcum.

Ploeg, J. D. van der, and A. Long. 1994. *Born from within: Practices and perspectives of endogenous development.* Assen, The Netherlands: Van Gorcum.

Plusquellec, H., C. Burt, and H. W. Wolter. 1994. *Modern water control in irrigation: Concepts, issues, and applications.* Irrigation and Drainage Series, Technical Paper no. 246. Washington, D.C.: World Bank.

Pradhan, R. 2000. Land and water rights in Nepal (1854–1992). In *Water, land and law: Changing rights to land and water in Nepal*, ed. R. Pradhan, F. von Benda-Beckmann, and K. von Benda-Beckmann, 39–70. Kathmandu: FREEDEAL; Wageningen: Wageningen University; Rotterdam: Erasmus University Rotterdam.

———., ed. 2003. *Legal pluralism and unofficial law in social, economic and political development.* Commission on Folk Law and Legal Pluralism. Papers of the XIIIth international congress, 7–10 April 2002, Chiang Mai, Thailand. Kathmandu: International Center for Study of Nature, Environment, and Culture.

Pradhan, R., F. von Benda-Beckmann, and K. von Benda-Beckmann, eds. 2000. *Water, land and law: Changing rights to land and water in Nepal.* Proceedings of a workshop held in Kathmandu 18–20 March 1998. Kathmandu: FREEDEAL; Wageningen: Wageningen University; Rotterdam: Erasmus University Rotterdam.

Pradhan, R., F. von Benda-Beckmann, K. von Benda-Beckmann, H.L.J. Spiertz, S. S. Khadka, and K. Azharul Haq, eds. 1997. *Water rights, conflict and policy.* Proceedings of a workshop held in Kathmandu, Nepal, 22–24 January 1996. Colombo: International Irrigation Management Institute.

Pradhan, R., and J. Brewer. 1998. Water rights in Nepal. Manuscript report prepared for International Irrigation Management Institute. Colombo: International Irrigation Management Institute.

Pradhan, R., K. A. Haq, and U. Pradhan. 1997. Law, rights and equity: Implications of state intervention in farmer managed irrigation systems. In *Water rights, conflict and policy*, ed. R. Pradhan, F. von Benda-Beckmann, K. von Benda-Beckmann, H.L.J. Spiertz, S. S. Khadka, and K. Azharul Haq, 111–134. Colombo: International Irrigation Management Institute.

Pradhan, R., and R. S. Meinzen-Dick. 2003. Which rights are right? Water rights, culture, and underlying values. *Water Nepal* 9/10 (1/2): 37–61.

Pradhan, R., and U. Pradhan. 2000. Negotiating access and rights: Disputes over rights to an irrigation water source in Nepal. In *Negotiating water rights,* ed. B. R. Bruns and R. S. Meinzen-Dick, 200–221. London: Intermediate Technology Publications.

Prahladachar, M. 1994. Innovations in the use and management of groundwater in hardrock regions in India. *Ecological Economics* 9: 267–272.

Rap, E., P. Wester, and L. Nereida Pérez-Prado. 2004. The politics of creating commitment: Irrigation reforms and the reconstitution of the hydraulic bureaucracy in Mexico. In

The Politics of Irrigation Reform: Contested policy formulation and implementation in Asia, Africa and Latin America, ed. P. Mollinga and A. Bolding, 57–94. Aldershot, England: Ashgate.

Ravesteijn, W. 1997. De zegenrijke heeren der wateren: Irrigatie en staat op Java, 1832–1942. Ph.D. dissertation, Delft University.

Regmi, A. 2001. Trajectories of regimes, regulations and rights from traditional to contemporary urban water uses in the Kathmandu Valley: A view from the window. Paper presented at the second conference of the International Water History Association, Bergen, Norway.

Repetto, R. 1986. *Skimming the water: Rent-seeking and the performance of public irrigation systems*. Research Report no. 4. Washington, D.C.: World Resources Institute.

Rinaudo, J. D., P. Strosser, and T. Rieu. 1997. Linking water market functioning, access to water resources and farm production strategies: Examples from Pakistan. *Irrigation and Drainage Systems* 11 (3): 261–280.

Ringler, C., M. W. Rosegrant, and M. S. Paisner. 2000. *Irrigation and water resources in Latin America and the Caribbean*. EPTD Discussion Paper 64. Washington, D.C.: Environment and Production Technology Division, International Food Policy Research Institute.

Roberts, S. 1998. Against legal pluralism: Some reflections on the contemporary enlargement of the legal domain. *Journal of Legal Pluralism* 42: 95–106.

Rodgers, C., S. M. Siregar, Wahida, B. Hendradjaja, S. Suprapto, and R. Zaafrano. 2001. Integrated economic-hydrologic modeling of the Brantas Basin, East Java, Indonesia: Issues and challenges. Paper read at the conference on Integrated Water Resources Management in a River Basin Context: Institutional Strategies for Improving the Productivity of Agricultural Water Management, Malang, Indonesia.

Rosegrant, M. W., and H. P. Binswanger. 1994. Markets in tradable water rights: Potential for efficiency gains in developing country water resource allocation. *World Development* 22 (11): 1,613–1,625.

Rosegrant, M., and R. Gazmuri. 1994. *Reforming water allocation policy through markets in tradable water rights: Lessons from Chile, Mexico and California*. EPTD Discussion Paper 6. Washington, D.C.: Environment and Production Technology Division, International Food Policy Research Institute.

Rosegrant, M. W., and C. Ringler. 1998. Impact on food security and rural development of reallocating water from agriculture. *Water Policy* 1: 567–586.

Ross, R. 1999. *A concise history of South Africa*. Cambridge: Cambridge University Press.

Roth, D. 1998. Land settlement, irrigation development and normative-legal complexity in the management and exploitation of land and water resources in Kabupaten Luwu. *Indonesian Environmental History Newsletter* 11: 8–10.

———. 1999. Local irrigation management in a public irrigation system: Balinese irrigators in south Sulawesi, Indonesia. *Water Nepal* 7 (1): 91–112.

———. 2003. Ambition, regulation and reality: Complex use of land and water resources in Luwu, South Sulawesi, Indonesia. Ph.D. dissertation, Wageningen University.

Roth, M., K. Wiebe, and S. Lawry. 1993. *Land tenure and agrarian structure: Implications for technology adoption*. Proceedings of a workshop on social science research and the CRSPs, University of Kentucky, Lexington, 9–11 June 1992. Washington, D.C.: United States Agency for International Development.

RSA (Republic of South Africa). 1994. *Constitution of the Republic of South Africa*. Cape Town: Office of the President.

———. 1997. *Water services act*. Cape Town: Office of the President.

———. 1998a. *Local government: Municipal structures act*. Government Gazette 402, 18 December 1998, no. 19,614. Cape Town: Office of the President.

——. 1998b. *National water act*. Government Gazette 398, 26 August 1998, no. 19,182. Cape Town: Office of the President.

——. 2000. *The Integrated Sustainable Rural Development Strategy*. Cape Town: Office of the President.

Sadeque, Zahir Sayed. 2000. Nature's bounty or scarce commodity: Competition and consensus over groundwater use in rural Bangladesh. In *Negotiating water rights*, ed. B. R. Bruns and R. S. Meinzen-Dick, 269–291. London: Intermediate Technology Publications.

Saleth, R. M. 1994a. Groundwater markets in India: A legal and institutional perspective. In *Selling water: Conceptual and policy debates over groundwater markets in India*, ed. M. Moench, 59–71. Ahmedabad: VIKSAT/Pacific Institute/Natural Heritage Institute.

——. 1994b. Towards a new water institution: Economics, law and policy. *Economic and Political Weekly* 24: A147–A155.

Salman, M. A. 1997. *The legal framework for water users' associations: A comparative study*. World Bank Technical Paper 360. Washington, D.C.: World Bank.

Salomon, F. 2002. Unethnic ethnohistory: On Peruvian peasant historiography and ideas of autochthony. *Ethnohistory* 49 (3): 475–506.

Sanbongi, K. 2001. Formation of case law and principles in watershed management. Paper read at Regional Conference on Water Law: Legal Aspects of Sustainable Water Resources Management. Sarajevo, Bosnia.

Santos, B. 1995. *Toward a new common sense: Law, science and politics in the paradigmatic transition*. London: Routledge.

Saravanan, V., and P. Appasamy. 1999. Historical perspectives on conflicts over domestic and industrial supply in the Bhavani and Noyyal basins, Tamil Nadu. In *Rethinking the mosaic: Investigations into local water management*, ed. M. Moench, E. Caspari, and A. Dixit, 161–190. Kathmandu: Nepal Water Conservation Foundation; Boulder: Institute for Social and Environmental Transition.

Schaffer, B., and G. Lamb. 1981. *Can equity be organized? Equity, development analysis and planning*. Brighton: Institute of Development Studies, Sussex University.

Scheer, S. 1996. Communication between irrigation engineers and farmers: The case of project design in north Senegal. Ph.D. dissertation, Wageningen University.

Schlager, E., and E. Ostrom. 1992. Property-rights regimes and natural resources: A conceptual analysis. *Land Economics* 68 (2): 249–262.

Schleyer, R. G. and M. W. Rosegrant. 1996. Chilean water policy: The role of water rights, institutions and markets. *Water Resources Development* 12 (1): 33–48.

Schulte Nordholt, H. 1986. *Bali: Colonial conceptions and political change 1700–1940; From shifting hierarchies to "fixed order."* CASP 15. Rotterdam: Comparative Asian Studies Program.

Scott, A., and G. Coustalin. 1995. The Evolution of Water Rights. *Natural Resources Journal* 35 (4): 821–979.

Scott, J. 1985. *Weapons of the weak: Everyday forms of peasant resistance*. New Haven: Yale University Press.

Seckler, D. 1993. *Privatizing irrigation systems*. Center for Economic Policy Studies Discussion Paper 12. Arlington, Va.: Winrock International Institute for Agricultural Development.

Sepúlveda, J. G. de. 1996 (1550). *Tratado sobre las justas causas de la guerra contra los indios*. Mexico: Fondo de Cultura Económica.

Shah, E. 2003. *Social Designs. Tank irrigation technology and agrarian transformation in Karnataka, South India.* Wageningen University Water Resources Series. New Delhi: Orient Longman.

Shah, S. S., and G. N. Singh. 2001. *Irrigation development in Nepal: Investment, efficiency and institutions.* Winrock international research report series in policy analysis in agriculture and related resource management no. 47. Kathmandu: Winrock International Nepal.

Shah, T. 1993. *Groundwater markets and irrigation development: Political economy and practical policy.* New Delhi: Oxford University Press.

Shah, T., and V. Ballabh. 1995. The social science of water stress: An exploratory study of water management institutions in Banaskantha District, Gujarat. In *Groundwater management: The supply dominated focus of traditional, NGO and government efforts,* ed. M. Moench, 42–53. Ahmedabad: VIKSAT/Natural Heritage Institute.

———. 1997. Water markets in north Bihar: Six village studies in Muzaffarpur district. *Economic and Political Weekly* 32 (52): 183–190.

Shah, T., V. Ballabh, K. Dobrial, and J. Talati. 1994. Turnover of state tube wells to farmer cooperatives: Assessment of Gujarat's experience, India. Paper presented at the international conference on irrigation management transfer, Wuhan, China, 20–24 September 1994.

Shah, T., I. Makin, and R. Sakhtivadivel. 2001. Limits to leapfrogging: Issues in transposing successful river basin management institutions in the developing world. In *Intersectoral management of river basins: Proceedings of an international workshop on integrated water management in water-stressed river basins in developing countries: strategies for poverty alleviation and agricultural growth,* Loskop Dam, South Africa, 16–21 October 2000, ed. C. L. Abernethy, 89–114. Colombo: International Water Management Institute and German Foundation for International Development.

Sharma, S. 2001. *Procuring water: Foreign aid and rural water supply in Nepal.* Kathmandu: Nepal Water Conservation Foundation.

Shurts, J. 2000. *Indian reserved water rights: The Winters doctrine in its social and legal context, 1880s–1930s.* Norman: University of Oklahoma Press.

SILT. 1997. *Operational procedural manual* (revised August 1997; updated June 2000). Second Irrigation Sector Project Loan no. 1437. Kathmandu: NEP (SF); Manila: Asian Development Bank, Manila; and His Majesty's Government, Nepal.

———. 2001. *Semi-annual progress report no 10.* SISP, project implementation unit. Kathmandu: His Majesty's Government, Nepal/MOWR/DOI.

Singh, Chatrapati. 1994. Research agenda for groundwater law in India. Paper presented at the international conference on water management: India's groundwater challenge. Ahmedabad: VIKSAT.

Skar, H. 1997. *La gente del valle caliente: Dualidad y reforma agraria entre los Runakuna de la sierra Peruana.* Lima: Fondo Editorial, Universidad Católica del Perú.

Slaats, H. 1999. Land titling and customary rights: Comparing land registration projects in Thailand and Indonesia. In *Property rights and economic development: Land and natural resources in South-East Asia and Oceania,* ed. T. van Meijl and F. von Benda-Beckmann, 88–109. London: Kegan Paul.

Slocum, R., L. Wichhart, D. Rocheleau, B. Thomas-Slayter. 1995. *Power, process and participation: Tools for change.* London: International Technology Publications.

Small, L. E., and I. Carruthers. 1991. *Farmer-financed irrigation: The economics of reform.* Cambridge: Cambridge University Press.

Sodemba, I., and R. Pradhan. 2000. Land and water rights in Thulo Sangrumba, Ilam. In

Water, land and law: Changing rights to land and water in Nepal, ed. R. Pradhan, F. von Benda-Beckmann, and K. von Benda-Beckmann, 101–128. Kathmandu: FREEDEAL; Wageningen: Wageningen University; Rotterdam: Erasmus University Rotterdam.

Solanes, M. 2002. *América Latina: Sin regulación ni competencia? Impactos sobre la gobernabilidad del agua y sus servicios.* Santiago de Chile : CEPAL.

Solón, P. 2003. La sangre de la Pachamama. Documentary. La Paz: Fundación Solón.

Soto, H. de. 2000. *The mystery of capital: Why capitalism triumphs in the West and fails everywhere else.* London: Bantam Press.

Spiertz, H.L.J. 1991. The transformation of traditional law: A tale of people's participation in irrigation management on Bali. *Landscape and Urban Planning* 20: 189–196.

———. 1992. Between cannibalism and pluralism: On the construction of legal frameworks in irrigation management in Bali and Sri Lanka. In *Law as a resource in agrarian struggles,* ed. F. von Benda-Beckmann and M. van der Velde, 89–110. Wageningse Sociologische Studies 33. Wageningen: Wageningen Agricultural University.

———. 2000. Water rights and legal pluralism: Some basics of a legal anthropological approach. In *Negotiating water rights,* ed. B. R. Bruns and R. S. Meinzen-Dick, 245–268. London: Intermediate Technology Publications.

Spiertz, H.L.J., and J. H. de Jong. 1992. Traditional law and irrigation management: The case of Bethma. In *Irrigators and engineers: Essays in honour of Lucas Horst,* ed. G. Diemer and J. Slabbers, 185–201. Amsterdam: Thesis Publishers.

Spiertz, J., and M. G. Wiber. 1996. *The role of law in natural resource management.* Nijmegen: VUGA.

Starn, O. 1992. Antropología Andina, "Andinismo" y Sendero Luminoso. In *Allpanchis* 39: 15–71.

Statistics South Africa. 1999. *Household Surveys.* Pretoria: Statistics South Africa.

Stavenhagen, R., and D. Iturralde, eds. 1990. *Entre la ley y la costumbre: El derecho consuetudinario indígena en América Latina.* Mexico City: Instituto Indigenista Interamericano e Instituto Interamericano de Derechos Humanos.

Steyl, I., D. B. Versfeld, and P. J. Nelson. 2000. *Strategic environmental assessment for water use: Mhlathuze Catchment, KwaZulu-Natal.* Pretoria: Department of Water Affairs and Forestry.

Sunaryo, T. M. 2001. Integrated water resources management in the river basin context: The Brantas River Basin, Indonesia. Paper read at the conference on Integrated Water Resources Management in a River Basin Context: Institutional Strategies for Improving the Productivity of Agricultural Water Management, Malang, Indonesia.

Sutawan, N. 1987. Farmer-managed irrigation systems and the impact of government assistance: A note from Bali, Indonesia. In *Public intervention in farmer-managed irrigation systems,* 49–69. Colombo: International Irrigation Management Institute.

———. 1998. *Peranan subak di era Reformasi: Dinamika petani.* Media informasi tentang sumberdaya air dan pertanian, diterbitkan untuk jaringan komunikasi irigasi Indonesia no. 32, Tahun X.

Sutawan, N., M. Swara, W. Windia, W. Suteja, N. Arya, and W. Tjatera. 1990. Community-based irrigation system in Bali. In *Irrigation and water management in Asia,* ed. W. Gooneratne and S. Hirashima, 81–147. New Delhi: Sterling Publishers.

Tamanaha, B. 1993. The folly of the "social scientific" concept of legal pluralism. *Journal of Law and Society* 20: 192–217.

Tankimyong, U., P. C. Bruns, and B. Bruns. 2002. *Towards polycentric governance: Challenges of managing water in the Mae Ping and Mae Yom river basins of northern Thailand.* Presented at the workshop on Asian Irrigation in Transition: Responding to the Challenges Ahead, Asian Institute of Technology, Bangkok, Thailand, 22–23 April 2002.

Teerink, J. R., and M. Nakashima. 1993. Water allocation, rights, and pricing: Examples from Japan and the United States. World Bank Technical Paper. Washington, D.C.: World Bank.

Theobani, M. 1998. Meeting water needs in developing countries: Resolving issues in establishing tradable water rights. In *Markets for water: Potential and performance*, ed. K. W. Easter, M. W. Rosegrant, and A. Dinar, 35–50. Boston: Kluwer.

Thomas, J., and M. S. Grindle. 1990. "After the decision. Implementing policy reforms." *World Development* 18 (8): 1,163–1,181.

Toledo-Llancaqueo, V. 1996. *Todas las aguas, el subsuelo, las riberas, las tierras.* Rehue, Chile: Temuco.

Torres-Galarza, R., ed. 1995. *Derechos de los pueblos indígenas: Situación jurídica y políticas de Estado.* Quito: Confederación de Nacionalidades Juchígenos del Ecuador/ Centro de Planificación y Estudios Sociales/Abya-Yala.

Trawick, P. 1996. La nueva ley de aguas: Una alternativa Andina a las reformas propuestas. *Debate Agrario* 28: 85–102.

———. 2003. Against the privatization of water: An indigenous model for improving existing laws and successfully governing the commons. *World Development* 31 (6): 977–996.

Tsur, Y., and A. Dinar. 1997. The relative efficiency and implementation costs of alternative methods for pricing irrigation water. *World Bank Economic Review* 11 (2): 243–262.

Ubels, J., and L. Horst. 1993. *Irrigation design in Africa: Towards an interactive method.* Ede, The Netherlands: Technical Centre for Agricultural and Rural Cooperation.

UNCDF (United Nations Capital Development Fund). 1998. *Managing the Nam Tan watershed.* UNCDF Project Brief. http://www.undplao.org/Projectfact/Watershed.pdf.

United States. National Water Commission. 1973. *Water policies for the future—Final report to the president and to the congress of the United States.* N.p.

Uphoff, N. 1986. Getting the process right: Improving irrigation water management with farmer organization and participation. In *Studies in water policy and management* 11. Boulder: Westview.

Uphoff, N., P. Ramamurthy, and R. Steiner. 1991. *Managing irrigation: Analyzing and improving the performance of bureaucracies.* New Delhi: Sage.

Urteaga Crovetto, P. 1998. Territorial rights and indigenous law: An alternative approach. In *The challenge of diversity. Indigenous peoples and reform of the state in Latin America*, ed. W. Assies, G. Van der Haar, and A. Hoekema, 275–292. Amsterdam: Thela Thesis Publishers.

Urteaga, P., and A. Guevara. 2002. *Legislación de recursos hídricos y derechos indígenas. Propuesta de investigación para el caso del Perú.* WALIR Phase 1 (1): 24–54. Wageningen: Wageningen University; Santiago, Chile: UN-CEPAL.

Urteaga, P., I. Vera, and A. Guevara. 2003. *Estudio sobre las reglas y regulaciones indígenas y consuetudinarias para la gestión de los recursos hídricos en el Perú.* WALIR. Wageningen: Wageningen University; Lima and Santiago: UN-CEPAL.

Velasco, H. G. 2001. *Water rights administration: Experience, issues, guidelines.* Rome: Food and Agriculture Organization of the United Nations.

Vermillion, D. L. 1986. Rules and processes: Dividing water and negotiating order in two new irrigation systems in North Sulawesi, Indonesia. Ph.D. dissertation, Cornell University.

———. 1991. The turnover and self-management of irrigation institutions in developing countries: A discussion paper for the new program of IIMI. Discussion paper. Colombo: IIMI.

———. 1995. Irrigation management transfer: Towards an integrated management revolution. In *Irrigation management transfer: Selected papers from the international conference on irrigation management transfer*, ed. S. H. Johnson, D. L. Vermillion, and J. A. Sagardoy. Rome: IIMI/FAO.

———. 2000. Water rights in the state of nature: Emergent expectations in an Indonesian settlement. In *Negotiating water rights*, ed. B. R. Bruns and R. S. Meinzen-Dick, 56–82. London: Intermediate Technology Publications.

Vermillion, D. L., M. Samad, S. Pusposutardjo, S. A. Arif, and S. Rochdyanto. 2000. *An assessment of the small-scale irrigation management turnover program in Indonesia*. Research Report 38. Colombo: International Water Management Institute.

Vidal, A. M. 1990. Derecho oficial y derecho campesino en el mundo andino. In *Entre la ley y la costumbre*, ed. R. Stavenhagen and D. Iturralde. Mexico City: Instituto Indigenista Interamericano / Instituto Interamericano de Derechos Humanos.

Villarejo, D. 1997. *Mendota executive summary.* http//www.whiteknight.com/ alliance/ mendota.htm.

Vincent, L. F. 1997. Irrigation as a technology, irrigation as a resource: A sociotechnical approach to irrigation. Inaugural lecture, Wageningen Agricultural University.

———. 2001. Struggles at the social interface: Developing sociotechnical research in irrigation and water management. In *Resonances and dissonances in development: Actors, networks and cultural repertoires*, ed. P. Hebinck and G. Verschoor, 65–81. Assen, The Netherlands: Van Gorcum.

Vos, J. 2002. *Metric matters: Water control in large-scale irrigation in Peru*. Ph.D. dissertation, Wageningen University.

Vyas, Rajnee. 1998. *The glory of Gujarat.* Ahmedabad: Akshara Prakashan.

Walker, J. L. and S. M. Williams. 1991. Indian reserved water rights. *Natural Resources and the Environment* 5: 6.

WECS (Water and Energy Commission Secretariat). 2000. *Water resources strategy formulation, phase II study*. First draft of water resources strategy: Main report, annex 6. Kathmandu: Water and Energy Commission Secretariat.

Wester, P. and J. Warner. 2002. River basin management reconsidered. In *Hydropolitics in the African world: A southern African perspective*, ed. A. Turnton and R. Henwood, 61–71. Pretoria: African Water Issues Research Unit.

Wiber, M. G. 1992. Levels of property rights and levels of law: A case study from the northern Philippines. *Man* (N.S.) 26: 469–492.

Williamson, O. E. 1996. *The mechanisms of governance.* New York: Oxford University Press.

Wolf, E. 1982. *Europe and the people without history.* Berkeley: University of California Press.

Wood, G. 1985. The politics of development policy labelling. *Development and Change* 16 (3): 347–373.

Wood, J. R. 1997. Changing institutions and changing politics in rural water management: An overview of three zones in Gujarat. Centre for India and South Asia Research, University of British Columbia. http://www.iar.ubc.ca/centres/cisar/WOOD/wood1.html.

Woodman, G. R. 1998. Ideological combat and social observation: Recent debate about legal pluralism. *Journal of Legal Pluralism* 42: 21–59.

World Bank. 1995. *Peru: A user-based approach to water management and irrigation development*. Report 13642–PE. Washington, D.C.: World Bank, Latin America and the Caribbean Country Department.

———. 1996. *Tradable water rights: A property rights approach to resolving water shortages and promoting investment*. P. Holden and M. Thobani. Policy Research Working Paper

1627. Washington, D.C.: World Bank, Latin America and the Caribbean Technical Department.

———. 2000/2001. *Attacking poverty: World development report 2000/2001.* New York: Oxford University Press.

World Bank / UNDP Water and Sanitation Programme. 2000. *The water supply and sanitation situation of the urban poor in Kathmandu Valley: Results of a research study,* volumes 1 and 2. Kathmandu: Lumanti Support Group for Shelter / Nepal Water for Health and Water Aid / Water and Sanitation Programme.

Wray, A. 1993. El problema indígena y la reforma del Estado. In *Derecho, pueblos indígenas y reforma del Estado,* 11–70. Quito: Abya-Yala.

Yoder, R. 1994. *Locally managed irrigation systems: Essential tasks and implications for assistance, management transfer and turnover programs.* Colombo: International Water Management Institute.

Young, R. A. 1986. Why are there so few transactions among water users? *American Journal of Agricultural Economics* 68 (5): 1,144–1,151.

Yrigoyen Fajardo, R. 1998. The constitutional recognition of indigenous law in Andean countries. In *The challenge of diversity: Indigenous peoples and reform of the state in Latin America,* ed. W. Assies, G. Van der Haar, and A. Hoekema, 197–222. Amsterdam: Thela Thesis Publishers.

Zoomers, A., and G. van der Haar. 2000. *Current land policy in Latin America: Regulating land tenure under neo-liberalism.* Amsterdam: Royal Tropical Institute.

Zwarteveen, M. Z. 1994a. *Gender aspects of irrigation management transfer: Rethinking efficiency and equity.* FAO Water Report no. 5. Rome: Irrigation Management Transfer.

———. 1994b. *Gender issues, water issues: A gender perspective to irrigation management.* Working Paper 32. Colombo: International Irrigation Management Institute.

———. 1997. Water, from basic need to commodity: A discussion on gender and water rights in the context of irrigation. *World Development* 25 (8): 1,335–1,349.

———. 1998. Identifying gender aspects of new irrigation management policies. *Agriculture and Human Values* 15: 301–312.

Zwarteveen, M., and M. Endeveld. 1995. Rural women's questions are agrarian questions: A discussion of the intellectual and political construction of realities of rural women. Paper presented at the conference on Agrarian Questions: The Politics of Farming Anno 1995. Wageningen, 22–24 May 1995.

Zwarteveen, M. Z., and R. S. Meinzen-Dick. 2001. Gender and property rights in the commons: Examples of water rights in South Asia. *Agriculture and Human Values* 18 (1): 11–25.

NOTES ON THE CONTRIBUTORS

VISHWA BALLABH holds a Ph.D. in agricultural economics from the Indian Agricultural Research Institute, New Delhi. His major area of work concerns the institutional aspects of natural resource management. He has coauthored and coedited several books, among which are *Farm Forestry in South Asia* (coedited with N. C. Saxena; New Delhi: Sage, 1995) and *Organising for Rural Development: Experience of an Action Research Project in Gujarat, India* (V. Ballabh et al.; Anand, Gujarat: Institute of Rural Management, 2001). He has been a consultant to several national and international development organizations. Presently he is working as RBI Chair Professor at the Institute of Rural Management, Anand, Gujarat, India (e-mail: vb@irma.ac.in).

PRANITA BHUSHAN UDAS is an agriculturist by training, with a master's degree in irrigation. Currently she is involved in Ph.D. research in Nepal, and is institutionally affiliated to Wageningen University, The Netherlands. Her current research is titled "Gendered Participation in Water Management in Nepal: Discourses, Policies, and Practices." Her working experience includes both the implementation of development programs and scientific research in Nepal and India. She has worked in rural communities with Eco-Himal and WATCH in Nepal; and Saciwaters, GLOCAL, and GIDR in India (e-mail: pranitabhushan@yahoo.com).

RUTGERD BOELENS is a lecturer and researcher with the Irrigation and Water Engineering Group at Wageningen University, The Netherlands. His research focuses on water rights, peasant and indigenous water control, legal pluralism, and interactive irrigation development, particularly in the Andean countries. Currently he coordinates the program on Water Law and Indigenous Rights (WALIR) on official and local water rights frameworks in Peru, Bolivia, Chile, Ecuador, and Mexico (comparative case: United States of America). He has published, among other things, *Searching for Equity: Conceptions of Justice and Equity in Peasant Irrigation* (with G. Dávila; Assen, Van Gorcum, 1998) and *Water Rights and Empowerment* (with P. Hoogendam; Lima, IEP / Van Gorcum, 2002) (e-mail: rutgerd.boelens@wur.nl).

BRYAN BRUNS is a consulting sociologist, specializing in participatory management of irrigation and water resources. He holds a Ph.D. in development sociology from Cornell University. He coedited *Negotiating Water Rights* (with Ruth
Meinzen-Dick; New Delhi: Vistaar, and London: Intermediate Technology Publications, 2000). Additional information and publications are available at his
Web site: www.BryanBruns.com (e-mail: BryanBruns@BryanBruns.com).

INGO GENTES is an independent consultant and researcher. He focuses on research and advisory work on water law and policies, social and rural development, sustainable natural resource management, and participation. At present,
he is responsible for the Chilean chapter of the WALIR-Program (coordinated by
Wageningen University / IWE, The Netherlands and UN / ECLAC, Chile), and
conducts research on water control and collective rights in Chile. He is also
affiliated to the Natural Resource and Infrastructure and Social Development
Divisions of the Economic Commission for Latin America and the Caribbean
(ECLAC), United Nations, and is public policy adviser for the German Association for Technical Cooperation (GTZ) (e-mail: gensil@netline.cl).

DAVID GETCHES is dean of the University of Colorado School of Law and the
Raphael J. Moses Professor of Natural Resources Law. Getches was executive director of the Colorado Department of Natural Resources, and founding executive director of the Native American Rights Fund (NARF). He has taught and
written extensively on water law, natural resources, and Indian law. As researcher in the WALIR program, he analyzes indigenous water rights under U.S.
legislation and in international law and conventions. His publications include
Water Resource Management (with A. D. Tarlock and J. N. Corbridge; Foundation Press, 2002); *Water Law in a Nutshell* (New York: Foundation Press West,
1997); and *Federal Indian Law* (with Wilkinson and Williams; New York: Foundation Press West Law School, 1998) (e-mail: LawDean@colorado.edu).

ARMANDO GUEVARA-GIL has a law degree from the Pontificia Universidad
Católica del Perú, Lima, and a master's degree in cultural anthropology from the
University of Wisconsin-Madison. Currently he is assistant professor at the Law
School at Universidad Católica del Perú, where he teaches sociology and anthro-
pology of law. He has done research on Hispanic colonial agrarian property,
Andean chiefdoms under Spanish rule, legal pluralism and water legislation,
and indigenous rights in Peru. He is the coordinator in Peru of the Water Law
and Indigenous Rights (WALIR) program (Wageningen University and ECLAC)
and is enrolled in a Ph.D. program of the University of Amsterdam, Faculty of
Law (e-mail: aguevar@pucp.edu.pe).

NITISH JHA is an anthropologist affiliated with the Madras Institute of Development Studies in Chennai, India. He is currently doing research on a groundwater regeneration movement in Chennai. Prior to this, he spent two years as a postdoctoral scientist with the International Water Management Institute (IWMI) in South Africa. His doctorate is based on fieldwork carried out in an irrigation community in Bali, Indonesia. His research interests include the governance of common property regimes; natural resource management in the context of socioeconomic development; multiple water use systems; and institutions and policies for integrated water resources management (e-mail: nitish_jha@yahoo.com).

BARBARA VAN KOPPEN is principal researcher on poverty, gender, and water in the International Water Management Institute (IWMI), and based in the Africa Regional Program in Pretoria, South Africa. Her work focuses on technologies, laws, and institutions that render water a tool for rural poverty eradication and gender equity. She has conducted action- and policy-research in Burkina Faso, Bangladesh, India, Nepal, South Africa, Tanzania, and the Netherlands. Before joining IWMI she has worked as a lecturer and researcher on "gender and irrigation" at Wageningen University, The Netherlands, and as Dutch volunteer in Burkina Faso (e-mail: b.vankoppen@cgiar.org).

RUTH MEINZEN-DICK is a development sociologist with a Ph.D. from Cornell University. She is now a senior research fellow at the International Food Policy Research Institute (IFPRI), conducting research on water policy, local organizations, property rights, and the impact of agricultural research on poverty. She coordinates the CGIAR System-wide Program on Collective Action and Property Rights (CAPRI). Her research focuses on India, Zimbabwe, Pakistan, Nepal, and Sri Lanka. Among her publications are *Negotiating Water Rights* (coedited with Bryan Bruns; New Delhi: VISTAAR; London: Intermediate Technology Publications, 2000) and *Innovation in Natural Resource Management: The Role of Property Rights and Collective Action in Developing Countries* (Baltimore: John Hopkins University Press, 2002) (e-mail: r.meinzen-dick@cgiar.org).

RAJENDRA PRADHAN is a Kathmandu-based anthropologist with varied research interests. He has studied religion among the Hindu Newars of Kathmandu, the care of the elderly in a Dutch village, and food beliefs and practices in southern Nepal. Over the last decade he has been involved in research on water rights and legal pluralism in Nepal. He is currently affiliated with the International Centre for the Study of Nature, Environment and Culture in Kathmandu. He has coedited several books, including *Water Rights, Conflict and Policy* (Colombo: IIMI, 1997); *Water, Land and Law: Changing Rights to Land*

and Water in Nepal (Kathmandu: FREEDEAL, 2000); and Law, History and Culture of Water in Nepal (FREEDEAL, 2003) (e-mail: icnec@wlink.com.np).

ANJAL PRAKASH was born in India and holds a Ph.D. from Wageningen University, The Netherlands. A graduate in social work with specialization in urban and rural community development from Tata Institute of Social Sciences, Mumbai, India, he is associated with VIKSAT in its groundwater management program. He is doing research on the politics of groundwater irrigation in north Gujarat. He has written several papers on the issues of equity and sustainability of groundwater resources. His Ph.D. dissertation was published as *The Dark Zone: Groundwater Irrigation, Politics and Social Power in North Gujarat*, New Delhi: Orient Longman, 2005) (e-mail: anjalprakash@yahoo.com).

AMREETA REGMI was born in Kathmandu, Nepal, and completed her initial studies in architectural engineering from Pulchowk Campus, Tribhuvan University, Nepal. She holds a master's degree in business administration from Brenau University, Gainesville, Georgia and a Ph.D. from the Irrigation and Water Engineering Group, Wageningen University, The Netherlands. She has worked with NGOs and various UN agencies in Nepal, Africa, and Asia, primarily in the water sector. She has published in various journals and books. Her dissertation is published as *Democratising Micro-hydel: Structures, Systems and Agents in Adaptive Technology in the Hills of Nepal* (New Delhi: Orient Longman, 2004). Currently she works as a municipal water services advisor in Jakarta, Indonesia (e-mail: aregmi@cbn.net.id).

DIK ROTH is a social anthropologist affiliated to the Law and Governance Group, Wageningen University, the Netherlands, where he teaches on the sociolegal dimensions of natural resource management. He has worked as a consultant on land reform and rural development in Luwu, Sulawesi, Indonesia. In the same region, he has done extensive research on migration, land reform, irrigation development, and local irrigation management, and has widely published on these topics. His Ph.D. dissertation will be published with KITLV Press. Currently he is involved in a research program on the dynamics of decentralization policy in Indonesia (e-mail: dik.roth@wur.nl).

PATRICIA URTEAGA is a lawyer and anthropologist. She has done research mainly on legal issues and on indigenous peoples in Peru. In her research she focuses especially on legal pluralism, local law, and the use and management of natural resources. She teaches at the law school of the Pontificia Universidad Catolica del Peru, and is a member of the Peruvian team of the Water Law and

Indigenous Rights (WALIR) program on official and local water rights frameworks in Peru (e-mail: purteaga@pucp.edu.pe).

MARGREET ZWARTEVEEN is a researcher and lecturer at the Irrigation and Water Management Group of Wageningen University, The Netherlands, and is also a member of the gender analysis group of this same university. She looks at the linkages between gender and water, mainly in rural areas and in relation to agriculture. Her work stretches from documenting and analyzing gendered rights and responsibilities in water management (among others in Nepal, Burkina Faso and the Andean countries) to the critical feminist analysis of water policies and professional water cultures. She has widely published on these topics (e-mail: margreet.zwarteveen@wur.nl).

INDEX